*The Schools
and the
Urban Crisis*

The Schools
and the
Urban Crisis / A Book of Readings

AUGUST KERBER and BARBARA BOMMARITO

Wayne State University

HOLT, RINEHART AND WINSTON
NEW YORK   CHICAGO   SAN FRANCISCO   TORONTO   LONDON

February, 1966

Copyright © 1965 by Holt, Rinehart and Winston, Inc.

Library of Congress Catalog Card Number: 65–14878

24894–0115

Printed in the United States of America

Preface

The greatest challenge facing public education today is that of
preparing students adequately for adult life in a complex and changing
urban society. In fact, the overwhelming and urgent problems of
urban education are posed by this challenge. In the great urban
centers across the nation, educators are finding this long-standing
and essential role of education an increasingly difficult one to fulfill.
The burgeoning problems besetting education occur at a time when
the nation is attempting as never before to equalize opportunities and
realize its human goals as an open and democratic society. But
education is committed to more than the democratic ideal. An urgent
need to avert social crisis has also placed enormous demands upon
public education. The urgency concerning the problems of urban
education is reflected throughout this book of selected readings.

One central purpose of this book is to account for the problems
that exist in public education by exploring the vast social changes
taking place today and to show how these changes have affected
education. Chapters One through Five deal with areas critical to
education. In each there is strong emphasis on the school's direct
relationship to the social texture of the urban community, because
the problems of education are not academic, as some critics would
have us believe; rather, the nature of educational problems is social.
The editors feel that there is need of such a study because those in
public education who seek to meet its challenges adequately must first
understand the nature and causes of problems currently frustrating the
aims of education.

Chapter One, "The Changing Urban Community," describes the
directions of contemporary urbanization. The opening selection by

Max Lerner, an outstanding historical account of America's evolution from a rural to an urban nation, sets the stage for the urban sociologists who follow. Community patterns and the ethnic composition of the central community are discussed by Mel J. Ravitz and Raymond W. Mack, respectively. Both articles are concerned with the problems found in the present urban setting. In the final selection of the chapter, Robert J. Havighurst discusses the need for preserving the mixed-class school, which is threatened with extinction by present community residential patterns.

In the second chapter most of the readings are drawn from educational journals. The authors are educators who write from firsthand experience in the schools of changing neighborhoods. The final selection is a government pamphlet reporting on an educational conference held in 1962. It, perhaps, best sums up the impact that current patterns of urbanization, as discussed in Chapter One, have had on education.

Chapters Three and Four both concern youth. The first of the two chapters presents selections by a newspaper reporter, an anthropologist, an educator, a sociologist, and a psychologist. Each approach is as valid as those in the companion selections. The chapter, taken as a whole, gives a meaningful composite of the American child and the urban forces that influence his level of achievement. Chapter Four is devoted to the special problem of alienated youth. The pressing problem of aimless youth, tagged "social dynamite" by James B. Conant, is one of the great tragedies of urban society. The selections, both general and specific, offer several explanations for the conditions that exist. Much has been said on the subject of juvenile delinquency. Our plea is for the many other young people who never protest overtly against the dehumanizing and emasculating urban forces to which they are subjected.

The teacher in a complex and diverse urban school system is a far cry from the stereotyped Miss Dove. She may reflect one of several aspects of our culture, as Margaret Mead points out in the opening selection of Chapter Five. It is no longer true that the social origins of teachers are mostly middle class, but Robert E. Doherty's article reveals some interesting findings about teachers' attitudes toward the working class. The articles by Bertrand Sandweiss and Robert H. Snow deal with the frustrating circumstances in education as they are experienced by the teacher. Although there are some excellent teacher-training programs in operation that are geared to special training for the inner-city school, the editors chose Miriam

L. Goldberg's article because it outlines the general aims of all teacher-training programs, both undergraduate and in-service, that have sprung up in recognition of the need for specialized teacher education.

Although urban education is viewed in operation throughout the entire metropolitan area, from the decaying vestigial center of the once-prosperous city to its far-reaching suburban tracts, the most pressing problems are those found in the central area of the city. It is here that the greatest social problems exist, and it is here that the institution of public education is looked to for the solutions. The social crisis, alluded to earlier, exists in awesome proportions in these depressed areas where the greatest energies of urban education are being expended today. For this reason a good part of the readings deal with the inner-city setting and the severely disadvantaged child who lives there.

Turning from problems and causes, Chapter Six deals with one phase of education's reaction and adaptation to the present situation in the inner city. No picture of urban education would be complete without an account of the stirring movement taking place today. Three programs aimed at alleviating unequal educational opportunities in depressed areas are set forth in the first four selections: the Higher Horizons Program in New York, The Flint Plan of community schools, and the Great Cities Project in both Philadelphia and Detroit. The last article, by Jack Cohn, describes how one school, taking part in the Higher Horizons plan, was able to improve the quality of its education.

It is difficult to justify Chapter Seven in the continuity of this book. However, its relevance is self-evident. As an emerging society, America is divided by power struggle and ideological conflict. Chapter Seven deals with some of the aspects of struggle and conflict that largely determine the policies and aims of education. The area is an entire field of study in itself; but these articles, with the exception of George D. Spindler's which discusses the source and nature of conflict, do not attempt to examine this aspect of the relation of education to the greater society in any great depth. Rather, the selections attempt to reveal the educator's stand on various controversial issues that deeply involve education.

The editors do not arrogate to themselves the answers to the problems discussed in this book, nor is the final chapter intended as a prescription for the ills of urban education. But we readily admit that the selections reflect our sentiments concerning directions of change and adaptation in education that we believe to be both sane and sound. We, like Roger L. Leatherman who discusses the explosion of learning, feel technical and specialized training are unrealistic tasks for public education. The comprehensive high school is as vital a part of public education as it ever was, perhaps more so in the midst of rapid technological change. Gerald W. Boicourt's article, concerning a need for greater decentralization of administration, reflects our opinion that educational resources are dissipated in the amorphous hodgepodge of school districts scattered across the modern megalopolis. The selection by B. Frank Brown on the nongraded high school, as well as that by Loretta B. Jones and Richard Wisniewski outlining a curriculum for slow learners, suggest a departure from the classroom regimentation that has become intensified in the large, bureaucratized urban school district. In the closing article, Harold Dunkel discusses the vital issue of education—the values it chooses to translate into actual curriculum and classroom procedure.

It is hoped that the reader may find among the many selections, which have been preceded by short editorial comments, some understanding of the dynamics of urban education and the challenges it has accepted. But well beyond the social and economic reasons given for helping young people toward a rewarding life is a plea for recognition of the human aspect of this complex problem. America's young have a right to the opportunities of this society for no other reason than that they are people. We speak from the frame of a social crisis, but that crisis is not the justification of education's challenge. The highest values and ideals of our society are the justification.

Detroit, Michigan　　　　　　　　　　　　　　　　A. K.
February 1965　　　　　　　　　　　　　　　　　　B. B.

The Contributors

Max Lerner is Professor of American Civilization and World Politics, Brandeis University. He is a nationally known author and syndicated columnist.

Mel J. Ravitz is Professor of Sociology, Wayne State University.

Raymond W. Mack is Chairman, Department of Sociology, Northwestern University.

Robert J. Havighurst is Professor of Education, the University of Chicago.

Clemmont E. Vontress is Director of Guidance, Crispus Attucks High School, Indianapolis, Ind.

Frederick Shaw is a Research Associate, New York City Board of Education.

Fern H. Jacobi is Principal, Hendley School, District of Columbia.

Alfred W. Beattie is Superintendent of Schools, Allegheny County, Pittsburgh, Pa.

Paul Zintgraff is Assistant Superintendent for Curricular Services, San Diego, Calif.

Richard Hammer is a staff writer for the *New York Times Magazine*.

Wilfred Smith is Professor of Sociology and Anthropology, Eastern Michigan University.

James S. Coleman is Professor of Social Relations, The Johns Hopkins University.

Dorothy Lee has been a member of the Anthropology Department at Harvard University.

Urie Bronfenbrenner is Professor of Psychology and of Child Development and Family Relationships at Cornell University.

Frederick C. Neff is Chairman, Educational Foundations Department, Wayne State University.

Earl C. Kelley is Professor of Education, Wayne State University.

Charles Stewart is Assistant Director, Human Relations Program, Detroit Public Schools.

Aaron Lipman is Associate Professor, Department of Sociology and Anthropology, University of Miami.

James B. Conant is President Emeritus of Harvard University and has held positions at some thirty-five universities.

David Riesman is Professor of Sociology, Harvard University.

Margaret Mead is Associate Curator of Ethnology, the American Museum of Natural History.

Robert E. Doherty is Associate Professor of Secondary Education, Cornell University.

Bertrand Sandweiss is Assistant Principal, Butzel Junior High School, Detroit.

Robert H. Snow is Program Administrator, Adult Education Division, University College, Syracuse University.

Miriam L. Goldberg is Associate Professor of Psychology and Education, Teachers College, Columbia University.

Morris Krugman is Associate Superintendent of Schools, New York City.

Aleda Druding is Superintendent of District Five Public Schools, Philadelphia.

Leo E. Buehring.

Carl A. Marburger is an Executive Administrative Assistant of the Special Program Division for the Improvement of Instruction, Detroit Public Schools.

Jack Cohn is Acting Principal, Public School 192, New York City.

George D. Spindler is Professor of Anthropology, Stanford University.

Dale Doak is Assistant Professor of Education, Ball State Teachers College, Muncie, Ind.

Leonard Gordon is Director of the Jewish Community Council Services, Detroit.

Alfred Meyers is Principal, Pershing High School, Detroit.

Cyril Tyson is a staff member of the Commission on Intergroup Relations, New York City.

Floyd Adams is Instructor, Department of Secondary Social Studies Education, Wayne State University.

Roger L. Leatherman is Associate Professor of Education, Eastern Michigan University.

Lee J. Cronbach is Professor of Education and Psychology, Stanford University.

Gerald W. Boicourt is Professor of Educational Administration, Wayne State University.

B. Frank Brown is Principal, Melbourne High School, Melbourne, Fla.

Loretta B. Jones is Instructor of Secondary Social Studies, Wayne State University.

Richard Wisniewski is Assistant Profesor of Educational Sociology, Wayne State University.

August Kerber is Chairman, Department of Educational Sociology, Wayne State University.

Barbara Bommarito is an Instructor at Wayne State University and a former teacher in the Detroit Public Schools.

Harold B. Dunkel is Professor of Education, the University of Chicago.

Contents

*The Schools
and the
Urban Crisis*

{Chapter One}

THE CHANGING
URBAN COMMUNITY

Over the past twenty years America has witnessed a marked
change in metropolitan life. The accelerated pace of urban
growth following World War II has been more than the final
throes of urbanization. The latter stages of urbanization have
occurred in the midst of rapid technological, social, and economic changes which have contributed to the emergence of
sprawling, amorphous metropolises. The newly affluent middle
class fled to the suburbs as a preferred way of life, leaving the
city proper to the in-migrant rural Negroes and Appalachian
whites who are not readily absorbed into the highly specialized
economy. The urban community today shows an increasing
ecological isolation of social classes and a widening gap between the living standard of the rising middle class and that
of the static lower class.

The city proper is faced with a welter of social problems
which have been generated in part by this situation. The
decentralization of business and commerce has emasculated
the once dynamic urban center. Slum and blight rush into the
vacuum created by a retreating middle class, and urban renewal runs a losing race against decay. The city lacks adequate
funds to meet rising operational costs, but finds that it must

compete with outlying independent communities for tax resources. Social agencies are overwhelmed by cases of the
unemployed and unemployable; the indigent who are displaced
by slum clearance; and the marginal and alienated who cannot
find identity, dignity, or aspiration in an urban society containing a complex of disparate nonintegrated roles and a lack of
primary relations.

This chapter gives a detailed account of how population
shifts, arising from changes in our society, have intensified and
created problems and how these problems affect urban education. Not all of the problems facing education today can be
explained in terms of demography, but this factor has become
a dominant theme in the current educational crisis.

---

*America is an urban nation. More than 61 percent of the
nation's population is concentrated in metropolitan areas, and
the percentage of city dwellers is still rising. In the process of
urbanization the city did not simply grow larger. It created a
new culture, a new way of life, and a new kind of man. This
new man no longer adapts to the elements. He interacts with
something quite different from seasonal change. He copes with
the changing technology and economy, social structure, and
attendant changes in ideology. These have become his more
immediate and dynamic environment.*

*Max Lerner traces the rise of the American city in the fol-
lowing selection from his book* America as a Civilization.
*In it he captures the anomalous mood of urban culture with
its "lights and shadows." One may find far more shadow than
light here. That is intentional. There is a crisis in urban life
today which stems from dramatic changes in our society.
Before setting out to examine this crisis as it affects urban
education, one major institution of the culture, we present first
this especially valid perspective of change and crisis.*

CITY LIGHTS AND SHADOWS / *Max Lerner*

America was formed in its present mold in the process of city building, and it is still true—even in the era of the suburban revolution—that wherever American places are being shaped anew the new forms irrepressibly move toward becoming cities. While making goods and making money, the American has become in the process a city maker as well.

Lewis Mumford, in his *Culture of Cities*, has traced with learning and passion the historical rise of the city as shelter, fortress, industrial center, mechanical way of life the stages toward "Megalopolis." In every civilization the rise of the big city has been a by-product of technical and industrial development. This has been true not only in Europe, whose cities grew big earlier than America's and whose population density is higher, but also in Asia, where the recent upsurge of population and the ferment of new forces have raised the size of the big cities staggeringly high. It is truer of the American city, however, that the rise of megalopolis has meant the accumulation not only of masses of people but of masses of power. The growth of the American city has gone along with—and been the product of—revolutions in production, motive power, transport, communications. Every transformation in the economy, including the rise of new industries and the changes from roads to canals to railroads to autos and aviation, and from steam to gasoline to electric and atomic power, has further complicated the web of city life. Yet the changes move inexorably, and as they occur they keep transforming the outer sky line and the inner structure and life of the city. Every new step in technology tends to destroy the inner forms of the cities on which they rest and which have made them possible, and on their ruins new forms arise.

The statistical growth line is by now familiar enough. In 1790 when the American nation first emerged it had no cities, large or small, that could compare with the glory of European cities. There were a few small "cities in the wilderness"—three between 10,000 and 25,000, two over 25,000, none as large as 50,000. Not until 1820 did New York have 100,000 and not until 1880 did it have a million people.

Max Lerner, "City Lights and Shadows," America as a Civilization. *New York: Simon and Schuster, Inc., 1957 . Copyright © 1957 by Max Lerner. Reprinted with the permission of Simon and Schuster, Inc., and Laurence Pollinger, Ltd., for Jonathan Cape, Ltd.*

By 1955 it had over eight million, five other cities were over a million, and twenty ranged from New York's vast mass to the roughly half million of Cincinnati, Seattle, and Kansas City. There were 106 cities of over 100,000. Putting the figures differently, the urban population by Census Bureau definition (those living in places of over 2,500) increased between 1940 and 1950 from around seventy-five million to around eighty-nine million, the latter figure representing almost two thirds (64 percent) of the total population; in the Northeast the proportion was some 80 percent, in the West 70 percent, in the South 50 percent. Add to this the fact that much of the nonfarming rural population is really urban, in the sense that it lives on the outskirts of metropolitan areas, with city jobs and values, and the urban percentage then goes as high as 80 to 82 percent for the whole nation. Taking a still different approach, and using 25,000 to 100,000 as the range for a small- and middle-sized city, there were seventeen million Americans living in 378 such cities in 1950, while there were forty-four million living in cities of over 100,000—some sixty-one million in all living in cites of over 25,000.

Each of these cities has a character and style of its own. New York and Boston are proud of their role as intellectual centers, but Chicago, "hog-butcher of the world," was the scene of a literary Renaissance in the early decades of the century and later became an educational center. A number of cities—San Francisco, New Orleans, Charleston— have a sure sense of their style and picturesqueness as carriers of a history-laden or exotic tradition, but Boston, Philadelphia, and Baltimore would make rival claims on that score. Some cities in turn are proud of their recent growth as boom towns—Los Angeles, Detroit, Houston, Dallas, Seattle, Portland; and in America the claim to boom is more swaggering than the claim to tradition. Most American cities owe their growth to industry and transport, yet Washington is what it is because it is the nation's capital; Los Angeles, the movie center of America, is also in an area of oil production and owed its original boom to the silver mining of the Sierras.

Emphasizing this, there is a danger of forgetting the strength of the agricultural hinterland out of which many of the American cities grew. They got their start as marketing centers for the products of the surrounding areas: Chicago and Kansas City became shipping centers for the steers of Texas and the Far West. But Pittsburgh and Cleveland owe most of their growth to iron and steel, and Detroit is the automobile center of America. Miami is the center of the vacationing and leisure industries, although recently it has been developing light industries less seasonal and precarious. In the East, cities like Boston, New York, Philadelphia, Charleston, and Atlanta got their start as strategic ports and others rose because they were at the convergence of the great trails and rivers or dominated high ground as forts. There are instances where a city of promising growth remained small while another grew into a metropolis, mainly because in laying out trans-continental railroads the line by-passed one and went through another. Thus many of the Western cities without natural location on rivers are mainly the result of the accident of transportation history, often aided by political pressure, land speculation, and outright bribery.

At some point in its history every American city has been a "boom" city, meaning the sudden spurt of growth when a particular city exerts a suction force upon people looking for opportunity, jobs, profits. Often this spurt of growth takes on a motive force of its own and threatens to run away with the city, outstripping its productive base. The great example of a synthetic boom was that of Florida in the 1920s when blueprint cities were staked out, with water systems, light-ing systems, and even community centers. Some later boomed again, and successfully; others remained as derelict reminders that a city can-not be wholly the creation of hope, hysteria, and paper profits. Even in the Paradise of real-estate values a city responds to organic laws of growth. When that growth has a valid base the initial boom will be succeeded by others in mounting succession. The original Chicago boom was that of a stockyard and railroad center; its later phases were those of farm-machinery manufacture, grain and commodity exchanges and speculation, and then war research and production. In Los Angeles a silver-mining boom was succeeded by an oil boom, a movie boom, and a war boom. In Houston and Dallas the booms were chiefly those of oil, real estate, and war industries. A smaller city like Norfolk grew originally as a port and then achieved a shipbuilding boom during World War II.

But the story of city growth is not summed up in the strategy of industrial location. Once the cities were established they exerted a suc-tion force on many diverse groups. Until World War I the city magnet drew immigrants from Europe and boys and girls from farms and small towns. In the forties and fifties it drew Negroes from the South and (in the case of New York) Puerto Rican immigrants. In most cases the trinity of motifs was comfort, opportunity, glamour.

The comfort motif was the answer a later generation gave to the harshness of frontier life that earlier generations had encountered. It was especially important for American women, who had found the frontier settlements bleak and welcomed the restoration of European comfort to the American situation. The middle class carried this motif further, and the calculated comfort of American heating, the American bathroom, and the garishness of the American hotel became symbols of "materialism" which the rest of the world first ridiculed, then envied and imitated.

Related to it is the glamour of city life. In the 1880s the magazine illustrations called it the "lure of the city." They depicted a country lad lying on a hillock, gazing longingly into the distance toward the towers and spires of the city. The mass city—Chicago, Detroit, Minneapolis, Cleveland, Pittsburgh, Boston, New York—was what the young men yearned for. It was their City of God. As for the young women, they turned toward the freedom and blandishments of the city and its romantic possibilities. It was in the cities that the young people hoped to find the excitement and fulfillment which the dynamism of their culture made them ask of life. Where people clustered together there was a greater choice of people, a chance to show one's beauty and wit to advantage, a chance for dress and gaiety, sexual adventure, love and marriage. The glamour of city life was part of the impulse back of the great migration from country to city in the past seventy-five years.

The greatest of the trinity of motifs was the idea of limitless opportunities for the young, strong, and able. Often the mass city proved to be a jungle in which many were destroyed and the survivors brutalized. But those who build a temple to the idols of success do not inquire too closely about the burdens of the sacrifices.

As a result of city living, Americans are becoming a people whose earliest memories are less apt to be of the farm or village or the main street of a small town than of pavements and movies, and swimming at the docks, and running in gangs, and "going downtown." They have had to get accustomed to the jangle of city sounds striking on the nerve centers, to new ways of dodging city traffic or of waiting it out patiently, to the complexity and pavements of the "asphalt jungle."

Why do they stand it? The answer is that many don't, hence the Great Exodus to the suburbs. For those who do, the city has become more than a convenience: it is a necessity. This is true for workers who must be near factories, railroad yards, and offices; for businessmen who must be near their markets and customers; for writers and artists, advertisers, workers in the big media, who must be near the centers of the nation's life.

The city is no longer a mode of comfort, as it was in its earlier phases. In some ways it has become the acme of discomfort—congested, traffic-stalled, smog-filled, shut out from sunlight, with scarcely space for breathing and no feel of soil beneath one's feet and no sense of the rhythm of the seasons. Any subway rider during the rush hours in New York can testify that city life has rigors challenging the frontier. This *ascesis* is made endurable (at least for the eggheads) because of the excitement of theaters, concerts, night clubs, restaurants, sports events, universities, art schools, which only the city can furnish and for which even the big media and the modern arts of mass reproduction are no substitutes. Beyond these amenities the core attraction of the city as a way of life is tension, movement, opportunity, and a swarming kind of warmth. A recent survey of Detroit, into which waves of workers have swept from farms and small towns, shows that most of them do not share the fashionable despair about city living. They like living in Detroit. It is as if there were an unlocalized yearning for what is big in size, dense in numbers, varied in type and stock of people, mobile, responsive. The cities are fed by this restlessness and grow through it.

Thus the American city as a way of life is the product not only of technical and economic factors but also of loneliness. It is here that the byzantine aspect of American city culture becomes important. What is involved is not only the quest for liquor and night clubs, late hours, sexual excitement and sexual opportunity. These are the more obvious garments of a Faustian hunger and an almost pathetic fear of being left out of things. The city is at once the product and symbol of human alienation and the longed-for antidote against it. It is the sum of all the signatures that a restless spirit has left on a people sensitive to experience. "This city," as E. B. White put it in a prose hymn to New York which is the distillation of the urban mood, "this mischievous and marvelous monument which not to look upon would be like death."

So dedicated an attachment does not exclude a sense of the realities of city life. White has said that there are three New Yorks—that of the natives, which gives continuity to the life of the city; that of the commuters, who use the city for business during the day and for evening forays but live in the suburbs; that of the migrants—the polyglot invaders from Europe, Africa and Asia, and from Puerto Rico nearer to home, and the youngsters coming from the Midwest to make a career and discover a universe. To some extent other cities are streaked with the same strata. The big cities offer a greater variation of ethnic stock and a heavier emphasis on the professional and intellectual classes.

But otherwise any American city contains, in replica, much the same pyramid of class and mass, of wealth and poverty, of conspicuous consumption and heartbreaking scrimping that American life as a whole contains. The difference is that in a city the contrasts are heightened because there are greater extremes at both ends and because the whole is brought within the compass of a single area.

At one end of the scale the big cities furnish the frame of American wealth and power. They provide the banking and financial mechanisms for the rest of the country, the centers of communication, the starting points of advertising, publications, and salesmanship. This does not mean that they are unproductive, since every big city owed its rise to some crucial relation to the American productive economy. But what the city adds as its own is the pecuniary frame of American society. This is where the money is, this is where the credit structure rests, and with the money and credit go the power and the glory.

Big cities are centers of absentee power, often holding the small ones in fief. In a medium city like Elmira, N.Y., for example, only a few of the big plants on which income and employment depend are locally owned. The others are subsidiaries of corporations with home offices in New York, Pittsburgh, Detroit. In Elmira even labor has an absentee structure of authority, because the national labor contracts on which the Elmira contracts are modeled are signed elsewhere, after negotiations that are carried on at conferences elsewhere. This absenteeism of ownership and control is especially true of the South and Far West, which are linked with control centers in the East and Midwest. A big city like Atlanta and a small city like Decatur, Ala. (pop. 25,000), bid anxiously against other cities for plants which will be the subsidiaries of absentee corporations. The chief function of chambers of commerce is to sell the city as a potential location for new industry. Newspapers, banks, mayors, and city administrations join forces to lure industry to the city. A corporation looking for a Southern plant close to cheap power will get bids from perhaps a score of cities offering hydroelectric power, cheap labor power, low taxes, and political favors. Once the city has the plant, it is dependent on a massive impersonal corporation that makes its decisions within the frame not of local conditions but of its whole empire. Face-to-face relations in the everyday area of job life become impossible. And when the corporation abandons the plant for a cheaper or more favorable spot, the effect on workers and merchants is devastating.

Although the gods whom it must propitiate for its destiny are not local deities but the gods of "business conditions," each city has its sense of welfare and catastrophe. The usual "community feeling" is a hopped-up, synthetic semihysteria called "boosterism." To be a "booster" is to sing your city's praises, push its wares, and defend its good name against defamers. It is an item in a spurious mythology of city promotion, tending to cancel out against the synthetic mythologies of the other cities. But at a time of general joblessness, the false front falls away and people feel caught in a common plight. The plants close down, the pay envelopes shrink, you buy on credit and face the threat of eviction notices. In such crises, or in the event of hurricane or flood disaster, the city discovers itself not just as a chance collection of atoms but as a whole whose parts are members of each other.

Despite the fond conviction abroad that all American cities look alike, each has its own characteristic architecture, its own sky line, its own style of building and of living, its own mood. Each has also its natural history, passing through a series of phases at each of which its characteristic style changed. Philadelphia and Boston, once the great political and cultural capitals of America, are now a mixture of the provincial and the ethnically pluralist. Several cities that started in a somewhat lurid fashion as centers of promiscuous frontier gambling and scarlet sex—such as San Francisco, Cincinnati, New Orleans— are now almost as respectable as their sister cities. From some cities, like Indianapolis, the stamp of rural provincialism is hard to efface. But others—Chicago, Cleveland, Cincinnati, Minneapolis, Kansas City, Louisville, Houston, Dallas—to which lecturers and theater troupes and concert companies used to come only as an act of condescension or uplift have become centers of regional culture.

Compared with the slow growth of the great cities of Europe, the American cities seemed to shoot up overnight. There were several turning points at which the efforts made to plan their growth might have taken hold and become a permanent part of the American scheme. For a time in the colonial America of Charleston, Annapolis, and Williamsburg some ideas of spacious planning were set in motion, but the Revolution interrupted them. After the emergence of the nation there were city plans in the air on a grand scale—not only for the Washington of Major L'Enfant but also for Boston and Philadelphia, and for the new frontier cities of Buffalo, Cleveland, and Detroit. But except in Washington and Savannah they came to little, largely because most cities were growing too fast to allow for the luxury of planned squares and open spaces at the city core, or for broad avenues fanning out on a radial pattern with houses well set back and with space between them. A New York study, which rejected such planning in favor of a cheaper and quicker gridiron pattern divided into uniform rectangles and subdivided with building lots, was later described by Edith Wharton as the expression of "a society of prosperous businessmen who have no desire to row against the current."

Once again, at the turn of the twentieth century, there was a Renaissance of city planning, sparked by the apprenticeship of American architects in Paris and by the Chicago Exposition of 1893. But while it yielded an influential Chicago plan and an attempt to put a beautiful façade on cities from coast to coast, under men like Daniel Burnham, Frederick Olmstead, and Charles McKim, the inertia of haphazard city growth was too great to arrest. What was called the City Beautiful movement caught the imagination and pride of American architects. It was a movement that dealt with state capitols, civic centers, universities, churches, and even railroad stations; eventually, inspired by the garden-city movement of England, it also left its impact on the layout of suburbs. Yet essentially its weakness was that it focused on boulevards and parks for the rich and did little about wider sidewalks and better quarters for the poor. "It had a lot of democratic phrases," writes William Wheaton, "but little democratic action."

A hundred years had elapsed between the city-planning movement at the turn of the nineteenth century and the one at the turn of the twentieth. Not only had vested interests become encrusted but so had habits of building, thinking, living. They were held fast by a century of custom and by greed and speed and the mistaken *laissez faire* that carried over from the realm of moneymaking into the realm of beauty, utility, and orderly growth. Still to follow were remarkable feats of city engineering and the building of skyscrapers, auto parkways, and thruways. But as for city planning, the movement was renewed so heartbreakingly late that it was no match for the strength of real-estate groups and the down-to-earth sense of the "practical" men. The American cities had already established their basic pattern of growth. By the time the Depression had stripped away the burnished surface of the cities and revealed the blight beneath, and governmental housing projects were started under the New Deal and new city planning commissions established, they could do little except operate within the accomplished fact of city history.

The core of that accomplished fact was planlessness. Most American cities had risen helter-skelter, wherever some convenience of location might place them or some rapacity push them. They grew up thus— grim and unlovely; often wrongly situated for health, huddling against tracks and wharves, clustered around railroad stations, stockyards, chemical factories, and power plants, with the scars of congested slums on them; swept by fires, vulnerable to epidemics, cradled often in low-lying areas periodically ravaged by floods; their air poisoned with smoke and polluted from the slag of the furnace: sprawling and crowded aggregates that grew by haphazard and piled-up wealth and excitement but offered large segments of their people a mode of living which was neither spacious nor gracious, with neither plan nor meaning.

To say the cities were without plan does not mean that their growth lacked any discernible principle. A group of thoughtful students of city development have tried ingeniously to uncover a theory by which planless growth unfolded in various cities according to somewhat similar patterns. It became clear, for example, that many cities had a central core—the downtown business and shopping district, with hotels, banks, theaters, movie houses, office buildings, and the City Hall; and that around this core the other areas were to be found—the warehouses, railroad yards, factories; the wholesale and light-manu-facturing districts; the blighted area with slums, rooming houses, and tenements (some of them once residences but later abandoned); the better low-cost houses of the skilled workers living near their work and the middle-class homes and the apartment houses; the heavy manufacturing district; sometimes an outlying business district; the "residential" area of bigger houses, set off from the street with trees and space around them; finally the suburban ring of commuters, including residential and industrial suburbs and comprising high and low incomes alike.

At first it was thought that the districts grouped themselves around the core in widening concentric zones, with the expansive energy push-ing from the center outward. Then with the coming of modern trans-port, a radial sector theory depicted the city as growing outward from the center along the lines of automobile and bus transportation, always away from low-lying, blighted, and dead-end areas toward higher and open country. Finally, to take account of the complex and bewildering growth of metropolitan cities, the theorists developed the idea of the multiple-nuclei city which grows around a number of cores.

Obviously all this was theorizing after the fact, and the naked fact was that the growth of the American city followed profitability and transport. The real arbiters of city growth were the railroad (which often pre-empted some of the best open space), auto traffic, and the real-estate promoter. It is these forces that dictated the shape of city growth far more than any city plan. To some this may seem evidence that American cities have grown organically rather than by some synthetic design, but haphazard growth is not organic. It is possible to provide for informal as well as formal features of growth, for variety as well as regularity, but the essential thing is to allow scope for both by taking thought.

In its layout the city tends to reflect the life history of its movements of immigration. The history of Brooklyn, for example, was that of successive migrations of Dutch, British, New Englanders, Irish, Jews, Italians, Negroes, Scandinavians, East Europeans, Syrians, Puerto Ricans, and even a colony of Mohawk Indians. They form a polyglot gridiron across the face of the city, with enough distinctness so that each section has its ethnic core and gives each neighborhood a sense of ethnic identity. This is why it has been said that in New York every street becomes a village, every area of ten or a dozen blocks becomes a neighborhood.

One of the results of the failure to take thought is the American city slum. Every big city had its slum area. Tolstoy's famous sentence—that all happy families are alike but every unhappy family is unhappy in its own way—applies inversely to cities: their gleaming and burnished streets belong uniquely to the city itself, but there is a deadly sameness about most slum areas. It is the universal quality of the scabrous areas where poverty and disease, delinquency and prostitution, walk together. The pattern of ethnic ghettos and race violence that had scarred some cities with blood and hate—among them Chicago, St. Louis, Detroit—comes out of elements that have a haunting similarity. The Negro slums in Atlanta do not differ much from those of Memphis, Birmingham, or Jacksonville. The Polish slums in Detroit, Buffalo, and Chicago are similar. The Mexican-American slums in San Antonio are worse than in Denver, but it is a difference of degree rather than of kind, and it is paralleled by the Barrio in New York City where the newly arrived Puerto Rican immigrants cluster.

William Bolitho once called the slums of Glasgow the "cancer of Empire," a phrase even better for the American slums, which are the blight on the gaudy flowers of American prosperity and power. The first buildings meant to house workers and immigrant families in the big Eastern cities were put up in the 1830s. They were followed by a dreary line of successors, each uglier and more macabre than what it replaced, with a greater population density and a blanker separation from the living needs of the time. They usually provided a higher profit return than the better housing units and were a continuing temptation to the exploiting of human helplessness. "I rent to the people no one else will take," said a Philadelphia "firetrap" landlord in 1956. Some of the slum houses were multiple dwellings encased in the old "balloon frame"; others were "three-decker" wooden tenements or rotting brownstones; still others were railroad flats stretching out endlessly in the "dumb-bell tenements," with windows looking out into narrow side courts; or they were five- and six-story walk-up tenements.

The 1940 Census revealed that in fact one third of American dwellings were substandard. As late as 1948 the head of the St. Louis Chamber of Commerce said that 30 per cent of the quarter million dwelling units in the city lacked bath and toilet; in 1950 it was possible for Alfred Roth, a Swiss architect teaching in St. Louis, to say of its slums: "I've been many times in the slums of London. I've seen the damaged areas of western Europe. But never in my life have I seen anything like this." Families everywhere lived doubled up and looked often into sunless shafts. Periodically the newspapers of Chicago or St. Louis or New York sent reporters out to survey the slums. They found a jungle of garbage cans spilling over, people living in dark basements, back yards, and vacant lots, with kids playing among tin cans and broken bottles, decaying dock areas and trash-laden river fronts, children growing up to delinquency. Along with the neighborliness that the poor never lose, they would also find hustlers and jackals, and amidst the overcrowding they might (if they were acute enough) find a dimension of loneliness and terror that no tenement law could isolate or prohibit. This is the aspect of city life that Nelson Algren's novels depicted, even in the 1950s.

No account of the mass city can exclude the pathos of life for the millions who don't get the prizes, the mean and scrubby struggle for a few scraps from the table of plenty, the wreckage of derelicts cast up by the unyielding tides of city struggle, the manic perversions and crimes, the organized preying on women, the conscription of children into vice. An American city shows to the defeated a different face from the one it shows the conquerors. With the slums come the vice areas, acknowledged and unacknowledged—those of brothels, "boarding houses," cheap hotels, saloons; those of narcotics addicts, whores, and pimps. It is for them that the Biblical words run true: "So shall thy poverty come as a robber, and thy want as an armed man."

What makes the slums ominous is that they represent a blight which, to a lesser degree, infects larger areas of the city as the restless movement of population shifts from one to another neighborhood. Land values in any particular segment of a big city are either moving up or down; neighborhoods are either gaining in prestige or getting "run down." Once they start to deteriorate the process moves with cumulative swiftness: the ethnic "undesirables" begin to make inroads, panic sets in, and soon the whole character of the area has shifted. As the new transition zones are swept by the crosswinds of ethnic struggle, the schools express some of the tension, and street fights break out. The exodus may be to other neighborhoods or it may be wholly out of the city to the suburbs. The vitality of neighborhood and city is drained.

Decay and blight have occurred, of course, in every phase of the city's cycle of growth. In the past they have been followed by renewal, where the old was continually displaced by the new. But the city today is asked to find the energies for renewal exactly when it is faced with pyramiding costs of government, throttling traffic, mounting crime, and a drain on its more prosperous and educated population (it is largely the lower income groups who remain because they have nowhere else to go). As its people join the Great Exodus to live in the suburbs, they remain as users of the city's services and facilities, but they are no longer taxed for them, getting a "free ride": thus far the efforts to combine the city and its suburbs into a single tax-and-governmental unit, to share the costs, burdens, and services of government in the metropolitan community, have failed. The suburbanite swells the throng who seek entrance to the city by car every morning and exit at night, clogging bridges, tunnels, and thruways, congesting the streets, snarling the traffic. Ironically those who live in the city all week join the monster auto rally on week ends, eager to get away for a day or two, and spending hours in traffic jams on the way out of the city and back.

Thus the mass city, which came into its present stature as a by-product of the revolutions in transport, finds itself being choked by the millions of artifacts the auto industry has created. The city seems to have become mainly a temporary stopover place for men and families in motion—which may explain why so many of the efforts at city replanning are geared to its traffic problems and its auto arteries. It is true that the network of roads leading, let us say, out of New York and Newark to the New Jersey Turnpike, was not only an engineering achievement but (seen from the air) of breathtaking beauty of design. But to rebuild cities mainly around road design and traffic clearance was to make man an adjunct of his creature, the automobile, and to lose sight of him as a human being needing roots in a living community. It meant undoing thousands of years of human evolution since the discovery of the wheel and making man the servant of the wheel, incomplete without it.

The American city is being replanned and rebuilt, but in what form, and with how much forethought, and with what image in mind of man and his needs? As the city core decays one would think it would not be too hard to buy up the deteriorated property and start afresh, with living quarters embodying what we know about the kind of work life and leisure life that will be within reach of the American family in the latter half of the century. But this is to reckon without the tenacity of vested institutions and habits of thought. The New Deal set in motion a sequence of housing projects that did more for slum clearance in a decade than had been done in a century. But the houses thus built had at least the same population density as the razed slums they displaced; and often they were built without adequate provision for neighborhood schools, churches, or markets or for pooled facilities for supervised play—which led Lewis Mumford to quote a sentence Patrick Geddes wrote in 1915: "Slum, semi-slum, and super-slum: to this has come the evolution of our cities."

The bleak, efficient, multi-story, barracklike apartment houses that are likely more and more to dominate the sky line of the big American cities are the expressions of the industrial organism, and their parallels will in time be found in the Communist societies of Moscow and Peiping as well as in capitalist New York. This is the skeletal frame within which industrial man is encasing himself, and here again the American has not so much created a distinctive pattern of man but foreshadowed the direction that industrial man is taking.

The new urban personality which is emerging in America is the product of the machine—but also of a good deal more. The machine aspects of city living are obvious enough. Who can forget the swift tunneling of the machine-as-subway in the earth, the scurrying of the machine-as-automobile over its surface, the exacting regularity of the machine-as-traffic-light, the droning of the machine-as-television, the stream of print emerging from the machine-as-press, the silent power and precision of the machine-as-dynamo? Who can escape the tempo of the mass city—hurrying to work, to appointments, to crises, to pleasure, to tragedy?

Yet what gives the city its character as living is not the tempo or discipline of the machine but the effort to reach for values beyond it.

The youngster becomes a member of the city gang, partly at least because the gang gives him a chance for a sense of belonging and feudal allegiance. Similarly with mechanized sports and amusements in the big city. Prize fighters pummel each other like gladiators before thousands; baseball contests are commercial events staged on schedule, with team standings calculated down to the fourth decimal point; movies and TV project the same *imago* on thousands of screens to the accompaniment of millions of fluttering pulses; choruses of dancing girls tap out their rhythms in night clubs with machinelike precision. Yet the big fact about all of them is not that they are mechanical, which is true enough, but that they furnish channels for mass emotion which relieve the tension of machine living.

Within this frame the city has developed a type of American character different from the type that De Crèvecoeur, De Tocqueville, or even Bryce depicted. It is less conditioned to the soil and the seasons, less religious, more skeptical about motives and chary of being "played for a sucker," less illusioned in the sense in which illusions—about friendship, work, sex, love, and God—provide an internal sustaining force for the personality. It has been psychologically hardened by innumerable brief encounters—in public schools, on subways and busses, in restaurants, in the course of shopping—which would become intolerable if one did not sheathe oneself against them with a constricted response. It is precocious about money matters and sex, since so many city people grow up in crowded quarters where few things are concealed from them. It is stoical in the face of hardship and the man-made catastrophes of economic life. It is not "urbane" except in the small groups in which one can afford to be generous, but it is much more likely to strip the jungle life of the city down to the nakedness of the human animal. It economizes time with an almost manic earnestness during the hours of business, only to waste it with equally manic intensity during the hours of pleasure and recreation. It lays stress (within limits) on individual traits of personality, on uniqueness in dress and sophistication in taste, on awareness, on the dramatic impact that the individual makes in his brief meetings with others. It has replaced fear by anxiety, and the concern about danger from elemental forces with a vague concern about security, safety, and the opinions of others.

What this means is that city living has carried men and women ever further away from their instinctual endowment. The city is not the root of the planlessness, the tensions, and the conformism of American life, but it is the envelope that encloses them. Or, to change the figure, the city is the battleground of the values of the culture.

In addition to its slums every city has its vice area and its crime problem. Whenever some vice inquiry has caught national attention or a newspaper puts on pressure or a city reform administration gets to power, the police force develops a spurt of energy. At such times there are "roundups" of petty criminals, prostitutes, or even the usual lodging-house population, and sometimes the more scabrous criminals also are kept moving and forced to seek other hunting grounds. But reform administrations are short-lived, and the ties between vice and politics, and between "rackets" and the respectable business elements of the city, are too close to be easily broken. In many cities the dynasty of political bosses started with the saloonkeeper who knew the weaknesses and tragedies of the slum people and built his political empire on the exchange of loyalty for favors. At a later stage in the dynasty, the boss may have become a contractor, dealing by a Providential coincidence with the very materials the city needed for its public works. There is scarcely a big American city whose administration is not at least marginally involved in this trinity of crime, political corruption, and business favors.

The city "machine" got its name because it operated with an impersonal efficiency to retain in power a group of political professionals who claim to know how to "deliver the vote." City crime is also mechanized, and the gangs, rackets, and shakedown outfits operate on a nation-wide plane. Yet in the case of both politics and crime the machine aspects can be overplayed. The political machine was usually run by a highly personal "boss" who gave a dramatic color to big-city corruption, as in the old days of Boss Croker in New York or more recently Boss Crump in Memphis or Boss Curley in Boston (it is Curley who is the protagonist of Edwin O'Connor's novel, *The Last Hurrah*). The function of the machine was to keep a firm hold on blocs of cohesive ethnic voters and thus capitalize on the inertia of the rest of the public. The relation of the political professionals to the ethnic blocs was mainly an emotional one of exchange of loyalties. The outward mechanism of the political machine conceals this inner structure of almost feudal allegiance—a structure of hierarchy, fealty to the overlords, and subinfeudation. Similarly the criminal machine reaches on the one side of the feudal gangsters, who are held together by greed and loyalty, and on the other side to the business community. The racket kings, levying their toll on the victims, are lawless versions of the "barons of the bags" who levy their toll on competitors and consumers.

But the problems of city government have now reached beyond crime and corruption. The big city generated administrative tasks which were never foreseen in the earlier years of American political thinking. Since the country was rural for most of its history, its political institutions were intended for small governmental units. The Founding Fathers could not have dreamed of a metropolitan unit like New York City, or of the web that it would spread from Westchester to Jersey City. The budget of New York City is higher than that of most state governments, and its administrative task is second only to that of the Federal government. It must run a huge police system, a school system that has to deal with Irish and Jewish children, Negroes and Puerto Ricans; it must run its subways through a Transit Authority, direct its bridge traffic through a Tri-Boro Bridge Authority, solve its harbor, truck, and air-line terminal problems through a Port Authority; it must run a network of public hospitals and clinics, a penal and prison system; it must deal with juvenile delinquency, run a set of magistrate's courts, and take care of the indigent who are "on welfare."

At best this involves an array of administrative services that can be only loosely held together. American cities have groped at once for the kind of technical civil service to be found in the Federal government, and for the kind of political leadership for which the American Presidency is the symbol. The city-manager movement, combined with the focusing of political leadership on the mayor, may convert city government into something a good deal better than what James Bryce lamented in his *American Commonwealth*.

The big fact about the mass city is that it has become so massive as to burst its bounds. It has become a "runaway city." New York, Cleveland, and Chicago each now contains a set of "satellite cities," which have developed their own civic pride and striven to become autonomous units within the larger metropolis. Yet the more difficult development has been that of the suburban communities which are functionally part of the metropolitan city but do not share its financial or administrative burdens. Like the single metropolitan area from Westchester to Jersey City, there are similar stretches through the industrial centers of Connecticut and Massachusetts, and around Buffalo, Pittsburgh, Chicago, and Los Angeles, where workers in chemical, automobile, and airplane factories cluster in a central city and in suburban communities that stretch for hundreds of miles in a continuous stream. These aggregates are not so much cities in the old sense but provinces in a larger industrial empire.

A number of American architects and planners have had a vision of how these monstrous masses can be kept within limits, the central cities renewed and replanned, the fringe growths contained, the whole turned into a set of decentralized communities each with an integrated pattern of work, residence, and recreation inside the far-flung larger frame. It is a moving vision, yet it would be surprising if Americans who had tolerated a planless past of the cities were to be converted—even under the spur of need—to a drawing-board-planned future.

In one area there are signs of concerted action—that of urban renewal. By 1955 there were 250 cities involved somehow in this effort, some to a minor degree, a number in a major way. They were starting to tear down the deteriorated parts of the central areas and rebuild them; they were taking steps to rehabilitate the indifferent areas; they were growing alert to the need for conserving the healthy ones. Except in cases like Pittsburgh and St. Louis, it was still being done without imaginative boldness, on a scale of cost suitable to the past and not to the staggering resources of the present. Yet the big fact was the emergence of the conviction that governments have a responsibility for city redevelopment.

Under the New Deal there was for the first time a clear recognition that the big metropolitan cities could not survive without Federal subsidies for crucial tasks, like housing, health, and unemployment relief, which affect the national interest. The countertendency was to follow the doctrine of states' rights and to give both the burden and the power to state governments. Since these state governments tend to be dominated by the rural members of their legislatures, the big cities fought this trend, feeling that their relationship should be directly with the Federal government.

The fact is that the growth of the metropolitan city has destroyed the base of the earlier version of federalism. A new equilibrium must be achieved between not just the center and the rim but between a whole new set of nuclear centers in the form of metropolitan cities as well as in Washington, and their rim in the rurally oriented state capitals. Hence a new alliance is emerging between city needs and Federal aid, to break the old dependence on the states. While Republican administrations are more reluctant than Democratic ones to push this alliance, they have recognized and continued Federal aid to private housing construction, to public housing, to slum clearance and the relocation of slum families, to community facilities like water and sewage. This aid, in turn, has spurred more comprehensive city replanning, and to feed the hope that in a generation or two the older city areas will be recast, the problems of the new runaway city will be grappled with, and both will become fitter places in which to live, work, and play.

I have talked entirely here of the city in peacetime. But after 1945 the atomic shadow darkened a good deal of city planning. The American mass city and the industrial stretch of the greater metropolitan city form an unparalleled target for atomic and radiation destruction. One answer has been that of the dispersal of the industrial concentration in the cities, so that the target would be more scattered. Actually, some kind of dispersal and decentralization has been taking place. Industries have tended to move out of the city itself to be nearer their source of labor supply in the suburbs. Department stores have established suburban branches. Retail stores have grouped themselves into shopping centers in suburban neighborhoods. But what this dispersal has done, desirable as it has been, has been to form a more or less solid line of industrial and population growth. It has burst the boundaries of the mass city, but it has not solved the problem of its survival in atomic war. The vulnerable areas still exist, but they have been stretched thinner. The "city panic" has not been wholly removed from the minds of millions of city and suburban dwellers, and it may be revived.

The firmest answer has been given by those who say that dispersal and burrowing in the ground may save lives but that they will not save civilization; that the city grew out of the expansive energies of America and that if the city does not survive a suicidal war the civilization itself may perish. The destinies of the two are intertwined, and the best way to save both is by the kind of affirmation from which the cities originally drew their strength.

———————

Traditionally, urban growth has had a drift of its own. Blight followed outward growth and slums followed blight, with population segments seeking their own respective socio-economic levels. Such change was gradual yet inexorable. Today urban renewal seeks to halt the "natural" drift and reclaim the inner city. Problems occur when urban renewal creates new patterns and directions in population shift which conflict with and catalyze traditional change. Mel Ravitz discusses some of the problems in population change and how

they are compounded by the changes in racial composition.
Within this discussion of change in urban population lies still
another dimension of change: the changing concept of the
urban community.

EFFECTS OF URBAN RENEWAL ON COMMUNITY RACIAL PATTERNS / *Mel J. Ravitz*

This paper seeks to explore the concept of urban renewal and its varying effects on existing and emerging racial patterns in the large metropolitan community.

Urban renewal is a new concept. Its widespread current usage among planners and laymen alike is a result of frequent Federal governmental mention. Urban renewal may be defined broadly as a joint local and Federal governmental program of financing, planning, and implementation to reconstitute our cities so as to make them physically more habitable for the millions who must and will continue to live in them. In a sense, urban renewal may also be viewed as recognition that the urban area is a vital national and local resource that cannot be permitted to deteriorate further.

As we begin an exploration of urban renewal and its influences on the racial patterns and programs of the city, it should be clear that renewal, as a phenomenon and a process, comes to an existing and ongoing city with its own social and physical characteristics and its own changes already underway. Indeed, in some instances, the renewal process simply intensifies existing characteristics and trends; in other instances it may interfere with them; and in still other instances, renewal may serve to initiate new characteristics and trends.

Bearing in mind then that the renewal process and its effects occur within an existing socio-cultural and physical matrix, it is appropriate first to sketch briefly some of the significant characteristics and trends of the metropolitan community. The characteristics and trends noted here are of Detroit, Michigan. The conclusions arrived at are valid for other cities only to the extent that the characteristics and trends, as well as the specific urban renewal activities and programs, which will also be described, are similar in these other American communities.

Mel J. Ravitz, "Effects of Urban Renewal on Community and Racial Patterns," Journal of Social Issues, *13, 4 (1957), pp. 38–49. Reprinted with the permission of The Society for the Psychological Study of Social Issues.*

CHARACTERISTICS AND TRENDS

Detroit, like other large cities, is composed of three main growth areas: an old central core, a large middle-aged area, and the newly developed sections and the suburbs. Within the old core of Detroit, for example, are about one hundred thousand dwellings, generally built prior to the turn of the century. Many show obvious signs of decay and obsolescence, and require clearance and redevelopment. Just outside this core area are three hundred thousand homes in middle-aged neighborhoods. These are the homes and neighborhoods in need of conservation and improvement to prevent them from becoming future slums. Finally, the third area of the city is composed of the newly developed sections near the boundaries and in the suburbs. The three hundred thousand new homes in these neighborhoods are in good condition at the moment, but they, too, can deteriorate if they are neglected.

In recent years Detroit has grown in almost fantastic fashion. Not only has it increased in population, but this population has spilled over the city boundaries, and there is a rapidly growing population now living in the suburbs, and in sprawling fashion beyond them. By the mid-60's, a majority of Detroit's roughly four million people will doubtless be living outside the city limits. This is hardly far-fetched, as since 1940 the total population of Detroit City increased by about 17 percent, as over against an increase in the Tri-County area (excluding Detroit City) of about 133 percent.[1]

Detroit's population is heterogeneous. Its largest distinguishable racial, religious, and ethnic groups are the Poles, the Italians, the Jews, the Negroes. Many members of each of these groups live close together in identifiable geographic areas of the city. Often this concentration of members of a particular group in a circumscribed area is misinterpreted to mean that these people live a life that is culturally separated from the rest of the community. While to some limited extent this may be true of Jews, and of some first generation Poles and Italians, it is not completely true of any of these peoples, and it is especially not true of the Negro.

Another obvious social characteristic of Detroit is the mobility of its population. The city itself is a result of population movement from the

---

[1] Estimates based on data gathered by Detroit Metropolitan Area Regional Planning Commission, Committee on Population, and on United States Bureau of Census, Census of Population, 1950, Detroit, Michigan, Vol. III, Chap. 17, United States Government Printing Office, 1952.

farms and countryside. This movement has been especially heavy during periods of war and war preparation: the early forties and early fifties. Many of these newcomers have been Negroes, who, because of insecure jobs and generally lower incomes, and because of formal or informal restrictions elsewhere, were forced to crowd into the oldest and most deteriorated areas of the city.

In addition to this rural to urban mobility, Detroit like other urban communities may be characterized by another type of movement: that from the interior—especially from middle-aged areas of the city—to its fringes or surburbs. What is essential to recognize about this movement is that it has not been simply random, individual, or isolated families who are moving out, but rather that one whole category of people is moving out, while another whole category is gradually moving into these interior neighborhoods, especially the middle-aged, conservation areas.

A graphic picture of the racial distribution of our growing metropolitan population is provided if we note that since 1940 the white population of Detroit City has actually decreased by about five thousand people. During the same time the Negro population of Detroit City has increased by about 290,000. About 23 percent of Detroit City's population is now Negro. During this same period since 1940, the white population of the Tri-County Area (excluding Detroit City) has increased by about 953,000, while the Negro population of that Tri-County area has increased by only 53,000. About 4.5 percent of the population of the Tri-County area is Negro.[2]

Particularly since the 1948 Supreme Court decision on restrictive covenants, this mass exodus has been taking place from many sections of our cities. To be sure, some of these people moving out are seeking larger or smaller houses, as the case may be, to meet the changing needs of the family cycle. Other people move because they want a more or less expensive home, depending on their different economic conditions, and depending on their need to "keep up with the Joneses." Moreover, many new families have formed, and have sought available housing where it could be purchased with the lowest down payment. Any of these reasons for moving is acceptable, given the mass values of our society. However, one of the most compelling single reasons why many of these people are moving from the middle-aged neighborhoods to the edge or out of the city is their fear of the Negro people

---

[2] Detroit Metropolitan Area Regional Planning Commission; and United States Bureau of Census. *Op. cit.*

moving in. Though their fear is frequently rooted in prejudice, it is nonetheless real to them. If people believe something is true, even if it is completely false, they will tend to act as if it were true. This principle is daily being demonstrated in our Detroit community, as we see many whites moving away because they believe terrible things will happen to them, their families, and their properties if they stay. Actual evidence from many places in every city shows that were they to stay, these dire things would not befall them. Especially is this true where it is middle-class Negro families that have moved in.

One trend of movement in our cities is of Negro families moving out of the blighted core area and into better neighborhoods; this movement will continue indefinitely, despite intimidation, until eventually Negroes are very widely distributed over the entire metropolitan area.

With these characteristics as background we may examine the various urban renewal programs more closely and consider their effects on the racial patterns of the community.

URBAN RENEWAL PROGRAM

As noted before, urban renewal has two main dimensions: a redevelopment or slum elimination aspect, and a conservation or slum prevention aspect.

The slum elimination program, of course, is intended to apply mainly within the old dilapidated core of the city; the slum prevention program is intended to apply to the middle-aged neighborhoods specifically, but also in modified form to the new growth areas.

Detroit's plans for redevelopment pay special attention to its Central Business District: the bulwark of its economic base. Projects totaling 100 million dollars of investment are underway in this area.

Application has been submitted to the Federal government for preliminary planning of a large scale medical center in an area where four major hospitals are presently located. Tentative plans call for a complete medical campus with new facilities for therapy, research, and housing for hospital personnel.

Industrial rebuilding is another fundamental phase of Detroit's redevelopment project. Presently in the planning stage is the first large scale effort of the city to replan a major land area for the modern housing and handling of today's industry.

These are some of the clearance projects Detroit has underway; however, redevelopment is just one aspect of urban renewal; the other is neighborhood conservation. Conservation is a blight-prevention program aimed at all of the non-clearance areas of the City, with most immediate concentration on a ring of middle-aged neighborhoods adjacent to and surrounding the older, inner core. Neighborhood conservation seeks to prevent the further encroachment of blight in those middle-aged neighborhoods considered still sound enough to be worth saving.

EFFECTS OF URBAN RENEWAL: REDEVELOPMENT

One effect of large-scale redevelopment has been, and will be, the displacement of thousands of people, especially Negroes, from the deteriorated areas in which they now live. Where are these people to go? Where will they relocate? This is not merely a matter of relocation of displaced people; it is essentially a matter of relocation of displaced Negro people. This is a pertinent distinction in the city, where we know that some whites are moving away because of the existence and presence of Negroes in their hitherto racially homogeneous areas. Will redevelopment renewal be the dynamic that helps push out of the city's core the many remaining Negro families not pulled already to the other areas of the city by the lure of more space, better houses, newer schools, more recreational facilities, and other, middle-aged area amenities?

The likelihood is great that most of these displacees will not return to the same old area. Much of the new housing in these old areas will doubtless be of a price beyond their reach. On these slum sites now stand, or will stand, much middle and upper middle income housing. Most of the former residents will have relocated elsewhere long before the new luxury housing is erected. Some will have moved to what public housing sites are available to them; others will have simply sought quarters a few blocks from their former homes, perhaps moving into an already overcrowded dwelling, which, obviously, will create a new slum, or worsen an existing slum condition; some few others may buy a house—often their first—in one of the middle-aged neighborhoods, the somewhat brighter, more spacious areas just beyond the slums, that beckon invitingly to those able to amass the requisite down payment. Some of those who are displaced, and who choose to relocate in these middle-aged neighborhoods, may not have the funds to do so; they may pool their resources, and together with one or more other families, seek to purchase one of the large middle-aged homes that characterize the conservation neighborhoods. The presence of any number of these conditions of over-crowding, often accompanied by an ignorance of urban ways, and by an abundance of lower class modes and mannerisms, prompt the middle class residents of these middle-aged neighborhoods, both Negro and white, to consider moving out even further towards the suburbs, sometimes into them. Thus, in centrifugal fashion, initiated by the momentum of redevelopment in the core of the city, wave after wave of people, first Negroes mainly, then both whites and Negroes, and then whites mainly are being pushed to relocate. Thus, redevelopment acts like a stone thrown in a pool to create a series of extending circles. The larger the stone, or the greater the scope of slum clearance, the more far-reaching the effect. This movement is not at all points a matter of racial prejudice and discrimination: Negroes in some instances move away from other Negroes, and whites move away from whites. Certainly, too, while there is much evidence of whites moving away from Negroes, this is only part of the picture. Complicating the entire issue is the factor of social class with its accompanying pressures. As displaced lower class families move into hitherto middle class neighborhoods, in many instances they bring with them overcrowding, different tenancy standards, rural folkways, and different speech, dietary, and dress customs. Upon such an invasion middle class families, quite apart from racial considerations (although in some instances these underly the manifest concerns), are often prompted to move to other residential quarters. Those who can afford to move do so; the others live and long for the day when they can escape. Usually the escape is to the fringes of the city or to the suburbs.

Another consequence of redevelopment renewal is to clear the central core of the city of some of its Negro population, and by virtue of middle and upper middle income housing proposed for the cleared land, to introduce potentially a new ecological arrangement, with middle and upper middle income families occupying former slum sites. This ecological rearrangement has been discussed elsewhere, but it should be considered as a legitimate outcome of redevelopment. It remains to be seen what the racial composition of this new middle class population will be. That there are many Negroes financially able to afford this housing is unquestioned. The questions, however, are whether this housing will be available on an open occupancy basis, and if it is, whether there will be a fair, unrestricted distribution of both Negro and white residents. In short, will whites in large number be willing to move into these middle income houses if Negroes are also permitted, with or without any kind of quota control?

Vast problems of social relationship especially centering in the school are part of this consequence of renewal. These problems stem principally from the fact that the first redevelopment projects comprise relatively small geographic areas. They are actually middle class areas carved out of, and contained within a surrounding sea of slums. One perplexing question is whether to seek to establish class-segregated schools to service the middle class families with school age children, or to have these middle class children attend existing schools in the nearby slum neighborhoods. As the redevelopment projects increase, and if they are contiguous, the problem might disappear as there would then be sufficient children to justify a new school plan that could service them alone. This would solve the immediate problem, but it would raise the theoretical question of whether such class segregation squares with the ideal American value of inclusiveness.

Redevelopment then has two main influences on population composition of the city. On the one hand it forces a great number of Negro families out of the slums of the central city, pushes them out either to other slums, or to the middle-aged neighborhoods. This in turn leads sometimes to overcrowding, and sometimes to a related outmovement of whites from the middle-aged areas. Sometimes both overcrowding and white exodus occur. On the other hand, redevelopment of the core of the city may be bringing back to the core those middle and upper income Negro and white families who desire the geographic advantages of inner city living, and who can afford the relatively high rentals. The net consequence of these interrelated results is to change the ecological pattern of the city, and to set in motion a far-reaching dynamic that may ultimately help loosen the lines of racial segregation that dominate many of our cities.

EFFECTS OF URBAN RENEWAL: CONSERVATION

In addition to the impact of redevelopment on the racial patterns of the city, we may note that the other dimension of urban renewal, conservation, is also related to these patterns, although in different ways. Some conservation neighborhoods are those into which many Negroes are now moving, and into which they have been moving, especially during the past decade. These neighborhoods are physically middle-aged, and many at present contain a racially mixed population. These neighborhoods generally represent one frontier of interracial relationships. In some instances the transition has been completed and the neighborhood is now all, or predominantly, Negro. It is one of these predominantly Negro conservation neighborhoods that middle class Negroes are beginning to leave as lower class Negroes enter. In other instances, the social class transition has not yet occurred, and the neighborhood is presently homogeneous with regard to class. In a few of the middle-aged, or conservation, neighborhoods no racial invasion has yet begun. Whether or not these middle-aged, or second layer, neighborhoods are invaded, and at what time they are invaded is influenced by a number of variables: their proximity to the core of Negro residency, the solidarity of the population presently inhabiting them, and the quality of their housing. Employing these variables, a series of hypotheses might easily be formulated. The following is an example of such hypotheses: middle-aged neighborhoods adjacent to the area of Negro residency, whose populations have a low degree of solidarity, and which contain comparatively low-quality housing, will be neighborhoods into which lower class Negroes tend to move first.

While the in-and-out population movement of these middle-aged neighborhoods has certainly been facilitated by the redevelopment phase of urban renewal, the conservation aspect of renewal has also had its effect. Conservation, it must be understood, is the blight prevention program that has, since 1954, become an increasingly significant dimension of renewal. Inasmuch as it is the newer of the two renewal programs, its influences have not had full opportunity to be felt. Nevertheless, in Detroit, where the conservation program is comprehensive and strongly supported by municipal government and an active citizens' committee, it is possible to note some significant effects on racial patterns.

The organizing experience in this pilot neighborhood suggested the following general hypothesis: that if Negro and white residents of a neighborhood become interested in such common concerns as the condition of their alley shacks or the lack of scouting opportunities, then the issue of racial difference diminishes, in at least overt importance. Evidence for this hypothesis was seen repeatedly in organizing this neighborhood. All blocks in the neighborhood had some Negro families. Most meetings were bi-racial. At early meetings it was often possible to see voluntary segregation in the form of the seating arrangements. On some occasions in the beginning, white residents inquired what the city was going to do about returning the neighborhood to its former all-white population. These questions gradually ceased, and it was also possible to notice a breakdown of the segregated seating pattern as interest in the program and concern with common problems came to the fore. Evidence exists that Negroes and whites have been and are communicating cordially at most block meetings, in committees, and at the neighborhood council. Occasionally they visit each other in their homes in order to get on with the paramount issues: how to improve their property, how to get people out to meetings, how to help the people whose homes are expected to be torn down, how to provide needed social services for the neighborhood. There seems to be a bare, gradual awareness on the part of some people that a more important matter than racial difference has come into their neighborhood. At least this seems to be true with some of those who attend block and neighborhood meetings; undoubtedly there is a selective process at work whereby those with strong prejudices stay at home, and wait to move away.

This consequence of a conservation program that includes careful citizen organization will serve mainly as a means of further educating both Negroes and whites to live together peacefully and cooperatively. Lessons learned in this kind of situation are useful both immediately and in the future when the pattern of residential racial segregation has broken down.

In the long run, however, this instance of cordiality between the races will be insufficient to keep very many of the white residents in the neighborhood. Some few will stay for a time because they cannot afford to leave; others will stay for a while to see the proposed public improvements which they have helped work for; others will stay because they are too old to move elsewhere; and some will also stay because they genuinely like their houses and don't want to leave. Ultimately, however, all the whites will pass away or will leave, as will many of the present Negro residents. They will all leave because of the invasion of the neighborhood by lower class Negroes seeking a place to live, and willing to overcrowd the large houses in the area to do so. The last whites will also have the additional reason that they are unwilling to be the only whites in a predominantly Negro neighborhood. This will be true even of those without children; indeed, most of those with children in the public schools have left long ago or are in the process of leaving as soon as possible. They are leaving even if they are racially unprejudiced; they are leaving for the same reason that the middle class Negroes are leaving: to find a school situation where their children will mingle with children of similar educational background and aspiration. In this regard we may suggest that predominantly white Catholic neighborhoods may show a high degree of solidarity longer than non-Catholic neighborhoods, because by sending their children to the Catholic schools, the parents avoid one of the major factors forcing otherwise unprejudiced families out of changing or mixed neighborhoods. This is incidentally a reason why many middle class Negro families, faced with the same situation and unable to move, are also sending their children to Catholic schools.

Pressure to move, then, is on the residents of the middle-aged conservation neighborhoods, as well as on the residents of redevelopment neighborhoods. This movement and search for housing by middle class whites and Negroes will tend to introduce an unending series of one- or two-family invasions of what have been up to now exclusively white neighborhoods. We may expect to read or hear about many more "racial incidents" in the areas just beyond the middle-aged neighborhoods. This outmovement from the conservation neighborhoods will be directly encouraged, of course, by whatever land clearance occurs in them as part of the physical replanning of the area. Some goodly portion of homes, regardless of condition, will be demolished to make way for necessary public improvements. Present residents of these homes will be displaced persons seeking housing, and they will turn not to the core of the city, but to the fringes and suburbs to search for homes. Ultimately, we may expect to find that Negroes are living in all the neighborhoods of the metropolitan area, wherever they desire to live and can afford to live. The generations-old pattern of housing segregation will at long last have been broken.

This, however, will not come about immediately or without difficulty. There are still whites living now in the fringes and suburbs who moved there in the first place primarily to escape Negro invasion of their former neighborhoods. These persons are organized into what are euphemistically called "protective" or "homeowner" associations. One of the central purposes of many of these groups is to prevent Negroes from buying or renting in their neighborhoods. In the long run, given the current values of our society and given, too, the clearcut decisions of the federal courts, these associations cannot win. But before they acknowledge defeat, they can and may cause considerable tension in our communities by organizing resident resistance every time a Negro family seeks to move beyond the very real, though invisible, lines that serve as present boundaries to Negro residency. The effectiveness of these organizations will be determined by the degree of previous preparation for interracial living that has gone on in any given neighborhood, the impartiality and efficiency of the local police force, and the financial ability of the members of these associations. At most, these associations can delay the time when Negroes move freely throughout the community. They cannot prevent this day from arriving: the direction has already been set by the basic values of the society at large. Indeed some of the white people, it must be noted, who now reside in these fringe areas are not there because they sought to avoid interracial housing situations; they are there because they felt they had to leave at last the predominantly Negro neighborhoods they lived in. Others are there because, given an FHA mortgage bias for new housing, the fringes or the suburbs were the locations in which they could best afford to purchase houses of the size and convenience they wished. These people constitute a potentially strong force within the presently all-white neighborhoods to facilitate the Negro invasion when it comes.

These are not mere speculations; observation of what is now happening in our major American cities supports these possibilities. Within twenty-five years we may find class rather than race the crucial segregating principle operative in our northern metropolitan complexes. This will have been brought about by the intermingling of many forces, one of the most important of which will have been the powerful dynamic of urban renewal in both its major applications: redevelopment and conservation.

Changes in urban life are affecting changes in the role of education. Today the school is more actively involved in its culture than it has ever been in the past. Many contemporary economic and social issues have come to be regarded as concommitant with educational issues. In the following article by Raymond Mack we see that traditional forces accounting for assimilation into urban life are no longer effective. With the changes in the ethnic fabric and the economy of urban culture comes a mandate for education. It must take upon itself the task of educating for assimilation. Time and exposure within the city are no longer enough.

THE CHANGING ETHNIC FABRIC OF THE METROP-
OLIS / *Raymond W. Mack*

> All dwellers in cities must live with the subborn fact of an-
> nihilation. . . . The city at last perfectly illustrates both the uni-
> versal dilemma and the general solution, this riddle in steel and
> stone is at once the perfect target scraping the skies and meet-
> ing the destroying planes halfway, home of all people and all
> nations, capital of everything, housing the deliberations by
> which the planes are to be stayed and their errand forestalled.*

E. B. White's characterization of the metropolis as "the universal
dilemma and the general solution" is perhaps as true of ethnic conflict
as of nuclear warfare. Today eight out of every ten Americans live
in or within twenty-five miles of a city of at least 25,000 people, and
the cities house in their concrete canyons the Little Italies, the Har-
lems, the Chinatowns, and the ghettos. At the same time that the
city shows us these ethnic pockets of segregated, unassimilated minorities, it boasts—in what we often disparage as the anonymity of urban
life—an acceptance of difference unknown in primitive or rural
societies, but evidenced in the uncritical acceptance of one another's
right to exist, which is typical of a milling city crowd.

A number of people may be defined as a minority by the dominant
population on grounds of race (i.e., that they are physically different)
or of ethnicity (i.e., that they are culturally different, that they share
a set of learned behaviors, such as language, religion, dress, or diet,
that set them off from the other members of the society). Despite the
noble efforts of social scientists to set up logical, meaningful, analytic
concepts, the whole issue is dreadfully confounded by two facts:
(1) Defining a race as a minority isolates them from the main stream
of the culture to such an extent that they tend to become ethnic, that is,
to develop patterns of behavior peculiar to the race; and (2) defining
an ethnic category as a minority leads the dominant people to attempt
to justify their discrimination by imputing some immutable characteristics to that minority; it is not unusual, therefore, for dominant people
to refer to ethnic minorities as "races." In short, the treatment that
they receive tends to make minority races ethnic, and people tend

* E. B. White, *Here Is New York* (New York: Harper & Row, 1949).

Reprinted by permission of Dodd, Mead and Company from Education in
Urban Society *by B. J. Chandler and Lindley J. Stiles. Copyright* © *1962
by Dodd, Mead and Company, Inc., New York.*

to call ethnic minorities races. Therefore, in the following discussion of the changing ethnic structure of metropolitan America, the word "ethnic" is used to connote both racial and cultural minorities.

Any consideration of the ethnic fabric of the metropolis must be essentially nationwide in scope for two reasons: (1) As has been pointed out in earlier chapters, the United States is rapidly becoming an urban society. (2) Historically, American minorities have, for the most part, been city-dwellers. The Negro was in the past an exception, but today a higher and higher proportion of Negroes is moving to urban areas. Analyzing the changing ethnic composition of the metropolis, then, involves examining the changing face of America.

The United States remains today a nation in which minorities comprise a significant proportion of the social structure. However the ethnic fabric of the society is undergoing extensive alterations. Who our minorities are, where they fit into the social structure, the rate at which they are encouraged to assimilate, and their impact upon such major institutions as education and government are all variables in a rapidly changing situation. We shall examine here what seem to be the two most important changes in the distribution of minorities in the American social structure. We shall then project four trends which seem to be a likely consequence of these changes.

THE WANING IMPORTANCE OF EUROPEAN MINORITIES

One striking change in the composition of American society is the declining significance of European ethnic groups. There are two reasons for this change: the number of Europeans entering the United States has decreased markedly, and those already here and their descendants are becoming assimilated.

Most of the people who became members of a minority in the United States did so as a result of voluntary migration. The primary source of voluntary migrants has been Europe—northern Europe before 1890, southern and eastern Europe since that time. Over 37 million immigrants have entered the United States in the past century. Fewer than one million of these came from Asia and Africa. In short, for the past century most of the country's minority population has been comprised of foreign-born immigrants of European extraction. This is no longer true. The children born in the coming decades will be the first in the history of the United States to be reared amidst a population that is over 95 percent native born.

The rate of assimilation of an immigrant into the dominant population is influenced by how recently he arrived, how different his native culture is from his adopted one, how concentrated he and his fellows are in one part of his adopted city or country, and whether or not he is physically different from the dominant population. All four of these assimilation-deterring factors add up to one thing: *How visible is he?* The more recently he has arrived, the less time he has to learn the language, mode of dress, and other culture patterns of the dominant group, and the more identifiable he is. The similarity of the culture in which he was reared to the one to which he has immigrated is a factor in his rate of assimilation for the same reason: the more different he is, the more identifiable he is. A large number of "different" people in one area are considerably more noticeable than a few would be. Because they are different and noticeable, they seem to be even more numerous than they really are. They are more likely to inspire fear, to be singled out as a threat to "our way of life," to have stereotypes built up about them, and to become objects of prejudice and discrimination. Concentration in the population makes them visible; visibility slows their rate of assimilation.

European immigrants have not been as visibly different as other minorities; consequently, they have been assimilated faster. The next generation of their descendants—native-born, playing in American city streets, attending American public schools, exposed to movies and television which explicitly and implicitly teach the ways and the desirability of American culture—are assimilated at an even faster rate than their parents and grandparents were. They are less concentrated in the population; they carry little of the burden of cultural differences; they are natives, not new arrivals; they are in most ways, not visibly different from the dominant people, and they therefore assimilate.

Does this combination of rapidly increasing assimilation with drastically curtailed immigration mean the end of ethnic minorities as a significant feature of the American metropolitan social structure? It does not. The waning of European immigration and the assimilation of the immigrant generation serves only to focus our attention more pointedly on our three new urban minorities.

THE NEW MINORITIES IN THE METROPOLIS

The second major change involving the place of ethnic groups in the social structure is the emergence of three new minorities in our metropolitan areas. The first of these are the Puerto Ricans. Legally the Puerto Ricans are not immigrants; they can pass freely from the island to the mainland without a passport, just as one would cross a state line. Sociologically, of course, they fall into the category of voluntary migrants, becoming a minority as they move out of the culture in which they were reared and appear—concentrated, newly arrived, culturally different, and visible—in a new land.

The Puerto Ricans are not widely distributed on the mainland, but are a peculiarly metropolitan problem. They are concentrated in a few large cities, most notably New York. By 1960 there were over 600,000 Puerto Ricans in New York City; to use a journalistic cliché, there were more Puerto Ricans in New York than in San Juan. Of the new minorities, the Puerto Ricans are the most like their European predecessors as immigrants in that they are marked off from the dominant population by language and religion. They have one difficulty, however, with which few of our previous minorities have had to cope: racial ambiguity. Some Puerto Ricans have physical characteristics considered in the United States to be white; others would be classed on the mainland as Negroes.

The second of the new minorities are not only English-speaking, they are also native-born. Furthermore, they are white. They are nonetheless an ethnic minority, unprepared by their upbringing, by the values and patterns of behavior they have learned, to be readily assimilated into the life of the metropolis. Southern white mountaineers, more commonly known as "hillbillies" or "Okies," are recent migrants to northern industrial cities and constitute an ethnic minority in several of them.

Like the Puerto Rican, the Southern white mountaineer has all the characteristics of an ethnic minority except the technicality of foreign birth. He comes from an area where the culture is different from that of the city, where different behaviors are rewarded and punished. He has recently arrived. He has come from a poor environment seeking economic opportunity, and hence will be found concentrated in an old, run-down section of the city. Both his speech and his behavior make him visible, and many people in the dominant population consider him inferior and undesirable.

The third new minority deserves most of our attention, since it is by far the largest. Everything we have said about the Southern white mountaineer as a minority applies to him, with one exception: he is more visible, and his visibility is not so easily shed, because he is Negro. It may be contended that the Negro is not a new minority; this is true, but he is a newly *urbanized* minority and hence is of concern to us here. To see that the Negro as an urban dweller is a new minority one need only note how ill-equipped our metropolitan areas are to deal with him. He compounds the problems of being racially visible with those of the rural person attempting to be integrated into an urban milieu.

Throughout the three centuries of Negro residence in the United States, most Negroes have dwelt in rural areas. As recently as 1900, 90 percent of the Negroes in the United States lived in the South, and over 80 percent of all Negroes in the United States lived in rural areas in 1900. By 1960, 73 percent of the Negroes were urban dwellers;[1] outside the South, over 90 percent lived in cities, which is to say that Northern Negroes are more urban than whites.

The change in the distribution of minorities in the metropolitan social structure can, then, be summarized as follows. For 150 years, European immigrants comprised most of our minority population; their most imporatnt learning task on the road to assimilation was the exchange of their native culture patterns for the ways of the Americans. Now, and for the foreseeable future, most of our minority population is composed of citizens of the United States: Negroes, Puerto Ricans, and Southern whites. Their assimilation depends upon adjustment to urban life, upon the exchange of rural values and behaviors for city ones. The overwhelming majority of them face the added block to assimilation of a visibly different skin color—a topic we shall pursue further in our discussion of the consequences of the changing ethnic fabric of the city.

We should note one other characteristic of these new minorities that is of importance in considerations of public policy. During the past few years, our newspapers and magazines have bombarded their readers with editorials and feature articles posing the frightening question of the impact on Northern city schools, neighborhoods, churches, governments, and other institutions of the flood of ignorant, unschooled, Southern migrants, both Negro and white. Such a rapid flow of uneducated migrants as the journalists deplore would create

---

[1] U.S. Department of Commerce, Bureau of Census, *Statistical Abstract of the United States* (Washington, D.C.: U.S. Department of Commerce, 1961), p. 30.

serious problems if it were to occur. However, the actual situation, like so many other "facts" about minority populations, is directly contrary to popular belief about it. As it happens, the in-migrants have a higher level of educational attainment than the resident urban population they are coming to join.

Of the resident population of the Chicago metropolitan area in 1950, for example, less than 15 percent had attended college. Of the in-migrant population to the Chicago area that year, over 30 percent —more than twice as many—had attended college. In-migrants present this favorable contrast with the resident population whether the data are considered as a total or broken down by race. That is, the Negroes who are arriving in the city have a higher level of educational attainment than the Negroes already there; the whites arriving have a higher level of educational attainment than the whites already there; all migrants arriving average more formal education than the present residents.

This is not startling information to a sociologist, because migrants are notoriously clustered in the younger age groups, and, in our society, younger people average more formal education than older people. It is apparently so startling to some of our journalistic friends as to be unthinkable, since they present us with thoughtful analyses of the magnitude of the problems which these uneducated migrants create without bothering to examine the 1960 Census.

The slowing of foreign immigration, the assimilation of European ethnic minorities, and the rise of a new, relatively well-educated urban minority most of whose members are racially visible—this drastic revision in our social structure should have some interesting sociological consequences. Let me state as propositions several reasonable hypotheses regarding the ethnic structure of American cities in the 1960's and 1970's.

HYPOTHESES REGARDING THE ETHNIC STRUCTURE

If the members of a society are to exclude some of their fellows from full participation in the culture and define them as a minority, the people who comprise the minority must have some visible characteristics by which they can be identified. The Negroes of the Ituri Forest can treat the pygmies as a minority because they can tell by a man's stature that he is a pygmy. New England Yankees can treat local French-Canadians as a minority because the latter's speech and family names set them off from the dominant people. A minority's identifiability may result from its members' speaking a different language, having a different skin color, possessing different eye color, or attending a different church from the people in the dominant category. In other words, minority populations can be different physically or they can behave differently, but one or the other is necessary if they are to be identifiable. And they must be identifiable if they are to be discriminated against as a minority; this is why the Nazis forced the German Jews to wear arm bands.

If it is his behavior that makes him identifiable, the member of a minority group can become socialized into a new culture and be assimilated. But physical differences are more permanent; if it is one's skin color that identifies him, no amount of socialization into the culture of the dominant category will remove him from minority status. So-called racial minorities are therefore less able than are ethnic minorities to lose their separate identity and escape their minority status.

Racial minorities, unlike ethnic ones, have been discouraged from total assimilation. Some states have laws against intermarriage between whites and Negroes or Orientals. All the culture patterns that keep racial minorities separate from the dominant category—segregated housing, schools, churches, and so on—are a deterrent to total assimilation, because total assimilation means that one is no longer identifiable as different. That would mean biological amalgamation and intermarriage.

THE RATE OF ASSIMILATION OF THE THREE NEW METROPOLITAN MINORITIES WILL VARY ACCORDING TO THEIR VISIBILITY

Identifiability is the key to the rate of assimilation and the degree of assimilation of a minority. The basic difference between European ethnic minorities and Asiatic and African racial minorities is the degree to which their identifiability is readily changeable. The Polish immigrant who learns English and changes his name will rear children who will not only not be identifiable as Polish, they will not *be* Polish. Their visibility as a minority depends upon culture patterns; if American culture patterns are substituted for Polish ones, their visibility as a minority is reduced to the vanishing point. But no matter how completely a Negro is American in his thoughts, language, religion, name, and behavior patterns, he is identifiable as a member of a minority because his visibility depends upon his physical features, not his learned behavior.

The Southern white mountaineers who currently seem such a

problem to Chicago and Detroit are therefore the most easily dismissed from our discussion of the new urban minorities. They are visible only because they are rural people from one region come to dwell in the cities of another region. As soon as they have learned the behaviors that are Northern and urban, and substituted these for the culture patterns that are Southern and rural, they will be assimilated.

Those among the Puerto Ricans whose racial ancestry allows them to be considered white will be the next fastest to assimilate. They have a little more to learn, a few more changes to make, than the Southern whites. Where the Southern white needs only to change his accent, the Puerto Rican must learn a new language. But so long as he does not look Negro, only the need to learn new ways of behavior blocks him from total assimilation.

The dark-skinned Puerto Rican, however, like the Southern Negro migrant to the city, remains a visible member of a minority no matter how complete his cultural assimilation. It seems safe to predict that those defined as racial minorities will be the last to assimilate, and that they will not do so in our lifetime or, for that matter, in our children's.

Since those socially defined as Negroes constitute our relatively permanent minority, the rest of my predictions will focus upon them.

THE SOCIAL DISTANCE BETWEEN DOMINANT AND MINORITY POPULATIONS WILL DIMINISH

Already we see evidence of a decrease in social distance between whites and Negroes. Polls by the National Opinion Research Center indicate that the views of white Americans on the intelligence and educability of the Negro have changed considerably in fifteen years. People were asked: "In general, do you think Negroes are as intelligent as white people—that is, can they learn things just as well if they are given the same education and training?"[2] In 1942, 50 percent of the Northern whites queried answered "Yes" to this question; by 1956, the proportion of Northern whites answering "Yes" had risen to 83 percent. Perhaps even more significant, the proportion of "Yes" answers among Southern whites increased from 20 percent in 1942 to 59 percent in 1956.

A recent Gallup poll asked: "If your [political] party nominated a

[2] Herbert H. Hyman and Paul B. Sheatsley, "Attitudes toward Desegregation," *Scientific American* (December, 1956), pp. 35–39.

generally well-qualified person for President and he happened to be a Negro, would you vote for him?" Thirty-eight percent of the respondents answered this question in the affirmative, with the "Yes" percentage running as high as 51 in the New England states. Even in the South, 22 percent of the voters say that they would support a Negro for President.

A great deal of sociological research indicates that social distance declines with increased socioeconomic status. The higher a person's occupational prestige, or the higher his income, or the more formal education he has, the less likely he is to be an ardent segregationist, or to condone violence as a weapon in dominant-minority relations. Social distance is least where both Negro and white have high socioeconomic status; social distance is greatest where both Negro and white have low socioeconomic status.[3]

Given the constantly increasing educational attainment of our population, both Negro and white, our steadily rising level of living, and the fact that the cities are drawing as in-migrants the better-educated members of the Negro minority, it seems reasonable to predict a decrease in social distance between the races in the coming decades. Most of the rationalizations justifying our treatment of the Negro as a minority are descriptions of lower-class behavior: poverty, disease, ignorance, irresponsibility, poor property upkeep, and so on. Most American Negroes must, at the present time, be objectively rated as occupying a low socioeconomic status. As more and more of them achieve the education, income, and behavioral prerequisites of middle-class "respectability," they will not automatically escape from their minority position, but the beliefs which justify keeping them at a caste-like distance will be greatly weakened.

This greater acceptance will, however, be one part of a paradox, opposed to our third proposition.

THE RAPID CHANGE IN THE STATUS OF THE NEGRO WILL BE ACCOMPANIED BY AN INCREASE IN INTERRACIAL CONFLICT

All that we know of the sociology of revolution indicates that— contrary to the popular fiction that people rise up against their masters when they are too downtrodden to bear further oppression—a group is most amenable to revolution when its status has been improving. Galley slaves do not revolt; they have neither the oppor-

---

[3] Frank R. Westie, "Negro-White Status Differentials and Social Distance," *American Sociological Review* (October 17, 1952), pp. 557–558.

tunity nor the strength. The French *bourgeoisie* overthrew the social structure not because they were a crushed and miserable minority, but because they had gained so many concessions and were doing so well that it seemed to them that their world might be an even better place if they took it over and ran it. The Thirteen Colonies which united to throw off the yoke of English oppression in the 1770's were probably the best and most generously governed colonies in the world at that time. The Russian serf lived for centuries under conditions of political and economic subjugation almost impossible for us to imagine, and was too busy just staying alive to question the justice of his lot, much less initiate any effective protest against it. But a series of political and economic reforms in the late nineteenth and early twentieth centuries vastly improved the status of the Russian peasant and culminated in the bloodiest revolution of this century.

Three conditions are necessary for intergroup conflict: the groups must be (1) in contact with each other, (2) in competition with each other, and (3) visible to each other. All three of these conditions will obtain in Negro-white relations in the United States in the coming years. Visibility we have discussed. The very conditions that define city life—crowding and rapid movement, for example—will throw the groups into a closer and more frequent contact than was customary when the Negro was a rural dweller. Every improvement within the status of the Negro throws him into more direct competition with the white. Visibility, contact, competition—all are intensified in the urban environment.

Add to these the uncertain definition of the situation, the ambiguity of role expectations that is a concomitant of urban life and of rapid social change, and you have an almost ideal situation for engendering conflict.

Because of the decreased social distance mentioned in our second proposition, it seems unlikely that this conflict will manifest itself in interpersonal violence, such as lynchings. It seems much more likely to occur as true intergroup conflict, for example, as street gang warfare. If we face the likelihood of conflict realistically, we may, with skill and care, be able to channel it into socially acceptable channels. One such channel—the political arena—seems likely to be used, whether or not for this deliberate purpose. It is with this that our fourth proposition is concerned.

THE CULTURAL LAG IN THE DEFINITION OF METROPOLITAN POLITICAL BOUNDARIES WILL ENABLE MINORITIES TO SEIZE CONSIDERABLE POLITICAL POWER

The pattern of urban growth which we so often refer to as new is, in several sociological essentials, the same pattern of urban growth which we have always had in this country. The oldest, least desirable housing has customarily been located in or near the centers of American cities; the newest, most desirable housing has been located beyond the city limits. We speak with wonder of man's newest social invention, the suburb. The new thing about having desirable housing away from the center of the city is that unrealistic political boundaries in metropolitan areas are separating the wealthier, better-educated citizens from control of their central city.

The fact that an increasing proportion of middle-class housing falls outside the city limits in most metropolitan areas has an obvious corollary: an ever-increasing proportion of the people inside the city limits are members of minority populations. Whereas only 12 percent of the people in the Chicago metropolitan area are Negro, 24 percent of the people within Chicago's city limits are Negro, and the percentage will probably increase in the future. This sort of trend makes speculation about a Negro mayor for Chicago more realistic, if no less startling, than it would be without the cultural lag in city boundary lines. Indeed, a mayor of New York who is either Puerto Rican or Negro, or both, seems very likely within the next twenty years. If this seems fantastic today, consider the probable reaction of a resident of New York City in 1920 had he been told that three candidates for mayor in 1950 would be the Messrs. Pecora, Impellitteri, and Corsi.

The four propositions reinforce each other. The variable rates of assimilation and the lessened social distance will allow increased political power for the Negro minority. Increased political power will make them more visible, hence retarding assimilation, but will confer higher prestige, thus decreasing social distance. At the same time, the bid for political power will intensify interracial competition and provide a fertile field for conflict, which in turn will interfere with assimilation, and so on.

SOCIAL CLASS DIFFERENCES WILL BECOME MORE NOTICEABLE AS CLASS BECOMES LESS EASILY MISTAKEN FOR ETHNICITY

From the sociologist's point of view, the bulk of the traits which most people cite as typical of a minority are actually characteristics of people in lower socioeconomic statuses. This is precisely why people are so frequently forced to defend their stereotypes by consigning some specific case to the category of "an exception to the rule." When someone who is convinced that Negroes do not take care of their property is driven west on Emerson Street in Evanston, Illinois, he has to concede that these Negroes are exceptions to the rule. When he tours West Madison Street in Chicago, he is forced to the conclusion that the whites there live like Negroes—but not like the Negroes in Evanston. A much simpler way to interpret these data is to note that lower-class people do not take as good care of their property as middle-class people.

Many class distinctions of this variety are bound to become more obvious as the social distance between dominant and minority categories decreases, and as people become less accustomed to viewing one another through race-colored glasses. Not the least of these is the strong tendency of public schools in metropolitan areas to be segregated—not necessarily by race, but virtually always by social class.

We are a long way from, but on the road to, grappling with the problem that where factory laborers' sons go to one school and company executives' sons attend another, separate facilities are inherently unequal.

Education is committed to transmitting the heritage of the greater culture. When a school enrolls only those children who live in a world seldom touched by any aspect of that culture, the task of education becomes a formidable one. This is one of the great issues of urban education today. The population shifts throughout the metropolitan area which cause increasing isolation and ethnic homogeneity of communities have threatened the mixed-class neighborhood school with extinction. Robert Havighurst presents a strong case for the need of the mixed-class school. Many of the opportunities education should offer cannot be provided in a lower-class school.

METROPOLITAN DEVELOPMENT AND THE EDUCATIONAL SYSTEM / *Robert J. Havighurst*

Metropolitan growth presents two major concerns. First, it has led to increased segregation on the basis of income and race. This segregation is a threat to democratic unity and educational opportunity, for slums or gray areas of the central cities breed political and social divisiveness and discontent. Second, space is not used properly. The location of industry, business, and dwellings have made the daily journey to work longer and more difficult than is really necessary for a large part of the population. The distance from residential areas to centers of leisure and cultural activity—theaters, museums, concert halls—is too great. Open space for recreation and for the enjoyment of nature has not been distributed so as to be available to the majority of the people.

Metropolitan developments have produced or intensified many social problems, most of which have had repercussions in education. The net effect has been to make the educational system less efficient and less effective in achieving its democratic goals. We shall call the complex of a central city and its surrounding suburbs a megalopolis and analyze some of its problems.

One major problem is increased socioeconomic and racial segregation of the population. As the total population of a megalopolis grows, the slum belt around the central business district becomes thicker. This is a result not only of the growth in total population but also of the concentration of lower-class people in areas of poorest housing, which are usually in the oldest parts of the city. Those who can afford to do so move away from the inner city as their economic circumstances improve. In general, working-class people whose income permits it move out of the slum district and take up residence farther from the center of the city, while people in middle-class districts of the central city move out to middle-class suburbs. Thus the ever-growing total population divides itself into a lower-class conglomerate at the center, with successively higher socioeconomic groups at greater distances and the upper-middle class and the upper class largely in the suburbs.

Robert J. Havighurst, "Metropolitan Development and the Educational System," The School Review 69, 4 (1961), 251–267. Copyright 1961 by the University of Chicago Press.

While this process goes on in the central city, the suburbs themselves become stratified into communities that are predominantly upper-middle class or lower-middle class, or upper-lower class. The city dweller who aspires to a house in the suburbs will find that the amount of money he can pay for a house determines the type of suburb he will live in. If he is employed as a manual worker in an auto assembly plant or an electronics factory fifteen miles out of the city, he is likely to make a payment on a two-bedroom bungalow in a real estate development that has hundreds of similar houses, all variants of one basic design, all on small lots with a plot of grass in front, a garage and a clothesline in the rear. He will live in a working-class suburb. If he is a lawyer with an office in the city, he will buy a ranch-type house on a large lot in an area where all the other houses are of similar type and cost, in a new section of a well-established upper-middle-class suburb with a reputation for good schools and a good country club.

One result of the segregation of lower-class boys and girls into elementary and secondary schools where they are exposed only to other young people of similar socioeconomic status is to deny them the stimulation of associating with middle-class youth in the school and the classroom. If lower-class boys and girls are in classes where a third or more of the pupils are from a middle-class family, they will be stimulated to keep up with the middle-class children in school-work, and they will also be in a position to form friendships and thus learn some of the social behavior and social values of middle-class children. But when lower-class youth are segregated in slum schools, they may lose these advantages.

Another problem in megalopolis is the weakening of civic and social relations between the various socioeconomic groups. While it has always been a principle of American democracy that all kinds of people should participate in the same schools and churches and political organizations, the growing segregation in megalopolis lessens the opportunity for this kind of interrelationship. Middle-class boys and girls grow up in antiseptic suburbs. Slum children grow up with no contact with middle-class children, with whom they might learn the art of co-operative citizenship.

Poverty in the central city is another problem. The central city suffers from a progressive economic downgrading of its population but must maintain increasingly expensive urban services—expressways, subways, schools, hospitals, many of which serve the entire population of megalopolis.

With the polarization of megalopolis into lower-class urban areas and middle-class suburbs comes a chronic state of cold war between the two sets of interests, with no authority in a position to bring about co-operation for the common welfare.

Problems of megalopolitan housekeeping becomes critical. Certain essential services are not readily available to some areas. New suburbs may have difficulty in getting fire protection, a water supply, and sewage disposal. The various police departments in a metropolitan area may not co-operate, and law enforcement may become lax. Transportation and traffic problems arise, and people have increasing difficulty in getting to places of work and recreation. The daily journey to work becomes more and more time-consuming, eating up the time gained by shorter working hours. Distances and difficulties of transport cut down freedom of movement.

Suburban slums arise in the unincorporated areas outside the central city. People living in these areas may have primitive sanitary facilities, insufficient water, inadequate fire protection, inadequate schools and other cultural facilities. Absence of a strong county or metropolitan government permits this kind of haphazard development.

Finally, there is the problem of the rustication of suburban dwellers. Middle-class suburban dwellers become almost parochial in their outlook and attitudes. Because of transportation difficulties they lose contact with the vigorous and variegated culture of the central city. Their children grow up in isolation from many of the educational influences of a great city.

Because of the many problems associated with metropolitan growth and megalopolitan complexity, it might be supposed that people would cease fleeing from the central city to the suburbs and instead remake slum areas into middle-class residential areas. This course is being urged, and urban renewal plans are under way to make the central city attractive for middle-class living. However, these efforts at urban renewal are meeting with difficulty, and the schools are at the heart of the difficulty.

People who have a choice as to where they will live in a metropolitan area look first at the schools if they have children. They generally want schools that have good standards of schoolwork and behavior. They also like schools that have new buildings and wide play spaces. Some who are prejudiced against non-whites, or fearful that the presence of non-whites will cause the neighborhood and the school to deteriorate, look for schools that are all white and likely to remain so. Others look for schools that have a mixture of races and economic levels, because they believe that such schools can teach their children democracy.

As more and more people, including working-class people, can choose among various places to live, they become more aware of and interested in school policies and school performance. Among other things, they try to sense the spirit, or ethos, of the school. Does it stimulate children to do well academically? Does it encourage children to want to finish high school and go to college? Does it have a program that is useful and interesting for children from all kinds of families? Does it provide a social life they like for their children?

There is a crude quantitative index, called the *status ratio*, which is useful for studying the ethos of a school. The status ratio is simply the ratio of the number of pupils from middle-class families to the number of pupils from working-class families. The ratio is $[2 \ (U + UM) + LM] \div [UL + 2LL]$. The number of pupils from the upper class and the upper-middle class is weighted twice as heavily as the number of pupils from the lower-middle class, and the number of pupils from the lower-lower class is weighted twice as heavily as the number of pupils from the upper-lower class.

The reason for weighting the number of pupils from the upper-middle class and the lower-lower class more heavily in the formula is that pupils from the upper-middle class are about twice as likely to go to college and to exhibit other forms of academic interest and achievement as youth from the lower-middle class are, while youth from the lower-lower class are only about half as likely as pupils from the upper-lower class to show these characteristics.

The *race index* is also an important indicator of the desire of middle-class families to send their children to a particular school. The race index is a ratio that shows the proportions of white and Negro children in a school. Middle-class parents are likely to favor an index of 1.5 or higher, or a proportion of 60 percent or more of whites. Negro middle-class parents might accept a lower ratio, but they generally favor a mixed or integrated school over a segregated one. Some white middle-class parents favor complete segregation, but most middle-class whites in northern cities would accept a school for their children that was stabilized at a race index of 1.5 and a status ratio of .6 or higher.

The most powerful factor in determining whether a family that can choose among places to live will stay in the central city or move to a suburb is the nature of the school to which its children will go. If the status ratio is close to a critical point, middle-class parents become anxious and start to think of moving away. This critical point depends on the attitudes and the experience of a particular parent and therefore is a subjective thing. The critical point also depends on the race index, the tradition of the school, the type of curriculum, and the quality of the teachers. However, among middle-class parents there is substantial agreement on the critical point—enough agreement to cause them to stream out of a school district as if by common agreement when the status ratio reaches a certain point.

Secondary schools are more vulnerable than primary schools to desertion by middle-class parents when the status ratio reaches the critical point. In a community where the residents represent a cross section of the American population in socioeconomic status the high school has a status ratio of about 1.0. The ratio is higher than that of an elementary school in the same type of community because a number of boys and girls from families of the lower class drop out of high school. In an upper-middle-class suburb the status ratio is very high. But in the central city the slums continually encroach upon high schools in formerly middle-class areas and reduce the status ratio. When the critical point is reached, there is a rapid flight of middle-class families that have children of high-school age.

The twin functions of the school—to mirror the present community and to aid the community in achieving its goals—are both called into action.

The policy of adaptation to existing metropolitan trends assumes that the future structure of megalopolis will follow present trends. The belt of the lower-class residential area around the center of the city will expand and grow thicker. The flight of middle-class families to the suburbs will continue. Suburbs will increase in number, size, and variety. Low-cost public housing will gradually make a physical improvement in the gray areas and result in physical renewal of slums. Expressways will give automobile owners quicker and more comfortable access to all parts of megalopolis. The present trend toward residential segregation by socioeconomic status will continue, together with at least as much racial segregation as now exists. Only a few small countertrends will be seen, such as the growth of working-class suburbs and the construction of expensive apartment houses near the center of the city for well-to-do people with few school-age children.

The major educational adaptations will consist of attempts to provide educational stimulation and opportunity for children in slum areas and programs for the identification and the separation of the abler children in special classes and groups in the school.

A multitrack system will be introduced to separate children into groups formed on the basis of learning ability and social status. In schools in slum areas or areas threatened by encroaching slums, the system will have the effect of maintaining at least one subgroup that has a fairly strong academic motivation. The children of higher social status tend to be placed in the superior group, an arrangement that makes the school more tolerable for their parents. Whatever the value of homogeneous grouping in helping children achieve according to their intelligence, and the alleged benefits are repeatedly questioned by research studies, there is no doubt that most teachers and parents favor a multitrack system in a school where the status ratio has fallen below the critical point. The multitrack organization gives middle-class parents and working-class parents who seriously want their children to get the most out of school some assurance that they will be given special help and special consideration.

Enrichment programs will be set up for working-class children who achieve fairly well. These programs will supplement the multi-track program. The more promising children will be placed in smaller classes and given special counseling and guidance, and their parents will be encouraged to take more interest in their education. The children will be given access to museums, libraries, theaters, and concerts. One widely known example of such an approach is the Higher Horizons Program of Junior High School 43 and the George Washington High School in New York City. This program has stimulated a considerable number of boys and girls to graduate from high school and to enter college who would not have done so if they had not received special attention. Financial assistance for college attendance is a necessary part of such a program.

Enrichment programs will be set up for culturally deprived children at the kindergarten-primary level. Several large cities are already trying programs that give special assistance in the primary grades of slum schools on the theory that many of these children lack stimulation from parents to read and to achieve well in school. If these boys and girls are not given special attention, they may fail to master the task of reading. For the first few years in school, they will stumble along. In time they will become confirmed non-learners and during adolescence, social misfits. These children can get a better start in school and thus a better start in life. The school can give these boys and girls the better start they need by assigning specially trained teachers to small classes, by using social workers or visiting teachers to bring home and school into contact, and by giving the children the enrichment that middle-class children are likely to get in their homes.

Work-study programs will be introduced for youth who are failing in school. Under present conditions about 15 percent of all boys and girls fail to grow up successfully through the avenue the school provides. At about seventh grade they react to school with apathy or hostility and aggression. In slum areas this group is likely to make up 25 or 30 percent of the young people. These boys and girls are alienated from the value of the school and other middle-class institutions. It is these boys and girls who make teaching difficult in seventh, eighth, and ninth grades, and who make junior high school and the early years of senior high school difficult for academically motivated youth in schools where the status ratio is below the critical point. For alienated youth, especially for the boys, a good deal of experimentation with work-study programs is now going on. The aim is to give the young people who take part a chance to grow up satisfactorily through the avenue of work. Most such programs commence with young people at the age of sixteen, when they may drop out of school if they wish. The programs appear to be having some success. Possibly better results will be achieved in programs that provide work experience as a part of the school program as early as age fourteen, or eighth grade.

Some people, including some educators, are not satisfied with accepting the present trends of metropolitan development and adapting the schools to them. They believe that the civic ills of metropolitan growth require fundamental urban renewal. These critics ask that a rational megalopolis be designed. They call for plans that will lead to new growth from the center of the city to the suburbs, with parks, shopping centers, libraries, churches, and schools organized to serve people near where they live, and with industry, the central business district, and the centers of residence linked by fast, comfortable transportation, public and private. Billions of dollars are already being spent on bold new shopping plazas, garden villages, high-rise apartment buildings, and expressways.

Urban renewal has the physical goal of restoring areas of comfortable middle-class living in the central city and establishing areas of comfortable, slum-free, lower-class living. Beyond this, urban renewal has the social goal of making the whole of megalopolis a good place for all kinds of people to live in. Leaders of urban renewal often say that their goal is to increase the range and the amount of choice people have among good ways to live.

Among specialists in city planning there is much discussion of the typical physical plan that will make megalopolis a good place to live. It is generally agreed that residential areas should be decentralized, that each area should be self-contained with respect to shopping facilities, schools, libraries, and churches. One type of arrangement is the galaxy, in which constituent communities are spaced more or less evenly over the territory, with a network of highways and transportation lines leading to areas of specialized activity, such as industrial sites, airports, freight docks, and financial centers. Another type of arrangement is the many-pointed star or wagon wheel, with residential areas radiating from a central business district, industry located in certain sectors of the star, and transportation routes leading out from the center, crisscrossing other transportation routes that circle the area at various distances from the center.

There seems to be agreement among city planners on two matters: first, megalopolis should consist of residential areas that meet nearly all the ordinary needs of family and cultural life; second, many residential areas should contain a cross section of the social structure, with people of the upper class, the middle class, and the working class living in the same area. In particular, it is felt that many residential areas near the central business district should be populated by middle-class as well as working-class people.

Several large cities have embarked on major programs of slum clearance with the aim of restoring cross-sectional communities in the central city. Chicago has such areas to the south, the southwest, and the northwest of the central business district. St. Louis has the Mill Creek Valley District, southwest of the city center. New York City has several such areas, including one north of Columbia University. In these and other places slum buildings have been cleared, and land has been made available to private builders for apartment buildings and single-family residences to be sold or rented to people who can afford to pay substantial prices and rents.

The future of these developments is uncertain, however, and further urban renewal is likely to be delayed until these experiments are evaluated. One major question is whether middle-class people with children will move into these renewal areas. Their decision will depend on their attitudes toward the schools. They may want new, modern school buildings, and in many places they will get them because the old buildings are obsolete. More important, they are likely to want assurance that the status ratio of the schools will be above the critical point. This assurance may be present for elementary schools, which serve relatively small areas, but not for secondary schools, which may serve both a renewal area and a large neighboring working-class area. The secondary school is likely to be the crucial element of the school system. The secondary school may well make or break programs for urban renewal.

Urban renewal of a fundamental nature will require major developments in school policy. The megalopolis of the future will probably have a single area-wide governing and taxing unit, with constituent local communities of fifty to a hundred thousand in population, each with its own local government. School policies and programs will be determined partly by an area-wide educational authority and partly by local community school boards. The following propositions concerning educational policy would seem to fit a rational plan for megalopolitan development:

1. A single area-wide educational authority with its own tax authority should be supplemented by local community school boards with authority to levy supplementary taxes for educational purposes.

2. A metropolitan area educational council or commission should work with the metropolitan area planning council on plans for establishment of new suburban school districts and area-wide educational institutions, such as a university, a teachers college, and technical institutions.

3. The area-wide educational authority should have responsibility for such educational functions as purchasing, teacher certification, pensions, the planning and the construction of school buildings.

4. The school board of the local community should administer its own school system up through the secondary school and probably through the junior college. It should provide a school program suited to community needs and should levy supplementary taxes if the area-wide tax support is inadequate.

Any metropolitan area that commits itself to a fundamental program of urban renewal needs to provide for a transitional period of perhaps twenty years. During this period the local communities would gradually become organized and separated from other communities by green belts, parks, and open spaces; and they would be linked by a system of highways and transportation routes:

Certain educational policies would need to be adopted for the transitional period. The policies should be aimed at stopping the flight of middle-class people from the central city. The goal should be self-contained communities of fifty to a hundred thousand in population, communities made up of a social cross section of the entire area. Some policies would be temporary, while others would become permanent policy for the megalopolis of the future. The principal transitional policies might well call for:

1. A set of regional high schools generously selective on the basis of intelligence and school achievement so as to be open to the top third of the high-school age group. Admission to these high schools should be controlled so that no school would have less than 60 percent white students and every school would have a status ratio higher than .6. By the end of the transitional period these schools would probably become comprehensive high schools serving local communities and open to all high-school students.

2. A set of work-study centers at the junior high school level for boys and girls who have demonstrated that they cannot profit from the regular academic high-school program. These centers should be located in junior and senior high schools but run on a separate schedule. They should enroll 10 to 20 percent of the school population at age thirteen or fourteen to sixteen, but enrollment should drop as the elementary schools improve their kindergarten-primary programs.

3. A set of general high schools with strong commercial and vocational training programs for young people who are not attending other types of schools. By the end of the transitional period they would probably merge with the selective schools into comprehensive high schools serving local communities.

4. Special attention at the kindergarten-primary level to children from culturally and emotionally inadequate homes so as to give these children as good a start in school as possible, thus reducing the number who would later go to the work-study centers.

5. A set of regional junior colleges so located that there would eventually be one in each local residential community.

6. An adult education program on an area-wide basis, a program that uses junior colleges and branches of the public library, a program that exploits the educative potential of the metropolitan area and seeks to make adult education available to all kinds of people.

Some of the adaptations now being made in great cities to the problems of metropolitan development can be fitted into a rational plan for urban renewal. There is no need for educators to take sides in a controversy between the two alternatives posed here—that of making the best of existing trends and that of working toward fundamental urban renewal. However, the choice of fundamental urban renewal requires more exercise of rational foresight, more thought about goals of megalopolitan development and about ways of reaching these goals. Educators can impede urban renewal by holding stubbornly to practices that were good before World War II but have now lost much of their value.

REFERENCES

Anderson, N. *The Urban Community: A World Perspective.* New York: Holt, Rinehart and Winston, Inc., 1959.

Berger, Bennet M. *Working Class Suburb.* Berkeley, Calif.: University of California Press, 1960.

Conant, James Bryant. *Slums and Suburbs.* New York: McGraw-Hill Book Company, Inc., 1961.

Drake, St. Clair, and Horace R. Clayton. *Black Metropolis.* New York: Harcourt, Brace & World, Inc., 1945.

Lund, S. E. Torsten. *The School-Centered Community.* New York: Anti Defamation League, 1949.

Lynd, Robert S. and Helen M. *Middletown and Middletown in Transition.* New York: Harcourt, Brace & World, Inc., 1929 and 1937.

Mumford, Lewis. *The Culture of Cities.* New York: Harcourt, Brace & World, Inc., 1938.

Passow, Harry. *Education in Depressed Urban Areas.* New York: Columbia University Press, 1962.

Petry, Ann. *The Street.* Boston: Houghton Mifflin Company, 1946.

Queen, S. A., and D. B. Carpenter. *The American City.* New York: McGraw-Hill Book Company, Inc., 1953.

Quinn, J. A. *Urban Sociology.* New York: American Book Company, 1955.

Rattan, V. W. "Industrial Progress and Rural Stagnation in the New South." *Social Forces,* 34 (December 1955), 114–118.

Walker, Charles R. *Steeltown.* New York: Harper & Row, Publishers, Inc., 1950.

PERIODICALS

Beers, H., and C. Heflin. *Urban Adjustments of Rural Migrants.* Lexington, Ky.: Agricultural Experiment Station, Bulletin 487, June 1946.

Burgess, Ernest W. "The Family in a Changing Society." *American Journal of Sociology,* LIII, No. 6 (May 1948), 417–422.

Burgin, R. W. *A Study of Literature Relevant to the Urbanization of*

Rural Southern Migrants. (An independent research paper.) Type-written form, May 1959.

Dodson, Dan W. "The Changing Neighborhood." *Educational Leadership,* 18 (May 1961), 497–501.

Druding, Aleda. "Stirrings in the Big Cities: Philadelphia." *NEA Journal,* 51 (February 1962), 48–51.

Havighurst, Robert J. "Metropolitan Development and the Educational System." *School Review,* 69, 251–267.

Hunter, M. C. "Stirrings in the Big Cities: Los Angeles." *NEA Journal,* 51 (April 1962), 18–20.

Weaver, Robert C. "Human Values of Urban Life." *Proceedings of the Academy of Political Science,* 27 (May 1960), 33–41.

Chapter Two

THE IMPACT OF URBANIZATION ON EDUCATION

Education has felt the full impact of the urban crisis. Mass population shifts have made the urban school district essentially one of culturally disadvantaged children, and educators have observed for some time, with increasing alarm, that neither the "tried and true" methods nor the latest pedagogical gimmicks are effectively reaching these children. The recent concentration of disadvantaged children in the urban schools has shaken education to its very foundations. Education can no longer make the distinction between the hewers of wood and the academically elite. The two-track curriculum becomes an absurdity when one third of the urban children are shuttled through only one track that leads to public subsidy of one sort or another. A redefinition of the role of education becomes necessary. Education cannot offer a curriculum intended to prepare students for life in their own community; the goals of society are to change such a community, not perpetuate it.

Beyond the city limits residents have learned that the "good life" they sought for their children comes at a high price. A residential suburb may be free of the social problems that accompany heavy industry; but the homeowner alone must finance an expensive school system which is expected to prepare his children for college or some other high-status position at all costs. The suburban homeowner often finances his schools reluctantly, clinging to the traditional values of private consumption and remaining suspicious of public consumption.

Here, too, education must redefine the community for which it prepares its students. The high mobility of our society requires education of a broad and liberal sort. Also, the newly developed residential community rarely has tradition or an established style of life to give unity and direction to the curriculum.

From the heart of the metropolis clear to its periphery the configuration of urbanization has been altering the role of education. Traditionally education lags behind its society, changes being brought about as it gradually adapts to outer pressures. Today education is adjusting from within in an unprecedented and constructive way.

Most migrants coming into the metropolitan center are rural Negroes. Many arrive severely disadvantaged, only to become more so in the impersonal press of contemporary urban life. Consequently, race has become an essential factor in the social, economic, and educational problems of the city. Clemmont Vontress discusses how this situation affects educational issues.

OUR DEMORALIZING SLUM SCHOOLS / *Clemmont E. Vontress*

A fed-up big-city school teacher resigned with this comment: "In public schools today the teacher is afraid of the principal; the principal is afraid of the superintendent; the superintendent is afraid of the school board; the board is afraid of the parents; the parents are afraid of the children; and the children are afraid of nobody."

Clemmont E. Vontress, "Displaced Negroes and Urban School," Phi Delta Kappan *(November 1963), pp. 77–81. Reprinted with the permission of Phi Delta Kappa, Inc.*

Such reaction, although tinged with humor, incisively describes one aspect of the much talked-about explosive social situations which swell in inner-cities. While many social institutions are subjected to critical analysis because of these potentially dangerous conditions, the severest scrutiny and the sharpest attack is reserved for the school. Perhaps this is because the school has for so many years been thought of as the panacea institution of a troubled society struggling to realize democracy for all its citizens. Not wishing to appear impotent as a social agency, it has attempted to be all things to all people. Lately, however, educators have gained new insights into what the school can and cannot do. They realize that no school system can overcome singlehandedly the social, cultural, and economic handicaps under which many children live in their non-school hours.

The retreat of whites from decaying city cores to segregated suburbs has become a salient social phenomenon. This exodus from the Negro-occupied inner-city has reached unbelievable proportions and no abatement is in sight. The annual white overflow from New York is 50,000; from Chicago, 15,000; and from Cleveland, 3,000.[1] As whites scamper, waves of Southern, country-bred Negroes move in. In 1895, Booker T. Washington revealed in his famous "Cast Down Your Buckets Where You Are" speech that one-third of the population of the South was Negro. Today, 43.5 percent of the country's 18,871,831 Negroes live outside the original Confederacy states.[2] Negro population density in major Northern cities is four times that of whites. Detroit is 28.9 percent Negro; Chicago, 22.9 percent; and Washington, D.C., 53.9 percent.[3] Some observers predict that by 1970 over one-half of all Negroes will live outside the South.

The Negro's presence in Northern urban areas has brought heretofore unknown racial problems to many cities. His "most visible racial traits which force themselves spontaneously upon one's attention"[4] and his un-city ways[5] have resulted in nationwide attention and

---

[1] Erwin Knoll, "The Truth About Desegregation in the Washington, D.C., Public Schools," *The Journal of Negro Education,* 28:92–113, No. 2, Spring 1959.

[2] G. Roberts, Jr., "Negro Education for What?" *New York Times Magazine,* November 19, 1961, p. 26.

[3] See Clemmont B. Vontress, "Parents of Segregation and Discrimination: Contributing Factors to Crime Among Negroes," *The Journal of Negro Education,* 31:108–116, No. 2, Spring 1962.

[4] Pitirim A. Sorokin, *Society, Culture, and Personality: Their Structure and Dynamics.* New York: Harper and Brothers, 1947, p. 183.

[5] Knoll, *op. cit.*

increased prejudice. Full integration into American society is still remote. Every small advance in one area is offset by a retreat in another.
Segregation by race is giving away to segregation by economic class.
Legalistically, advances have been made; economically, more severe
pressures and restrictions for the vast majority of Negroes are apparent. Automation, calling for technically trained workers, now excludes
most poorly educated, unskilled Negro workers from the ranks of the
employed. Since unemployed parents are in no position to assist their
children in furthering their education, a degrading, self-perpetuating
cycle of poverty sets in. Although laws may not prohibit a Negro from
entering certain places of business, money—that is, the lack of it—
will. For the vast majority of Negroes, equality will be realized only
when they can compete economically. Successful job competition depends on education. Thus, finding ways to keep Negro youngsters in
school is just as urgent as passing laws to "open doors" through which
only the employed pass. Unless Negro children stay in school, the
poverty-stricken, crime-riddled inner-city will remain the unhappy
staging center for black DP's destined for a life of misery and shame.

In spite of steps toward school integration, the majority of Negro
children will continue to attend all-Negro schools located in all-Negro
neighborhoods.[6] These schools serve the cramped victims of residential segregation. Overcrowded all-Negro areas constitute cultural
Siberias, stifling educational initiative. In general, the conditions under
which Negro children are expected to receive an "equal" education
are demoralizing to parents, teachers, and administrators, not to mention the children themselves.

DEMORALIZED PARENTS

Criticism of the apparent indifference of Negro parents toward
education and the public schools is demoralizing to those criticized.
Educators lament that homes are not measuring up to their original
responsibility. Parents and children who are seldom at home at the
same time have become strangers. Home has become a rest-stop where
family members fill up, rest up, clean up, and are off again. Mothers
and fathers are remiss in disciplining their children and in encouraging
them to study. This analysis of the home situation, although accurate
in many cases, is unfortunate, for it seemingly absolves schools of
further responsibility. Further, in failing to delimit the problem, it dis-

---

[6] Loren Miller, "Home Sweet Segregated Home," *The Journal of Negro
Education,* 28:142–144, No. 2, Spring, 1959.

torts the truth. Middle-class homes whose goals and aspirations are compatible with those of middle-class oriented schools have not abdicated their responsibility, for the most part. Urban-suburban population shifts have created socio-racial stratifications which now force into bold relief thousands of victimized lower-class Negroes who, because of continued psychological isolation from the dominant group, are cultural strangers.

In general, lower socio-economic families are characterized by material deprivation and low standards of conduct. Although they are many-generation Americans, their culture is not the dominant culture; it is lacking in stimulating content, for they have suffered their outsider status so long in so many ways. High proportions of their children began school with little on which to build a good education.[7] Language differences and the verbal problems children experience can be illustrated by the second-grader who dejectedly reported, "Ma, I ain't going to school any more."

"Why not?" inquired her mother.

"Cause it ain't no use. I can't never learn to spell. The teacher keeps changing the words on me all the time."

Lack of familiarity with the language of the school and its textbooks is handicapping to slum children. In this respect the child is not unlike his parents, who also find it difficult to understand and communicate with those who seek to change their offspring. Teachers, both Negro and white, represent another culture. They dress differently, talk differently, think differently, and appreciate differently. Negro parents come to look upon them as partially responsible for their hunger, pain, and entrapment in the ghetto. They are especially suspicious and critical of Negro teachers, who they feel are in cahoots with whites seeking to further confuse, deny, and suppress them.

It should not be supposed, however, that all slum parents are alike. Some are victims of what Galbraith[8] calls "case poverty." They are too lazy, drunk, or mentally deficient to care what happens to their children. Demoralized and frustrated out of debauchery or ignorance, they are quick to blame anyone but themselves for their unfortunate situation. Often looking upon their children as unanticipated although appreciated commodities, they may connive to keep them out of school

---

[7] Robert W. Smuts, "The Negro Community and the Development of Negro Potential," *The Journal of Negro Education,* 26:456–465, No. 4, Fall, 1957.

[8] John K. Galbraith, *The Affluent Society.* Boston: Houghton-Mifflin Co., 1958, p. 325.

to help "keep the family going." On the other hand, parents who are victims of "insular poverty" are cognizant of what is happening to them; but they are powerless to combat the forces that confuse and ensnare their lives.[9] Indeed, it would be a shock to some of the whites who criticize the conditions in which many Negroes live to find out that the people most dissatisfied with slum conditions are the people who live in them, who are entombed in ghettos in a caste of pigmentation. Parents representative of this group try to provide for their brood but are powerless to overcome the negative forces operating against them. Women without husbands work long, hard, monotonous hours to afford bare necessities for their offspring. They would like to be more active in the PTA, but their lack of time and energy deny them the opportunity. Often their status in society results in a lack of appreciation for middle-class values, including education. Thus they feel little allegiance to the school and have little faith in what it can do for their children, since it has meant so little in their own lives.

WHY NEGRO TEACHER MORALE IS LOW

Added to the educational impotence of slum schools is the demoralization of many teachers who staff them. In major Northern cities, most Negro teachers, regardless of qualifications, are shuttled off to teach in ghetto schools. Denied an opportunity to come in contact with the full range of learning abilities, many of them become tired, discouraged, and disgruntled.[10] To them school is not an enthusiastic learning center where everybody is academically alert, where people desire to learn something now because it is worth knowing. Instead, it is a place where a major part of the teacher's time must be devoted to maintaining discipline among children who never before have known it. Thus it is often felt that years of excellent preparation go for naught.

There are other reasons why the morale of Negro teachers is often low. Many of them did not plan to teach in the first place; they were forced by discrimination into this traditional Negro white-collar job.[11] Through their education and association many have become psychologically "white" and are repelled by having to work and rear their children in segregated communities. In many cases, they send their own children to other schools, because of the obvious deficiencies of

---

[9] Ibid., p. 326.

[10] Martin Mayer, "How Alive Is Your High School?" Seventeen, 22: 120–3, February, 1963.

[11] Omar Carmichael, "Is Voluntary Integration the Answer?" U. S. News and World Report, 4:46–50, October, 1956.

the schools in which they teach or because they fear the influences of lower-class children on their own. Further, Negro teachers are frequently very sensitive to and critical of their Negro administrators who must play "both ends" (kow-towing to white superiors while appeasing and engineering co-workers) to insure the smooth operation of the school.

In general, Negro teachers appear to be ambivalent toward all-Negro schools. Many express disappointment over the performance of their students. Others, becoming defensive of their schools, keep from students and parents the fact that all-Negro schools are inferior to those where white children go. Holding their white counterparts in high esteem, they often feel that it is prestigeful to teach in predominantly white schools.[12] Few, however, leave the comfort and security of their own race even when the opportunity is available.

The challenges of slum schools call for better teaching. "Better teaching" implies enthusiasm and willingness to experiment and to grow on the part of the teacher. If Negro children continue to receive an inferior education in inner-city schools, it is not because Negro teachers do not measure up to white teachers, as Carmichael[13] boldly stated in 1956; rather, it is because shuttled-off teachers are discouraged and disgusted with the practice of assigning Negro teachers to all-Negro or predominantly Negro schools. Although they have not quit on the job, they are seriously demoralized. Integrating teachers now may help to arrest this creeping lethargy. The interests and attitudes of white and Negro teachers can be shared. The elimination of this ethnic educational in-breeding on the faculty level should also revive interest in learning on the part of students. They will see integration in action and may soon come to rededicate themselves to striving for achievement in spite of their race.

THE NEGRO PRINCIPAL: MAN IN A TRAP

To assume that the principal of the slum school is less demoralized than parents and teachers is to be unaware of the facts. The Negro principal must respond to the expectations of the superintendent, who is generally white, and to his teachers, who are usually Negro. This dual responsibility creates an ethnic dilemma for him. If he responds

---

[12] Willard E. Gandy, "Implications for Integration for the Southern Teacher," *The Journal of Negro Education*, 31:191–197, No. 2, Spring, 1962.

[13] Carmichael, *op. cit.*

to the expectations of the superintendent and neglects those of his co-workers, he may incur severe criticism from his teachers and the wider community as well, since teachers assume many roles outside the classroom.

The responsibility entrapment causes many top-level administrators to exculpate themselves while giving pupils and parents a false impression of what they are getting for their money.[14] Fearful of criticism from superiors, Negro school administrators are often more interested in presenting a "good front" than they are in ascertaining the real capabilities of their students and teachers.[15] This, in part, may be why slum schools have become harbors of incompetent teachers and prisons for inept students. Principals often stock-pile passionate and vituperative replies to hurl at those who imply that their students do not measure up.[16] They thus dilly-dally away precious psychological time and expend vital energy defending "Negro Education," thereby falling into a snare set by the white power structure seeking to contain the Negro student in separate schools.

Especially frustrating to the Negro principal is the often ill-defined role of the white subject-matter supervisors who work within the school, but who are under direct supervision of the superintendent. While this ambiguous situation is disconcerting to most principals, it is especially obnoxious to the Negro principal, who may feel surrounded by white spies who may cost him his job. To say that the principal of an all-Negro slum school has a difficult job is to put it mildly.

THE POSITION OF THE STUDENT

Let us now look for a moment at the position of the student. The typical slum school, although located in the inner-city, is still middle-class oriented. Its goals are therefore antithetical to the focal concerns of the youth it serves. Having to meet the expectations of this educational institution for over one-half of their waking hours is frequently intolerable. Their own poverty and the resultant necessity to work part-time, their lack of privacy at home, and the remoteness of school-set goals prevent them from concentrating on study. The longer they stay in school the more discouraged they become. Many who do not become truant merely sit out their lessons, stolidly awaiting the drone of the

---

[14] L. W. Jones, "Social Unreadiness of Negro Youth," *Saturday Review,* 45:81–83, October, 1962.

[15] *Ibid.*

[16] *Ibid.*

bell and their release from suffering. Others, finding self-restraint no longer possible, express themselves in the only way they know how—through toughness, smartness, and excitement, thereby invoking immediate condemnation from their captors.

Students who are able to meet the expectations of the school are often unwilling to put forth the effort, for they are aware that an education is likely to be useless. Even with a college education, they may be forced to drive municipal busses, bell-hop, wait tables, or work in post offices. Seeing no escape from the racial trap, they look forward not to more education but to adult work and marriage.

Students who want more education may recognize that the academic odds are against them. Their unfamiliarity with the official language in which most tests are written is a barrier to qualifying for competitive college scholarships, most of which are based on test scores. It was reported that in 1956 not a single Negro was among the 5,000 or so winners or runners-up in the National Merit Scholarship Qualifying Test.[17] Although a great deal of work has been done to indicate the cultural bias of tests, this method of determining who shall get college scholarships is likely to continue for some time.

The explosive character of the inner-city situation is easy to see. Youngsters no longer able to withstand the confinement of classrooms are roving the streets night and day looking for their kind of excitement—crime and destruction. To them, nothing is inviolable. Incapable of achieving in school and unsuccessful in finding work, wandering dropouts often live by the code, "Fair is foul, and foul is fair." Stealing, destroying, assaulting, they do not or cannot conform to the expectations of the dominant society.

Citizens, associating idleness with norm-violating behavior, have become concerned over the alarmingly high dropout rates among teenagers. Parents, teachers, and community leaders often hurl accusations and recriminations at each other. Although disagreement abounds on the dropout question, there is a general consensus that since youngsters without a high-school diploma are locked out of the labor market, the best place for them is in school, even though many cannot read or write well enough to achieve a modicum of success. If they are different as a result of their impoverished background, they should be treated differently, some propose. Advocates of this approach say that vocational training programs designed to meet the employment opportu-

---

[17] Stanley E. Ballinger, "Of Testing and Its Tyranny," *Phi Delta Kappan*, 44:176–180, No. 4, January, 1963.

nities in the community should be provided.[18] However, this viewpoint has come under attack by educators who view automation with increasing alarm. They maintain that traditional vocational training will serve neither the interests of the economy nor the Negro. Unskilled and semi-skilled workers are being replaced rapidly by machines. Moreover, to provide a special kind of education for minority youth is to make more rigid the caste which they and their parents have known for so long. In the American society, integration means competition, and successful competition requires equal education. Without it, true equality in other areas will never be realized.

MUCH TO BE DONE—QUICKLY

If we intend to do more than continue the make-believe of educating countless slum children who will eventually become wards of the state, much has to be done and done quickly. The slum community must be mobilized to exert whatever resources may be there. Parents must be taught to demand quality education. This means demanding quality teachers, administrators, and school board members. To compensate for the poor state of affairs in slum schools, more money must be spent on them than on schools which serve middle-class communities. Teachers should be given incentive pay for teaching in slum schools. How else are quality teachers to be kept in run-down inner-city schools?

At the school level, teachers and administrators must work to win back alienated parents, who have come to associate schools with the "they" in their lives, the people who somehow determine what happens to them. If parents will not come to school—and there is some reason to believe that they will not—the school must go to them. "Education Appreciation" workshops may be set up in neighborhood churches, regardless of denomination or the state of repair of the church. The main thing is to make contact and gain the psychological leverage for social action. Parents must learn that education is the salvation for themselves and for their children.

Negro educators who continue to defend "Negro Education" should examine their positions carefully. Would it not be more fruitful to stand up for quality education instead? Negro education teeters on excuses; quality education competes on equality.

The slum school curriculum needs re-examination. Special attention

---

[18] James B. Conant, "False Education for Many Slum Children?" *Ladies Home Journal*, 79:6, January, 1962.

must be given to the teaching of reading, since it is impossible to learn without being able to read. All teachers must become teachers of reading.

Since the slum child's world has been devoid of books, the whole school must become a library. Every classroom should have its own library, not locked in clear-glass bookcases but readily available on open shelves. Children must be able to find books on any subject which is of even the slightest interest to them.

An examination of the curriculum is incomplete until teachers have taken a look at themselves. The importance of this is realized if it is accepted that the Negro child needs to develop a sense of identity, a pride in being Negro, in being black. If the teacher himself is anxious about being Negro, he is an ineffective purveyor of faith, courage, and pride in being Negro. The school curriculum must help the child discover who he is and what he is. A course in Negro history may be effective in helping the student acquire a historical frame of reference. A course in the psychology of adjustment may be an immediate way to heal wounded personalities, bleeding from self-pity, shame, and a lack of courage to achieve.

Guidance counselors are needed in greater numbers in slum schools. If the counselor-student ratio in the average middle-class school is 1:300, it should be 1:150 in the slum school. The Negro child is alienated from himself, from the school, and from those who remind him of himself. He needs to find identity in a white world. Coming from predominantly matriarchal homes, Negro boys and girls grow from the experience of a counseling relationship.

There are many pressing social needs indeed, but none seems nearly so important as searching for ways to give slum boys and girls a reason for staying in school.

The number of children we fail to educate in urban schools is appalling. Frederick Shaw points out that this problem is rapidly becoming a crisis. If the schools do not effectively solve this problem, the city will face greater social problems at a later time.

EDUCATING CULTURALLY DEPRIVED YOUTH IN URBAN CENTERS / *Frederick Shaw*

The number one problem faced by urban teachers today is how to offer culturally deprived youth an education that meets their needs. In 1950, about one child out of ten attending public schools in the nation's fourteen largest cities was culturally disadvantaged. In 1960, the proportion had risen to one of three. Some authorities believe that by 1970 it may be one out of two. These figures underscore the urgency of the problem.

The purpose of this article is to trace the origins of the problem, show how some of the nation's larger school systems are trying to handle it, and explore the issues involved.

In terms of sheer numbers, American population movements in the middle years of this century dwarf the tribal invasions of the early Middle Ages and the westward surge in American history. During the years 1940 through 1960, for example, more than twenty-six million people were added to the populations of the suburbs of our large cities. The entire country did not contain that many people in 1850.

By 1960, about 62 percent of all Americans were concentrated in 212 "standard metropolitan areas." Such a region is defined by the Bureau of the Census as "one or more contiguous counties containing at least one central city of over 50,000 population as the core of an economically and socially integrated cluster of people." In more colorful language, these areas have been called a "galaxy of urban solar systems." The combined population of these metropolitan areas now exceeds 108 million inhabitants, and almost one-third of the nation now lives in suburban areas.

Suburb and central city, however, have not grown at the same pace. Between 1950 and 1960, the outskirts of our great cities grew by more than seventeen million, an increase of 47.2 percent. At the same time, the central cores gained scarcely four million, only 8.2 percent. Millions have deserted the central areas for the suburbs, seeking attractive homes and surroundings, more play space for children, and lower taxes. Those who left were usually in the above-average income brackets, for they could afford to buy a house and pay commuting

Frederick Shaw, "Educating Culturally Deprived Youth in Urban Centers," Phi Delta Kappan (November 1963), pp. 91–93, 96–97. Reprinted with the permission of Phi Delta Kappa, Inc.

costs. The poorer families, of course, were unable to build or purchase homes or rent "garden apartments."

As a result, some of our more affluent suburbs have tended to become homogeneous in economic status and occupation, and sometimes in ethnic background as well. Dan W. Dodson, professor of educational sociology at New York University, has pointed out the consequences of this selectivity. Suburbanites, he declared, lead an "antiseptic" way of life: "nice families, segregated into nice homes, away from the pollution of both industry and the heterogeneous masses of the inner city."

Economic homogeneity can operate most advantageously for a community's educational system, if its affluent citizens are school-minded and willing to tax themselves. Some of the best American school systems today are found in wealthy suburban areas. School districts near New York, Chicago, and Philadelphia have built up top-ranking systems. They have pioneered in teaching methods, school administration, and school architecture. Schools like these are sometimes called "lighthouse schools," because they serve as beacons to guide less favored communities in educational progress.

Who replaces suburban-bound citizens in the core cities? Throughout American history, the chief source of unskilled urban labor has been Europeans. Today, trans-Atlantic immigration has been reduced to a trickle, and the principal newcomers are natives of the Western hemisphere. Thousands of Puerto Ricans and Negroes from our Southern states have settled in such Northeastern cities as Newark and New York. Southern Negroes and Appalachian whites have migrated to Baltimore, Detroit, Cincinnati, Chicago, and other cities in the Middle West, Mexican-American and reservation Indians have flocked to western cities, such as Oakland, California, and Phoenix, Arizona. Between 1950 and 1960, New York City lost about 1,300,000 middle-class whites, a population greater than that of Cleveland, Ohio. They were replaced by 800,000 Negroes and Puerto Ricans, an underprivileged group larger in size than Washington, D.C. New York's experience in the Fifties was not typical in numbers, but it *was* characteristic of population shifts other major cities have experienced.

James B. Conant believes that the "very nature of the community determines what goes on in the school." The neighborhoods in which these immigrants settle are often characterized by bad housing, high population density, and a lack of privacy. Incomes tend to be low and uncertain, and many residents may be on public relief rolls. Most have limited vocational and economic competence and low social and economic expectancy. Not infrequently, the community lacks trained leadership. Crime rates are high and conditions ripe for juvenile delinquency. Cultural resources are minimal. Family patterns are disoriented.

Neighborhoods of this kind have a marked impact on their schools, for the children who live in such areas are poorly prepared and poorly motivated for formal education. Mel Ravitz, professor of sociology at Wayne State University, has explained why the conventional courses taught in urban schools often seem to have little relevance for them:

> Many of these children of the depressed areas come from home situations that are deplorable, where the primary need is for the services of a nurse, a dentist, a dietician, where there is abject poverty, where there is much physical overcrowding in poor housing, where many kinds of psychological problems beset members of the family. Often, too, the families are split, with the mother assuming responsibility for both parents. Even if the family is not split, the controls that once applied in the rural setting have been broken in an urban setting that is hostile, uncaring, anonymous, and which has forced the restructuring of the family. The parental images the children now see are images of despair, of frustration, and of enforced idleness. It is absurd, too, for a middle-class teacher to set these children down each day to try to focus their attention on ancient history or on the multiplication table or on nouns or verbs, when simple good common sense demands a concern with situations and circumstances under which these children live, conditions which they cannot ignore sufficiently to concentrate on what to them are really otherworldly matters.[1]

Research studies have consistently shown lower average IQ's among children in such depressed areas than those from more favored homes. Often scores on such tests decline as the children grow older. Here are the median scores in certain disadvantaged districts in New York City: grade one—95; grade three—92; grade six—87; grade eight —82.

Children from low socio-economic areas also tend to fall farther and farther behind their peers in achievement. In one large district in New York, the average child was found to be retarded one year in reading in the third grade, almost two years in the sixth, and two and one-half in the eighth.

---

[1] Mel Ravitz, "The Role of the School in the Urban Setting: Depressed Areas." Paper delivered at Work Conference on Curriculum and Teaching in Depressed Urban Areas, Teachers College, Columbia University, July 2–13, 1962.

These children often have great difficulties in personal adjustment. Delinquency is more concentrated, and destructive aggression more widespread in problem areas; psychoses and completely disabling breakdowns are disproportionately high. One reason is that they receive relatively little of the ego satisfaction, the rewards, and the feeling of belonging that society has to offer. Almost from the very beginning, however, many fail to master the conventional curriculum. This lowers their already shaky self-esteem. School dropouts are also highest among children from neighborhoods of this kind, and relatively few go to college.

Basically, these children have the same drives for achievement, recognition, and acceptance as their peers; but deficiencies in early experiences and in motivation, and frequently family and social difficulties as well, weigh the odds against academic success. Often their parents work at jobs requiring little education, and the children get the impression that school is not particularly important in preparing them for life. These influences seem to weigh most heavily on the boys. In low socio-economic areas, they consistently score lower on intelligence tests and achievement tests than the girls.

Difficulties like these are further aggravated by the high turnover of newcomers in the schools. Children frequently shift from neighborhood to neighborhood and from school to school, disrupting their own schooling as well as the education of their less-traveled classmates. In Manhattan, where the pupil population of the elementary schools is higher than 76 percent Negro and Puerto Rican, the mean mobility rate in a recent year was 51 percent. In three schools that were almost completely Negro, the turnover was 100 percent that year.

Some authorities believe that the whole environment in these slum areas must be improved and that the schools must play a vital role in this endeavor. What they need is more special services, greater efforts to help pupils solve their personal problems, and a boost in their parents' cultural aspirations. This is precisely what the Great Cities Grey Areas School Improvement program and the Higher Horizons program have set out to do. Each will be discussed in turn.

The "great cities" include the fourteen largest public school systems in the country. Ten are now experimenting with the Grey Areas program, assisted by the Ford Foundation. Program aims are to help disadvantaged children in many ways: to raise their school achievement levels, to identify and help able youngsters, to raise the level of their aspirations, to equip them for modern urban life by developing their competencies, to increase parental responsibility, and to mobilize community support in their behalf.

When James B. Conant visited slum schools in big cities, he found teachers and administrators struggling against "appalling odds." These schools are too difficult and the rewards too small for many teachers. As a result, the need for teachers in such schools tends to outrun the supply.

Measures have been taken to help the teachers in these schools. Alertness courses, some partly on open-circuit TV, have trained teachers in such areas as the techniques of teaching reading. Specially trained coordinators recently conducted a training program for teachers of non-English-speaking children. Finally, teacher assistants have taken over some of the teachers' burdens. Volunteers provided by the Public Education Association have assisted classroom teachers for several years. A key part of this experiment has been helping pupils improve their reading and giving special assistance to the non-English-speaking child.

Some teacher preparatory institutions have attempted to inculcate future teachers with the idealism of the Peace Corps. Hunter College, a municipally supported institution in New York, has been developing a promising program of training teachers to staff multi-problem schools. Student volunteers are assigned to a particular school in a depressed neighborhood, usually in Harlem. They familiarize themselves not only with the schools but with the community as well. They visit Negro homes, read Negro newspapers, confer with community leaders, talk with local ministers, and inspect local housing projects, hospitals, and police stations. They observe teachers for two weeks before they gradually "break in" to a regular classroom assignment. More thorough than most pupil-teacher courses, this program includes mutual exchanges of experiences among student-teachers, periodic conferences with key personnel in the school, and intensive guidance by the Hunter College teacher preparatory staff. Comprehensive preparation of this kind helps ready them for later service in schools in depressed areas. It enables them to face their tasks with realism and understanding instead of shock and frustration.

The "Bridge Project," conducted at Queens College, another college-level municipal institution, is a demonstration project established to discover how teachers can be prepared to help slum children learn. (Bridge stands for "Building Resources of Instruction for Disadvantaged Groups in Education.") Its approach is many-sided. Three recent graduates of the teacher-training program, for example, will teach the same classes in a Negro neighborhood continuously for the entire three years of junior high school. Secondly, an experiment in supervision centers about a "coordinating teacher," who will suggest possible improvements in teacher preparation and supervision in schools of this kind. Finally, new teaching techniques and a modified organization of subject matter are being tried out.

We have only a beachhead of knowledge on how to teach disadvantaged children. The college experiments and demonstration projects described above are hopeful signs. Intelligent efforts are being made to prepare teachers to handle assignments of this kind with confidence and skill.

In the past, one of the principal tasks of the American public schools has been to assimilate and Americanize the European immigrant and to help him take his place in an industrial society. Today it is to educate millions of newcomers in the slums of our big cities. The preservation of our democratic way of life, the demands of our economy, and the mental health of our people all require that we learn how to educate their children effectively. Thomas Jefferson hoped this nation would remain agricultural, because he distrusted city mobs. If millions of newcomers in our big cities are alienated because they are inadequately prepared to cope with the dynamics of urban living, Jefferson's prophecy may be partly realized.

Again, this country has been shifting to occupations that require more skill. With automation already on the horizon, the demand for unskilled labor is inevitably declining and the need for trained workers is rising. This suggests that we must look to the culturally deprived to fill shortages of skilled manpower. Otherwise, declares Conant in an oft-quoted remark, we are "allowing social dynamite to accumulate in our large cities." More than half the youth in some slum neighborhoods, he discovered, were unemployed.

Finally, we must offer these children the best opportunities to develop a wholesome respect for themselves and society. Failure to do so will inevitably produce heavy costs, in the form of police protection, courts, jails, and mental institutions. It will surely be less expensive, in the long run, to organize schools which can meet the needs of disadvantaged youth.

The neighborhood school in the changing urban culture does not see its problems as generic, nor does it deal with them as such. So far we have viewed the changes in urban life and education in sociological perspective. In this article by Fern Jacobi the situation is described in curricular perspective. Changes in a school program, if they are to be more than capitulation, must attempt to maintain a high level of learning experiences for the student. The positive results of West School's efforts are encouraging. Adjustment does not necessarily have to be, as it unfortunately is in some schools, an increase in discipline and a decrease in expectation.

CHANGING PUPILS IN A CHANGING SCHOOL / *Fern H. Jacobi*

"Once nine hundred children went to school here." The retiring custodian of West School was speaking 16 years ago when, as neophyte principal, I first came to work in the community. "That was when the neighborhood was young."

But "young" neighborhoods grow up. At the time he spoke, only 400 children were attending. Later, in 1954, numbers had dwindled to less than 300, and West's "grandchildren"—offspring of parents who had attended the school—frequently enrolled. Meanwhile, small changes were taking place in the area as urbanization forces crept slowly out from the center of the city. The neighborhood kept neatly manicured lawns, proud and gracious homes. Yet, here and there on the edges were evidences of a creeping blight—hedges left untrimmed, or worn through by careless feet, a crumbling porch, homes converted into small business enterprises.

OUR COMMUNITY CHANGES

Most of the parents were still "salt of the earth," stable, friendly people providing a background of cultural experiences for their children and cooperating with their school and community. Almost half were Jewish people, ambitious for their children and generous with time and money. As time went on changes were noted in the occupa-

Fern H. Jacobi, "Changing Pupils in a Changing School," Educational Leadership *17 (February 1960), pp. 283–287. Copyright © 1960 by the Association for Supervision and Curriculum Development. Reprinted with the permission of the author and The Association.*

tion of the fathers. The percentage of professionals dropped, and more children from lower middle class homes attended. Differences began to be noted in the background of the children. The span of intelligence level widened. Mothers went to work outside of the homes—some because of economic necessity, others to provide for their children the luxuries of life, or a college education. Soon there appeared in the windows a dark face or two. In the back yards little Negro children played quietly together. Slowly, conducting themselves with decorum and dignity, upper class Negroes moved into some of the homes on quiet streets. We had Negro neighbors.

Later, after integration, we were to know these people better as kind and loving parents and as cooperative patrons of the school. Now, however, we learned little about them except through an occasional confidence from the earlier residents, "I used to step out to get the milk in the morning in my robe, but our new neighbors never do that, so I have stopped doing it now."

In September 1954 West opened as an integrated school. The enrollment soared. Three classes were opened the first year, and two each succeeding year. Now children from parents in all occupational classes came. The widest disparities were noted in cultural background. We had become in truth a small "melting pot" from which, with other similar schools, the liberties of future generations of Americans of all races must be forged.

OUR CHILDREN DIFFER

Our children's range in intelligence was tremendous—at one time from 68 to 167 IQ! In many cases there was an educational lag of one to six years in reading achievement. "Sixth grade" children tested in reading from grade 1.4 to 9.0. For many years past our children testing high average in intelligence had ranked far above the national norm in reading. Now our reading achievements dropped down far below national norms. Faculty morale slipped to a low ebb. Our Negro teachers were eager to learn new methods and willing to share with us their understanding of Negro children. But even they grew discouraged with achievements.

The problem of discipline reared its ugly head. Freedom in classroom and corridor sometimes became license. Indirect methods of control were of no avail. Hall and playground duty became difficult tasks for experienced teachers and thwarting for the inexperienced.

White and Negro teachers were working together—many with the pride of long years of successful experience, working harder than any of us had worked in all our lives before. Were we failing in our duty to these children and so to our country?

WE ACCEPT THE CHALLENGE

The words of Abraham Lincoln in his Address to Congress in 1863 leaped to new life within our minds: "The dogmas of the quiet past are inadequate to the stormy present. The occasion is piled high with difficulty, and we must rise to the occasion. As our case is new so we must think anew and act anew. We must disenthrall ourselves and then we shall save our country."

We decided to "think anew and act anew." The methods by which we had established a good school in other days with outstanding character development and achievement in our children were unequal to the stormy present. We began to "disenthrall ourselves," and it wasn't easy.

We resolved to hold fast to our high standards, to learn more about our present pupils, and to experiment with different methods of work.

WE SEEK NEW DIMENSIONS

It was not easy to gain clear understandings about our children. We were plagued by oversized classes and high rate of mobility.

We studied our children in class, on the playground, in their homes, and in the community. We invited parents for long conferences which revealed family values, mores, and methods of home discipline. We learned that in some homes beating was the form of punishment accepted by both parent and child. In school, without fear of physical reprisal, children often worked out their aggressions and thwartings with results not at all conducive to pupil progress.

We learned, too, from these conferences that the insistent demand for more and more homework from homes, cultured and uncultured, was tied to ambition for the children, to a lack in many instances of sound recreational patterns, and not infrequently to a desire to use the homework to substitute for family discipline.

We learned that false and too sweeping generalizations on the part of Negroes about whites, and on the part of whites about Negroes, created tensions. Sometimes rejection was experienced by young children. A young mother wrote to explain a sudden rebellious attitude of her daughter to her kind and capable white teacher: "In January we moved here from a block in which Phylicia was one of the most popular children in the area. She had almost too many friends, if such is possible. Never a dull moment. Then abruptly we bought a home, moved to a block where not one little girl has been allowed to play with Phylicia although at first all have attempted friendliness. Reared in an atmosphere where only behavior has counted, the rejections of the past months have been a great shock to Phylicia and she is still confused. She could not understand the 'sudden' color distinctions, especially since her own complexion is fair and people have always 'made a lot over her.' After our talk this morning, Phylicia went to school probably feeling quite rebellious toward an image of Susan's (a rejecting playmate's) mother. As a result, she associated Susan's mother with you probably (through no fault whatever of yours)."

We studied pupil records. We saw broken homes, children living insecurely, in many instances with neither parent. We saw frequent changes of schools as economic necessity forced families to move from one school area to another.

As a faculty we shared our knowledge and understanding of the children. We asked for, and gave advice and help to each other. Sometimes the teachers served as my consultants. We used our master teachers, white and Negro, as group leaders, policy planners, helpers to new teachers.

As we learned more about our children we saw changes in their reactions to us. Faces of children in trouble lost the "dead-pan" look and came alive with changing emotions as they sought with us a solution to their problems. Children in trouble trusted us. Rude, negative answers to questions diminished in number and violence. Often the truth, even though damaging, was told at the start of a conference, and a healthy emotional tone was established for the improvement of the situation and of the child.

WE "ACT ANEW"

Coincident with our deepened understanding of our children came changes in methods of teaching. Frequent evaluation meetings were held. In these, our faculty took an honest look at our methods and their effect on the learning of our children.

Both our experience with the children and the low test scores in paragraph meaning showed us that our children needed consistent and sequential development of concepts. Through trips and other firsthand experiences as well as with books and visual aids we developed concepts in science, in social studies, in math, and the arts. "Milk really does come from a cow!" said a sixth grade girl aide helping a second grade group on their trip to a farm, "and a cow is so big!"

We worked constantly for improvement in pronunciation and enunciation. In our oral English work, in spelling and in phonetics related both to reading and to spelling, we worked to improve speech habits.

Each teacher learned to make an informal reading inventory and used this technique to group her children for instruction in reading.

We made assignments on the level of each group—very simple factual ones for slow groups and, for those more highly endowed, assignments involving fine discrimination, critical thinking, and interpretation.

It was early evident that some form of ability grouping was necessary. It was completely unrealistic, for instance, to give a sixth grade teacher a class of sometimes 40 children, ranging in IQ from 73 to 167, and in reading level from 1.4 to 9.3.

We wanted, however, to avoid the undemocratic complications of the old XYZ ability groupings—with consequent parental pressure to put each child, no matter how limited, in the highest group. Rather we developed a policy which we called Overlapping Ability Grouping. We used reading level as our main criterion, but also considered mental age and social maturity. Miss A, who had the fastest learners, had also a few high average ones. Miss B had a high average to low average range. Miss C had the slowest ones with some low average children. Not a perfect system, of course, but under it grouping for reading instruction could be done on three levels usually, and so each child could read at his instructional level. Yet since there was no hard and fast delineation between groups, parents seldom asked for changes of placement. A truly democratic grouping is one where each child's needs, social and intellectual, can most nearly be met.

We gave our children the kind of discipline they needed—firm and kind—with external controls established first and leading to internal controls. We found something in every child that we could honestly praise. We feel that a child needs *something to live up to, not to live down*.

We provided many opportunities for pupil leadership through Patrols, Girl Aides, and school and classroom committee work. We made every opportunity to overcome the handicaps under which some of our children live—social, moral, intellectual, and economic—and to make school a happy place for them to live and to work in.

OUR CHILDREN ACHIEVE

We had worked prodigiously. We had studied, planned, evaluated as a faculty. Early in the year 1958–59 there were some evidences that a degree of success was crowning our efforts. We knew that many of our children had achieved a high level of self-control in halls, in classrooms and on the playground. Some of them had developed outstanding leadership. But what about reading and understanding? There were evidences throughout the year in books read, in teachers' tests and in semi-standardized commercial tests that our children were achieving very well. By now we were almost afraid to believe it.

At the start of the year the fifth grade tests (Stanford KM) disappointed us. We felt that in one class they did not reveal the children's true ability. So two months later we gave 30 children the Stanford M, a comparable test. Increments ranged from $-.1$ year to 3.6 years with the mode from one to two years (instead of the expected .2 increment). These results to some extent increased our confidence in the job we were doing. Our Superintendent and our Department of Pupil Appraisal were much interested in the results of our second test.

In March 1959, our sixth grade pupils were tested with the Stanford Reading Test, Intermediate Form. Results indicated that in all subjects West sixth graders averaging 100 in IQ were well above national norms. Concerning our reading achievements Dr. Carl Hansen, our Superintendent, said in his "Summary of the Desegregation Experiences in the Public Schools of the District of Columbia for the Notre Dame Conference (May 8, 1958)":

> An illustration of superior growth is found in the summary of achievement gains (in reading) made by three classes of sixth grade students in the West Elementary School, March 1959, over their fifth grade placement in the fall of 1957.
> The West School, formerly all white, has an enrollment of 572 Negro and 84 white pupils, a faculty of 12 white and 8 Negro persons.

Class A	Fifth grade median	6.3
	Sixth grade median	8.7
	Mental maturity	7.7
Class B	Fifth grade median	4.5
	Sixth grade median	7.2
	Mental maturity	6.5

Class C[1] Fifth grade median   4.5
            Sixth grade median   6.4
            Mental maturity   6.2

How well have we succeeded in educating these youngsters? Improvement in achievement tests is only one index. It is difficult to evaluate the major factors—the growth in poise, in self-discipline, the development of cultural background and interests, the growing desire of the children to learn, to understand, the constant use of the public library, and the increase in pleasure and pride in their school.

Over and over again in their letters evaluating their school the children refer to it as a respected school or as a school with a good reputation. They recognize that the program involves more than the skills. "The teachers teach us right from wrong." Pamela, a sixth grader in Class B, writes: "I think that West is a wonderful school. I like it because I know that I can be well educated. I also like it because I have such a nice teacher. Another reason why I like West is because I not only learn to read, write and do arithmetic, but I have learned how to make friends and keep them. I have learned that when someone picks a fight with me, to walk away. I have learned all that from West School's teachers and my principal."

Through the years, our community has changed, and the children entering our school have reflected these changes. Our faculty has accepted the challenge of a changing school, has reached out to new dimensions in understanding children, has held to high standards while adapting methods of work to the learners' needs.

Population shift in the urban center has had its repercussions at the outer periphery. Alfred Beattie reminds us that the suburban school has been affected too. The current attention given to social and educational issues indigenous to the inner city tend to obscure problems of suburban education. The former rural and township districts beyond the city proper have become independent districts of the metropolis itself. Their school systems have become expensive institutions, operating in those areas that draw many young families with children of school age. These seldom-regarded districts sur-

---

[1] Actually, Class C was a part of a 5th–6th grade class. There were 12 sixth grade children placed there by their addresses, since the school area had changed and this group was to transfer to another school.

rounding the city are engaged in the education of a large proportion of metropolitan youth. Inadequate financing is a major problem.

CHANGING SCHOOL NEEDS IN SUBURBAN AREAS / *Alfred W. Beattie*

The problems of educating children in suburban school districts are not unique. School directors and administrators in suburban areas, like all school directors and administrators, are trying to accomplish our national requirements for better educated and vocationally competent citizens. They want to reduce the number of dropouts. They wish more talented pupils to prepare for the professions. They are beginning to recognize that occupational training must be provided for those whose formal education ends with high school. Current writings tend to give the impression that the most difficult educational problems are in the large cities. At least one national foundation is awarding substantial grants to city school districts to finance team teaching projects and other techniques for culturally deprived children. Some city school districts employ persons to lobby in the general assemblies of their states for a larger share of state funds. However, I doubt that city school districts must provide educationally for culturally deprived or racial groups which do not exist in the suburbs. I am not aware of a competent study which establishes that financing schools, including special programs for deprived children, is more burdensome or requires greater effort on the part of the residents of cities than on residents of suburban communities. Ordinarily, city school districts tax industrial plants, stores, office buildings, warehouses, and other nonchild-producing real property. Similar sources of revenue do not exist in many suburbs. The suburbs tax homes, wages, amusements, dead transfers, and individuals. In city school districts, only part of the city is slum. The remainder of the city has strength to match federal funds for redevelopment or to maintain a competitive educational program. I am not minimizing the difficult financial and human problems of city school districts. I wish to emphasize that the problems encountered in educating youth in cities are problems in the suburbs also.

Alfred W. Beattie, "Changing School Needs in Suburban Areas," American School Board Journal *(August 1962), pp. 11–13. Reprinted with the permission of The Bruce Publishing Company.*

TYPES OF SUBURBAN SCHOOL DISTRICTS

At the risk of oversimplification, I propose to divide suburban school districts into three groups. The first group includes municipalities which were queens. Today they are old and tired, or they are aging and tiring. The second group includes municipalities which are growing or are not showing signs of aging. The third group includes undeveloped communities which are not attracting builders or buyers.

The educational problems of the one-time queen communities are extremely difficult. Usually these communities were centers of business, culture, recreation, and education for neighboring municipalities. Most of these communities were secondary school centers for their neighbors. Money and pupils from surrounding municipalities added to local money and pupils enabled the boards of school directors to build up respected high school programs. At the same time, other forces were destroying the queen communities. Houses became old, outdated, and in need of repairs. Lack of parking space choked business. The proximity of industry with the accompanying air pollution accented the appearance of shabbiness. Importation of culturally deprived persons to provide labor during war production years changed these communities culturally and educationally. The automobile accelerated the decline. Young citizens and particularly the young professional people built their homes in the neighboring rural communities and commuted. Finally, the old queens could no longer accommodate all the pupils from neighboring communities. Then, the new communities built high schools. The queens lost income and pupils, and began to retrench. Continuing migration of the young citizens, accompanied by an influx of older citizens and culturally limited families, accelerated the queens' decline. Finally, industry moved out to get more space and to be part of growing communities. Eventually, these communities became depressed areas whose residents oppose higher taxes. The educational program became minimum and inadequate.

The second group of suburbs includes areas which are being subdivided and developed. These are the communities in which mass builders are operating. New homes, small down payments, and initially low taxes attract young families. New communities require water, streets, sewers, churches, and schools. Roughly, 1600 families require a 12 room, kindergarten elementary school. Six thousand families need a 750 pupil junior high school. Twelve thousand families require a 1200 pupil senior high school. The proportion of the districts' income necessary to amortize indebtedness for building grows and grows. Eventually, school boards must choose between economizing on teachers' salaries, textbooks, libraries, visual aids, and other pre-requisites to excellent educational programs, or raising taxes further. Too frequently, they choose to economize.

Retirement of debt and payment of interest are not the only ex-penditures which reduce funds available for extending educational opportunities. Families purchasing homes in suburban townships want cement or asphalt streets, but they refuse to purchase sidewalks. However, these same parents demand that the entire municipality be taxed to provide free transportation to school on the grounds of safety. In Allegheny County, transportation will cost more than 1.9 million dollars this year. Transportation expenditures are, beyond doubt, becoming a serious financial problem in suburban school districts. They are reducing funds available to improve the quality and quantity of educational opportunities while children are in school.

A third group of suburbs does not attract builders or buyers. These municipalities are neither farming nor residential. They do not have access to expressways. Strip mining or deep mining operations make some unattractive and expensive to develop. City water is not avail-able. Mining destroyed the underground water resources. They are depressed areas. Children residing in these communities are culturally deprived.

Some of you may consider me somewhat pessimistic about the educational program in suburban communities. All of you can point to wealthy suburban school districts which have none of the symptoms I have described. They have excellent educational programs. The salary schedules attract very capable teachers. These communities, however, are exceptions. Usually, they are the home communities for upper-salary bracket industrial, business, and professional men. The communities were pre-planned and zoned to attract people in high-income brackets. Nevertheless, these communities have dropouts, square pegs in round holes, emotionally disturbed, and the socially unaccepted. Children must accept college preparatory programs. Citizens pay handsomely for their schools.

The flood of families into the suburbs brings with it the social values of the greater city. The sleepy township or rural junction of yesterday is caught unaware in the sudden shifts

*that occur in the various institutions. The rapidly expanding
school system may be concerned with meeting the immediate
needs of facilities and space for its students and have little
opportunity to realign itself with the changed community. Such
a lag creates conflicts and obscures vision and direction. Paul
Zintgraff discusses some of the problems of this nature which
beset the rapidly expanding residential suburb.*

BEDROOM COMMUNITIES AND THE
SCHOOL / *Paul Zintgraff*

The rapid and unprecedented transition from city to suburbia has
created changes in the political, economic and cultural fabric of the
community. Since the schools are an integral part of the community,
it is trite but important to point out that they are directly affected
by such changes.

The explosive nature by which bedroom communities develop
creates a chain of related problems for education. No segment of the
curriculum or administration escapes the pressure of accelerated
growth. The effect of cultural shifts on the purposes of the school, the
problem of faculty disunity, the need for personnel, the demand for
insightful leadership, and the financing of schools are a few of the
important and more difficult problems inherent in the schools of the
bedroom community.

CULTURAL SHIFTS

The infiltration of a large number of new families into a small
suburban area in some instances has had a disorganizing effect. The
leadership structure of the old community may be threatened by the
invasion of new families with different backgrounds, interests, status
and orientation. There is a tendency for lines of social stratification
to develop rapidly. Purchasers of the project homes may be thought
of as "invading foreigners" by the older residents. Community problems created by rapid growth, such as the need for recreational
facilities, additional utilities, improved streets and more schools, may

Paul Zintgraff, "Bedroom Communities and the School," Educational
Leadership *(February 1960), pp. 292–297. Copyright © 1960 by the
Association for Supervision and Curriculum Development. Reprinted with
the permission of the author and The Association.*

become symbols of attack on the old community. Consequently, conflict, disunity and social fermentation are likely to develop.

The older residents of the community may look at the newcomers as being disloyal to the traditions which have been established over the past years. This feeling may be reflected in their attitudes toward school growth and curricular change. They recall the good old days when the school was small. The curriculum was simple, for it grew out of the needs of a largely rural society. Now they have pupils in their schools with many different educational plans, career aspirations, and abilities. The once simple curriculum no longer fits the needs of the new community. The school program must be broadened to encompass many more facets if all of these demands are to be met. This involves the modification of old purposes and the inclusion of new ones. Problems arising out of these changes in purpose can easily become emotionally lashed to the conflict of the old versus the new.

FACULTY DISUNITY

Naturally this curriculum function cannot take place if the teachers are emotionally involved in the community disunity. In many situations this problem exists because of the very way in which the bedroom community develops. When a flood of new teachers is added to the staff each year, a problem of adjustment develops for the teachers who have served the district for many years.

New teachers bring new ideas founded in the experiences they have had in universities and public school systems throughout the country. Coupled with this are the frustrating demands made by the influx of new students and their parents. These factors threaten the security of the teacher whose experience during the past years has been limited to the less impelling needs of a stable community. At the same time the new teachers have not yet found their place in the community or the school and have variant points of view concerning the direction of the school program. This is fertile ground for the development of a serious split within the faculty—the old versus the new.

NEED FOR PERSONNEL

Unfortunately, an in-service program cannot be developed without an adequate staff to direct it. This identifies another problem of the enlarging suburb. Because of the financial demands, it is difficult and often impossible to find enough money to hire the number and caliber of needed administrative and curriculum assistants. For example, in one California county a suburban district of 970 A.D.A.[1] will hire more teachers next year than a stable neighboring district of 10,280 A.D.A. Yet the latter has 13 district staff professional members while the former has two and a half.

Actually, in such a district the demand for help is greater while it is growing than when it has reached its full complement of students and teachers. This is true because problems occurring during a district's rapid growth are pressing and demand immediate decisions. Unfortunately they come at a period when personnel and time are extremely limited—yet such decisions become the policy for the future. Unless the chief administrator has the assistance of an adequate district staff, he can ordinarily give little attention to curriculum development. The urgency and complexity of administrative detail make it almost impossible for him to see the total program in proper perspective.

In some cases, this lack of attention to a district-wide program will result in individual schools' organizing their own programs. This makes it possible for schools in the same district to go in many different directions. In other cases no attempt is made to develop a unified program and teachers are permitted to drift. In both situations this results in a disorganized program. To bridge the gap in some areas the services of the state department of education or an intermediate unit such as a county department of education are available. These agencies may offer general consultants, specialists and educational survey teams trained to give direct assistance to educational and lay groups. However, the amount of benefit to be realized often depends upon how well the local district is organized to take advantage of the services.

Another problem directly affecting the development of the curriculum of the suburban school district is that of adequate school financing. The expeditious growth of the school district demands tremendous increases in the amounts of instructional materials and supplies. The need for additional classrooms becomes a problem of major concern.

ADEQUATE FINANCING

Once the children start arriving, the district finds itself faced with extensive construction costs. At this point the school board employs its full taxing power and finds the demands can only partially be met.

---

[1] Average daily attendance.

There is a false assumption made by many that the influx of large numbers of students from homes of above-average income produces sufficient revenue through local taxes to support the growth. There is a significant difference between the wealth of families as a factor in supporting education and real property as a tax base. The assessed valuation of homes is relatively much less than that of business and industrial property. Consequently, revenue from property tax in a district containing few businesses, little or no industry, and many family dwellings reduces the per pupil revenue. This is the situation in nearly all bedroom communities. Adequate school financing demands a balance between homes, business and industry if schools are to continue to obtain most of their income from local taxes.

A possible solution to this problem lies in establishing a broader tax base as a source for school revenue. One way of accomplishing this is by placing a greater portion of the financial burden on the state or perhaps federal government.

Another possible alternative to lessen the financial burden on suburban schools is through district reorganization. By this means the boundary of a district could be extended to include areas supported by business and industry so that the balance between homes, business and industry is brought about. Unfortunately, the usual problems involved in district reorganization tend to arise in exaggerated forms in bedroom communities.

LEADERSHIP

Neither of these two solutions, more federal and state support or district reorganization, lies entirely within the jurisdiction of any individual district. Consequently, immediate escape is not possible. Yet the lack of adequate financing makes it impossible for most bedroom community districts to house pupils properly, provide sufficient materials, acquire adequate staff, or to pay salaries that will attract experienced professional leadership.

To cope successfully with the problems thus far identified, bold and strong leadership on the part of the chief administrator is particularly needed. The superintendent of the once small school district may lack the adaptability, imagination, experience and energy to give constructive and insightful leadership when his district is hit with the influx of students and problems. When this situation exists, the pressures will eliminate an unprepared superintendent.

This is unfortunate for both the man and the school district, for he is usually not relieved of his responsibilities until a multitude of problems have developed. Consequently the new superintendent finds himself faced not only with the mounting problems of the future, but the problems of the past which are closely tied to the emotions of his staff and community. The new administrator must recognize that he is subject to being the victim in this situation. He will be well advised to learn the causes of tension, recognize that prejudices exist, and identify the reasons for the differences in the community. His job becomes one steeped in human relations and directed toward assisting diverse groups to find ways of working together. He must be a social engineer attuned to the human climate. At the same time he must not sacrifice sound educational practices to gain personal favor in the community. Only strong professional leadership can withstand such a test.

This article has identified a few of the problems inherent in rapidly growing suburban school districts. The suggested solutions to these problems are based on a premise that the school in a bedroom community can be an effective force for acculturation and that the school cannot be considered apart from the cultural fabric of the community. The school has an important role in weaving the thread of this fabric into a harmonious whole.

The role of the urban school is clearly spelled out in this government pamphlet. The image of the school in the midst of these socioeconomic issues, as seen by national leaders and educators, is one of total involvement and commitment. It is pointless to ask just how much can be expected of education— just as pointless as the pleas from perennialists for a return to the clearly defined limits of an education for the elite. The field of education has accepted a dual role—keeping the best of the past, yet actively working in a changing present for a better future.

EDUCATIONAL PROBLEMS AND URBANIZATION /

The past two decades have been years of mounting crisis for cities. The "urban sprawl" has burst the traditional organizational boundaries to cross the administrative and legislative jurisdictions that once were an effective basis for providing urban services and facilities. As a result of this situation, joint Federal-State-local efforts to stem the decay and disorientation of unplanned urban growth have been initiated, particularly with respect to urban housing and transport, and have now become so significant as to constitute a major new dimension of the Federal system.

Efforts of educators have been largely restricted to local educational jurisdictions in attempting to deal with the impact of these new urban developments. Furthermore, Federal action with regard to other urban problems has sometimes been taken without systematic consideration of possible implications for educational facilities and has tended to create added difficulties for the city schools. It was this aspect of the urban educational problem that prompted the U.S. Office of Education to bring together city superintendents and Federal officials concerned with various aspects of urban planning.

Disappearing Taxable Property

One of the crucial problems is the diminishing amount of taxable property, particularly in large cities, which results in part from the activities of the Federal Government in the cities—the increasing demand for acreage for freeways, public housing, etc. In the case of property removed from tax rolls and condemned for construction of freeways and traffic arteries, the lost revenue cannot be recovered. In the case of housing projects, an annual payment is agreed upon in lieu of taxes, although a considerable amount of time may elapse before this payment is available to schools. Also, the payment often amounts to a lower figure than the school tax paid by a private apartment development and, indeed, in many cases lower than the taxes from the original properties which housed a much smaller pupil population. In urban renewal areas of the city it may be many years before the full

"Educational Problems and Urbanization" (originally entitled, "The Impact of Urbanization on Education"), Summary Report of a Conference (May 28–29, 1962). Washington, D.C.: U.S. Department of Health, Education and Welfare, Office of Education, Pamphlet No. OE-10021.

amount of taxes from redeveloped land is available. Yet successful renewal requires great capital investment in new schools. Thus the need for educational services may increase while public payments for such services decrease.

DETERIORATION AND DECLINE OF REAL PROPERTY

Large numbers of homeowners who could afford to maintain their property have left the cities for the adjacent suburbs. Tenants have replaced homeowners and real property has deteriorated and declined. The cumulative effect of these conditions, added to the aging of property within the city, results in ever-decreasing property valuation per pupil.

COORDINATION OF FEDERAL PROGRAMS AT LOCAL LEVEL

The coordination of the efforts of Federal agencies could be improved at the local level. These agencies have often worked at cross purposes in relation to one another and to the locality. For example, school and public housing officials have not engaged in enough joint planning. While in some instances joint scheduling of housing and school facilities is impossible, more often this lack of coordination indicates that local school and housing officials remain in the isolation of their sphere of activity and thereby defeat at least temporarily the goals of both programs. There is also a need for more sensitive and coordinated planning of highway programs. Approval of federally aided highway programs in metropolitan areas should be contingent upon their consistency with adequate, comprehensive development plans for the area.

HEAVY IMPACT IN ONE AREA
WILL BE FELT THROUGHOUT THE SCHOOL SYSTEM

All programs that uproot large numbers of people from the city compound the difficulty of the school's job throughout the city. The displaced people crowd other facilities in numbers and ways that are hard to predict. Sometimes they bring with them problems and needs quite different from those of the existing clientele. To prepare for these changes requires money and a great deal of planning.

HIGH MOBILITY AND PHYSICAL CHANGE

There is a higher transiency rate in the congested areas of the city, and city schools reflect this in their high rates of pupil turnover. This mobility, together with the effect of urban renewal and highway projects, is making long-range school planning in the large cities very complex. Under these circumstances, school planning depends on a better understanding of the demographic structure of the city and the way it affects and is affected by the physical changes caused by public action.

REPLACEMENT OF SCHOOL FACILITIES

School facilities in the city are often condemned for urban renewal, highway construction, or other public purposes. It is all too convenient to take school property for public purposes, for the process of condemnation is usually easier and cheaper than if the property were in the control of private homeowners. Yet the school system has to look to the replacement of these facilities and receives little aid or interest from the agency which caused the displacement.

The role of the attractive school as a catalyst in the creation of new neighborhoods, and as an anchor to hold older neighborhoods in central city areas, must be made clear. These neighborhoods are dependent upon their ability to attract families who already have a wide range of housing choices. Their attractiveness depends largely on a school program of high reputation.

COORDINATED PLANNING BETWEEN LOCAL GOVERNMENT UNITS

The community is a socioecenomic unit, but the independence of the various functional parts of the local government may belie this fact. The independent status of the school system, for example, makes necessary a conscious effort toward coordination and cooperation because the local government is not highly centralized. Effective coordination will result in planning and scheduling public facilities and action, which will benefit the school system and all other parts of local government. Perhaps the best examples of the benefits possible from such coordination can be found in localities which have successfully and fully included the schools, as well as other parts of local government, in the step-by-step development of plans and programs for the future of the city and for its renewal.

CHILD WELFARE AND THE FEDERAL GOVERNMENT

WISE USE OF RESOURCES

The United States is as richly endowed in human resources as it is in material wealth. It has not utilized all these resources wisely.

The task that must be undertaken now, through education, is to make the most of these human resources. The magnitude of the problem is indicated by:

a. *Larger youth population.* The high birthrate in the post-war years means that youth services will be overwhelmed by the number of youngsters needing these services.

b. *Higher delinquency rates.* Over the past 12 years, the rates of delinquency have been rising faster than the child population. Even if these rates do not increase in the next 10 years, correctional services will be taxed by the large number of cases of delinquency.

c. *Changed labor force requirements.* There is now less demand for the unskilled laborer and greater need for the skilled technical and professional worker than formerly. In a complex technological society young people must have sound basic training which will permit them to adapt quickly and easily to new tasks as the economy changes.

d. *More school dropouts.* Despite the greater need for trained workers in the future, we can expect 7½ million school dropouts by 1970. Many of them will constitute a pool of discontented and alienated workers whose labor no one will seem to want.

SLUM CONCENTRATION OF YOUTH PROBLEMS

These youth problems, like other social problems, are not evenly distributed throughout our society. Crime, alcoholism, drug addiction, poverty, illiteracy, disease, unemployment, and broken families are found in the city slums in massively greater degree than in society as a whole.

PROBLEMS OF A CHANGING POPULATION

The United States has grown in the last century from a predominantly rural country to a Nation whose population is two-thirds urban and growing more so. Urbanization causes profound problems in education as well as in other fields. People migrating to the large cities come largely from the rural South. They come to a mode of life and an environment alien to them. They come with serious educational disabilities. Those who do not adjust readily soon develop antisocial attitudes in the classroom and outside of school. The situation constitutes a grave educational problem and an added financial burden as the schools try to meet the needs of these people who require an increasingly larger share of special services offered by counselors, social service workers, attendance officers, psychologists, doctors, nurses, psychiatrists, and others.

LACK OF MOTIVATION

There is a lack of motivation on the part of many in-migrant children whose educational experience has often been mediocre, who lack academic skills, and whose language deficiencies in many instances produce a forbidding barrier to school achievement. They require extensive remedial help to prevent their dropping out of school.

The largest reservoir of undeveloped talent in America lies in the slums of our cities. These children are as important, in themselves and to the future of this country, as any other children. At the present time they constitute resources which are being almost altogether wasted. The greatest gift schoolmen can give these children is success in school. One of the things educators can do to insure this success is to give more attention to the specialized training and compensation of teachers assigned to central city schools to educate and guide these children of the slums.

ROLE OF THE OFFICE OF EDUCATION

The Office of Education intends to play an increasingly vital role in critically examining the problems involved in the impact of urbanization on education. Through research conducted by specialists in the Office, through its consultative services, through the basic statistics and facts it provides, and through such additional legislative authority as may be enacted by the Congress, the Office will seek new approaches and new applications in line with the educational demands which are manifest in large city school systems.

EDUCATION AND ORIENTATION FOR WORK

YOUTH UNEMPLOYMENT

The unemployment rates in the 14-21 age group are usually twice as high as those of the labor force as a whole, both in prosperous times and in recession periods. The drying up of low-level skilled jobs will be accentuated by automation. It has been estimated that one million youth between 16 and 21 years of age are unemployed and out of school. This represents a waste of manpower and results in frustration for young people. Meanwhile, they deteriorate and become fertile ground for delinquency and for foreign ideologies.

DECREASING EMPLOYMENT OPPORTUNITIES

There are fewer opportunities out of school for those who are poorly prepared to fit themselves for jobs. Wage scales, employment regulations, automation, and competitive prices reduce the chance to be hired as a novice and to learn on the job. Machines take over simple jobs. Wage scales are set for the experienced, productive employee. Seniority in layoff and rehiring, workmen's compensation, and other provisions make it generally uneconomic for an employer to hire inexperienced and untrained employees.

THE SCHOOL'S ROLE IN OCCUPATIONAL PREPARATION

Vocational education programs and attitudes toward vocational education have not kept pace with occupational changes, especially in the cities. Present vocational programs do not prepare for many occupations that can be entered with less than high school completion; they tend to center on programs leading to high school graduation, although many pupils, especially in the central areas of the city, do not complete high school. Those of least ability—the mentally retarded and the reluctant learners—should be trained before they leave school for the less skilled jobs. Those who have more ability, but in the past have held unskilled jobs, will have to learn new skills as greater proportions of the work force are prepared for high-level skilled and professional positions. An upgrading of preparation for work at all levels of ability is essential.

Occupational preparation involves the entire school program, not just that portion usually labeled vocational education. Pupils succeed or fail in their occupations fully as much because of their lack of competence in communication, their quantitative thinking, their care of self, their understanding and use of environment, and their habits of citizenship, as from their specific preparation in the vocational programs of their schools. Every teacher, then, is in essence a vocational educator.

OCCUPATIONAL PREPARATION OF WOMEN

The changing role of women in the work force implies the need for many vocational programs to reassess the preparation of girls and to expand their opportunities for vocational preparation. The percentage of women 14 and over who are gainfully employed has risen steadily, from about 25 percent in 1940 to about 35 percent in 1960.

MOTIVATING POTENTIAL DROPOUTS

Realistic occupational choice and meaningful preparation for that occupation play a crucial role in motivating the potential dropout to continue in school long enough to achieve this goal, or to prepare for a job in which he can earn the money to continue his education for a vocation requiring still greater preparation. The first job for which the student prepares should not be looked upon as his ultimate occupational goal.

EARLY VOCATIONAL DECISIONS

The argument advanced by many educators that secondary school pupils should avoid early vocational decisions and devote their energies to a broad general education is supportable only for some pupils. A learner's motivation often depends on whether he sees the significance of what he is learning to what he wants to do. Many a pupil looks upon much of schooling as a delaying tactic to keep him from the chance to earn money, the spending of which he can control. Embarkation upon courses designed to prepare him for a particular job makes sense to him and he is willing to learn as a means to earn. Keeping this opportunity open to the pupil while he gains enough insight and maturity to make the shift to higher vocational objectives complicates vocational program planning, but it helps to keep students in school and to prepare them for work.

NEED FOR UNBROKEN LINE BETWEEN SCHOOL AND JOB

If schools are to be effective in reducing the number of dropouts and in preparing young people with salable skills, students must be assured that they will not face a dead end when they leave school. It is crucial that young people feel they have a contribution to make to society no matter what their level of skill, and that meaningful job opportunities be provided even though they may have to come through subsidized work programs. An unbroken line between leaving school and entering a job must be established.

MANPOWER DEVELOPMENT AND TRAINING ACT

The Manpower Development and Training Act of 1962 (Public Law 87–415) holds promise for the unemployed who need and desire retraining or additional training to improve their skill. Its purpose: to "appraise the manpower requirements and resources of the Nation, and to develop and apply the information and methods needed to deal with the problems of unemployment resulting from automation and technological changes and other types of persistent unemployment." This Act was designed to cope with problems which exist to a major extent in urban centers, areas we might call unemployment-impacted. Two major reservations, however, are emphasized by large city school officials. First, the aid comes through the States—and often the States' fiscal programs are not suited to the special problems of large cities. Second, Federal support for the program will be halved in 1965; thereafter the city or State will be expected to provide half the cost. Except for a recent (1962) New York State school support program, States generally have not recognized that the per pupil expenses in city school systems are greater than the average. Nor have they taken into account the fact that vocational education is more expensive per pupil than are the usual nonvocational programs. Even though the city schools provide expensive special and vocational education (at a relatively higher cost per pupil than is often experienced in rural and suburban areas) their State per pupil reimbursement may be no higher than or not as high as that provided to rural and suburban schools.

REFERENCES

Fattu, Nicholas. "Education and Technology." Unpublished report, Institute of Educational Research, Indiana University (Bloomington, Ind.), pp 1–3, 9.

Grambs, Jean D. *Education in a Transition Community*. New York: National Conference of Christians and Jews, 1955.

"The Population Bomb." Pamphlet Published by the Hugh Moore Fund (New York), pp 5–9.

Sutton, Elizabeth. *Knowing and Teaching the Migrant Child*. Washington, D.C.: National Education Association, Department of Rural Education, 1960.

Thompson, Ronald B. "Implications of Impending College Enrollments." *Current Issues in Higher Education*. Washington, D.C.: Association for Higher Education, 1954, pp 42–47.

PERIODICALS

Beegle, J. A., and D. Halstead. *Michigan's Changing Population*. East Lansing, Mich.: Agricultural Experiment Station, Bulletin 415, June 1957.

Beegle, J. A., and J. F. Thaden. *Population Changes in Michigan:*

With Special Reference to Rural-Urban Migration. 1940–1950. East Lansing, Mich.: Agricultural Experiment Station, Bulletin 387, October 1953.

Earle, Clifford. "Overpopulation: New Threat to Survival." *Presbyterian Life*, May 1, 1959, pp 6–8.

{Chapter Three}

URBAN INFLUENCES ON AMERICAN YOUTH

Today's urban youth grows up among forces of change. Even in the enduring slums young people learn a way of life that has become more dysfunctional in the wake of a changing economy. It has been observed in our urban society that the institution is taking over more and more of those responsibilities once belonging to the home. This is especially the case in the inner city, where the welfare of the child is in the hands of the settlement house, social agency, and school. These institutions offer the only opportunity to learn the skills needed for life in the greater culture. The traditional avenues of escape from poverty have been shut off by increased technology and specialization. The influences of the institution, however, are unable to offset those of the community and peer subcultures. The latter, especially, enlists strong allegiance from its members.

The adolescent subculture is a unique phenomenon of contemporary society. Even in communities where adolescent behavior is not overtly antisocial, young people adopt from their peer group social values and attitudes that are sometimes in a conflict with those of the school and the adult community. The partial estrangement of American youth from the greater society poses problems for secondary education.

Schools are faced with the dilemma of "reaching" its youth through channels of their own interests and thereby possibly reinforcing the anti-intellectualism that underlies much of the adolescent value structure.

American education must not only adapt to an emerging society it must also adapt to an emerging young American— one who is exposed to a society of vanishing absolutes, who is destined to play more complex social roles, and who is reared in a climate of "other-direction." The child, like his society, is also changing.

———————————

Slum children live among social—and antisocial—forces that are alien to the surrounding community. This is one reason it is so difficult for the teacher to fully appreciate the world view of life and self that students acquire from this environment. Richard Hammer has written an extremely telling report of life in a slum area.

REPORT FROM A SPANISH HARLEM "FORTRESS" / *Richard Hammer*

An 18-year-old who has lived there all his life describes the world of one block.

The people will tell you that this block is a fortress. Its walls are invisible; they are inside the mind, built by the people who live on the block and by society outside. But the walls are as real as if they were made of mortar and stone; they keep 3,000 people locked up inside, afraid, and they keep most outsiders away, afraid.

The block is in the middle of Spanish Harlem, a section of New York that runs roughly from 96th Street to 118th Street between Fifth Avenue and Park Avenue. As events constantly make clear, the area is seething. To the outsider, it is a strange and unfamiliar and often frightening world—one he can never know on his own and one he can understand only partially even with the most expert help.

Recently I met a young man, 18 years old, for whom Spanish Harlem is home. He was born on the block on which he lives and has

Richard Hammer, "Report from a Spanish Harlem 'Fortress,' " The New York Times Magazine, *January 5, 1964. Copyright © 1964 by The New York Times Company. Reprinted with permission.*

spent his entire life on it, in the same small apartment he now shares with his mother, widowed for 10 years, three brothers, three sisters and three other relatives. From all outward signs, Hiram Gonzales (this is not his name) could be a typical 18-year-old from his block. He has grown up in its poverty and faced discrimination all his life because his skin is dark and he is recognizably of Puerto Rican descent. Twice he has dropped out of high school, once from vocational high school in Brooklyn and later from an academic high school in Manhattan.

But Hiram is articulate beyond his education and background, made so by self-education and by an innate brightness and intelligence, and he has thought long and hard about what it is like to grow up and live in Spanish Harlem. He also has a goal and the talent and determination to realize it: he wants to be a professional photographer and he is driven by a desire to return to school and then go on to college. And he has the sensitivity to see into and beneath the sights and sounds and texture of the life around him.

For several nights, we sat together and talked. At first, he was hesitant and wary, looking for something in the interviews other than interest in him and his problems. "To tell you the truth, man," he said later, "I dislike white men because I feel all the injustice that I, my family, my mother, my friends . . . you know, that all of us have gone through." Later, as respect and trust grew, Hiram led me through his world.

"When you walk through my block," he said, "probably the first thing you realize is that there are a lot of people on the streets all the time, from early in the morning to late at night. You'll see that the buildings are old, almost falling apart, but a lot of people have hung curtains in the windows.

"If you are an observing person, you'll notice prostitutes waiting for guys with money, most of them white men from downtown. You'll see drug addicts just moving nowhere; you'll see dope peddlers practically passing the stuff right out in the open. You'll see incidents of theft, you'll just walk along and see them. You'll see a lot of things that are wrong by moral standards and by the moral laws of the rest of society.

"But, man, ever since I was a little kid, this was my block, the block of the fellows who live in it. It was our property and we govern it and we make our own laws and no outsider or no people who don't live in the block can tell us what to do. There are a lot of people who come up and they try to tell us. But, man, they don't understand, they're living in some kind of dream.

"Their standards and ideas don't belong on this block. Because we've been made to feel like we're different, like we don't fit, like we don't belong any place but on our own crummy block. And there's nobody up here who's going to listen until the white man lets us become a part of his society outside, and I don't mean just a couple of guys who are really exceptional, who've got a lot of brains, but I mean everybody who can make it."

One of the things the rest of society has to understand, Hiram thought, was that the people on his block are not different or strange. "To live on my block," he said, "is to live anywhere where there are a lot of people who are poor and who don't have any place else to go. There's a lot of pain and a lot of sorrow, but underneath there's also a lot of glory and happiness and love. Sure, there are a lot of problems on my block, and maybe more problems than a lot of other places. And everybody on the block knows that you think we brought all the problems with us. Well, man, we didn't. The problems were all here before the people came, or anyway, the things that made the problems. For every unjust act done by the people in my neighborhood, there was an unjust act, directly or indirectly done to these people by society."

By indirect, Hiram meant the often unthinking attitudes of whites. "There was this white woman from downtown," he said, "who sometimes came into the neighborhood to help my mother when she was sick. One day, this woman said to me, 'Now, I don't have anything against the Irish or the Italians, but I just don't like most Negroes and I don't like most Puerto Ricans.'

"Now, man, even though she was helping us when we needed help, I got damn mad. 'Now, just a minute,' I said to her, 'how many Puerto Ricans or Negroes do you know? How many do you associate with? Where do you come off saying something like that?'

" 'Well,' she told me, 'I see lots of Negro and Puerto Rican boys hanging on the street corners who look tough, and I'm afraid of them.'

" 'You go out to Bedford-Stuyvesant and you'll see plenty of white boys hanging on the street corners who are just as tough; you go anywhere where people have to live in this kind of filth and you'll see the same damn thing. When you and your kind first came here, you weren't any better.' "

Later, Hiram said, "You know, I'd like to move all the people from Scarsdale, N. Y., right into my block, into the same apartments where some of them have to pay maybe $70 for a couple of crummy little rooms for 10 or 11 people and have to share a bathroom in the hall with the door falling off. Let them live in a place where somebody throws a tire in the furnace and stinks out the place and then the cops come along and tell you that it's nothing and laugh when they're telling you.

"I'll tell you, I think they'd make just as much of a mess as we do, maybe more, because we're used to it, we're used to dodging those weak spots in the floors and not leaning on the wall because it will fall in.

"I don't think those people from Scarsdale could take it. In Scarsdale, the first things the kids learn are how to read and write; that's taken for granted. In my neighborhood, the first things the kids learn are how to fight and steal and not take any crap from anyone. We grow up knowing about narcotics, I mean we don't even remember when we didn't know about them, and everybody just takes that for granted.

"In my block, there are five places where you can buy marijuana cigarettes and I know, even though he's never said anything, that my little brother who's 14 knows where most of them are, that he's known for a long time."

I suggested that nobody forces the kids to use narcotics. "Of course nobody comes up to us and says, 'Man, here's some pot, you got to take a drag; man, here's some horse, you got to shoot.' But, man, these little kids look at the teen-agers who are using, and they look bigger, and, man, they can laugh and forget everything that's around. So, the little kids think, 'That's a tough man; he's great.' And then they see the pushers and racketeers in their $50 shoes and $100 suits, driving a big car, and they think, 'Man, he's tough; he's into some money and he's doing good.' So, when the pusher talks, they listen."

Hiram told me that by the time the boys on the block get to be 20 probably 95 percent of them have tried some kinds of drugs and about 40 percent of them are hooked.

"We aren't fooling ourselves," he said, "when we try drugs. We know what can happen. When I was 13, I saw somebody die of heroin. I went up to the roof of the house next door . . . I think it was to fly my kite . . . anyway, when I came out the door I nearly fell over these addicts who were sort of sitting around in the hallway next to the door. They saw I was only a kid, so they kept right on shooting.

"All of a sudden, I heard a lot of rumbling and this one guy leaped out through the door and started running and turning and jumping all over the roof. Man, he still had the needle sticking in his arm. His friends, and they were still half asleep, sort of staggered out and grabbed him and held him down until he was quiet; then they started walking him back and forth to keep him awake. After a while, they sent me downstairs to get some milk, and more people began coming up to try to help. But nobody could do nothing, and by the time the ambulance got there, he was dead."

Most of the young people in Spanish Harlem are bitter and disillusioned. They sit on the stoops because there isn't anything else most of them can do, and they play cards and they joke. "Our goal is to have a good time, to keep having fun so we don't have to think," said Hiram. "You know what we're doing? We think we're sending the world on its own way while we go on ours. But we know, and, man, that's the trouble, we know that we can't send the world away, that we're part of the world and the world is looking down at us and snarling and laughing at us."

Isn't there, I asked, a desire to get out of the block and into that world to stop that sneering?

"Man, when I was a kid, I used to have dreams that maybe I'd be a scientist and discover all kinds of things. But they were only dreams; when I woke up, there wasn't anything real about them, there couldn't be anything real about them. I've never seen a scientist; I don't understand anything about them; there aren't any scientists, or anybody else who has a big job, on my block so I haven't got the least idea of what they're like. It's hard to even picture them mentally. These things are so far above us they aren't real. They're like a cloud that looks solid until you grab into it and find it falls apart in your hands."

The boys on the block feel that even with an education they have no hope of realizing any dreams. "I know guys with a diploma who start looking for jobs. You know what they can get? A stockboy or a delivery boy or something like that, but not something where they feel they can move ahead.

"I've got a friend who wants to be a mathematician and he's a real smart guy. But when he graduated from high school, an academic one, too, not a lousy vocational one like most of us dropped out of, he went looking for a job so he could make the money to go to college. Nobody had nothing for him. Finally, he answered an ad for a lousy busboy's job at a crummy cafeteria.

"You know what they told him? They told him that he had too much education, that they were afraid he would quit. Now this kid would have worked like hell because he needed the money; but he couldn't even get that crummy job, a job any fink who didn't even know how to read could handle."

So most of the boys just sit. They are convinced that if they went back to school, it would not assure them of a decent job; besides, they are disenchanted with the schools themselves. "When I reached sixth grade, I couldn't read," said Hiram. "The teachers, most of them, didn't give a damn."

The school, instead of revealing the world, merely mirrored the world the young people from the block already knew. "But when I was in seventh grade, I went to a Catholic school for a year. They put a kind of wrench in my mind and opened it a crack and I began to see that there was a world outside my block. Man, that school cared, about me and about everybody, and they wanted to teach and they wanted me to learn.

"Then I went back to public school because, man, the work just got too hard and I wasn't ready for it. In public school, the only thing the teachers wanted was quiet. If they thought we didn't want to learn, they would sit there smoking and reading and if you got out of line, sometimes they'd curse at you: 'You little spic, sit down.' "

But in that school Hiram's horizons were broadened by one teacher of a subject he hated, English. "One day, the teacher came in and played us 'The Three Penny Opera,' and there was something about this 'Mack the Knife' character that really hit us. We asked him to play it over and over, and the next day he brought in 'West Side Story,' and every day he played us records for a while. Then he began to read to us. He read 'The Old Man and the Sea,' 'The Most Dangerous Game,' and a lot of others.

"Now, man, we weren't angels after that; we still carried on, maybe even more because we were getting some freedom, but when that man asked for silence, he got it, and when he began to suggest things, they began to move."

While there were some who managed to get an education, Hiram explained that they paid a terrible price for it. They had to be the teacher's pet, and this put them at the mercy of their fellows, who were not slow to deal out fitting punishment. For most, however, "this was the white man's education, taught the way the white man wanted it taught, without giving it any meaning for us. It was routine, do this and do that, and today we try to escape routine all the time. And it was using things from the white man's world which didn't mean anything to us or things that were so completely against everything we knew that we laughed at them. They even had books telling us what great guys the cops are.

"Now look, man, I know that most cops are just doing their jobs and trying to protect people most of the time. But I've grown up admiring people, I mean admiring, who would fight back at cops; to some extent, I still admire them. Why, I think that if right now, right this minute, a cop walked into this room and told me to do something, I don't think I'd do it, just because he was a cop."

This is the way Hiram and his friends see the law. "In my neighborhood, the cops feel that they're superior to the people, and man, they let us know they think they're better than us. They walk into our homes and look around and tell us to open up, and we're afraid, and I mean afraid, to do anything or say anything. We just do what the cops say.

"And they'll come walking down the street and see us sitting on the stoop, and you know what they do? They come up to us, asking us who we're going to rape next and what job we're planning to pull, and then they tell us to get moving. Man, it can be our stoop, right in front of our house, with our mothers watching out the windows, and the cops are cursing and, man, even demanding that we show them identification."

Another group of "outsiders," youth board and social workers, also rank low in the opinion of the block, Hiram said. "They're all around the neighborhood and most of them are rat fink types. They act like they think that we're not human. They think they've got all there is and all they've got to do is convert us to think and do what they think and do. Then, everything will be just great. But, man, these jerks pop up in the morning with their little briefcases and they cut out for their homes a hell of a way away around 5 or 6 at night, and that's it. If you ever are nuts enough to go to one of them, they hand you the old crap, 'Now, son, you shouldn't feel that way.'

"Now, look, I don't think these guys mean any harm. I think the least thing they want is to do any harm. But harm comes in many forms."

So Hiram and the people on the block have come to distrust those who arrive with good words and offers of help. They feel that they have only themselves to depend on, that only within their group is there reliability.

"As bad as things are here," Hiram said, "in my lifetime I have seen more good things on this block than I have seen bad. On my block, people help each other and most of them do the right things, for themselves and for everybody. Man, I have seen thieves help thieves; I have seen thieves help other guys; I have seen guys who have to rob for a living, and I mean really rob because they don't have any other way, I have seen them give their money to make another guy a little happier.

"I have seen an addict—and this guy was nearly crying for a fix and practically running across the street to get one—stop and shove his last $3 in the shirt pocket of another guy who was married and had a lot of kids but couldn't find a job and didn't have any money. And this junkie went walking away, kicking himself and cursing, 'Now, why the hell did I do that?'

"Now, man, this may not sound like much, but that one incident, for me, could equal 50 unjust things, because it shows that these people do have concern about each other, even though it may be hard for them to show it or express it or maybe even to understand it."

The people on the block are not unconscious of the horror and the filth and destitution around them. They know that it is bad, and at times, they talk of leaving it, though few ever do. But now, today, most of them are afraid. They are afraid because their block is going; all around, new housing projects have risen and this is almost the last block to remain unchanged. It will not remain so for long, and the people know it. Hiram said that most of them would not be able to get into the new projects; some because they wouldn't be able to afford the rents, some because they have an addict or a criminal in the family and the rules of projects forbid such tenants.

"The people are going to have to move, like up to the Bronx, and the landlords know that these people are going to need houses, so instead of $50 they'll make it $70 or $100 an apartment; they're already doing it.

"Man, this is the end of my block," said Hiram. "This is something that we all evade; like, this has been going on for five years. All the other blocks have been going, and this has been in my mind, in everybody's mind, but I haven't really given it any thought, but it scares me. I fear it. But wherever, any place, there is poverty and minorities like us, you will find another block like this one, with all the same problems and the same horrors that we have. Maybe that's where we will have to go. Forget it, man, let me live in this rathole that I have now, that I know, instead of some other new rathole that I don't know."

The most undesirable qualities of our culture realize themselves through the slum child with blind determinism. Wilfred Smith offers to the school the only alternative it has if it is to educate these children—"unteach" the slum set toward life. He also suggests the only alternative to the greater society if it is to attain its ideal—stop rationalizing the existence of slums and break the vicious cycle beyond the classroom.

POVERTY AND THE CHILD / *Wilfred Smith*

In the biblical quotation, "The poor ye shall have ever with you," many find a conclusive description and prescription of reality. Stars collect in varying quantities in space, the ductility of Toledo blades varies, and the middle class mothers of Stamford, Connecticut spread the toilet training of their female children over a range of months. Chance is of the essence of things, but chance follows the laws of probability, sorting most of the phenomena of nature according to the normal curve. And, it follows, the relative wealth of human beings, like the varying amounts of swill ingested at a trough by a farrow of piglets, must follow the law.

A surprising array of untested assumptions, inconsistencies of thought, and unwarranted conclusions lie in the above reasoning. The views of people on poverty and ignorance are strangely mixed, but most would agree on the inevitability of ignorance, of a continuing reservoir of human suffering stemming from any change whatever in human affairs. Probably the greatest single cultural barrier to the elimination of poverty—or broadly speaking, human need—is just this acceptance of the inevitability of human need. It serves as a rationalization for not doing what has become possible. It makes for a self-fulfilling prophecy, an ever repeated cyclical causation in which poverty breeds poverty.

A clear example of the problem of progress—or the hope of attaining the unattainable ideal, some would say—is that of the slum, or the slum child. In the slum child we have a quandary posed by the ambivalence of values in our society. Perhaps the problem is insoluble, but it appears to us that it can be solved within the hearts and minds of men. The basic problem is this: We have enough knowledge and technology to give each person a higher standard of living, but many

Wilfred Smith, "Poverty and the Child," unpublished paper, 1964. Reprinted with the permission of the author.

cannot or will not fulfill the requirements of the context which would give them this higher standard. The value of individualism, which includes the right not to choose the advantages of modernity, is set against the values of materialism, rationalism, and social sensitivity which offers the means of improvement. What can be done to break this log jam—the cycle of poverty begetting poverty, the sequence of generation permanently on welfare?

Why do not the slum people do something to improve themselves—get better jobs, more education, more skills in managing themselves constructively? If they freely chose to do such things, our catechism of laissez-faire economics informs us, they would improve. Since they do not so choose, the judgment is, they are hopeless and helpless, and must be written off, or paid for in minimal welfare checks. The simplified notion is that "in the nature of things" some will be shiftless, vicious, or incompetent. Such a simplified "either-or" view we reject. The problem is much more complicated—but not insoluble. But the solution must be as complex as the problem.

One way to understand the complexity of the problem is to understand the subjective feelings of the slum child. This child is the cultural unit, the packet of culture carried from one generation to the other. What he feels about his environment is the outstanding, salient fact about him, his moment-to-moment acts of will. Such understanding can never be perfect about another person. Very likely, the person is never quite clear within himself. But we can communicate and learn to a remarkable extent what is going on inside the person. This understanding is helpful toward, but not a sufficient solution of the next phase of the problem—that of causing the person to change in some overt ways and become "progressive." We need to understand a slum child from the "inside," with the purpose of discovering the salient reality of the individual. The solution of the problem requires the elimination of human need, of having in existence masses of poorly fed, poorly housed, poorly educated people who do not get fair treatment from the rest of our society, socially or economically.

Since culture is among other things a picture of reality, our problem is to get slum children to change their pictures. They must get new pictures, and must motivate themselves and develop a whole new feeling tone about the new pictures. They have not only to learn new symbols, but must experience feelings about the new symbols so that we can say they have "internalized" the new feelings, and have an entirely new set of qualitative experiences toward these new symbols. They have to not only learn, but to unlearn. The difference is between a cultural experience of plotting death to enemies, and that of planning experiences with friends who had been the enemies. Furthermore, these planned experiences with friends must be such that they will lead to more complicated, peaceful, and sometimes radically, new mechanisms of enjoying social life.

The great obstacles of overcoming "slum thinking" and human cultural needs then, lie in the following areas:

1. The slum children and adults need to unlearn the content of many prevailing symbols.

2. They must unlearn the emotional involvements, self-identifications, and value-attitude constitutions toward their slum culture patterns.

3. They must correspondingly learn the new symbols of the greater culture and modern world citizenship.

4. They must correspondingly internalize values and identifications of the idealized culture.

5. They must develop the social processes and structures to effectuate the first four learnings.

6. The society of participation and communication—potentially all mankind—must act and react supportively with the slum dwellers in developing the material, interpersonal, and cultural benefits which lead to continuing growth toward the ideal of unity of mankind and the elimination of poverty in all its aspects.

An adolescent subculture has emerged from a changing society, and it has profound influence on its members. James Coleman has found that American youth do not emulate the goals of education. If education is to be effective, it must find ways to break through the closed circuit of the peer group.

THE ADOLESCENT SUBCULTURE AND ACADEMIC ACHIEVEMENT / *James S. Coleman*

Industrial society has spawned a peculiar phenomenon, most evident in America but emerging also in other Western societies: adolescent subcultures, with values and activities quite distinct from those of the adult society—subcultures whose members have most of their important associations within and few with adult society. Industrialization, and the rapidity of change itself, has taken out of the hands of the parent the task of training his child, made the parent's skills obsolescent, and put him out of touch with the times—unable to understand, much less inculcate, the standards of a social order which has changed since he was young.

By extending the period of training necessary for a child and by encompassing nearly the whole population, industrial society has made of high school a social system of adolescents. It includes, in the United States, almost all adolescents and more and more of the activities of the adolescent himself. A typical example is provided by an excerpt from a high-school newspaper in an upper-middle-class suburban school:

SOPHOMORE DANCING
FEATURES CHA CHA

SOPHOMORES, this is your chance to learn how to dance! The first day of sophomore dancing is Nov. 14 and it will begin at 8:30 A.M. in the Boys' Gym. . . .

NO ONE is required to take dancing but it is highly recommended for both boys and girls. . . .

If you don't attend at this time except in case of absence from school, you may not attend at any other time. Absence excuses should be shown to Miss _____ or Mr. _____.

In effect, then, what our society has done is to set apart, in an institution of their own, adolescents for whom home is little more than a dormitory and whose world is made up of activities peculiar to their fellows. They have been given as well many of the instruments which can make them a functioning community: cars, freedom in dating, continual contact with the opposite sex, money, and entertainment,

James S. Coleman, "The Adolescent Subculture and Academic Achievement," American Journal of Sociology, 65 (1960), 337–347. Copyright © 1960 by The University of Chicago Press.

like popular music and movies, designed especially for them. The international spread of "rock-and-roll" and of so-called American patterns of adolescent behavior is a consequence, I would suggest, of these economic changes which have set adolescents off in a world of their own.

Yet the fact that such a subsystem has sprung up in society has not been systematically recognized in the organization of secondary education. The theory and practice of education remains focused on *individuals*; teachers exhort individuals to concentrate their energies in scholarly directions, while the community of adolescents diverts these energies into other channels. The premise of the present research is that, if educational goals are to be realized in modern society, a fundamentally different approach to secondary education is necessary. Adults are in control of the institutions they have established for secondary education; traditionally, these institutions have been used to mold children as individuals toward ends which adults dictate. The fundamental change which must occur is to shift the focus: to mold social communities as communities, so that the norms of the communities themselves reinforce educational goals rather than inhibit them, as is at present the case.

The research being reported is an attempt to examine the status systems of the adolescent communities in ten high schools and to see the effects of these status systems upon the individuals within them. The ten high schools are all in the Midwest. They include five schools in small towns (labeled *0-4* in the figures which follow), one in a working-class suburb (*6*), one in a well-to-do suburb (*9*), and three schools in cities of varying sizes (*5, 7,* and *8*). All but No. *5*, a Catholic boys' school, are coeducational, and all but it are public schools.

The intention was to study schools which had quite different status systems, but the similarities were far more striking than the differences. In a questionnaire all boys were asked: "How would you most like to be remembered in school: as an athletic star, a brilliant student, or most popular? The results of the responses for each school are shown in Figure 3-2,[1] where the left corner of the triangle represents 100 percent saying "star athlete"; the top corner represents 100 percent saying "brilliant student"; and the right corner represents 100 percent saying "most popular." Each school is represented by a point whose location relative to the three corners shows the proportion giving each response.

---

[1] I am grateful to James A. Davis and Jacob Feldman, of the University of Chicago, for suggesting such graphs for presenting responses to trichotomous items in a population.

The schools are remarkably grouped somewhat off-center, showing a greater tendency to say "star athlete" than either of the other choices. From each school's point is a broken arrow connecting the school as a whole with its members who were named by their fellows as being "members of the leading crowd." In almost every case, the leading crowd tends in the direction of the athlete—in all cases *away* from the ideal of the brilliant student. Again, for the leading crowds as well as for the students as a whole, the uniformity is remarkably great; not so great in the absolute positions of the leading crowds but in the direction they deviate from the student bodies.

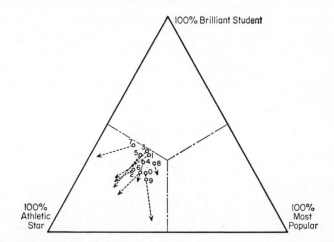

Fig. 3-2. Positions of schools and leading crowds in boys' relative choice of brilliant student, athletic star, and most popular.

This trend toward the ideal of the athletic star on the part of the leading crowds is due in part to the fact that the leading crowds include a great number of athletes. Boys were asked in a questionnaire to name the best athlete in their grade, the best student, and the boy most popular with girls. In every school, without exception, the boys named as best athletes were named more often—on the average over twice as often—as members of the leading crowd than were those named as best students. Similarly, the boy most popular with girls was named as belonging to the leading crowd more often than the best student, though in all schools but the well-to-do suburb and the smallest rural town schools (*9* and *0* on Figure 3-2) less often than the best athlete.

These and other data indicate the importance of athletic achievement as an avenue for gaining status in the schools. Indeed, in the predominantly middle-class schools, it is by far the most effective achievement for gaining a working-class boy entrée into the leading crowd.

Similarly, each girl was asked how she would like to be remembered: as a brilliant student, a leader in extracurricular activities, or most popular. The various schools are located on Figure 3-3, together with arrows connecting them to their leading crowd. The girls tend slightly less, on the average, than the boys to want to be remembered as brilliant students. Although the alternatives are different, and thus cannot be directly compared, a great deal of other evidence indicates

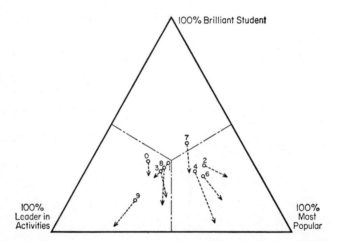

Fig. 3-3. Positions of schools and leading crowds in girls' relative choice of brilliant student, activities leader, and most popular.

that the girls—although better students in every school—do not want to be considered "brilliant students." They have good reason not to, for the girl in each grade in each of the schools who was most often named as best student has fewer friends and is less often in the leading crowd than is the boy most often named as best student.

There is, however, diversity among the schools in the attractiveness of the images of "activities leader" and "popular girl" (Figure 3-3). In five (9, 0, 3, 8, and 1), the leader in activities is more often chosen as an ideal than is the popular girl; in four (7, 6, 2, and 4) the most popular girl is the more attractive of the two. These differences correspond somewhat to class background differences among the schools: 2, 4, 6, and 7, where the activities leader is least attractive, have the highest proportion of students with working-class backgrounds. School 9 is by far the most upper-middle-class one and by far the most activities-oriented.

The differences among the schools correspond as well to differences among the leading crowds: in schools 2, 4, and 6, where the girls as a whole are most oriented to being popular, the leading crowds are even more so; in the school where the girls are most oriented to the ideal of the activities leader, No. 9, the leading crowd goes even further in that direction.[2] In other words, it is as if a pull is exerted by the leading crowd, bringing the rest of the students toward one or the other of the polar extremes. In all cases, the leading crowd pulls away from the brilliant-student ideal.

Although these schools vary far less than one might wish when examining the effects of status systems, there are differences. All students were asked in a questionnaire: "What does it take to get into the leading crowd?" On the basis of the answers, the relative importance of various activities can be determined. Consider only a single activity, academic achievement. Its importance for status among the adolescents in each school can be measured simply by the proportion of responses which specify "good grades," or "brains" as adolescents often put it, as a means of entrée into the leading crowd. In all the schools, academic achievement was of less importance than other matters, such as being an athletic star among the boys, being a cheerleader or being good-looking among the girls, or other attributes. Other measures which were obtained of the importance of academic achievement in the adolescent status system correlate highly with this one.[3]

If, then, it is true that the status system of adolescents *does* affect educational goals, those schools which differ in the importance of academic achievement in the adolescent status system should differ in

---

[2] This result could logically be a statistical artifact because the leaders were included among students as a whole and thus would boost the result in the direction they tend. However, it is not a statistical artifact, for the leading crowds are a small part of the total student body. When they are taken out for computing the position of the rest of the girls in each school, schools 2, 4, 6, and 7 are still the most popularity-oriented, and school 9 the most activities-oriented.

[3] Parenthetically, it might be noted that these measures correlate only imperfectly with the proportion of boys or girls who want to be remembered as brilliant students. These responses depend on the relative attractiveness of other ideals, which varies from school to school, and upon other factors unrelated to the status system.

numerous other ways which are directly related to educational goals. Only one of those, which illustrates well the differing pressures upon students in the various schools, will be reported here.

In every social context certain activities are highly rewarded, while others are not. Those activities which are rewarded are the activities for which there is strong competition—activities in which everyone with some ability will compete. In such activities the persons who achieve most should be those with most potential ability. In contrast, in unrewarded activities, those who have most ability may not be motivated to compete; consequently, the persons who achieve most will be persons of lesser ability. Thus in a high school where basketball is important, nearly every boy who might be a good basketball player will go out for the sport, and, as a result, basketball stars are likely to be the boys with the most ability. If in the same school volleyball does not bring the same status, few boys will go out for it, and those who end up as members of the team will not be the boys with most potential ability.

Similarly, with academic achievement: in a school where such achievement brings few social rewards, those who "go out" for scholarly achievement will be few. The high performers, those who receive good grades, will not be the boys whose ability is greatest but a more mediocre few. Thus the "intellectuals" of such a society, those defined by themselves and others as the best students, will not in fact be those with most intellectual ability. The latter, knowing where the social rewards lie, will be off cultivating other fields which bring social rewards.

To examine the effect of varying social pressures in the schools, academic achievement, as measured by grades in school, was related to IQ. Since the IQ tests differ from school to school, and since each school had its own mean IQ and its own variation around it, the ability of high performers (boys who made A or $A-$ average)[4] was measured by the number of standard deviations of their average IQ's above the

---

[4] In each school but 3 and 8, those making A and $A-$ constituted from 6 to 8 percent of the student body. In order to provide a correct test of the hypothesis, it is necessary to have the same fraction of the student body in each case (since IQ's of this group are being measured in terms of number of standard deviations above the student body). To adjust these groups, enough 6's were added (each being assigned the average IQ of the total group of 6's) to bring the proportion up to 6 percent (from 3 percent in school 3, from 4 percent in school 8).

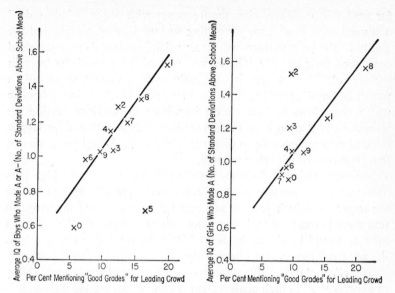

Fig. 3-4, left. IQ's of high achieving boys by importance of good grades among other boys.
Fig. 3-5, right. IQ's of high achieving girls by importance of good grades among other girls.

mean. In this way, it is possible to see where the high performers' ability lay, relative to the distribution of abilities in their school.[5]

The variations were great: in a small-town school, No. *1*, the boys who made an *A* or *A*— average had IQ's 1.53 standard deviations above the school average; in another small-town school, No. *0*, their IQ's were only about a third this distance above the mean, .59. Given this variation, the question can be asked: Do these variations in ability of the high performers correspond to variations in the social rewards for, or constraints against, being a good student?

Figure 3-4 shows the relation for the boys between the social rewards

---

[5] The IQ tests used in the different schools were: (0) California Mental Maturity (taken seventh, eighth, or ninth grade); (1) California Mental Maturity (taken eighth grade); (2) SRA Primary Mental Abilities (taken tenth grade); (3) California Mental Maturity (taken ninth grade; seniors took SRA PMA, which was tabulated as a percentile, and they have been omitted from analysis reported above); (4) Otis (ninth and tenth grades; taken eighth grade; Kuhlman Finch (eleventh and twelfth grades, taken eighth grade); (5) Otis (taken ninth grade); (6) California Mental Maturity (taken eighth grade); (7) California Mental Maturity (taken eighth grade); (8) Otis (taken ninth or tenth grade); and (9) Otis (taken eighth grade).

for academic excellence (i.e., the frequency with which "good grades" was mentioned as a means for getting into the leading crowd) and the ability of the high performers, measured by the number of standard deviations their average IQ's exceed that of the rest of the boys in the school. The relation is extremely strong. Only one school, a parochial boys' school in the city's slums, deviates. This is a school in which many boys had their most important associations outside the school rather than in it, so that its student body constituted far less of a social system, less able to dispense social rewards and punishments, than was true of the other schools.

Similarly, Figure 3-5 shows for the girls the IQ's of the high performers.[6] Unfortunately, most of the schools are closely bunched in the degree to which good grades are important among the girls, so that there is too little variation among them to examine this effect as fully as would be desirable. School 2 is the one school whose girls deviate from the general relationship.

The effect of these value systems on the freedom for academic ability to express itself in high achievement is evident among the girls as it is among the boys. This is not merely due to the school facilities, social composition of the school, or other variables: the two schools highest in the importance of scholastic achievement for both boys and girls are 1 and 3, the first a small-town school of 350 students and the second a city school of 2,000 students. In both there are fewer students with white-collar backgrounds than in schools 9 or 3, which are somewhere in the middle as to value placed on academic achievement, but are more white-collar than in schools 7 or 4, which are also somewhere in the middle. The highest expenditure per student was $695 per year in school 9, and the lowest was little more than half that, in school 4. These schools are close together on the graphs of Figures 3-4 and 3-5.

It should be mentioned in passing that an extensive unpublished study throughout Connecticut, using standard tests of achievement and ability, yielded consistent results. The study found no correlation between per pupil expenditure in a school and the achievement of its

---

[6] For the girls, only girls with a straight-A average were included. Since girls get better grades than boys, this device is necessary in order to make the sizes of the "high-performer" group roughly comparable for boys and for girls. Schools differed somewhat in the proportion of A's, constituting about 6 percent of the students in the small schools, only about 3 percent in schools 6 and 7, 1 percent in 8, and 2 percent in 9. In 8 and 9, enough girls were added and assigned the average grade of the 7 (A—) group to bring the proportion to 3 percent, comparable with the other large schools. The difference, however, between the large and small schools was left.

students relative to their ability. The effects shown in Figures 3-4 and 3-5 suggest why: that students with ability are led to achieve only when there are social rewards, primarily from their peers, for doing so—and these social rewards seem little correlated with per pupil expenditure.

So much for the effects as shown by the variation among schools. As mentioned earlier, the variation among schools was not nearly so striking in this research as the fact that, in all of them, academic achievement did not count for as much as other activities. In every school the boy named as best athlete and the boy named as most popular with girls was far more often mentioned as a member of the leading crowd and as someone to "be like," than was the boy named as the best student. And the girl named as best dressed, and the one named as most popular with boys, was in every school far more often mentioned as being in the leading crowd and as someone to "be like," than was the girl named as the best student.

The relative unimportance of academic achievement, together with the effect shown earlier, suggests that these adolescent subcultures are generally deterrents to academic achievement. In other words, in these societies of adolescents those who come to be seen as the "intellectuals" and who come to think so of themselves are not really those of highest intelligence but are only the ones who are willing to work hard at a relatively unrewarded activity.

The implications for American society as a whole are clear. Because high schools allow the adolescent subcultures to divert energies into athletics, social activities, and the like, they recruit into adult intellectual activities people with a rather mediocre level of ability. In fact, the high school seems to do more than allow these subcultures to discourage academic achievement; it aids them in doing so. To indicate how it does and to indicate how it might do differently is another story, to be examined below.

Figures 3-2 and 3-3, which show the way boys and girls would like to be remembered in their high school, demonstrate a curious difference between the boys and the girls. Despite great variation in social background, in size of school (from 180 to 2,000), in size of town (from less than a thousand to over a million), and in style of life of their parents, the proportion of boys choosing each of the three images by which he wants to be remembered is very nearly the same in all schools. And in every school the leading crowd "pulls" in similar directions: at least partly toward the ideal of the star athlete. Yet the ideals of the girls in these schools are far more dispersed, and the leading crowds "pull" in varying directions, far less uniformly than among the boys. Why such a diversity in the same schools?

The question can best be answered by indirection. In two schools apart from those in the research, the questionnaire was administered primarily to answer a puzzling question: Why was academic achievement of so little importance among the adolescents in school 9? Their parents were professionals and business executives, about 80 percent were going to college (over twice as high a proportion as in any of the other schools), and yet academic excellence counted for little among them. In the two additional schools parental background was largely

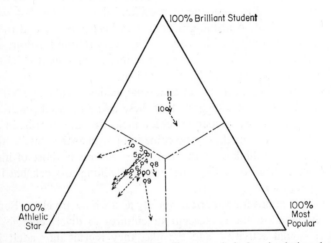

Fig. 3-6. Positions of schools and leading crowds in boys' relative choice of brilliant student, athletic star, and most popular (two private schools included).

held constant, for they were private, coeducational day schools whose students had upper-middle-class backgrounds quite similar to those of school 9. One (No. 10) was in the city; the other (No. 11), in a suburban setting almost identical to that of No. 9. Although the two schools were added to the study to answer the question about school 9, they will be used to help answer the puzzle set earlier; that of the clustering of schools for the boys and their greater spread for the girls. When we look at the responses of adolescents in these two schools to the question as to how they would like to be remembered, the picture becomes even more puzzling (Figures 3-6 and 3-7). For the boys, they are extremely far from the cluster of the other schools; for the girls, they are intermingled with the other schools. Thus, though it was for the boys that the other schools clustered so closely, these two deviate sharply from the cluster; and for the girls, where the schools already varied, these two are not distinguishable. Furthermore, the leading crowds of boys in these schools do not pull the ideal toward the star-athlete ideal as do those in almost all the other schools. To be sure, they pull away from the ideal of the brilliant student, but the pull is primarily toward a social image, the most popular. Among the girls, the leading crowds pull in different directions and are nearly indistinguishable from the other schools.

The answer to both puzzles, that is, first, the great cluster of the

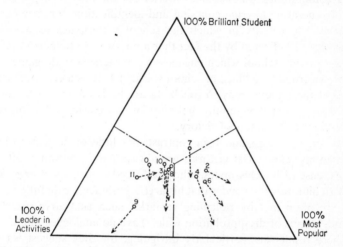

Fig. 3-7. Positions of schools and leading crowds in girls' relative choice of brilliant student, activities leader, and most popular (two private schools included).

boys and now, in these two additional schools, the greater deviation, seems to lie in one fact: the boys' interscholastic athletics. The nine public schools are all engaged in interscholastic leagues which themselves are knit together in state tournaments. The other school of the first ten, the Catholic school, is in a parochial league, where games are just as hotly contested as in the public leagues and is also knit together with them in tournaments.

Schools *10* and *11* are athletically in a world apart from this. Although boys in both schools may go in for sports, and both schools have interscholastic games, the opponents are scattered private schools, constituting a league in name only. They take no part in state or city tournaments and have almost no publicity.

There is nothing for the girls comparable to the boys' interscholastic athletics. There are school activities of one sort or another, in which most girls take part, but no interscholastic games involving them. Their absence and the lack of leagues which knit all schools together in systematic competition means that the status system can "wander" freely, depending on local conditions in the school. In athletics, however, a school, and the community surrounding it, cannot hold its head up if it continues to lose games. It *must* devote roughly the same attention to athletics as do the schools surrounding it, for athletic games are the only games in which it engages other schools and, by representation, other communities. These games are almost the only means a school has of generating internal cohesion and identification, for they constitute the only activity in which the school participates *as* a school. (This is well indicated by the fact that a number of students in school *10*, the private school which engages in no interscholastic games, has been concerned by a "lack of school spirit.") It is as a consequence of this that the athlete gains so much status: he is doing something for the school and the community, not only for himself, in leading his team to victory, for it is a school victory.

The outstanding student, in contrast, has little or no way to bring glory to his school. His victories are always purely personal, often at the expense of his classmates, who are forced to work harder to keep up with him. It is no wonder that his accomplishments gain little reward and are often met by ridiculing remarks, such as "curve-raiser" or "grind," terms of disapprobation which have no analogues in athletics.

These results are particularly intriguing, for they suggest ways in which rather straightforward social theory could be used in organizing the activities of high schools in such a way that their adolescent subcultures would encourage, rather than discourage, the channeling of energies into directions of learning. One might speculate on the possible effects of city-wide or state-wide "scholastic fairs" composed of academic games and tournaments between schools and school exhibits to be judged. It could be that the mere institution of such games would, just as do the state basketball tournaments in the midwestern United States, have a profound effect upon the educational climate in the participating schools. In fact, by an extension of this analysis, one would predict that an international fair of this sort, a "Scholastic Olympics," would generate interscholastic games and tournaments within the participating countries.

*As our society becomes increasingly complex, impersonal,
and divergent, it becomes increasingly difficult for children to
learn acceptable behavior for the countless roles they must fill.
The school, therefore, attempts to teach some social skills. Yet
Dorothy Lee finds wide discrepancy in text material concerning various areas of our culture. If society contains confused
images of the wife, husband, or family, how can the school
present them any more clearly?*

DISCREPANCIES IN THE TEACHING OF AMERICAN CULTURE / *Dorothy Lee*

The study on which this paper is based was initiated in an attempt to
discover what cultural values, concepts, and attitudes are presented
to the growing generation in the school.[1] The subject matter included
in the Home Economics program, and occasionally under Family Life
Education, was chosen because this includes generally most of what
anthropologists cover under the term culture. It is concerned with
helping the student to develop a healthy personality through participation in human relations in the home and the community and to develop
into a mature and healthy adult, who will establish a home where
democratic, happy co-operative living will prevail. Skills and understanding and knowledge necessary for homemaking are taught under
this program. Behavior at home and outside the home is discussed, as
well as personal ethics, social intercourse, friendship, and marriage.

The study was made through an analysis of teachers' manuals and
guides;[2] and early in the study it became apparent that often there
was a wide discrepancy between the objectives of the program and
their implementation. A similar discrepancy was present in the presentation of areas of culture, as, for example, between the skills of homemaking and the relations and values in homemaking, or between the

---

[1] This paper is a by-product of a pilot study on American values and
concepts made possible by a grant from the Humanities Division of the
Rockefeller Foundation.

[2] The manuals and guides used for this study are referred to by code
number. The list will be supplied by the author of this paper on request.

---

self and society. The family of one's birth and the family to be made through marriage appeared to contain discontinuous values. Work and leisure, duty and fun, the given and the chosen were presented in an exclusive dualism of opposition.

The discrepancy existing between theory and implementation, as well as between the areas of home living and of homemaking skills, is expressed variously in discontinuities and dualisms, which, though more pronounced in the older manuals, are still present to an extent in the newer ones. A discussion of family life and marriage from a course of study designed for high school, published in 1950, will illustrate this point. This course is offered because:

> We are living now in a changing society. The family patterns and traditions of yesterday no longer hold true in the world of today. . . . Plainly, people do need help in understanding the real values of life; in appreciating the very real treasure of the family . . . they need help in preparing for marriage in order to live fully, richly, and satisfyingly. The justification for the teaching of courses in the schools in human relationships is found in that last sentence. [3]

The main objective of the course is stated as follows: "To promote the founding of . . . ideal homes. . . ." For this the individual needs a healthy personality; and the basic social needs for the personality are best met in the family unit. The family is of "immense importance in the emotional development" of the individual; therefore, the course includes units which are to help the student develop his personality through the human relations in the home. The lesson on Family Relationships has as its first objective to "help the student to understand the meaning of the co-operative, the sharing; the democratic home. . . ."

How is the student's home life actually to be used in helping him found an "ideal home"? In the lesson on Family Relationships there are three more objectives stated:

> 2. . . . To realize the purpose of restrictions.
> 3. . . . To realize his contribution to family conflict.
> 4. . . . To help the student know ways of improving family life, of reducing conflict.

And the name of the lesson has as subtitle: "Family Relationships: Conflicts—Ways of Improving."

The lesson apparently attempts here to teach its material in terms of specific problems to be solved, specific things to do. And the problematic material is characteristically negative: not something had, to be enjoyed, but something to be achieved or solved or ameliorated. To teach in terms of problems has long been considered an effective method; the problem delimits, makes concrete, clarifies. But in selecting this method the manual necessarily suggests the presentation of family life as negative, thus going counter to its avowed intention. Family life is presented as not good and there is no suggestion that the student is to be helped to indulge in it and be emotionally nourished. He is to relate himself to it in terms of adjusting to it, correcting its evils, improving it, rather than enjoying it. Home life is full of conflict and restriction. In this lesson, the question posed as: "Why do parents act as they do?" is spelled out as "Why do they 'always' say no?" The brother-sister relationship is covered in one question, "What can a boy or girl do about a 'pesky' sister or brother . . . ?" and under one subheading, "Sister-sister, brother-brother, brother-sister conflicts." This is the picture which the course presents of "the very real treasure of the family" which it is to help the student to appreciate.

In using his family experience to develop into an adult who can found an ideal home, the student is to be urged to learn "to get along." He is to recognize restriction, improve relations, resolve conflicts so that he can "get along" with others and himself. Of the six "immediate and specific objectives" given for the course, four are to help the student "to get along." It is a negative objective, satisfied with a minimum which lacks positive values; it does not go beyond the elimination of the undesirable. It is corrective rather than creative. The most dynamic and positive phrasing in which this "getting-along" sphere of human relations is expressed is represented by statements such as the following: "A substitute for that tried and true method of getting along— desire and effort—has never been found. . . . Try to attain the live-and-let-live attitude, and see . . . the achievement in maturity it will mean, even its relationship to preparation for marriage." This minimal phrasing of goals is certainly not what this course of study wants to convey to the growing generation as American culture.

The American ideal of the maximum is expressed only when speaking of the future, of the homes which the students themselves will establish with a chosen mate. This future family life is presented in positive value terms, full of creativity. In the one lesson on Family Relationships, the term "get along" occurs seven times; in the eight lessons on dating, courting, engagement, and marriage, it occurs, I think, only once. And what is impressive here is the large number of times when the "get along" attitude is absent, replaced by terms implying spontaneity and value (the italics throughout the following are added): "You *enjoy* the thought of being his wife." "You work out disagreements as they appear, for your relationship is more *important* than being right." "You are *willing to do personally anything* to make it [the marriage] succeed." "You are *willing and eager* to share with him in everything." Now the student is to be helped to establish an "ideal home" where happy family life is maintained, by being helped to develop emotionally and mature through experiencing human relations in his family. How can the meager and stingy soil of the "get-along" relationships bright forth anything so vital?

"Family living" in the present and "marriage" in the future also differ in the way "sharing" is presented. "To be willing to share" is one of the signs of maturity listed in the course, and sharing is mentioned often throughout the course; the student is to be helped to understand "the meaning of the cooperative, the sharing." However, only in the marriage relationship is it *sharing in*, as in the last quotation given. In the life which develops the attitudes that would make this possible, it is always a *sharing*. And sharing, without the *in*, is diminishing and dividing; it is concerned with fairness, atomistically pitting one individual against another. It is in this respect the opposite of *sharing in*, which enhances in the very act of sharing.

The writers of this guide, faced with the task of presenting good marriage, give a picture of a warm, positive, creative, agentive relationship, full of value and without utilitarianism. But in trying to show the student how to relate himself with his present family, they face a dilemma. They would like to show him how to find emotional nourishment, value, and security here. Yet often this is a situation in which he is not accorded an agentive role, where he has no opportunity to create; it is a given, and often for him its predominant quality is one of dissonance and conflict. So the solution is to guide the student in resolving this conflict, understanding the basis of the restrictions, "getting along" with the least possible friction.

As a result, the course suggests that creativity in human relations be taught through the medium of situations which allow only of correction, and a positive attitude, through relations which are phrased as negative and restrictive. It has to teach the American in speaking of hobbies. This guide suggests that the unit entitled Food for Family Fun be correlated with the unit on Family Relations; a year-long unit called Food for Family Health precedes this, but no suggestion is made as to its being connected in any way with family relations. In another manual, only leisure occupations are called "enriching [5]"; and only in connection with leisure did I find the words "joy" and "satisfaction" used.

The one value, apart from "nutritional value," implemented through the teaching of the skills needed for routine work in homemaking is "the value of saving time and energy," or the "value of time and money management." And this value is negative, tending not toward deriving satisfaction from the process, but toward the opposite. It helps shorten the process, which has been called a "meaningful experience" in the list of objectives, but is actually presented as preoccupation with the meaningless. In doing their work girls are urged to "perform house-keeping duties using both old and new equipment; compare results of experiment as to time, energy, and efficiency [8]." Relative enjoyment is apparently not to be considered as a factor in the evaluation. The human relations differential between the mechanical dishwasher and the family dishpan is not discussed. What is important is that the *must* be diminished, leaving more time and energy for the chosen.

It is so important, in fact, to diminish this *must* of everyday living that many of the manuals urge the "sharing" of work not as a good and rewarding experience in itself, but as a means of increasing leisure time, particularly, of course, for the mother. In one manual, the objective of "sharing responsibility" is implemented as "sharing household duties to allow for leisure [10]." In another we read,

> *Appreciation of fact that sharing home tasks means some leisure time for all.* Problem: Report on sharing care of rooms in homes and on sharing mother's special tasks.
> *a.* How mother used that extra free time.
> *b.* Good times made possible by working together. [7]

Another way to escape from the valueless given is to make a special occasion of what is otherwise a routine task, for example, ideal of the maximum—"willing to do . . . anything," "eager to share in every-thing"—through experiences phrased as minimal.

This type of unresolved dualism is found generally between the given and the chosen, the areas of the *must do* and the *free to do*. The skills used in homemaking are presented as a *must*, to be recognized and accepted. For example, a textbook tells the student "We must have a working knowledge of nutrition. We must know what foods. . . . We must apply what we know. . . . [1]"

The following are stated objectives for the "Clothing Unit" in one of the manuals:

> Recognition that some seams need no finish.
> Recognition of order of work as important.

Recognition of effect of laundry and pressing on appearance.
Realization of need for fixing good habits.
Appreciation of need for good habits. [7]

This, like the family of one's birth, is in the area of the given, to which the student is to be led to adjust minimally and not necessarily with joy. There is no social value in this, there are no "good times." Value and freedom lie in the chosen, the leisure-time activity, the hobby, the special occasion (the italics are added):

Problem 4: *Discuss* values of remembering family birthdays, other *special* days.
Problem 5: Discuss the *problems* of brother-sister relations. [4]

The chosen is something that I *can* do (I am free to do or not do) rather than something I *should* do (I am not free not to do). For example we have (italics added), "What responsibility in my home *should* I share?" and, farther down in the same section, "How *can* I help my family *enjoy leisure* time? [8]"

It is in the area of the chosen that value lies. During leisure time, one is free to choose one's occupation; this then may contain "fun" or other value. Consequently, there is a dualism between work and leisure. The word "enjoy" is used rarely, if ever, in connection with the regular work or life of the home. In one manual I found it used only once, when "to enjoy work [3]" is given in a list as one of the characteristics of maturity. In one guide, which suggests courses, lessons, and units for six grades, the word "enjoy [9]" is used twice to my knowledge, both times to prepare a picnic instead of the usual lunch. Instead of following established procedure passively, the individual can, in this way, exercise initiative and spontaneity, and be agentive in creating the special.

In all the writing there is repeatedly this suggested escape from the routine to the special, from work to leisure, when the good is to be introduced:

Housekeeping is an important part of the spirit that makes a home. . . . The end product of effective housekeeping is comfortable living. Comfortable living affords time for leisure. . . . [1]

Being without value the work of ordinary home life is not dynamic and provides no emotional nourishment, no feedback. This, like all the good, comes through leisure:

Happy family life is essential to the welfare of individuals and nations as well. . . . Total health, mental and physical, has its

foundations in the habits established in home living. . . .
Recreation is doing things for fun. Out of fun comes relaxation
and renewal of energy for all we must do.

It is in the special that social values lie, and through these are they
implemented. The section on Thinking of Others, in the seventh-grade
homemaking course given in one of the manuals, states the following objectives:

> 1. An interest in doing things for others.
> 2. To learn ways girls can do thoughtful things for others.
> [These are implemented through the following means:]
> 1. Events that call for special thoughtful attention to others.
> 2. Ways of remembering special times.
> 3. Simple refreshments for an "afternoon at home."
> 4. Decorations and favors for special occasion. [4]

The list continues through eleven objectives all dealing with the special.
Another manual teaches "consideration for others and willingness to
compromise," entirely through the problem. "Sharing facilities for
entertainment: 1. Radio, 2. Other entertainment [7]." In one high-
school course "Good Citizenship" is presented as "positively practiced [5]" only during one's leisure.

Family feeling, unity, loyalty, come through sharing occasions of
fun. "The strong feeling of love and respect in a modern family is the
result of playing together more often than working together," according to one textbook.

> The greatest satisfaction is derived from the companionship of
> the people who live there [the family] and the pleasures they
> enjoy together. . . . It would be wise to adopt the slogan: "The
> family . . . that plays together stays together." . . . Good times
> shared by the family group result in a better understanding of
> each other and therefore promote family unity. [1]

At no time are the operations involved in everyday homemaking
presented as areas where spontaneity might be given range. Initiative
and creativity are listed, in one manual, only in the section on Fun
with the Family, under the subtitle "Cultivating Hobbies [10]." In
another manual, there is a leisure-time unit listed under "Clothing [7]"
and only here is the development of originality mentioned.

Another dualism implicit in the manuals is that between self and
society. The student is urged to develop herself by acquiring and developing, in the main, traits which meet with the approval of others: to
achieve "a pleasing voice, a pleasant expression [5]," to find an answer
to the question, "How can I be popular with others? [4]" This means

that standards and criteria for personality and conduct are to be sought outside the self. The emphasis seems to be on the development of the "other-directed," to use Riesman's term. One manual lists a unit which "might be called personality and good grooming [7]"; and, in general, personality is defined largely in terms of manners, grooming, and adherence to accepted conduct:

> Personality Development Objectives: Desire and ability to know and use approved social customs and good manners. Make and keep friends. Possess good personality traits. Problems:
>
> a. Get along with people by having good manners.
> b. How to develop good manners at home.
> c. Careful grooming to make you pleasing at first sight.
> d, e, f, g, h deal with being a good guest and a good hostess and having a good voice.
> i. How to be popular, and make and keep friends. Five points listed under this deal with good manners, two with dating procedures, five with how to behave in public. [4]

Such a person, who has good manners and behaves acceptably on social occasions, has "the ability to get along with people [which] not only increases your chances of having a good time but also contributes to success in every phase of living [4]." Another manual lists:

> General Objectives: [of unit which "might be called personality and good grooming."]
> 1. Realization of the importance of good personal appearance and the development of a good personality for successful living.
> 2. Knowledge of how to behave in a socially acceptable manner. [7]

One manual lists seven objectives for the unit which helps the individual in personality development. Of these, two are:

> 1. Understands the importance of knowing current customs.
> 2. Practices some ways of acting which are socially accepted. [6]

Another manual states as one of its objectives "Appreciation of and a desire for a pleasing personality." A "pleasing" personality is not necessarily good, or strong, or mature, or relaxed, one which satisfies an internal standard; it is an externally directed one, which succeeds when it pleases another. This stress on the teaching of good grooming and acceptable manners comes, to some extent, in response to a felt need and reflects the social mobility of this society; it will probably remain, even after the disparity between a good personality and a pleasing personality has been overcome.

There is another way in which society is presented as external to the self: it is to be used for the meeting of the needs of the self. A unit for the eighth grade, entitled "Being a Likeable Person in Your Own Home," states as one of its objectives the teaching of the student to look "for ways in which family life contributes to success." In the same manual, in a unit for the ninth grade, entitled "Feeling Successful in High School Years," the students are to become aware of "ways in which school and community are contributing to their success [6]." In another manual, relationships within the family, "contacts," and "cooperation" are urged on the student for the development of a "truly effective personality [5]." Consistent with this conception of the self, as external to society, a course is divided into sections on: *helping myself,* and *helping others.*

The goals and values of the self are also phrased in terms of externality. Its qualities and traits are spoken of as possessed and acquired. Time and energy and even habits are mentioned as "managed" or "used" by the self. One manual states as its first objective

> Ability to use wisely available human and material resources such as time, energy, health, money, attitudes, and understandings. [8]

It follows that the self, as presented here, is not an internally growing unit, but one which increases through accretion, so that personal development is a matter of "acquiring desirable traits."

In one manual, the unit on "Growing Up" lists the following among seventeen "needs and interests" (italics are added):

> To *better* understand one's self and others.
> Make *more* of own decisions.
> Buy *more* of own things.
> Assume *more* responsibility for behavior.
> Find ways to *improve* personality.
> Be *more* popular. [10]

Much of this is, of course, abetted by a language which makes it extremely difficult to refer to growth and development except in terms of accretion, increase, and improvement. Thus even emotional maturity itself may be phrased as external, a goal to be achieved, not a becoming. One manual which uses the phrase, "the child *grows into* [italics added] adult situations," nevertheless presents maturity as "a goal that pays the highest dividends." It speaks of the individual who "pays too high a price for the security he gains by withdrawal or by aggression," thus giving the impression that security, also, is something external to be bought at a price. Continuing this phrasing of externality it tells how some individuals maintain a discrepancy between the goals they set for themselves and "the energy they are willing to expend." An individual who has "a sense of values" knows that "there is a price to pay and is willing to pay for value received [11]."

The self is clearly conceived as external to its life process when we come to the discussion of planning. Managing the time and energy of the self by planning one's work is presented as one of the main objectives in a variety of areas. Out of forty-eight "behavior changes sought" through the unit on "Clothing" in one manual, seven mention "planning and the management of time [9]." In another manual, out of five objectives to be met in four to six weeks of teaching, one is "learn to save time [4]." In a unit on "Foods for Special Occasions," covering two pages, a manual mentions "plan" eighteen times and "time management" three: "Plan work efficiently, and manage time well" . . . "the value of planning" . . . "plan and carry out" . . . "plan time schedules" . . . "plan market order [7]" . . . and so forth. "Careful planning helps make the task easier," states another manual; *"Value of Planning Care of the House:* 1. Saving time, 2. Saving energy [10]."

In general, planning is taught in connection with the given, the required work. Here there is to be no wasted motion or wasted time; no exploring and no randomness of operation. Time saved from this area is time for leisure and fun; energy saved means energy for leisure-time activity, and this may be used for exploring. One manual, however, carries planning into the chosen: leisure time itself can be planned and managed to the advantage of the self. A student can use leisure time to earn money, for example, and, in this way, meet three objectives:

> 1. Realization that what she does today is important to tomorrow's success.
> 2. Realization that success in the school, home, and community are related.
> 3. Finding out what are opportunities for part-time jobs.

The student is told, in effect, that if she wants to succeed tomorrow she should plan carefully so that even the leisure time of today may contribute toward this end. This manual quotes students' reports on how their free time was used, and lists some of the answers giving "satisfactory" ways (italics added):

> Drove out in the country *in order to see the sunset.*
> Read a book that *has been recommended.*
> Did some typing for a neighbor for pay to build up a fund *for a definite purpose.*

No random driving in the country, nor exploring in lanes, no exploring in the realm of books, no building up a fund and then discovering something to spend it on. No exploration, no adventure is quoted as desirable, even in this "free" time. Time is "wasted" when one is "day-dreaming instead of attending to the present"; when "one talks idly for long times." It is "not wasted" when "talking idly to someone in order to be better acquainted." Yet when does one discover that one wants to be better acquainted? Planning beforehand would save time, as "knowing what radio program you would like to listen to and when they come." Yet how does one discover the unknown and unpredictable?

The discrepancies, discontinuities, and unresolved dualisms listed in this paper are implicit in a program which is the result of accretion. The program is in constant process of revision and integration; when it becomes a unit some of these discrepancies will probably disappear. Others, however, are inherent in the very structure of a mobile society and in a culture which values change. It is possible, then, that in presenting the adult role in terms of discontinuity and exclusive dualism the writings examined here are merely faithfully presenting American culture.

Many readers will undoubtedly see origins of Riesman's other-directed crowd and Whyte's Organization Man in Urie Bronfenbrenner's Changing American Child. Many may find this trend objectionable, but we cannot blink the facts of growing empirical evidence; the personality of the American child is changing. The school's traditional image of him is evolving into a myth.

THE CHANGING AMERICAN CHILD—A SPECULA-TIVE ANALYSIS[1] / Urie Bronfenbrenner

A QUESTION OF MOMENT

It is now a matter of scientific record that patterns of child rearing in the United States have changed appreciably over the past twenty-five years (Bronfenbrenner, 1958). Middle class parents especially have moved away from the more rigid and strict styles of care and discipline advocated in the early Twenties and Thirties toward modes of response involving greater tolerance of the child's impulses and desires, freer expression of affection, and increased reliance on "psychological" methods of discipline, such as reasoning and appeals to guilt, as distinguished from more direct techniques like physical punishment. At the same time, the gap between the social classes in their goals and methods of child rearing appears to be narrowing, with working class parents beginning to adopt both the values and techniques of the middle class. Finally, there is dramatic correspondence between these observed shifts in parental values and behavior and the changing character of the attitudes and practices advocated in successive editions of such widely read manuals as the Children's Bureau bulletin on *Infant Care* and Spock's *Baby and Child Care*. Such correspondence should not be taken to mean that the expert has now become the principal instigator and instrument of social change, since the ideas of scientists and professional workers themselves reflect in part the operation of deep-rooted cultural processes. Nevertheless, the fact remains that changes in values and practices advocated by prestigeful professional figures can be substantially accelerated by rapid and widespread dissemination through the press, mass media of communication, and public discussion.

Given these facts, it becomes especially important to gauge the effect

[1] This paper draws heavily on results from a program of research being conducted by the author in collaboration with Edward C. Devereux and George J. Suci. The contribution of these colleagues to facts and ideas presented in this paper is gratefully acknowledged. The research program is supported in part with grants from the National Science Foundation and the National Institutes of Health.

Urie Bronfenbrenner, "The Changing American Child," *Journal of Social Issues*, *17*, 1 (1961), 6–17. Reprinted with the permission of the author and *The Society for the Psychological Study of Social Issues*.

of the changes that are advocated and adopted. Nowhere is this issue more significant, both scientifically and socially, than in the sphere of familial values and behavior. It is certainly no trivial matter to ask whether the changes that have occurred in the attitudes and actions of parents over the past twenty-five years have been such as to affect the personality development of their children, so that the boys and girls of today are somewhat different in character structure from those of a decade or more ago. Or, to put the question more succinctly: has the changing American parent produced a changing American child?

A STRATEGY OF INFERENCE

Do we have any basis for answering this intriguing question? To begin with, do we have any evidence of changes in the behavior of children in successive decades analogous to those we have already been able to find for parents? If so, we could take an important first step toward a solution of the problem. Unfortunately, in contrast to his gratifying experience in seeking and finding appropriate data on parents, the present writer has, to date, been unable to locate enough instances in which comparable methods of behavioral assessment have been employed with different groups of children of similar ages over an extended period of time. Although the absence of such material precludes any direct and unequivocal approach to the question at hand, it is nevertheless possible, through a series of inferences from facts already known, to arrive at some estimate of what the answer might be. Specifically, although as yet we have no comparable data on the relation between parental and child behavior for different families at successive points in time, we do have facts on the influence of parental treatment on child behavior at a given point in time; that is, we know that certain variations in parental behavior tend to be accompanied by systematic differences in the personality characteristics of children. If we are willing to assume that these same relationships obtained not only at a given moment but across different points in time, we are in a position to infer the possible effects on children of changing patterns of child rearing over the years. It is this strategy that we propose to follow.

THE CHANGING AMERICAN PARENT

We have already noted the major changes in parental behavior discerned in a recent analysis of data reported over a twenty-five year period. These secular trends may be summarized as follows:

1. Greater permissiveness toward the child's spontaneous desires
2. Freer expression of affection
3. Increased reliance on indirect "psychological" techniques of discipline (such as reasoning or appeals to guilt) vs. direct methods (like physical punishment, scolding, or threats)
4. In consequence of the above shifts in the direction of what are predominantly middle class values and techniques, a narrowing of the gap between social classes in their patterns of child rearing.

Since the above analysis was published, a new study has documented an additional trend. Bronson, Katten, and Livson (1959) have compared patterns of paternal and maternal authority and affection in two generations of families from the California Guidance Study. Unfortunately, the time span surveyed overlaps only partially with the twenty-five year period covered in our own analysis, the first California generation having been raised in the early 1900's and the second in the late '20's and early '30's. Accordingly, if we are to consider the California results along with the others cited above, we must make the somewhat risky assumption that a trend discerned in the first three decades of the century has continued in the same direction through the early 1950's. With this important qualification, an examination of the data cited by Bronson et al. (1959) points to still another, secular trend—a shift over the years in the pattern of parental role differentiation within the family. Specifically:

5. In succeeding generations the relative position of the father vis-à-vis the mother is shifting with the former becoming increasingly more affectionate and less authoritarian, and the latter becoming relatively more important as the agent of discipline, especially for boys.

"PSYCHOLOGICAL" TECHNIQUES OF DISCIPLINE AND THEIR EFFECTS

In pursuing our analytic strategy, we next seek evidence of the effects on the behavior of children of variations in parental treatment of the type noted in our inventory. We may begin by noting that the variables involved in the first three secular trends constitute a complex that has received considerable attention in recent research in parent-child relationships. Within the last three years, two sets of investigators, working independently, have called attention to the greater efficacy of "love-oriented" or "psychological" techniques in bringing about desired behavior in the child (Sears, Maccoby, and Levin, 1957;

Miller and Swanson, 1958; 1960). The present writer, noting that such methods are especially favored by middle class parents, offered the following analysis of the nature of these techniques and the reasons for their effectiveness.

Such parents are, in the first place, more likely to overlook offenses, and when they do punish, they are less likely to ridicule or inflict physical pain. Instead, they reason with the youngster, isolate him, appeal to guilt, show disappointment—in short, convey in a variety of ways, on the one hand, the kind of behavior that is expected of the child; on the other, the realization that transgression means the interruption of a mutually valued relationship. . . .

These findings [of greater efficacy] means that middle class parents, though in one sense more lenient in their discipline techniques, are using methods that are actually more compelling. Moreover, the compelling power of these practices is probably enhanced by the more permissive treatment accorded to middle class children in the early years of life. The successful use of withdrawal of love as a discipline technique implies the prior existence of a gratifying relationship; the more love present in the first instance, the greater the threat implied in its withdrawal (Bronfenbrenner, 1958).

It is now a well established fact that children from middle class families tend to excel those from lower class in many characteristics ordinarily regarded as desirable, such as self-control, achievement, responsibility, leadership, popularity, and adjustment in general.[2] If, as seems plausible, such differences in behavior are attributable at least in part to class-linked variations in parental treatment, the strategy of inference we have adopted would appear on first blush to lead to a rather optimistic conclusion. Since, over the years, increasing numbers of parents have been adopting the more effective socialization techniques typically employed by the middle class, does it not follow that successive generations of children should show gains in the development of effective behavior and desirable personality characteristics?

Unfortunately, this welcome conclusion, however logical, is premature, for it fails to take into account all of the available facts.

[2] For a summary of findings on social class differences in children's behavior and personality characteristics, see Mussen, P. H., and Conger, J. J., *Child Development and Personality*. New York: Harper, 1956.

SEX, SOCIALIZATION, AND SOCIAL CLASS

To begin with, the parental behaviors we have been discussing are differentially distributed not only by socio-economic status but also by sex. As we have pointed out elsewhere (Bronfenbrenner, 1961), girls are exposed to more affection and less punishment than boys, but at the same time are more likely to be subjected to "love-oriented" discipline of the type which encourages the development of internalized controls. And, consistent with our line of reasoning, girls are found repeatedly to be "more obedient, cooperative, and in general better socialized than boys at comparable age levels." But this is not the whole story.

. . . At the same time, the research results indicate that girls tend to be more anxious, timid, dependent, and sensitive to rejection. If these differences are a function of differential treatment by parents, then it would seem that the more "efficient" methods of child rearing employed with girls involve some risk of what might be called "over-socialization" (Bronfenbrenner, 1961).

One could argue, of course, that the contrasting behaviors of boys and girls have less to do with differential parental treatment than with genetically-based maturational influences. Nevertheless, two independent lines of evidence suggest that socialization techniques do contribute to individual differences, *within the same sex*, precisely in the types of personality characteristics noted above. In the first place, variations in child behavior and parental treatment strikingly similar to those we have cited for the two sexes are reported in a recent comprehensive study of differences between first and later born children (Schachter, 1959). Like girls, first children receive more attention, are more likely to be exposed to "psychological" discipline, and end up more anxious and dependent, whereas later children, like boys, are more aggressive and self-confident.

A second line of evidence comes from our own current research. We have been concerned with the role of parents in the development of such "constructive" personality characteristics as responsibility and leadership among adolescent boys and girls. Our findings reveal not only the usual differences in adolescents' and parents' behaviors associated with the sex of the child, but also a striking contrast in the relationship between parental and child behaviors for the two sexes. To start on firm and familiar ground, girls are rated by their teachers as more responsible than boys, whereas the latter obtain higher scores on leadership. Expected differences similarly appear in the realm of parental behavior: girls receive more affection, praise, and companionship; boys are subjected to more physical punishment and achievement demands. Quite unanticipated, however, at least by us, was the finding that both parental affection and discipline appeared to facilitate effective psychological functioning in boys, but to impede the development of such constructive behavior in girls. Closer examination of our data indicated that both extremes of either affection or discipline were deleterious for all children, but that the process of socialization entailed somewhat different risks for the two sexes. Girls were especially susceptible to the detrimental influence of overprotection; boys to the ill effects of insufficient parental discipline and support. Or, to put it in more colloquial terms: boys suffered more often from too little taming, girls from too much.

In an attempt to account for this contrasting pattern of relationships, we proposed the notion of differential optimal levels of affection and authority for the two sexes.

The qualities of independence, initiative, and self-sufficiency, which are especially valued for boys in our culture, apparently require for their development a somewhat different balance of authority and affection than is found in the "love-oriented" strategy characteristically applied with girls. While an affectional context is important for the socialization of boys, it must evidently be accompanied by and be compatible with a strong component of parental discipline. Otherwise, the boy finds himself in the same situation as the girl, who, having received greater affection, is more sensitive to its withdrawal, with the result that a little discipline goes a long way and strong authority is constricting rather than constructive (Bronfenbrenner, 1960).

What is more, available data suggest that this very process may already be operating for boys from upper middle class homes. To begin with, differential treatment of the sexes is at a minimum for these families. Contrasting parental attitudes and behaviors toward boys and girls are pronounced only at lower class levels, and decrease as one moves up the socio-economic scale (Kohn, 1959; Bronfenbrenner, 1960). Thus our own results show that it is primarily at lower middle class levels that boys get more punishment than girls, and the latter receive greater warmth and attention. With an increase in the family's social position, direct discipline drops off, especially for boys, and indulgence and protectiveness decrease for girls. As a result, patterns of parental treatment for the two sexes begin to converge. In like manner, we find that the differential effects of parental behavior on the two sexes are marked only in the lower middle class.

It is here that girls especially risk being over-protected and boys not receiving sufficient discipline and support. In upper middle class the picture changes. Girls are not as readily debilitated by parental affection and power; nor is parental discipline as effective in fostering the development of responsibility and leadership in boys.

All these trends point to the conclusion that the "risks" experienced by each sex during the process of socialization tend to be somewhat different at different social class levels. Thus the danger of overprotection for girls is especially great in lower class families, but lower in upper middle class because of the decreased likelihood of overprotection. Analogously, boys are in greater danger of suffering from inadequate discipline and support in lower middle than in upper middle class. But the upper middle class boy, unlike the girl, exchanges one hazard for another. Since at this upper level the more potent "psychological" techniques of discipline are likely to be employed with both sexes, the boy presumably now too runs the risk of being "oversocialized," of losing some of his capacity for independent aggressive accomplishment.

Accordingly, if our line of reasoning is correct, we should expect a changing pattern of sex differences at successive socio-economic levels. Specifically, aspects of effective psychological functioning favoring girls should be most pronounced in the upper middle class; those favoring boys in the lower middle. A recent analysis of some of our data bears out this expectation. Girls excel boys on such variables as *responsibility* and *social acceptance* primarily at the higher socio-economic levels. In contrast, boys surpass girls on such traits as *leadership*, *level of aspiration*, and *competitiveness* almost exclusively in lower middle class. Indeed, with a rise in a family's social position, the differences tend to reverse themselves with girls now excelling boys.[3]

TRENDS IN PERSONALITY DEVELOPMENT: A FIRST APPROXIMATION

The implications for our original line of inquiry are clear. We are suggesting that the "love-oriented" socialization techniques, which over the past twenty-five years have been employed in increasing degree by American middle class families, may have negative as well

---

[3] These shifts in sex difference with a rise in class status are significant at the 5% level of confidence (one-tailed test).

as constructive aspects. While fostering the internalization of adult standards and the development of socialized behavior, they may also have the effect of undermining capacities for initiative and independence, particularly in boys. Males exposed to this "modern" pattern of child rearing might be expected to differ from their counterparts of a quarter century ago in being somewhat more conforming and anxious, less enterprising and self-sufficient, and, in general, possessing more of the virtues and liabilities commonly associated with feminine character structure.[4]

At long last, then, our strategy of inference has led us to a first major conclusion. The term "major" is appropriate since the conclusion takes as its points of departure and return four of the secular trends which served as the impetus for our inquiry. Specifically, through a series of empirical links and theoretical extrapolations, we have arrived at an estimate of the effects on children of the tendency of successive generations of parents to become progressively more permissive, to express affection more freely, to utilize "psychological" techniques of discipline, and, by moving in these directions to narrow the gap between the social classes in their patterns of child rearing.

FAMILY STRUCTURE AND PERSONALITY DEVELOPMENT

But one other secular trend remains to be considered: what of the changing pattern of parental role differentiation during the first three decades of the century? If our extrapolation is correct, the balance of power within the family has continued to shift with fathers yielding parental authority to mothers and taking on some of the nurturant and affectional functions traditionally associated with the maternal role. Again we have no direct evidence of the effects of such secular changes on successive generations of children, and must look for leaders to analogous data on contemporaneous relationships.

We may begin by considering the contribution of each parent to the socialization processes we have examined thus far. Our data indicate that it is primarily mothers who tend to employ "love-oriented"

---

[4] Strikingly similar conclusions were reached almost fifteen years ago in a provocative essay by Arnold Green ("The Middle Class Male Child and Neurosis," *American Sociological Review*, 1946, 11, 31–41). With little to go on beyond scattered clinical observations and impressions, Green was able to detect many of the same trends which we have begun to discern in more recent systematic empirical data.

techniques of discipline and fathers who rely on more direct methods like physical punishment. The above statement must be qualified, however, by reference to the sex of the child, for it is only in relation to boys that fathers use direct punishment more than mothers. More generally, . . . the results reveal a tendency for each parent to be somewhat more active, firm, and demanding with a child of the same sex, more lenient and indulgent with a child of the opposite sex. . . . The reversal is most complete with respect to discipline, with fathers being stricter with boys, mothers with girls. In the spheres of affection and protectiveness, there is no actual shift in preference, but the tendency to be especially warm and solicitous with girls is much more pronounced among fathers than among mothers. In fact, generally speaking, it is the father who is more likely to treat children of the two sexes differently (Bronfenbrenner, 1960).

Consistent with this pattern of results, it is primarily the behavior of fathers that accounts for the differential effects of parental behavior on the two sexes and for the individual differences within each sex. In other words, it is paternal authority and affection that tend especially to be salutary for sons but detrimental for daughters. But as might be anticipated from what we already know, these trends are pronounced only in the lower middle class; with a rise in the family's social status, both parents tend to have similar effects on their children, both within and across sexes. Such a trend is entirely to be expected since parental role differentiation tends to decrease markedly as one ascends the socio-economic ladder. It is almost exclusively in lower middle class homes that fathers are more strict with boys and mothers with girls. To the extent that direct discipline is employed in upper middle class families, it tends to be exercised by both parents equally. Here again we see a parallelism between shifts in parental behavior across time and social class in the direction of forms (in this instance of family structure) favored by the upper middle class group.

What kinds of children, then, can we expect to develop in families in which the father plays a predominantly affectionate role, and a relatively low level of discipline is exercised equally by both parents? A tentative answer to this question is supplied by a preliminary analysis of our data in which the relation between parental role structure and adolescent behavior was examined with controls for the family's social class position. The results of this analysis are summarized as follows: . . . Both responsibility and leadership are fostered by the relatively greater salience of the parent of the same sex. . . . Boys tend to be more responsible when the father rather than the mother is the principal disciplinarian; girls are more dependable when the mother is the major authority figure. . . . In short, boys thrive in a patriarchal context, girls in a matriarchal. . . . The most dependent and least dependable adolescents describe family arrangements that are neither patriarchal or matriarchal, but equalitarian. To state the issue in more provocative form, our data suggest that the democratic family, which for so many years has been held up and aspired to as a model by professionals and enlightened laymen, tends to produce young people who "do not take initiative," "look to others for direction and decision," and "cannot be counted on to fulfill obligations" (Bronfenbrenner, 1960).

In the wake of so sweeping a conclusion, it is important to call attention to the tentative, if not tenuous character of our findings. The results were based on a single study employing crude questionnaire methods and rating scales. Also, our interpretation is limited by the somewhat "attenuated" character of most of the families classified as patriarchal or matriarchal in our sample. Extreme concentrations of power in one or another parent were comparatively rare. Had they been more frequent, we suspect the data would have shown that such extreme asymmetrical patterns of authority were detrimental rather than salutary for effective psychological development, perhaps even more disorganizing than equalitarian forms.

Nevertheless, our findings do find some peripheral support in the work of others. A number of investigations, for example, point to the special importance of the father in the socialization of boys (Bandura and Walters, 1959; Mussen and Distler, 1959). Further corroborative evidence appears in the growing series of studies of effects of paternal absence (Bach, 1946; Sears, Pintler and Sears, 1946; Lynn and Sawrey, 1959; Tiller, 1958). The absence of the father apparently not only affects the behavior of the child directly but also influences the mother in the direction of greater over-protectiveness. The effect of both these tendencies is especially critical for male children; boys from father-absent homes tend to be markedly more submissive and dependent. Studies dealing explicitly with the influence of parental role structure in intact families are few and far between. Papanek (1957), in an unpublished doctoral dissertation, reports greater sex-role differentiation among children from homes in which the parental roles were differentiated. And in a carefully controlled study, Kohn and Clausen (1956) find that "schizophrenic patients more frequently than normal persons report that their mothers played a very strong authority role and the father a very weak authority role." Finally, what might best be called complementary evidence for our inferences regarding trends in family structure and their effects comes from the work of Miller, Swanson, and their associates (1958; 1960) on the differing patterns of behavior exhibited by families from *bureaucratic* and *entrepreneurial* work settings. These investigators argue that the entrepreneurial-bureaucratic dichotomy represents a new cleavage in American social structure that cuts across and overrides social class influences and carries with it its own characteristic patterns of family structure and socialization. Thus one investigation (Gold and Slater, 1958) contrasts the exercise of power in families of husbands employed in two kinds of job situations: a) those working in large organizations with three or more levels of supervision; b) those self-employed or working in small organizations with few levels of supervision. With appropriate controls for social class, equalitarian families were found more frequently in the bureaucratic groups; patriarchal and, to a lesser extent, matriarchal in the entrepreneurial setting. Another study (Miller and Swanson, 1958) shows that, in line with Miller and Swanson's hypotheses, parents from these same two groups tend to favor rather different ends and means of socialization, with entrepreneurial families putting considerably more emphasis on the development of independence and mastery and on the use of "psychological" techniques of discipline. These differences appear at both upper and lower middle class levels but are less pronounced in higher socioeconomic strata. It is Miller and Swanson's belief, however, that the trend is toward the bureaucratic way of life, with its less structured patterns of family organization and child rearing. The evidence we have cited on secular changes in family structure and the inferences we have drawn regarding their possible effects on personality development are on the whole consistent with their views.

LOOKING FORWARD

If Miller and Swanson are correct in the prediction that America is moving toward a bureaucratic society that emphasizes, to put it colloquially, "getting along" rather than "getting ahead," then presumably we can look forward to ever increasing numbers of equalitarian families who, in turn, will produce successive generations of ever more adaptable but unaggressive "organization men." But recent signs do not all point in this direction. In our review of secular trends in child rearing practices we detected in the data from the more recent studies a slowing up in the headlong rush toward greater permissiveness and toward reliance on indirect methods of discipline. We pointed out also that if the most recent editions of well-thumbed guidebooks on child care are as reliable harbingers of the future as they have been in the past, we can anticipate something of a return to the more explicit discipline techniques of an earlier era. Perhaps the most important forces, however, acting to redirect both the aims and methods of child rearing in America emanate from behind the Iron Curtain. With the firing of the first Sputnik, Achievement began to replace Adjustment as the highest goal of the American way of life. We have become concerned—perhaps even obsessed—with "education for excellence" and the maximal utilization of our intellectual resources. Already, ability grouping, and the guidance counselor who is its prophet, have moved down from the junior high to the elementary school, and parents can be counted on to do their part in preparing their youngsters for survival in the new competitive world of applications and achievement tests.

But if a new trend in parental behavior is to develop, it must do so in the context of changes already under way. And if the focus of parental authority is shifting from husband to wife, then perhaps we should anticipate that pressures for achievement will be imposed primarily by mothers rather than fathers. Moreover, the mother's continuing strong emotional investment in the child should provide her with a powerful lever for evoking desired performance. It is noteworthy in this connection that recent studies of the familial origins of need-achievement point to the matriarchy as the optimal context for development of the motive to excel (Strodtbeck, 1958; Rosen and D'Andrade, 1959).

The prospect of a society in which socialization techniques are directed toward maximizing achievement drive is not altogether a pleasant one. As a number of investigators have shown (Baldwin, Kalhorn and Breese, 1945; Baldwin, 1948; Haggard, 1957; Winterbottom, 1958; Rosen and D'Andrade, 1959), high achievement motivation appears to flourish in a family atmosphere of "cold democracy" in which initial high levels of maternal involvement are followed by pressures for independence and accomplishment.[5] Nor does the prod-

---

[5] Cold democracy under female administration appears to foster the development of achievement not only in the home but in the classroom as well. In a review of research on teaching effectiveness, Ackerman reports that teachers most successful in bringing about gains in achievement score for their pupils were judged "least considerate," while those thought friendly and congenial were least effective. (Ackerman, W. I., "Teacher

uct of this process give ground for reassurance. True, children from achievement-oriented homes excel in planfulness and performance, but they are also more aggressive, tense, domineering, and cruel (Baldwin, Kalhorn and Breese, 1945; Baldwin, 1948; Haggard, 1957). It would appear that education for excellence if pursued single-mindedly may entail some sobering social costs.

But by now we are in danger of having stretched our chain of inference beyond the strength of its weakest link. Our speculative analysis has become far more speculative than analytic and to pursue it further would bring us past the bounds of science into the realms of science fiction. In concluding our discussion, we would re-emphasize that speculations should, by their very nature, be held suspect. It is for good reason that, like "damn Yankees" they too carry their almost inseparable sobriquets: speculations are either "idle" or "wild." Given the scientific and social importance of the issues we have raised, we would dismiss the first of these labels out of hand, but the second cannot be disposed of so easily. Like the impetuous child, the "wild" speculation responds best to the sobering influence of friendly but firm discipline, in this instance from the hand of the behavioral scientist. As we look ahead to the next twenty-five years of human socialization, let us hope that the "optimal levels" of involvement and discipline can be achieved not only by the parent who is unavoidably engaged in the process, but also by the scientist who attempts to understand its working, and who—also unavoidably—contributes to shaping its course.

REFERENCES

Brameld, Theodore. *Minority Problems in the Public Schools*. New York: Harper & Row, Publishers, Inc., 1946.

Cohen, Albert. *Delinquent Boys: The Culture of the Gang*. New York: The Free Press of Glencoe, 1955.

Eells, Kenneth, *Intelligence and Cultural Differences*. Chicago: University of Chicago Press, 1951.

Eissler, Ruth S., and Anna Frued. *The Psychoanalytic Study of the Child*. Vol. II. New York: International Universities Press, 1956.

Estvan, Frank J., and Elizabeth W. Estvan. *The Child's World—His Social Perception*. New York: G. P. Putnam's Sons, 1959.

Frazier, E. Franklin. *The Black Bourgeoisie*. New York: The Free Press of Glencoe, 1957.

Competence and Pupil Change," *Harvard Educational Review*, 1954, 24, 273–289.)

Frazier, E. Franklin. *The Negro Family in the United States*. Chicago: University of Chicago Press, 1939.

Riessman, Frank. *The Culturally Deprived Child and His Education*. New York: Harper & Row, Publishers, Inc., 1962.

Weaver, Robert. *The Negro Ghetto*. New York: Harcourt, Brace & World, Inc., 1948.

Whyte, William Foate. *Street Corner Society*. Chicago: University of Chicago Press, 1943.

PERIODICALS

Association for Supervision and Curriculum Development. "Disaffected Children and Youth." *Educational Leadership,* 20 (February 1963), pp. 291–318, 337–353.

Ashley, Walter E. *The Society of the Streets*. New York: Ford Foundation, 1962, 49 pp.

Boutwell, William D. "What's Happening in Education? Culturally Deprived Child." *PTA Magazine,* 57 (October 1962), 11.

Byerly, Carl L. "Pupils Who Do Not Respond." *Educational Leadership*, A. S. C. D. (February, 1963), pp. 309–314.

Capps, G. S. "Diverting Our Social Dynamite." *Journal of Home Economics,* 53 (November 1961), 756–758.

Caravello, S. J. "Drop-Out Problem." *High School Journal,* 41 (May 1958), 335–340.

Cohn, Werner. "On the Language of Lower-Class Children." *School Review,* 67 (Winter 1959), 435–440.

Della-Dora, Delmo. "Culturally Disadvantaged: Further Observations." *Exceptional Children,* 29 (January 1963), 226–236.

Hunt, R. R. "Job Upgrading: Rehabilitation for the Dropout." *Phi Delta Kappan,* 40 (February 1959), 219–220.

Chapter Four

PROBLEMS OF YOUTH AND COMMUNITY

Many American youth occupy a marginal position in our society today. More adult than child, the adolescent is denied the genuine roles of adult responsibility and contribution to his society because the changing economy has no need for him as a producing member. Urban society offers him few other realistic ways to achieve status and find an acceptable identity. And so he plays the adult game of sex, sociability, and consumption in the frame of his peer culture, which may give him a highly distorted view of society.

The school does little more than hold the displaced youth in custody, deferring the time when he must look for a dead-end job in a society that finds him expendable. Like the greater culture, formal education is unable to offer him acceptable identity or status. He is frustrated, passive, nonproductive, or openly hostile in the school as well as in the community. Understandably, the displaced youth is not warmly received by his teachers, even though he is urgently counseled to remain in school and get an "education." Only in his peer group can he find acceptance, achievement, and status. Lacking social power, he must also rely on the peer group as his only organ of social protest.

There is more in this situation than grist for the mill that grinds out polemics against contemporary society. This is a criminogenic setting which is bound to claim a good proportion of urban youth and, consequently, of the city's human resources. This social problem, as it exists in education, is beyond solution if it is perceived in isolation as that of the school dropout. Perhaps no other aspect of the urban crisis makes as strong a case for the need for education to become more realistically and logically related to the other agencies and institutions of society.

One of the most crucial issues today in urban education is that of the dropout or "token graduate." Because of the economic conditions in our country today many youth are not readily absorbed into the mainstream of business and commerce. In a time when more and more students go on to higher education and technical training, the dropout finds that his culture has no need of him. It is a paradox that in these times, when we are dedicated to more education for all, there is a widening gap rather than a closing one between social strata. Much has been said about this situation as a curricular as well as an economic problem. Frederick Neff examines the issue through a grid of social values prevalent in urban culture today. We are still a long way, says the author, from the ideals of democracy.

"LET THEM EAT CAKE" / *Frederick C. Neff*

I

Two or three decades ago the American public school was engaged in a singular and somewhat inspired experiment: it had undertaken to be all things to all youngsters—i.e., to meet all the needs of all its pupils. Following the lead of John Dewey, education began to perceive that learners were more than disembodied minds—obviously, they also had hands and hearts. Today, however, this outlook seems already to belong to the long ago and the far away. Despite the fact that the

Frederick C. Neff, "Let Them Eat Cake," The Educational Forum *(May 1964), pp. 405–412. Reprinted by permission of Kappa Delta Pi, an Honor Society in Education, owners of the copyright.*

concept of the totality of learning has never been refuted, it has now become fashionable to regard "the whole child" as no more than a cliché and to narrow the curriculum once again to administer to the almost exclusively "intellectual" needs of youngsters.

Not only is the American public school moving away from the goal of educational breadth, but it is also showing signs of yielding to the influence of those who have urged an imitation of European educational systems, which cater—not equally to the needs of all boys and girls—but primarily to the needs of the so-called academic-minded. Like Woodrow Wilson's vision of a working League of Nations, the early attempt at comprehensiveness on the part of the school may have been too idealistic—it may have attempted too much too soon. But with the new élitism[1] that is now upon us, with its concomitant failure to make adequate provision for other than the strictly academic talents of our young people, we are confronted with an alarming rate of school dropouts, for whom a narrowly academic regimen provides little or no challenge.

When, within the range of normal abilities, any particular segment of the school population is singled out for special consideration and the curriculum is reconstructed accordingly, some other group of youngsters is bound to suffer. When physical education, vocational training, or practical arts are over-emphasized, youngsters with academic bents are placed at a disadvantage; conversely, youngsters whose abilities lie in the area of manual skills are likely to be "eased out" of school into the growing army of dropouts—the unneeded and the unwanted—when the school, often under the protective guise of the "pursuit of excellence," makes only token provision for their special talents. The traditional concern of American schools has not been simply with academic prowess—admirable though that may be; its goal has been the over-all education—vocational, cultural, academic, economic, and social—of *all* the youngsters of *all* the people, whose talents, interests, and needs reflect the diversity of a free, multi-group society. When curriculum-makers, perhaps at the prodding of vested pressure groups, inaugurate certain courses and water down or delete others in order to favor the incipient Latin scholar at the expense of the potential draftsman, they are tampering, not merely

---

[1] Cf. the views of such writers as Robert M. Hutchins, Mortimer Adler, Albert Lynd, Arthur Bestor, Mortimer Smith, Russell Kirk, Jacques Barzun, Hyman Rickover, Max Rafferty, James Koerner, and others.

with the curriculum, but with a fundamental precept of the American way of life, viz., the intrinsic worth of every citizen, and his right to prepare for and to engage in a legitimate vocational pursuit commensurate with his capacity to do so.

Nor does an increased emphasis upon science, especially when it takes the highly specialized form of technology, provide suitable outlets for the talents and needs of the majority of our school-age boys and girls. Ever since the Russians launched their first Sputnik, American education seems to have proceeded on the assumption that technological proficiency was the acme of human aspiration, the aim and end of human living. The democratic way of administering to the needs of every boy and girl was suddenly changed, and, abetted for a while even by the academicians, education became geared to producing budding technologists—whose function apparently was to assist America to become first in the conquest of space—and to fostering among others at least an appreciation of the importance and magnitude of the task. Following the example of the Russians, we have made of every astronaut a national hero. It seems never to have occurred to educational revisionists that beating the Russians to outer space might be a rather paltry substitute for the historic American goals of freedom, justice, and equality for all. One is tempted to ask, in the spirit of the Scriptures, For what profiteth it a nation if it gain outer space and lose its own soul?

Indeed, one cannot but wonder whether the schools are any longer guided by a singleness of purpose that takes into account a long-range implementation of what used to be rather reverently referred to as the democratic ideal. Whatever charges might be made against the influential thinkers of a few years back—Dewey, Bode, Kilpatrick, Counts, Childs, and others—at least they did not apologize for gearing education to a continuous realization of the free way of life, and the clarity with which they spelled out their goals remains unsurpassed. A great sea change has occurred since the days when the practice and realization of democracy—of such grand ideals as justice, equality, brotherhood, and freedom—constituted criteria for educational excellence. Today we aim at other things, and the phenomenon of "education" and prejudice co-existing in the same individual seems not especially shocking or inconsistent, even when the individual happens to be the governor of a state with considerable jurisdiction over its school and university policies.

II

Ours is often called an "age of anxiety," and not without reason. The frustration from which we suffer stems largely from our attempts to "hitch on" new values to an older value scheme with which they are basically incompatible. We have attempted to compromise our values instead of to reconstruct them. The blurred-over conflicts between creationism and evolution, between church and government, between moral principles and human conduct, between the rights of capital and the rights of labor, between religious dogma and birth control, between national sovereignty and international accord are but a few examples of the cleavages that beset us. Our attitude seems to be that if we but look in another direction such problems might go away. A popular topic for sermons is "Why Worry When You Can Pray?" Yet only an over-aged boy scout could pretend that God's in his heaven—all's right with the world, that every cloud is guaranteed to have a silver lining, or that Providence is going to see to it that everything turns out all right in the end.

It is in such a confused and disturbing world that today's adolescent is being asked to take his place. Despite all the stout talk of their elders, sensitive adolescents (of whom there are probably more than we acknowledge) are likely to "see through" the shallowness that characterizes the adult world of morals, values, and professed ideals. The youth of today is often more honest about what life means than his more pretentious and sophisticated parents. He senses the discrepancies between our so-called beliefs and our everyday conduct. Like Holden Caulfield in *The Catcher in the Rye*, he is disenchanted with the adult world of make-believe—of profit-making, of sex, of "phonyness"—and would rather be preoccupied with more serious concerns—like what happens to the ducks in Central Park when winter comes and the lake freezes over.

The maladjusted youth of today was not "born that way." He is maladjusted because he is at war with a society that has not bothered to prepare a place for him. While there are, of course, psychopaths whom society cannot afford to turn loose in its midst and for whom it cannot find a constructive role, we are speaking here of the teen-ager who has turned from society, not because of any inborn tendency to be anti-social, but because he feels pushed out, unwanted, and inferior. The drive-in "rumble," the party-crashing, the "drag race," and the gang war are but outward manifestations of deep-seated hostilities. They are the symptoms, not the ailment, and to trace the roots of the problem would require much careful analysis. But we do know from what meager probing has been done that very often the teen-ager is a "rebel without a cause," angry at no one or nothing in particular, yet seething with a fury because of the inferior status role into which life has thrust him. The fact that he is often inarticulate about why he does what he does, that he can point to no culprit in particular, only makes his plight the more frustrating and his actions the more resentful.

III

Our values are awry, confused, and inconsistent—and the teen-ager senses it. He represents in focus the plight of the adult world, and rebellion under a precarious system of values is sooner or later inevitable. Whereas the rebellion of youth is often violent, the rebellion of the alienated adult often expresses itself through such channels as, for example, the avant-garde nihilism of the existentialist movement. When, with Sartre, the existentialist announces that God is dead and that man is "on his own," he utters it not so much as a proclamation nor even as a resignation, but rather as the unadorned discovery that man's destiny is within man's power to shape and that invocations to metaphysical Being or beings will no longer suffice. From the reconstructed theism of Tillich, Barth, and Niebuhr to the atheistic-agnosticism of Russell, Sartre, and Camus there is rebellion against smugness, dogmatism, and protective self-assurance. At the other end of the scale are the back-to-God movements—strong in their emphasis upon piety, conformity, and "sweetness and light." Religious conservatism ranges all the way from the organizational dogmatism of a Cardinal Spellman, to the literal-mindedness of a Billy Graham, to the peace-of-mind "unguentism" of a Norman Vincent Peale. At its best it appears to offer a kind of spiritual sustenance—especially to the sick, the aged, and the weary; by its critics it is charged with representing not much more than a soporific, and with being deceptively unreal and pathetically out of touch with contemporary knowledge.

Nevertheless, in this age of anxiety young people need desperately a stable yet viable system of values, as attested by the eagerness with which most of them are wont to discuss their value concerns. Perhaps more than the adult might realize, youth is vaguely aware of the outmodedness of the pious clichés of the past. But it is we adults who are more aware than youth of the tenuous and still-experimental nature of the thought systems of the future. It is into this unsettled and unsettling situation that we turn our teen-agers loose—many of

them unprepared to accept the fact of a changing world, others unschooled in respecting the solid wisdom of the ages. When the experience of trying to become oriented to doubtful adult mores is further
complicated by the problem of finding a job without adequate training,
we have all the ingredients of "social dynamite."

IV

Among the so-called underprivileged youth of our country the
meaning of life is usually earthy—it is defined largely in terms of job
opportunities and bread-and-butter values. Life assumes meaning in
so far as airy abstractions are kept at a minimum and jobs are or
will be available that are commensurate with training and ability.
The line between present training and future placement had best be
kept taut, lest the teen-ager lose interest and become discouraged.
Among overprivileged young people, in whom a disdain for work,
especially for manual activities, has been deviously cultivated, the
meaning of life is less easily defined, and their values are often less
tangible. Like those of their less privileged brothers, their values seem
to be geared neither to themselves as individuals nor to society at large,
but to their own "in-groups." Overly ambitious parents of Suburbia
often set standards of academic achievement for their children that
are so unrealistic that they engender rebellion, hostility, depression,
and even suicide; or they are so permissive that their children rebel
against a lack of discipline and of reasonable standards of conduct.

After his forty-room summer home in Southampton, New York,
had been wrecked by about a hundred young people from socially
prominent families of Boston, New York, and Philadelphia, Financier
Robert M. Harriss had this to say: "I'm disheartened, to tell the truth.
I just feel like—well, I just wonder what the country's coming to.
It was shocking and terrible that the youth of our country should do
such wanton destruction. Yet it is not the destruction that worries me
most but the fact the privileged youth of our country should set such
a horrible example."

Rebellion appears to stem from feelings of not being wanted, of not
being needed. It is symptomatic of what is coming to be called
anomie—meaning "ungoverned"; hence, a sense of feeling rootless,
unattached, and alienated. Both privileged and underprivileged youth
are too often "unemployed"—in the more technical sense of the term.
Both feel, as a result, a lack of status; and destruction, stealing,
"rumbles," and violence provide attention-getting devices whereby

society is compelled to sit up and take notice. On the other hand, youth who are employed in jobs and other worthwhile pursuits accumulate a self-respect that dispels any proclivities toward delinquency.

The irony of the situation is that, while too many people are without jobs, there are at the same time too many jobs without people to fill them. In the city of Detroit, for example, the discrepancy between training (or the lack of it) and job opportunities is illustrated by the fact that, while there are thousands of jobs available in the metropolitan area, 60,000 persons are in need of gainful employment.

> There is an urgent need for skilled workers of all types. There are hundreds of openings in the lower-paying service trades. Opportunities for professional people have never been better. The tragedy both in Detroit and across the nation is that few among the army of unemployed are qualified to fill them. They lack either training or experience, or both. The bulk of the jobless are teen-agers on the job market for the first time, older people and illiterates.

At the national level the picture is equally grim. In a statement to the House of Representatives Subcommittee on Education, Commissioner Francis Keppel recently reported that:

> Jobs filled by high-school graduates rose 30 per cent, while jobs for those with no secondary education decreased 25 per cent in the past decade.
>
> One out of every three students in the fifth grade now drops out of school before high-school graduation. Only two of every ten now graduate from college.
>
> Almost a million youths drop out of elementary and secondary schools each year. Of these, 250,000 fail to complete elementary school.
>
> Over 23 million Americans eighteen years of age and older have completed less than eight years of schooling.
>
> One of every ten workers who failed to finish elementary school is unemployed today, compared to one out of fifty college graduates.

Vocational schools, at least in their presently constituted form, have not provided an answer to the problem. School officials have often regarded the vocational school as a place to dump youngsters who are behavior problems or potential delinquents. As a consequence, it has often been difficult to secure top-flight teachers to teach in these schools. Moreover, what skills pupils have picked up in vocational schools have often been so pathetically behind the times—due in part to outmoded equipment—that it has been remarked that vocational schools actually teach students to be unemployable. Only now is it becoming possible to channel Federal funds for vocational education into other than the traditional areas of agriculture and home economics.

No single element in the complex problem of gearing education to meet the needs of present-day society can be dealt with in isolation. Despite the abuse and ridicule that have been heaped upon the sort of education that aimed at "life adjustment," the fact remains that every teen-age delinquent is a person who has failed to adjust to life as prudence and decency require that it be lived. Yet even a "socially adjusted" youngster may at the same time be lacking in the equipment necessary for moving ahead in a particular occupation or profession. Moreover, a youngster may have his mind so thoroughly "cultivated" that he has a disdain for any sort of manual effort and may go through life unable to cope adequately with the simplest practical problems that daily confront him. And a vocational training that neglects to prepare the learner to comprehend his cultural heritage and to assume the duties of responsible citizenship represents an equally segmented practice.

V

In being overly concerned with "intellectualism," we have pretended that every learner is a nice, obedient, diligent, bright, interested boy or girl—a story-book Dick or Jane. We have been urged to put aside such trivial concerns as health, preparation for earning a livelihood, and home problems, and instead to cultivate disembodied "minds," which, once trained, are supposed to enable their possessors to cope with every type of problem with equal ease. We have allowed an intellectual élitism gradually to displace education for the vocations and common life pursuits despite the fact that, according to James B. Conant, only about fifteen percent of our high-school population are equipped to partake of and to profit from a strictly academic brand of education. We seem to have assumed that it is better for a boy to quit school and roam the streets than that the curriculum give serious attention to "non-status" courses like auto mechanics. We have committed the fallacy of equating intelligence with academic-mindedness and stupidity with hand-mindedness.

It might be well occasionally to remind ourselves that the activity known as intelligence is, after all, an activity, and not an entity. It has to do with how we behave, act, conduct ourselves—it is not what we *own*, but what we *do*. Every conceivable form of intelligence involves a doing, and much of this doing involves some sort of manipulation. The skilled violinist, surgeon, sculptor, painter, writer, draftsman, technician, auto mechanic—all work, in various ways, with their hands; and all such work involves, in various ways, intelligence. While it is quite proper to compare the intelligence of a surgeon with that of other surgeons, of a painter with that of other painters, or of an electrician with that of other electricians, it does not follow that the intelligence of a writer is to be compared with, say, that of an engineer. The old Greek notion that intelligence is strictly a matter of contemplation, that activity is somehow inferior to contemplation, and that contemplation is virtually a form of inertia is completely alien to the democratic aspiration.

It now behooves us to engage in a concerted effort to make the public school—and especially the public secondary school—truly comprehensive. In addition to increasing the variety of subjects offered, it might be wise also to inaugurate the practice of individual pupil program scheduling with extensive counseling and to adopt an administrative policy of approving dropouts only for emergency reasons.[2] Above all, the modern high school needs to become an institution where both the most abstruse kinds of intellectual curiosity are aroused *for those so talented* and the most practical vocational skills are fostered *among those so oriented*. In a "multiversal" society we need both; and there is no supportable reason why an *equivalent* respect and dignity should not be attached to these differing kinds of intelligence. That the hand-minded and the academic-minded represent distinctive abilities is a fair appraisal. But when epithets of derision are associated with one and of approbation with the other, our very democratic and religious foundations are threatened; for, apart from what a person's legitimate talents may be, a fundamental postulate of the free way of life is to respect the intrinsic worth and dignity of every human being—social "status" notwithstanding. We have with us the artistically inclined and the mechanically inclined, the scientifically talented and the poetically talented, the experimenters and the researchers, the specialists and the generalists—all of whom represent proper facets of a pluralistic society. It is only when one of these groups is branded "better" and another "worse" that a democratic precept is breached and an insidious "classism" is abetted.

We can no longer afford not to be bothered with the square pegs,

---

[2] These policies have been successfully adopted in the Red Lion Area School of York County, Pennsylvania. See *Phi Delta Kappan*, XLV (October, 1963): 64.

the maladjusted, and the dropouts. We can no longer "let them eat cake." Ignored, unloved, and unwanted, little wonder that they eventually rebel. A hated group, they in turn become hateful, just as respected youngsters in turn become respectful. In final appraisal, the basic issue throughout is a problem of values—and of the conflicts that lie therein. Important as it may be, no amount of reshuffling of the curriculum can substitute for confronting the issue of how to recapture the vision that is democracy and, through courageous teachers, for relaying and sharpening that vision among those who learn.

Earl Kelley vividly describes the school experiences of potential dropouts. These youth are as untouched by the educative processes while in school as they are long after they leave. Many remaining in school do not necessarily learn the skills needed to become self-sufficient contributing members of the community. A question arises from this discouraging picture. How is any young man to have purpose and aspiration if the school itself holds none for him?

THE DROPOUT—OUR GREATEST CHALLENGE / *Earl C. Kelley*

There is much interest presently concerning the young people who are leaving our high schools before graduation. This is known as the "dropout problem." Concern with this problem is not confined to school people, but appears throughout our mass media—newspapers, magazines, television. Especially at the close of summer, newspapers often run articles exhorting our young to go back to school. They quote statistics to show how much better off the holder of a high school diploma is than one who does not have one. The appeal seems to state that if a young person will just hang on grimly until the band plays *Pomp and Circumstance*, doors to the good life will swing wide.

Earl C. Kelley, "The Dropout—Our Greatest Challenge," Educational Leadership 20 (February 1963), 294–296, 318. Copyright © 1963 by the Association for Supervision and Curriculum Development. Reprinted with the permission of the author and The Association.

Some of those who decry the dropout situation are the same people who tell us that we give out too many high school diplomas to students who do not deserve them, and complain because, they say, the diploma has no meaning any more. Some suggest meeting this problem by giving the unworthy ones special diplomas that will show that they are inferior. Sometimes we even establish an inferior colored paper so that the quality of the diploma can be detected from afar. At this moment it occurs to me that we might at last have found a use for the skin of the black sheep. We could give these youngsters black sheep-skins. This idea falls down because there are not enough black sheep to supply diplomas to all who do not deserve regular ones. Perhaps the geneticists could solve the problem.

Nevertheless, the problem of having so many of our young leave school is a serious one, and I, for one, am grateful for the increasing interest of lay people in it. The problem is quite humiliating to school people, because these youths leave us with nothing else in mind. If there were plenty of jobs for our young, this would constitute a choice, but when they leave us for nothing else, it is hard to take. I question whether any commercial enterprise could continue as a going concern if it lost over a third of its business every year.

WHAT IS THE COST?

The cost to society and to individuals of so many leaving our schools is hard to calculate. Some of the dropouts, having nothing to do, become delinquent; others withdraw into mental illness. The economic loss to society for delinquency and mental illness is staggering, and getting worse every year. The loss in self-respect suffered by those who find no place in our culture may cripple them for the rest of their lives. Who can compute the cost of a life wasted in comparison with a life well lived? How calculate the damage done to family and friends?

The *Saturday Evening Post* (March 12, 1962) published an article by Kohler and Fontaine entitled, "We Waste a Million Kids a Year." Some of these live in your own home town. Human waste is our greatest extravagance.

But we are here concerned with the large percentage of our young who have dropped out but are still in school. If we visit a secondary school class and look at the faces of the young people, we will see that in many cases the outstanding characteristic of the members is that they are not involved in what is going on. Most of them are going through motions to please their elders. Some are just sitting. Some are engaging in behavior which can only be interpreted as a protest. The latter are our "discipline problems."

While we have many studies of dropouts, we do not know much about the matter, because we have no way of including the dropout who stays in school. All we seem able to do is to count bodies, but physical presence does not mean presence of the whole person.

These young people are doing very little, learning very little; at any rate they are not learning much of the curriculum. We hear a good deal about how much homework a high school youth should do, but studies have shown that these youths do not do any homework. They have lost contact with what is going on in school, and are just passing time.

It is concerning this group that we get the complaints of employers and college teachers about the youths who hold diplomas but do not know anything. These are the ones for whom the curriculum has been "watered down." It seems never to have occurred to adults that if a soup does not taste good in the beginning no amount of water will improve the flavor. The need is for a fresh and different soup.

It is good that these dropouts have stayed in school, because they have to be somewhere, and even though they eschew the curriculum, they are better off in school than they might be if they removed their bodies. They get good out of associating with their peers. They can enjoy many activities which are closed to the physical dropout. But this is not enough. They desperately need an education too.

RESPONSE TO PRESSURE

Why do these dropouts stay in school? Mainly, I think, because of the enormous parental and cultural pressure. It is "the thing to do." If they leave school, their fathers and mothers would be too embarrassed. The neighbors would wonder about their basic intelligence and whether or not the condition is hereditary. There isn't anything else to do anyway, so, all things considered, they decide they may as well stay in school, hoping that the teachers won't bother them too much. It seems that the quiet, well-behaved ones have entered into an unspoken truce with their teachers: "If you don't bother me, I won't bother you."

The adult reaction to the young people who cannot become involved with what we have decided they should care about is usually blameful. "If they were any good they would like what I've planned for them."

We reward the ones who can and are willing to do what we want, and punish those who will not (cannot). Thus while these dropouts continue to stay in school, their concepts of self continue to take a beating, so that it is possible that they are actually less able for having stayed.

I do not think there is very much that we adults do unless we see the reason for doing it, feel able to do it, and preferably have had some small part in the planning of it. I believe that young people are quite like us in this regard. They need to be able to see that their school work is worth doing, and that it comes within the scope of what they feel able to do. They do not have to have their own way, but, like us, they are more enthusiastic about what they have had a hand in planning than they are about things that adults plan for them. This is especially true since it seems to them that adults really live in another world.

If involvement is necessary, then we must involve these youngsters. This will call for the abandonment of many of our sacred cows, because when young people choose, there is no guarantee that they will choose what we had in mind. As for myself, I have some things I think everyone should know. But they don't and they obviously are not going to, so I might just as well relax.

Not only must each learner be involved but he must be free to be involved in his own way. Perhaps the best-proven fact in educational research is that each human being is unique. We will have to make it possible for unique learners to do different things and to come out with different learnings. They come out with different learnings now, and always have, but we teachers have not yet accepted this fact. This failure to accept the obvious and inevitable spoils the lives of many teachers.

People do things with goals in mind. The envisioned goal is the valid reason for doing anything. Children and youth are people. In general, the younger the person, the more immediate the goal must be. When we tell an elementary or junior high school child that if he does not do what we tell him to, he will not be able to go to college, he is not likely to be impressed. He has to have a better reason than that, and it seems likely that we may have to modify what we are doing.

When we urge youth to stay in school, or to return to school to do what has already been found wanting, we sell a shabby piece of goods. I would like for all of them to stay in school if for no other reason than there is no other place in our society for them. Just to "stick it out," however, will not do them very much good. What we could say is that "if you will stay with us, we will try something different, something that makes sense to you."

If he stays, he will of course get a "credential" or diploma which may be of some use to him. It is a poor substitute for an education. This is especially true if, as sometimes happens, we then give him a spurious diploma, saying in effect, that he really did not graduate after all.

WHY NOT TRY?

There is nothing new in the foregoing; certainly nothing new to supervisors and curriculum directors. If it is true that people have to be involved, that learners are unique, that goals have to be reasonably near, why don't we do more about it? What are we afraid of?

I have asked this question many times. Often the answer is, "We don't know how." Superintendents and principals tell me they would like to have good core classes, for example, but they do not have anybody who knows how to do it.

It seems to me that if our profession requires us to do something we do not know how to do, then we must learn how. This applies to the teaching profession as a whole. We will have to be satisfied with small beginnings at first, because, not knowing how, we must learn in small ways at first. We can expand on these small beginnings until we *do* know how.

The dropouts, in school and out, are legion. In some ways, they seem faceless. Our society being what it is, they have no place in it, except in school. They are wasting their time, often deteriorating rather than improving. They constitute our greatest waste. They can give us our greatest opportunity.

The quest for an answer as to how to prepare youth for a selective and specialized world of work leads some searchers to the very psyche of the youth himself. The problem of failure on the part of the school is compounded by a self-concept of failure within some young people, says Charles Stewart.

SELF-IMAGE: AID OR DETERRENT? /
Charles Stewart

I think it is probably obvious to most of us here who represent one service agency or another in the community, that the kinds of movement, the kinds of motion, the kinds of mobility and transition that were implicit in the first presentation have very serious implications for all of us who are concerned primarily with continually increasing the productivity of the total population.

I would try, however, to move us a little closer to a scrutiny of people themselves, and particularly young people. I would select, from among the many things that are becoming clearer to us as we learn how to ask questions better and how to be searching and probing in the area of self-concept, two rather simple things that I wish to emphasize this morning: One of them is that the determinants of self lie in the total socio-cultural setting in which the organism is operative. The second is that there is a simple, direct relationship between the way in which one feels about himself, and the nature and quality of his goals.

As clinical and research evidence accumulate in the fields of anthropology, sociology, psychology and psychiatry, there is strong support for the notion that interlocking complexities of modern living, form, as it were, a web of life tending to induce a dull and torpid conditioning detrimental to general realization of harmonious and satisfying designs for living. Kluckhohn and Murray put it this way, "for a variety of reasons: lack of money, lack of ability, social barriers, defects of character and deficient environment, very few individuals are capable of satisfying their needs."

Many people, we observe, learn to depress their levels of aspiration, or learn to accept substitute goals, so that their needs may become realizable. This phenomenon is especially important here in that it points to the inner or private world of the individual, to his particular self system. The tendency to depress levels of aspiration after a series of failures or to accept alternate goals to appease needs for goal satisfaction, indicates the presence, within the organism, of a tension-

Charles Stewart, "Self-Image: Aid or Deterrent?" Proceedings of a Conference, Education for Opportunity: Opportunity for Education. *Unpublished address (February 1961), pp. 6–9. Reprinted with the permission of the author.*

reducing system. Such a system would be the psychological counterpart of the physiological function sometimes called homeostasis.

The physiologist tells us that specific mechanisms in the body function to maintain a state of relative balance or equilibrium. Given the bare necessities for bodily health, these organs perform their relatively simple functions well in a relatively stable internal environment. If physiological imbalance does occur, often a small, tastefully flavored pill will restore order. The brain, operating in the self system, has a much more difficult job. It must learn continuously how to improvise new and socially acceptable ways of dealing with the external environment. It must learn to do so more effectively than other people do or, if not this, to reduce its acquired craving for prestige and self-enhancement.

Ideally, it may be said that one's aspirations take shape in a general context of activity, teleological in design, and directed toward a more adequate realization of his innate capacity for being; that is, experiencing life more richly, more creatively, more luxuriantly. When inability of the self system to cope with the external environment causes psychological imbalance, the cures may range all the way from reduction of aspiration level to institutional care and treatment. Significantly, environment, as a cooperating factor in human development, appears to have markedly different effects on individuals in the same culture. Why do a limited few react to a slum-ridden and poverty-ridden environment in such a manner that the very conditions which they deplore serve as a spur to achievement, while the larger number of their fellows succumb to the pervasively enervating influence of the same environment?

A basic problem inheres in this question: how can one see the creative possibilities of his environment, however limited or bountiful, so as to realize ever novel, self-energizing and resourceful ways of bringing out his sense of being at as many points as possible? Inherent here, too, is the fact that more people are passive, rather than active, participators in this dynamic process of culture change. More people fail to realize the wonder and beauty of their own uniqueness and individual personalities because identification with cultural convention is so thorough and so complete.

The fascinating fact is that this phenomenon of passive or active participation can be observed at every status level among variant ethnic groups, sub-cultures, and caste systems. Benedict, Mead, and others have helped us to understand how inexorably culture influences personality development. What is, perhaps, not so readily recognized is the effect upon levels of aspiration or even the awareness of aspiring tendencies in people whose individuality is so completely submerged in the mechanism of cultural change that the psyche is but dimly, if ever, perceived.

Western culture, replete with its divergent standards and modes of conduct presents, to individual consciousness, such a welter of stimuli amidst a confused, mechanical bustle, that human development manifests amazingly subtle and complex patterns. The immediate environment is an important factor in shaping so plastic a being.

The question arises: if there are favorable habitats and favorable forms of association for animals and plants, then why not for men? It is not surprising that children from favorable homes and communities show more zest for academic achievement, more insight and emotional expansiveness and higher levels of aspiration than low-status children. Low status children, who are prevented from participating fully in the cultural benefits and rewards necessary to encourage endeavor, are quite apt to reduce their aspiration level. It is among the low status children that passive participation in the cultural process is most prevalent. To what extent is the more passive participant suffering from a kind of cultural ennui and conditioning which dulls his sensitivity? To what extent was Goethe right when, appalled by the grossness and ugliness of the commonplace he said: "that which cramps us all, the habitual commonplace."

The influence of hope and expectancy play a vital part in human experience. Allport notes, "in all human relations, familial, ethnic, international—the engendering power of expectancy is enormous." When hope or expectancy is abandoned, there is no desire to continue, no will to do. The startling psycho-genic effect of voodoo death illustrates, in an extreme, a conditioning of self which may account for the helpless emotional response of individuals doomed to voodoo death.

Richter, accepting the possibility of voodoo death, set up experiments, trying to place limiting values on this preconception. He found that if he trapped healthy, wild rats in a leather bag which provided sufficient air for their living purposes but kept them trapped, they struggled for awhile and then gave up the struggle and died. Why did they die? Not for lack of air, not for lack of stored chemical energy in their muscles. What physiological and psychological processes were involved here? He found that if he repeated the same experiment only this time after the animal had made a struggle, he was temporarily liberated then trapped again, the second time the struggle goes on to complete exhaustion—a much longer period of time than the initial struggle.

The implications of these experiments for individuals living in an atmosphere overcharged with fear and frustration, hopelessness, and misery, seem clear enough. Since children in deprived minority groups are not exposed to the enspiriting effects of an enriched atmosphere and lush environment, it can be expected that their ambitions and what is required to satisfy them will, in most instances, be adversely affected. It can be expected that there will be manifestations of reduced drive toward achievement and a corresponding lack of zest for acquiring the skills necessary to obtain social rewards and life satisfaction.

In the classroom, it can be seen that well-adjusted children seem capable of setting levels of aspiration which are satisfying, challenging, and subject to change as acquired skills and abilities render previous levels obsolete or no longer appealing. Such activity is regenerative, supplying rewards and satisfactions which fortify the quest toward creative expansion of their talents. The attainment of homeostatic balance in this manner is offset by a predisposition to establish a measure of imbalance through the risk-taking behavior in the struggle to surmount more difficult barriers to progress. The re-establishment of equilibrium merely sets conditions for further striving for more difficult and prized goals, the ultimate of which is never realized and ever recedes into the future. Thus, the individual develops a habit of accepting insecurity as the only way toward independent security. For these well-adjusted children, there seems to exist an ideal level of aspiration as distinguished from the realistic or attainable level acquired by the organism to maintain an adequate tension-reduction system. It can be noted also that this desirable form of adaptive behavior is less likely to obtain among children in the lower income groups; lower thresholds of educational motivation are the pattern for underprivileged groups and their levels of aspiration seem to bear a correspondingly low ratio.

Low-status children have a more difficult task learning the social instigations and rewards which attach to insecurity as a motivating factor among children of higher status. We must learn how to motivate children, low-status children in particular, and adults and we must learn how to do this by means of socially adaptive anxieties. In order to make low-status children anxious to work hard, study hard, save their money, accept stricter sex morals, our society must convince them of the reality of the rewards at the end of the anxiety-laden climb.

To the middle class child who learns well and climbs fast, the prestige awards appear large, certain and relatively near.

Our society cannot hope, therefore, to educate the great masses of deprived people in any really effective manner until it has real rewards to offer them for learning and enduring the necessary anxiety. If Negro children stem from a local sub-culture which is in a state of log, they will not reflect the same sense of self-worth or self-regard as children from higher status groups where command over the immediate environment is encouraged as an essential means of progress toward self-determination. With reduced motivation for employing energy in the pursuit of educational objectives valued by the superordinate group, it may be expected that Negro children would achieve at a lower level in school, that their uncertainty about themselves and their potentialities would be reflected in their levels of aspiration. It seems clear that there is a need to help underprivileged children and Negro children, perhaps, in particular, to gain a measure of self-insight sufficient to support a feeling of quiet confidence in themselves as well as an abiding belief in themselves as adequate human beings. It is clear enough also, that the school can play a tremendously important role in this process.

Unfortunately, our present knowledge of this role potentiality yields but crude and inferential notions as to how the school can compensate for deprivation and perversive influences of defective homes and neighborhoods. It is at this point that total community skills and planning become necessary. It is an awesome task, but unavoidable if we are to approach full utilization of our vast human resources.

Aaron Lipman is concerned with the problems of youth in still another context: cultural lag. Technological advance and subsequent growth of urban culture occurred so rapidly that many attitudes and values lag far behind in the grass roots of rural life. Certain concepts of virility which remain today are dysfunctional. During adolescence a person develops a new sense of self-awareness and self-acceptance that is necessary for maturity. Our changing culture has made the task of growing to manhood increasingly difficult.

CULTURAL LAG AND MASCULINITY /
Aaron Lipman

A major part of the process of socialization involves learning the common value system of the society. This value system (which, when internalized, becomes the core of conscience) defines ideal goals, or ends of action, for the individual. Through socialization the individual learns those expected behavior patterns (roles) appropriate to certain statuses, with the type of early socialization dependent to a great extent on the kind of adult position for which the individual is being prepared. Since there is a reciprocal interaction between the school and the society in which it operates, a general aim of education is to facilitate this process of socialization, and to thus prepare the student for the world around him, both socially and occupationally.

What are some of the values emphasized in today's society, and what are the behavioral attributes necessary to attain these values? It has been stated that our urban industrial society approaches a universalistic-achievement orientation; the major emphasis of this achievement is in the occupational sphere. In this occupational system, intellectual abilities have assumed an ever-increasing importance. Today's new industries have comparatively few jobs for the unskilled or semi-skilled, and this tendency will be accelerated when, in the future, automation upgrades the nature of many more jobs.

The reality of this emphasis on brains rather than brawn or manual skill is attested to by the differential rewards offered each: Lipset has shown that consistently throughout our culture, for the male, the "head" occupations (where there is manipulation of abstract symbols and words, as well as manipulation of people) generally lead to higher incomes than do the manual occupations. Since in legitimate occupations, status rewards usually correlate closely with monetary rewards, there is evidence that urban industrialized societies place high value on occupations requiring intellectual ability and high educational attainment; its practitioners are generally granted the highest statuses and the best incomes. ". . . educational achievement is the main source of occupational achievement in a bureaucratized industrial society."

Surely by the time young men have reached the stage of second-

Aaron Lipman, *"Cultural Lag and Masculinity,"* Journal of Educational Sociology *(January 1962), pp. 217–220. Reprinted with the permission of the* Journal.

ary school, there should be some reflection in their attitudes of this adult world for which they are being prepared. We find, however, that young people's values show an inverse relationship to those that are functional for the society at large. Thus, in a recent questionnaire, when boys at ten different schools were asked, "How would you most like to be remembered in school: As an athletic star, a brilliant student, or most popular," the majority preferred to be remembered as athletic stars; most popular came next as a choice, and the least valued category was "brilliant student."

Physical prowess and excellence in sports—non-intellectual abilities—are highly valued by the youth, while the culture at large needs the inculcation of intellectual values in order to continue to operate most efficiently. How can we account for this discrepancy, and can anything be done to bridge these divergent views?

The value system that stressed the attribute of physical prowess was directly anchored and functionally related to a frontier and rural society. In this rural pattern, the masculine role consisted of the ability to actively manipulate concrete entities such as tools and animals, in the male's participation in farming, building, hunting, and fishing. The rural male was an active participant in a perpetually dynamic battle to control the elements; understandably, then, physical prowess was highly idealized, for the skills associated with this physical prowess could be transferred to farming, building, hunting, and fishing. Also, since industrialization had not emerged, the possession of great physical strength meant the ability to more successfully fight, conquer, and organize one's environment. Small wonder, then, that the farmer or frontiersman emphasized brute strength, toughness, physical endurance, and outdoor pastimes close to nature, i.e., hunting, fishing, etc.

As jousting tournaments in the medieval era were functionally related to education for the military, this outdoor emphasis was functionally related to education for the rural male's occupational sphere. Proficiency attained in these "extra-curricular" activities helped facilitate occupational skill, and was therefore highly valued.

The rural ideal, then, was the "manly" man. We can see how this ideal worked in a functional manner for the culture; it was the "manly" men who could best perform in a rural setting, therefore it was most sensible to encourage the young to internalize this ideal.

Unfortunately, we find that this ideal has survived our rapidly changing social patterns. Lynd indicates, for example, that Middletown believed that " 'red-blooded' physical sports are more normal recreation for a man than art, music, and literature." This ideal continues to exist at a time when it is not merely functionless, but actually dysfunctional and detrimental to the emergent new patterns consistent with the industrialized culture of today.

Technological evolution has almost eliminated the need for manliness of the old type. Whereas formerly the frontier or farm challenged the physical hardiness of the individual, the contemporary industrial challenge is now to his ingenuity in the creation of new, improved, mechanical and automated machines. The entire trend of cultural evolution has meant a decrease in emphasis on biological brawn, with a greater emphasis on man-made tools inspired by the brain. On an occupational level, how could one possibly equate muscle-power with atomic energy?

From a strictly functional standpoint, then, since we have seen that the necessary traits for the occupational system have changed drastically, the popular conception of the ideal man for the age should also undergo a drastic alteration. That this has not happened, and that people still perpetuate the old rural ideal of manliness, represents one of the most serious cultural lags of our time—certainly, one with direct implications for the education of young men in our society.

In this disparity between the old rural ideal of manliness and the new urban reality, for example, can be found the reasons for much of the disciplinary problems associated with today's young men. Talcott Parsons has pointed out that "farm boys tend to be 'good' in a sense which is not typical of their urban brothers," whereas the urban boys are more apt to be "recalcitrant to discipline and defiant." The rural patterns of proving manliness are still accessible to the farm boy. However, the urban male's attempt to prove his maculinity becomes a rather difficult task in an urban society, since there are few institutional means for achieving this end. (The search to prove his masculinity is imperative at this time, because the adolescent is also groping for emotional emancipation from his parents.) The result has been, not the development of new urban patterns, which are sorely needed, but instead, improvisations on the old rural ones. Thus, for example, hardiness and physical stamina, once useful attributes, have become translated into "toughness." The once-real physical dangers of a frontier environment, which necessitated courageousness and calm nerves, have been replaced by games like "chicken," or lawbreaking, which also demand a measure of physical bravery. The young man is still saddled with these "physical" expectations although our urban society has made it virtually impossible for him to fulfill them in an orderly, methodical, approved fashion.

This cultural lag, then, is dysfunctional in two important ways: not only does it interfere with the demands and needs of an urban industrialized society for more and more highly trained intellects (one-third of the nation's brightest high school graduates do not go on to college), but it seriously impedes the socialization of our young men by denying them a societally sanctioned means of entering the real world of the adult male (not the world they conceive to be adult and grown up).

In the rural culture, the young male entered the adult world gradually; he participated in it from a very early age, in a manner commensurate with his abilities. During this process, his father served as a direct model; other males were also readily accessible, and it was thus possible for the youth to make a realistic identification with adult males during his adolescence. The young man could also understand the type of work the men did, and could look forward to full participation, once he becomes sufficiently mature.

The adolescent male in a rural culture, then, could prove his manliness in easily-accessible, societally approved ways, and gradually earn a recognizable niche in the adult world. He was able to identify with his father in the occupational sphere, and could understand the basic processes in which he was engaged.

In contemporary urban society, however, no such occupational continuum exists for the adolescent. There is an abrupt transition for him, from boyish irresponsibility to the demands of the first real job. Adult male models have become largely inaccessible, including the important father figure. The males work away from home, and even if the young sons could follow them to the office, the boys might not readily understand the nature of the work in which their fathers were engaged. The occupations are now urban and abstract, involve the manipulation of words and symbols, and require training which the fathers and neighboring males can no longer transmit to the young.

Some of these changes (such as specialization and complexity of job) are integrally related to an urban industrialized society, and any attempt to alter them would necessitate a drastic change of our entire social structure. The cultural lag under discussion, however, where rural values of manliness still persist in an urban society, can be eliminated through an acceleration in the change of values. With channels of communication as highly developed as they are at present, "the mass media can be a strong force influencing the images held by the general public." We need new, positive, urban-oriented values, which would articulate the needs of both the culture and the young men seeking a proper, direct way to enter it, where boys would idealize and attempt to emulate the intellectual as much as they do the football or baseball player. This does not mean to suggest that physical fitness standards, in terms of bodily health, be abandoned; however, the needs of neither our society nor our youth are being met, when the worst epithet one can hurl at a present-day high school student is "egghead."

The problem of giving our young a valid and meaningful education is not entirely curricular. Within our society is the ethos that demands honest labor in return for self-respect, yet the economy of this same society values the adolescent only as a consumer. Many of our youth, caught between these traditional and emergent forces, go unheeded in a social limbo.

SOCIAL DYNAMITE IN OUR LARGE CITIES: Unemployed, Out-of-School Youth / James B. Conant

I submit that the existence in the slums of our large cities of thousands of youth ages 16-21 who are both out-of-school and out-of-work is an explosive situation. It is social dynamite.

In preparation for this Conference, a few special studies were conducted in slum areas of large cities to find out what the facts really were. In a slum section composed almost entirely of Negroes in one of our largest cities the following situation was found. A total of 59 percent of the male youth between the ages of 16 and 21 were out of school and unemployed. They were roaming the streets. Of the boys who graduated from high school 48 percent were unemployed in contrast to 63 percent of the boys who had dropped out of school. In short, two-thirds of the male dropouts did not have jobs and about half of the high school graduates did not have jobs. In such a situation, a pupil may well ask why bother to stay in school when graduation for half the boys opens onto a dead-end street?

An even worse state of affairs was found in another special study in a different city. In a slum area of 125,000 people, mostly Negro, a sampling of youth population shows that roughly 70 percent of the

James B. Conant, "Social Dynamite in Our Large Cities," Vital Speeches, July 1, 1961. Delivered before the Conference on Unemployed, Out-of-School Youth in Urban Areas, sponsored by the National Committee for Children and Youth, Washington, D.C., May 24, 1961. Reprinted with the permission of Vital Speeches, City News Publishing Company.

boys and girls ages 16-21 are out of school and unemployed. When one stops to consider that the total population in this district is equal to that of a good-sized independent city, the magnitude of the problem is appalling and the challenge to our society is clear.

I do not have to remind this audience of the fact that the fate of freedom in the world hangs very much in balance. Our success against the spread of Communism in no small measure depends upon the successful operation of our own free society. To my mind, there is no question that a healthy body politic necessitates a sound economy and high employment. The history of Communism shows that it feeds upon discontented, frustrated, unemployed people. The present unemployment rate nationwide is roughly 7 percent for all age brackets, but unemployment among youth under 20 years of age is 20 percent, or three times greater than the nationwide rate for all workers. These young people are my chief concern, especially when they are pocketed together in large numbers within the confines of the big-city slums. What can words like "freedom," "liberty," and "equality of opportunity" mean to these young people? With what kind of zeal and dedication can we expect them to withstand the relentless pressures of Communism? How well prepared are they to face the struggle that shows no signs of abating?

In a slum area where over half the male youth are unemployed and out of school we are allowing a grave danger to the stability of our society to develop. A youth who has dropped out of school and never has had a full-time job is not likely to become a constructive citizen of his community. Quite the contrary. As a frustrated individual he is likely to be anti-social and rebellious. Some of this group of youth will end as juvenile delinquents. No one would claim that providing full employment for youth in the large cities would automatically banish juvenile delinquency, for we all realize that the causes of this problem are complex and there is no one solution. However, I suggest that full employment would have a highly salutary effect. Moreover, I offer the following hypothesis for professional social workers and sociologists to demolish; namely, that the correlation between desirable social attitudes (including attitudes of youth) and job opportunities are far higher than between the former and housing conditions, as measured by plumbing facilities, heating, and space per family.

Leaving juvenile delinquency aside, the existence of gangs of unemployed out-of-school youth in some neighborhoods of our large cities creates social problems acute enough by themselves. The adverse influence of the "street" is largely a consequence of the existence of these gangs. I doubt if anyone familiar with a slum district would deny that, if all the male youth by some miracle were to find employment, the social climate would change dramatically for the better. Some juvenile delinquents would remain, gangs might not wholly disappear, but the whole attitude of the neighborhood would alter in such a way as to make more effective the teacher in every classroom.

Unemployment is bad anywhere. Adult unemployment is grievous because it usually involves the loss of support for an entire family. In rural areas, towns and small cities, one might say that solving the unemployment of adults has the top priority; unemployment of youth may be pushed aside by some people as relatively unimportant. But in the slums of the largest cities I would say the drastic reduction of unemployment of male youth under age 21 is a greater need.

Consider for a moment the long-run consequence of persistent failure of underprivileged youth to find work. Leaving aside the human tragedies involved in each individual instance and looking at the matter solely in terms of the welfare of our free society, one sees the special position of the large-city slums. The boys brought up in slum neighborhoods, even if they came to the big city from the country as children, are conditioned to street life with all that this life implies. Out of work and out of school since they turned 16, these youth behave in ways that may have serious political consequences; similar behavior of youth in smaller cities would be far less serious. It is a matter of geography in the last analysis. Three factors are significant: first, the total size of the group of youth to whom I am referring— the larger the group, the more dangerous; second, the density of the population—the number of frustrated youth per block; third, the isolation of the inhabitants from other kinds of people and other sorts of streets and houses.

If one compares the slum areas in the largest cities with similar districts in small cities, the difference as regards those three factors is clearly evident. The youth in the big-city slums dwells in the midst of a mammoth social complex. The surrounding city extends for blocks and blocks. The business and industrial areas hem in the impoverished youth. In the case of the Negro, added to all the negative influences of a slum is the absence of any evidence that there is a pathway out. In spite of the high mobility of the family unit or perhaps because of it, a tone is set by constant talk and the prevailing attitude of the older people. And the tone is not one to encourage education or stimulate ambition. The unemployed floaters on the street are walking evidence to all the youth that nothing can be accomplished through education, that the door of the neighborhood schoolhouse indeed opens on a dead-end street.

Let me emphasize that, in my opinion, there is no reason why this should be the case. I know there are those who maintain that, on the average, Negro children are inferior to white children in academic ability. I have seen no evidence to support any such contention. In considering the relative abilities of whites and Negroes, let us examine the situation in an all-white slum in a city of considerable size. A careful study of a group of children in grade 4 of one such school showed that their average achievement level was a full year below their grade placement—a typical situation in any slum area.

What the teachers in this school have to contend with is shown by a report from the principal. Perhaps the greatest handicap to good school work is the high mobility of the white population in the area. In this school mobility is very high; it is not uncommon in similar schools to have a turnover of the entire enrollment in one school year.

The principal writes, "When a residential area composed of large, old homes formerly occupied by owners and single family groups changes, economically and socially conditions of general deterioration begin. Absentee owners rent the property by single rooms or small so-called apartments of two or three rooms to large families. . . . Such conditions attract transients (who either cannot or will not qualify for supervised low income housing), the unemployed, the unskilled and unschooled, and the distressed families whose breadwinners have either just been committed to prisons or mental institutions or who have but recently been released from such. The only possession most of these families have is children. . . . In such an environment all forms of evil flourish—the peddling of dope, drunkenness, disease, accidents, truancies, physical, mental and moral handicaps, sex perversions involving children . . .

"The parents of at least one-third of the children are either in penal institutions, are on probation, or have prison records. At least 100 children are on probation to the Juvenile Court. There has not been a day since I've been at the school that there has not been one or more children in detention at the Juvenile Court . . .

"Less than 10 percent of the children have private doctors or dentists. A dental examination of 900 children in the fall of 1959 reveals only forty-four free of cavities. The eyes of every child in the school were examined and about 300 showed some vision defects, and thirty had such serious vision loss that they were referred for partially-seeing teaching. At least one-third of the children are on welfare rolls or are recipients of very small social security and/or veteran benefits checks. In many cases, however, the neediest children . . . are those who cannot qualify for any dependency grant.

"Unless a school is able to educate its children so they may become competent and responsible citizens its work is a temporary stop gap that relieves immediate suffering only. Although the school is the only organization that has instruction as its primary responsibility, when a noble hearted teacher faces a barefoot, hungry, sick, distressed child, the result is an endless chain of efforts to relieve such a child.

"We realize that little or nothing can be done for or with the parents of the children who face such serious problems in their homes. These problems directly affect the child's health, attendance, emotional and personal adjustment, his learning and his progress (or lack of it) in every respect. In all probability at least one-half of our children will be school dropouts. In our opinion the children need, desperately, for desirable development, in addition to good schools— good homes, churches and communities."

I am quoting from an official report which, in acknowledging the generally low achievement of the white children in this school, makes the interesting statement that "There is no reason to believe that these students as a group are inherently or genetically less capable than average students, but apparently because of some types of experiences in their lives they have been unable to develop their intellectual skills." The belief expressed in the first part of this sentence can hardly be based on anything firmer than an assumption as to the genetic uniformity of white children whose ancestors have for several generations lived in the United States. Such an assumption, of course, leaves out of account the possibility of a selective process occurring over the generations as some tended to move to one type of occupation and settle in one type of community. However, since I see no way of investigating the role of selective migration, I would be inclined to let the assumption stand unchallenged. *Only I should argue strongly that to date we have no evidence to indicate that the assumption should not be broadened to include both white and Negro students.* For all the contrary evidence, namely the poor work in school and low scores on tests made by Negroes, is based to a large degree on the performance of children in what are essentially slum conditions. Consequently, I start with the belief that, given a satisfactory socioeconomic background and educational opportunity, Negro children can be just as successful in academic work as any other group. You are all aware of the dramatic success that has been achieved in more than one instance in raising the aspirations and achievement levels of slum children.

The difference between the Negro slum of today and the slums of the Northern seaport cities of sixty years ago is a difference that deserves attention. The worries I have expressed about the continuation of present conditions may appear to be neutralized by contemplating the record of the past. Big cities have always had slums. In the United States it has been possible for people to raise themselves by their own bootstraps in the course of a generation. Why be alarmed about the present situation? Such a complacent projection of the past into the obscure future is fallacious for several reasons. First and foremost is the fact that in the past most of the inhabitants of slums were recently arrived white foreign immigrants. They knew that their predecessors for generations had worked their way out of poverty in the cities. They were convinced that they could do likewise. The almost complete lack of such conviction—a consequence of the tragic story of the Negro in the United States—is the outstanding characteristic of youth in the Negro slum. Second, a foreign immigrant came from an impoverished but stable society, for the most part a peasant society with its own ancient mores. The pride of family and often strong church connections were social cement that kept the slums from being complete social jungles in spite of the fact that the dwelling conditions were often far worse than they are today. Lastly, for most of the period of our history, labor shortages rather than labor surpluses were characteristic. Particularly, unskilled laborers were in demand. When this was not so, namely, in the depression years, organized society had to step in on a large scale to bolster up the tottering social structure. Today, automation has affected the whole employment scene; there is much less demand for unskilled labor. Racial discrimination makes unemployment chronic for the Negro male North and South. In short, neither in terms of the kinds of people involved nor in terms of the economic and social setting is there much resemblance between the slum districts of 1900 and those which are the sore spots of our modern cities.

What was especially shocking to me in my visits to the large cities in the last school year was the discovery that the employment of youth is literally nobody's affair. To be sure, there are groups concerned with various aspects of the problem, but no single agency in any of the cities has the data as to the unemployment picture in that city. There is little up-to-date information about youth unemployment even city-wide and only the estimate of school people about the slum neighborhoods. Seldom are figures available to distinguish between the unemployed who are high school graduates and those who have dropped out of school before completing the twelfth grade. Most important, it is not possible to say with any accuracy how the unemployed youth are distributed among various neighborhoods. There is much to be done in the gathering of reliable statistics. The problem of unemployed youth in the large cities is in no small part a Negro problem. We do not facilitate its solution by trying to find phrases to hide this fact. And it is largely a Negro problem in the North because of the discrimination practiced quietly but extensively by employers and labor unions. In an effort to overcome this unjust and nationally dangerous discrimination, people must not shrink from publishing statistics, unpleasant as they may be. How can we improve a situation if we are deprived of knowledge of what the situation really is? And it is my hope that in this Conference this problem of setting forth the facts will be thoroughly explored in a spirit of goodwill.

At this point I imagine many of you who are well aware of the nature of the appalling problems in the big cities are wondering just how I became concerned about the social problems of the big city. Therefore, I thought I might take a few moments to explain my interest and to describe briefly the situations I found which have caused my great concern.

The subject of my first report, *The American High School Today*, was the widely comprehensive high school found in independent cities that were not part of a large metropolitan complex. Aside from some short comments, I ignored both suburban schools and big-city schools, both of which by my definition tend not to be widely comprehensive because they often do not include a wide variety of elective programs. In the college-oriented suburb there is not likely to be interest in vocational programs, and in the big cities the existence of separate vocational schools also means a restriction of the elective program in the general high school. However, in conjunction with my study last year of junior high school education, I decided to take a more detailed look at schools in metropolitan areas—at schools in slums and suburbs, if you will. In the large metropolitan areas of New York, Philadelphia, Detroit, Chicago, St. Louis one has no difficulty in locating examples of both. In some cases twenty minutes drive will enable a person to go from one to the other. A visit to the high school serving each community will open the eyes of a visitor to the complexities of American public education. Their basic problems are quite unlike, and these differences spring from the differences in the nature of the families being served. One lesson to be drawn from visiting a well-to-do suburb and a slum is all important for understanding American public education. That lesson is that to a large degree what a school should do and can do is determined by the status and ambitions of the majority of the families within the community. I drew this conclusion after either my staff or I had visited metropolitan schools in and around many of the largest cities in the nation—New York, Los Angeles, Chicago, Detroit, Philadelphia, Baltimore, St. Louis.

In the suburban high school from which 80 percent or more of the graduates enter some sort of college the problems are the mirror image of those in the city slums, where as many as half the students drop out of school prior to graduation. The task with which the school people must struggle in the city slum is, on the one hand, how to prepare the youth for getting and keeping a job as soon as he or she leaves school and, on the other hand, to encourage those who have academic talent to aim at a profession through higher education. The task thus stated seems simple. In fact, as you all know, the difficulties are enormous. The improvement of conditions in the slums is only in part a school problem, but the role of the schools is of the utmost importance. I am not nearly so concerned about the plight of the suburban parents whose offspring are at present having difficulty finding places in prestige colleges as I am about the plight of parents in the slums whose children drop out of school or graduate without prospects of employment. The latter is a much more serious social phenomenon, and too little attention has been paid to it.

Visits to a wealthy suburb and impoverished slums only a few minutes away jolt one's notions of the meaning of equality of opportunity. On the one hand, there is likely to be a spacious, modern school staffed by as many as 70 professionals for 1,000 pupils; on the other hand, one finds a crowded, often dilapidated and unattractive school staffed by 40 professionals for 1,000 pupils. Expenditure per pupil in the wealthy suburban school is likely to be over $1,000; often it is less than half that in the slum school. To my mind, in view of the problems one finds, conditions in the slum school necessitate more staff and more money than in the suburban school.

Leaving aside the suburban communities, I would like now to point up some of my observations in the large cities, especially in the slums, where my staff and I made special efforts to visit schools. In each of the cities we visited, one can find neighborhoods composed of various minority groups. Many of these are areas now designated as "culturally deprived," or "culturally different" but which in my youth would have been more simply designated as "slums." The schools serving such neighborhoods have to be visited in order for one to understand the nature of the tasks which the teachers face.

The slum areas of certain big northern cities are today largely inhabited by Negroes who have recently moved from the South hoping to improve their lot. The economic changes in the South which have forced this migration are too well known to require elaboration. The Negro is being displaced as a farm laborer, and, being unable because of discrimination to obtain other employment in the section where he was born, he becomes a migrant headed North. Between 1950 and 1960 the proportion of Negroes living in the South dropped from 60 percent to 52 percent. St. Louis is said to be the first stopping point for many who make the journey, though the school people in Chicago, Detroit, Philadelphia, Baltimore, Washington, or New York indicate that their problems with the recently arrived Negroes from the South are quite as great as those which confront their colleagues in St. Louis. New York State now has the largest Negro population of any state in the Union.

The growth of Negro slums in big cities is alarming. I wish that I could do more than direct attention. For without being an alarmist, I must say that when one considers the total situation that has been developing in the Negro slums since World War II, one has reason to worry about the future. The building up of a mass of unemployed and frustrated Negro youth in congested areas of a city is a social phenomenon that may be compared to the piling up of inflammable material in an empty building in a city block. Potentialities for trouble —indeed, possibilities of disaster—are surely there.

Let me start by describing a slum that might be in any one of several of the large cities I have visited. The inhabitants are all Negroes and with few exceptions have entered the city from a state in the Deep South anywhere from the last month to the last three years. Even the elementary schools serving this neighborhood are plagued by the mobility of the families. Often the composition of a grade will alter so rapidly that a teacher will find at the end of a school year that she is teaching but few pupils who started with her in the fall. In one school, I recall the principal stating that a teacher absent more than one week will have difficulty recognizing her class when she returns. The mothers move with their offspring from room to room from month to month and in so doing often go from one elementary school district to another; I am told that resident tenements look more like transient hotels. I write "mothers" advisedly, since in one neighborhood, by no means the worst I have seen, a questionnaire sent out by the school authorities indicated that about a third of the pupils come from family units (one hesitates to use the word "home") which had no father, stepfather, or male guardian. Less than one percent of the parents graduated from college; 10 percent of the parents graduated from high school; only 33 percent completed the elementary school; and another 32 percent did not go that far. Contrast the situation in which a third of the parents have not completed elementary school with that in a high-income suburb where as many as 90 percent of the parents have bachelor's degrees, if not graduate degrees.

These Negro slums seem to vary considerably as regards the social mores. In some there are very bad gangs with gang warfare among the boys. There are also vicious fights outside of school between girls. The condition in one such neighborhood was summed up to one of my staff by a principal of a junior high school who said even he was shocked by the answers to a questionnaire to the girls which asked what was their biggest problem. The majority replied to the effect that their biggest problem was getting from the street into their apartment without being molested in the hallway of the tenement. He went on to say that the area had a set of social customs of its own. The streets are full of unemployed men who hang around and prey on the girls. The women are the centers of the family and as a rule are extremely loyal to the children. The men, on the other hand, are floaters. Similar reports from principals and teachers can be heard by the attentive and sympathetic visitor to the Negro slums of any one of several cities.

I have so far referred only to white and Negro slums. In addition, a few words are necessary to point out that in some cities, New York in particular, there are slum areas inhabited by recent arrivals from Puerto Rico. In these sections, the problems are similar to those I have described but complicated by the difference in language. Unlike the American Negro from the South, these recent arrivals bring with them a set of social mores closely associated with their own methods of communication. At the same time, they often, if not always, come with children whose schooling has been bad. Clearly the problem of teaching these Puerto Rican children involves both a reading problem and a problem of teaching a foreign language. These problems are so special I shall not attempt to discuss them here. One hardly needs to point out that the existence of these problems adds one more complication to the tasks confronting the administrators and teachers in New York City schools. Add to these tasks the possibilities of interracial hostility and gang warfare between Negroes and Puerto Ricans and the resentment of both toward the whites and one has a veritable witches' brew which comes to boil with unsavory vehemence in certain schools in certain areas—particularly in the junior high school years. The amazing feature of the whole situation is that pupils make any progress in schools in certain areas of the city.

One only needs to visit the type of school I am now describing to be convinced that the nature of the community largely determines what goes on in the school. Therefore, to attempt to divorce the school from the community is to engage in unrealistic thinking, which might lead to policies that could wreak havoc with the school and the lives of children. The community and the school are inseparable. For example, I have walked through school corridors in slum areas and, looking into classrooms, have seen children asleep with their heads on their hands. Is this situation the result of poor teachers without either disciplinary control or teaching ability? No, the children asleep at their desks have been up all night with no place to sleep or else subject to unbelievable family fights and horrors through the night. Checking into one case, a principal told one of my staff that after climbing six flights of a tenement he found the boy's home—one filthy room with a bed, a light bulb, and a sink. In the room lived the boy's mother and her four children. I might add that it is not unusual for teachers in these schools to take home with them children with little or no place to go at night. I would ask suburban parents to ponder the contrast between the lives and the education of their children and the lives and education of the boys and girls in the schools I have been describing. It is after visits to schools like these that I grow impatient with both critics and defenders of public education who ignore the realities of school situations to engage in fruitless debate about educational philosophy, purposes, and the like.

I use the phrase "social attitudes," including attitudes of youth, to try and sum up my impressions of what I have heard so often from the teachers in grades 1 to 8 in slum neighborhoods. As one teacher said to me, "We do quite well with these children in the lower grades. Each of us is, for the few hours of the school day, an acceptable substitute for the mother. But when they reach about 10, 11, or 12 years of age, we lose them. At that time the 'street' takes over. In terms of schoolwork, progress ceases; indeed, many pupils begin to go

backward in their studies!" What can be done to offset the demoralizing attitude of "the street" in the worst of the slums? Not much that
lies within the province of the school authorities alone. Here is where
the social agency people, the juvenile court people, the churches—
all the various groups represented at this Conference come into
the picture.

This last thought leads me to say that thus far I have spoken in
negative terms for the most part, describing my own sense of shock
at the slum conditions in our large cities, especially as these conditions
relate to education and employment. So important are these problems
that in putting together a final report for the Carnegie Corporation
I decided to publish a small book that will contrast the wealthy suburban schools and the slum schools. In this small volume I shall try to
create a set of anxious thoughts in the minds of conscientious citizens
who while living in the suburbs may work in the cities. I wish that I
had many more constructive proposals to make than I now have, and
I am hoping that this Conference, composed of people thoroughly
familiar with slum problems, will come up with positive, constructive
ideas that will lead to solutions. There are clearly many areas of concern. Among the more important are racial discrimination; employment practices of labor and management; Federal-State laws including
insurance rates and wage scales; lack of jobs, as well as changing types
of employment because of automation and the necessity for more
highly skilled workers; the role of the schools in preparing youth for
employment, especially average and below-average youth, and in helping them make the transition from school to work; the coordination of
the efforts of the schools, the employers and labor unions, and the
various community agencies that have a hand in promoting youth welfare; the role of the public sector of the economy at the local, state, and
federal level in providing employment if the private sector of the economy is unable to do so. All of these questions are complex and controversial but will, I sincerely hope, be thoroughly aired at the various
Workshop meetings in this Conference.

In closing, I should like to express my own views on a very few of
the subjects just mentioned about which I feel strongly. In the first
place, there are those who would say that what goes on in the schools
should not have any direct connection with the community or the
employment situation. I completely reject this idea. The school, the
community, and the employment picture are and should be closely tied
together. I am not impressed by the holding power of a school as a
criterion of its quality, but neither am I impressed by the argument

that a boy who fails to get along in school ought to drop out. It all depends. The situation in which a boy drops out of school only to roam the streets is quite different from the situation in which a boy drops out and finds satisfactory employment. Full-time schooling, for certain youths through grade 12 may be good or bad depending upon the employment picture. What goes on in the school ought to be conditioned in large measure by the nature of the families being served, the vocational plans and aspirations of the students, and employment opportunities. To sum up, *I submit that in a heavily urbanized and industrialized free society the educational experience of youths should fit their subsequent employment.* This should be so whether a boy drops out of school in grade 10, after graduation from high school, or after graduation from college or university. In any case, there should be a smooth transition from full-time schooling to a full-time job.

This is an ideal situation admittedly and one which is at present approached only in the learned professions and in a few instances the occupations for which undergraduate college courses provide the necessary training. In the case of the learned professions, those in charge of the last stage in the educational journey—the professors of law, of medicine, and those who direct the research of candidates for the Ph.D.—have usually a sense of responsibility for their students based on their own passionate interest in promoting the best interests of their profession. Graduates of some undergraduate professional courses in some institutions are also often assisted in finding employment. Engineering is perhaps the best example. With the present shortage of teachers, professors of education have no difficulty in finding jobs for their students. While the universities or colleges do not accept responsibility for the placement of their graduates, many, if not all, spend time and money in helping the young man or woman to find a job. In many cases the subsequent career is followed with interest and assistance is provided in re-employment. Sixty years ago the situation was very different. Concern with placement of college and university graduates was a product of the depression years. The change, I believe, has been important and in the best interests of both the individual and society. For the college graduate who has received a general or liberal education without majoring in a professional or semi-professional field, many difficulties of finding a suitable job will remain. Still, by and large, one can say at the college and university level a considerable fraction of the youth involved make a smooth transition from education to a job.

When we examine the situation at the high school level, we find quite a different state of affairs. Although in many high schools a half or more of the graduates seek employment immediately on graduation, only in a few cities does one find an effective placement service. And I make this statement without intending any reproach to either social agencies or to guidance counselors. The obligations of the school should not end when the student either drops out of school or graduates. At that point the cumulative record folder concerning a student's educational career is usually brought to an end. It should not be. To my mind, *guidance officers, especially in the large cities, ought to be given the responsibility for following the post-high school careers of youth from the time they leave school until they are 21 years of age.* Since compulsory attendance usually ends at age 16, this means responsibility for the guidance of youth ages 16 to 21 who are out of school and either employed or unemployed. It is with the unemployed out-of-school youth that I am especially concerned—especially the boys, for whom the unemployment problem is more severe than for girls. This expansion of the school's function will cost money and will mean additional staff—at least a doubling of the guidance staff in most of the large cities; but the expense is necessary, for vocational and educational guidance must be a continuing process to help assure a smooth transition from school to the world of work. The present abrupt break between the two is unfortunate. What I have in mind suggests, of course, a much closer relationship than now exists between school, employers, and labor unions, as well as social agencies and employment offices.

There is no question that the school people in the large cities face a gigantic task in their efforts to prepare youth from impoverished homes for useful lives as responsible citizens and productive workers. I have the heartiest respect for the dedicated men and women who with limited means and facilities are doing the best job they can to overcome the adverse influence of the home and street in the big-city slum. As one of my associates who had spent the best years of his life as principal of a suburban public high school put it, "I visited junior high schools in New York City in some of the worst areas. I expected to find blackboard jungles; instead I found schools with high morale, tight discipline, imaginative principals and teachers." My own visits were largely confined to similar schools in Chicago, Detroit, and St. Louis, and my admiration for what is being done in those cities is equal to that of my colleague for what he saw in New York City.

Not that all problems have been solved. Far from it, as you all know. Reading is the essential tool for success in school and on the job, and although in this area much has been done, much remains to be done, particularly with respect to gaining the interest of the parents in the success of their children, reducing class size, and providing for more remedial reading teachers. Decentralized administration in the big cities is surely a step in the right direction by bringing the schools closer to the people. A new look is needed at vocational programs, especially for the below-average students who are rejected by the vocational people and academic people alike. Much remains to be done for the future dropout to ease the break between school and job. It appears that the only jobs available for unskilled workers in the decade ahead will be in service occupations, a fact of considerable importance in educational planning. As you all know better than I, many of the large cities have made attempts to prepare these youths for work. Adult education courses, work-study programs of various sorts—these are all evidence of a continuing interest of the schools in furthering educational opportunities for out-of-school youth and ought to be expanded. Finally, I have been told many times that an important obstacle in improving the education of slum children is the fact that the teachers who may have taught in schools for a number of years with a certain kind of student body suddenly find themselves engulfed by slum children whom they do not understand and for whom they fail to recognize the need for changes in the curriculum. In many cases, a re-education of the teachers becomes necessary.

In short, there is much that schools are doing but much more that they should do. Money in many instances is the key—remedial reading teachers, smaller classes, guidance counselors cost money. I have already noted the vast disproportion between the amount spent per pupil in the wealthy suburbs and that spent in the slums of the big city.

But even if the schools were to improve their services drastically, there would still remain what seems to me the crux of the situation— the presence or absence of employment opportunity. Whereas I have indicated my conviction that the problems of Negro education are no different from those of all underprivileged socio-economic groups, the problems of Negro employment are distinctly different. The enforcement of anti-discrimination laws has proved a most difficult undertaking. I have heard it said that only those projects which are supported by public funds can really be operated on a truly non-discriminatory basis. Therefore, it seems to me that unless local management and labor take up the challenge, it may be necessary for Congress to appropriate funds for public work programs to alleviate the problem of unemployment among youth 16 to 21 in the large cities. In view of the past discriminatory employment practices by both management and labor, action at the federal level may become a necessity. Even if there were no discrimination, it might become a necessity if the private sector of the economy is unable to provide sufficient jobs.

In conclusion, let me repeat my sense of shock as I contemplate conditions in our big cities with respect to youth in slum neighborhoods. The problems are the result of a social situation, the roots of which run back to the days of slavery and the result of an economic problem which is in part a reflection of the total unemployment situation and in part a result of racial discrimination among labor unions and employers. To improve the work of the slum schools requires an improvement in the lives of the families who inhabit these slums, but without a drastic change in the employment prospects for urban Negro youth, relatively little can be accomplished. I close by urging that our large-city problems be analyzed in far more detail than in the past and with a far greater degree of frankness. Neighborhood by neighborhood we need to know the facts, and when these facts indicate a dangerous social situation the American people should be prepared to take drastic measures before it is too late. I wish this Conference all success as it tackles this extremely urgent and perplexing problem of unemployed, out-of-school youth in our large cities.

David Riesman's observations of our emerging society are sobering. It is not only poverty that denies youth the opportunity to fully participate in and identify with the genuine values of society. Such opportunity is lost in abundance, too. Goals of education must incorporate more than opportunity in order to share in the "good life."

THE SEARCH FOR CHALLENGE / *David Riesman*

I want to discuss the problem of discovering challenge in what Galbraith calls the "affluent society," challenge when the older challenges based on the subsistent society and the struggle for sheer survival are no longer imperative. One of the perspectives I want to use is cross-cultural, and we shall look at an anthropological example. Another is

David Riesman, "A Search for Challenge," Abundance for What? *New York: Doubleday & Company, Inc., 1964, pp. 349–367.*

historical, and we shall look at ourselves as we were in an earlier day—this, too, is cross-cultural. The third perspective is genetic, in which I shall ask what sorts of challenges are requisite at what stages of one's own life cycle. This is a vast topic. I don't bring to it the erudition of a Toynbee or an Alfred Kroeber, but on the contrary I shall bring to it some observations and free associations in the hope of stimulating further thinking.

Periodically throughout Western history men have imagined that collective as well as individual life could be better, or at least less bad. In times of chaos and of war they dreamed of social stability and hierarchy, as Plato did in *The Republic*, or as Sir Thomas More did in his *Utopia*. Myths of heaven refracted the popular weariness of toil, short life, illness and social disorganization. Periodically, too, men could be mobilized for revolt against plainly oppressive conditions, once these conditions had lightened enough to make them seem less than divinely given. For the ills that have plagued man have been such nightmares that men at all but the lowest levels of brutishness could grasp the possibility of being less badly off, once they *were* less badly off. Today, however, we are faced with a paradox: the United States and a few other rich countries have caught up with many Utopian ideals while at the same time literal belief in heaven has almost vanished. In this country people suffer less from nightmarish misery than from the more subtle disorders previously buried by the harsh struggle for existence.

We can see an analogue to this development in the short career of psychoanalytic therapy, which is about 50 years old. When Freud began, patients came to him who were suffering from hysteria, from paralyzed arms, from inability to talk, from obvious symptoms. By helping them internalize what they had externalized, that is, what they had (so to speak) thrown into an arm, it was relatively easy and even speedy to cure them. Today, in contrast, one sees such cases only, for instance in this country, among immigrant Poles in Pittsburgh or among rural southerners in West Virginia. Many therapists go through their entire lives without ever seeing such a case. People come to analysis today who do not suffer from an external subsistence problem, from a paralysis. Their limbs work and their sexual organs work, but somehow life doesn't live up to its billing for them; they carry on an unrepressed interior dialogue, but it bores them. Often, I might add, all they do is include the analyst in the dialogue and bore him. They need, usually without knowing it, a new vision and not merely a new way of talking about themselves; in fact, I was talking the other day with an analyst who said that patients talked today, as was no surprise, very freely indeed about any of the things that in Freud's day they would have considered private and intimate.

Yet, as we all know, most of the rest of the world would trade places any day with the rich American and trade its miseries for his neuroses. An ironic instance are the Manus whom Margaret Mead revisited several years ago, twenty-five years after her first field trip in 1928. When she had first been there the Manus had been a Stone Age people; then had come World War II and their island had been a staging area for American troops. When she arrived, the Manus had just finished throwing out a Catholic mission on the ground that the mission was trying to get them to adjust slowly to the ways of the West, whereas they wanted to take over the distance to modernity in one big jump. They thought the white people in the mission were patronizing them, holding out on them, trying to ration the blessings of industrial society. You can imagine the position of the mission which was saying in effect, "It isn't just so wonderful to be Westernized, and take it easy." For the Manus the effort to act like Americans was a heroic challenge; one, in fact, which produced a revolutionary leader, Paliau, a man of enormous strength and determination. For him, it was a new religion to become Americanized.

The Manus, like many South Pacific peoples, had had their craze of cargo cults in which traditional objects had been thrown in the ocean in the fond belief that planes or boats would come, piled high with the white man's goods, if only the Manus would propitiate the cargo by appropriate action. Even where the cargo cult does not take such open and violent form, it exists. A few years ago I met a Burmese doctor who had come to the University of Chicago to study technological change. I asked him why he, a gentle and speculative man, had left his homeland on such a quest; and he replied that once the peasants in the rice fields had seen American movies and Cadillacs they would never be quiet again until they had them too. In his book *The Passing of Traditional Society*, Daniel Lerner discusses interviews which were done a few years ago in seven countries of the Middle East. In these the theme that life in America is more modern and, hence better, comes up again and again—whatever the political hostilities toward America, one finds this lure among Egyptians and Syrians and others who are politically, ideologically, violently antagonistic to America and yet admire it. The dream of America—the dream of plenty—is shared by people at all levels, and it is also rejected on religious and traditional grounds by many who are obviously and plainly influenced by it. The conflicts are only about the rate of speed with which one should move to plenty and the mode, and the Malthusian handicaps and how they are to be overcome, and the values to be reintegrated by doing so. And all this is new and exciting to peoples to whom it happens, but it is not new to the West—we have had it.

In fact, we can today in some considerable degree measure the backwardness of a social class or a nation by the extent to which America provides it with a model of Utopia. For the intellectuals of Europe and of India, for instance, America is more to be feared than admired, distrusted than copied. The collapse of the image of America as a vision of Jeffersonian equality and of orderly democracy has been enormously rapid and is not merely the result of Communist propaganda. One factor is the shutting off of immigration after the first World War, which doused the hopes of millions of south Europeans and Levantines that they might find a personal Utopia in the United States; and in these interviews of Professor Lerner's one finds this also coming up again and again—people who have uncles in America from Syria or Turkey and who would like to come here and can't.

The more vociferous Americans themselves, moreover, in desperate search of a self-justifying ideology, have been tempted to identify *the* American way with their own tendentious misinterpretations of our economy as one of free enterprise, or to boast of American technological virtuosity or of the workingman's standard of living. This last might appear to appeal to workingmen in some places, but it does not appeal to the elites whose own frustrated materialism is all too well acted out on their behalf by strident Americans.

I have in the last years talked to a good many non-Americans who, like the Burmese doctor, are visiting this country in the hope of hastening the economic development of their own lands, and they have gone home again with an ambivalent feeling: can they reduce poverty, cut the birthrate, start cumulative economic growth, all without arriving at the American destiny—that is, arriving at the place we are now, from which the next steps are opaque—once the novelty wears off?

I would be giving the wrong impression if I were understood to contend that there is no Utopianism in present-day America. There are first of all many conservative people, maybe some here, who find in the American past an adequate image for the future: they contend that if only we balanced our budgets, spanked our kids, worked hard and uncomplainingly, tore down all the teachers colleges—all would be well. And there are many others who find in the huge distance we still have to travel toward economic, and especially toward racial equality, enough challenge for their lifetimes—and in a sense it is enough. Likewise, the effort of the Communist bloc to overtake America has given still other Americans of both major parties the short-run aims of a coach whose all too confident team has lost a game—the feeling that with a little discipline and locker-room talk, along with better scouting and recruiting for scientists, all will be recouped. Perhaps the major benefit thus provided for Americans is the renewed conviction that there is a game and that winning it can give meaning to life. In my opinion none of these, not even the generous one of getting rid of the residues of inequality, is sufficient to mobilize social energies to take the next obscure steps in American life that would bring us a measure of international security and more adequate social goals for an age of plenty.

In this situation many of the most sensitive and truly disinterested young people have given up the larger societal goals to pursue what I might call the Utopianism of private life. It is in the family first of all, and beyond that in the circle of friends and neighbors, that one looks for Jeffersonian simplicity, an idyll of decency, generosity, and sensibility. Much of the confusion in current discussion is due to failure to distinguish between the high quality of these personal goals of young people and the low quality of our social aims. That is, if one is looking at the texture of individual life in America, this country is harboring, despite all surrounding miasmas, extraordinarily fine enclaves whose tone, though not ascetic, has something in common with the outlook of Utopian colonies in the last century, or with Hopi pueblos, or with the spirit of some of our great nineteenth-century dissidents, whether Melville or Whitman, William James or Bellamy. In many past epochs of cultural greatness the dichotomy between an avant-garde few and the brutalized many was taken for granted and would occasionally perpetuate itself for long periods. But in the United States today the contrast between the private Utopianism that I have spoken of and the general low level of vision in the general population and in its political activities seems to my mind both less tolerable and less viable for the long term. With the growth of interdependence within and between nations, private virtues, if they do not actually become public vices, become almost irrelevant—beautiful gardens at the mercy of fallout. I don't expect every young person to take part in the development of a more inclusive Utopia than "familism," but I would like to see a better proportion achieved between private and public visions; indeed, I believe that private life would be enriched and in a way become more meaningful if the two spheres were both more forcefully cultivated.

When I spent a summer in the Soviet Union twenty-seven years ago, I met many eager young Communists who had enthusiastically junked all private aims in the communal enterprise of "building socialism." Amid a Philistine culture made desolate with slogans, they *were* building socialism in an all too literal sense, i.e., they were building dams, railroads, factories, and machine tractor stations and Communist Party apparatus. They brought to their work the zeal of pioneers and, as a blueprint for their own activities, the model of American industrial achievement. At the Stalingrad tractor plant, then barely beginning to produce, I saw fanatical young Stakhanovites (I guess the term "Stakhanovite" is unknown to many undergraduates today; that is a kind of Russian version of an Eagle Scout) working with tremendous zeal in the midst of a mass of sullen peasants, new to industry and by no means reconciled to its restrictions. I had gone over with a group of American students, some of whom found this spectacle in contrast to the America of the depression marvelously exhilarating. It was a battle with simple rules and clear goals, or so it seemed, and, in fact, the reports from Stalingrad in *Pravda* and *Izvestia* were couched in the language of battle—so many tractors had been turned out that week on the Stalingrad front, or there were that many defeats in the battle for electrification, and so on. I thought then, and I still think now, that the tasks confronting Americans are more exhilarating but also more problematical. It would be child's play for us to build the Turk-Sib Railway or the Dneprostroi Dam, although, as I shall indicate later, every child should have this opportunity. We have to make our own model of the future as we go, in a situation which is new historically.

Young children are somewhat less firm in their control of and by the given ways of seeing reality, and I want now to turn from the general and cross-cultural problem I have been discussing, of how one finds or how one fails to find a new vision, to the genetic one, that is, to see what forms of challenge can be expected in the different ages of man from childhood to maturity. Observers of children's play, such as Piaget and Erik Erikson, have commented on children's desire for mastery, the integrative quality of much play. The studies of these men lend some support to the belief that children at certain stages of development can be freer in their aesthetic sensibility and their formation of concepts than in earlier more literal, and later more conventional stages. Other students of childhood (notably Ernest Schachtel in his paper "On Memory and Childhood Amnesia") have noted the ability of great artists, such as Proust or Paul Klee, to recapture the codifications of childhood without going crazy: ability, that is, to retranslate the freedom and imagination of childhood into adult terms. Percival Goodman, an architect, and Paul Goodman, a novelist, have shown that kind of freedom and imagination in their neglected and out-of-print book *Communitas*, where they employ the traditions of Utopian thinking and the customs of other cultures to create several kinds of social and architectural designs for the future of America. In fact, they employ the model of children's play in much of their discussion. But I don't know any case where a researcher has systematically asked children before their teens to depict the sort of world they would like to live in, that they would find exhilarating, or invented a game which would call on their conceivable abilities for making cultural kaleidoscopes. (We have, of course, games which children play which simulate the adult world as it is, such as Monopoly, and *Mad* magazine recently suggested that children might also play other adult games, for instance, "alimony"—player who reaches Reno first wins—"draft dodger," and "make-out"—in which boy chases girl. Here once more the macabre is easier to evoke than the Utopian.)

Moving on now from children and adults, I want to mention one example of approaching Utopia through the techniques of social science—an example that, I fear, shows how little these techniques can contribute at present. I have in mind a recent study done at The University of Michigan for the Michigan Bell Telephone Company in which a group of articulate adults were invited to let their imaginations roam free, and to tell trained interviewers what sort of things they would like to see in the "world of tomorrow." Out of 126 interviews, mainly with well-educated respondents, there were, in fact, few suggestions which were at all visionary. Respondents want a machine which will bring them the morning newspaper from the doorstep. They want conveyor-belt highways and drive-in supermarkets and automatic car controls. They want a personal air-conditioning unit inside their clothes. (This reminded me of Aldous Huxley's novel *Antic Hay*.) Or they want a machine which will bring them any sight, sound, smell, or climate they choose without having to go out to find it. They want to be able to bring back fond memories at will, and to erase annoyances at will. One wants a device to look a doctor over without going to his office, another a device to make it easy to complain to a supercilious sales person, or another a gadget to allow one safely and anonymously to bawl out somebody. One wistfully asks, and here is one of the few quasi-political suggestions, for some means of making suggestions to the legislative government (that's his term) and still another says, "I want to be able to visit relatives and friends without missing church." One wants "more variety in my daily living—a surprise every day."

If such wishes can be called Utopian at all, they are once more very private; they are seldom connected with any plan for the development of the individual's powers, let alone any plan for society more extensive than that of the person who wanted whole cities covered with plastic to keep out the weather. Many of the suggestions represent what I have sometimes called the cult of effortlessness. I speak of it as a cult, for I don't believe that most Americans not presently overworked seek this nirvana with steady passion. But it is striking that in the interviews, and perhaps reflecting their relaxed form, no one seems to wish for obstacles, for challenges, for things that take time and require effort.

Children assuredly are seldom like that unless they are sick: they are often a problem for parents and other adults, and for people who have to enforce parental rules too, because they have energy to burn. To some extent, children fall back on the nearly universal culture of games, for which they need only modest equipment and a modest tradition which they fondly elaborate. Last December at the American anthropological meetings I saw films from New Guinea showing children at play—they kicked balls, climbed trees, imitated adult ceremonies, including a complete funeral with a dead chicken as corpse. They also slid down mountains on homemade sleds, not on snow (this was in the tropics) but on sand or grass. And as I watched them I recalled my experience when I lived a few years ago in Kansas City. My home was near a park where gangs of young people from well-to-do homes would gather in their parents' cars at night in search of, as it seemed to me, non-existent mountains. With much screeching of voices and brakes, they would tear around in their parents' Buicks and Oldsmobiles at 80 miles an hour. I don't know how many of you recall the movie *Rebel without a Cause*, in which comfortable California teenagers sought even more desperate challenge than driving, as if they had to initiate each other in the absence of more formal initiation rites. What is left in such children of the Utopian impulse is soured and is only negative; all that is open for them is the road ahead. Such young people hang suspended between the traditional games of children and those which war and work and some new and some old kinds of play provide for adults.

It is hard to imagine a culture like ours suddenly turning every adolescent into an artist who finds challenge in creative exploration, although some hot-rodders seem to me to be sculptors in metal and inventors as well, whose cars of tomorrow have sometimes been imitated by Detroit. Considering the emphasis currently put on sports, it is surprising how small is the proportion of high school students who actively engage in them; there are, I would surmise, as many dropouts from the athletic program as from the academic one. The community and the coaches alike interest themselves for the most part in the valuable players of team sports and only a few high schools have adequate teaching and equipment outside the squads for the major sports. The Y and the Boy Scouts do ancillary and often important work, but often the slow and awkward boys have little encouragement, and the girls none at all. At the wheel of a car, however, as we all know, many boys and many people who are perennially boys seek to make up for deficiencies in other sports as well as for lack of challenge in other areas of life.

No doubt extremely inventive children could find other alternatives, but when I was in Kansas City I kept thinking that it made a difference that there were no nearby mountains where these young people could go skiing or climbing and fulfill in that way the desire of young people to test and extend themselves, the recurrent romanticism and individualistic Utopianism of the young. I am quite sure that if mountains were plunked down near Kansas City, many of these high school youngsters would go there to ski and climb. Of course they would not have invented the idea, but the mountain would still create its own demands on them once the idea existed. We all of us know young people who look as if under ordinary conditions they couldn't walk a step if they could drive for a block, yet go to Aspen or Wisconsin or Vermont on weekends and spend a day or two in often bitter cold weather schussing down mountains. It seems to me that as a social policy for full employment the country might build other things than armaments and superhighways and might move mountains to Kansas City for the youth of that city and other such cities to tackle.

Moreover, I believe that building the mountains, and the ski trails and firebreaks to go with them, would provide another challenge for these young people. Many parents today try to discipline and harden and teach discipline to their children with chores or paper routes, but in our society the young, always sensitive in such matters, are quick to realize that the work they are asked to do is after all not really necessary but could be done with machines. The experience the psychoanalyst Allen Wheelis describes so movingly in his book *The Quest for*

Identity of being forced by his father in the South to cut the grass with a razor blade all one summer as an exercise for the will—such an occurrence seems impossible today. Yet the testing that parents and adults no longer provide, the children still seek; it cannot be provided institutionally. That is, can we think of any organized way of locating snowy mountains needing to be cleared as well as skied down, any way of connecting the young person with others in the way that the age grades of a primitive tribe connect him and get him to go through initiation rites together? Such a rite tells the young person, "Now you're a man, no question about it"; and may require in addition that the young person bring back, not an impersonal paycheck or a piece of consumer goods equipment, but a personal totem and even a personal vision or a command for the whole tribe. Compulsory military service seems to me the closest thing for some young people in wartime, and even during peace. But save for a brief spell of basic training, compulsory military service seems to me to be training in nonwork and more or less impatient time killing. Although some privileged young men do enter the Army with the thought of experiencing a common democratic fate, the military situation today is so fantastical that most recruits don't enter service, thank goodness, with any zeal or any spirit save resignation, or at best the hope for some relevant training. Moreover, the avoiding of service raises moral dilemmas just as service itself does. For the privileged who are studying physics or clinical psychology or something else of presumptive usefulness, there must always be the question whether their motives for choosing this career are contaminated by draft dodging, just as they may feel they married the girl for the same reason. Is there any meaningful as well as moral equivalent for basic training which could be applicable to all and to women as well as to men?

One partial answer has received insufficient attention, partly because it was blotted out by World War II and the ensuing full employment, and partly because we are careless of small social experiments although not of small scientific ones: I am referring to a variation of the CCC Camps. (I wonder how many in this audience know what they were? "CCC" stands for Civilian Conservation Corps, and if you do not know this, it is a sign of the enormous gap that separates postwar from prewar America.) The CCC was one of the many improvised relief measures, like the WPA, but its aim was conservation of lands and forests—and, as a by-product, people. Young men out of work and in need could enlist and go to camp in the country where they would clear trails, install soil conservation ponds, build firebreaks, and so on.

Many privileged young people have a desire for this kind of experience, as manifested in Quaker work camps, at Antioch, and in other ways. And there was founded in Vermont during this period a variation, for such boys, of the CCC camp, called Camp William James. Its founders were Dorothy Thompson, Eugen Rosenstock-Huessy, a Dartmouth philosopher, and a few other people who felt that the CCC experience should not be limited to the desperately poor. It attracted Dartmouth students and Bennington girls and others whose needs were psychological rather than alimentary. Camp William James was an appropriate name, for James was passionately concerned with the moral tone of the elite who were his students at Harvard and eager to find in the moral life forms of discipline other than the juvenile hunting of men and beasts he despised in Theodore Roosevelt and would have distrusted in Hemingway. I never had the good fortune to attend Camp William James, but I have known a number of people whose lives have been deeply affected by their experience there. Some of these people today look back on that experience as a naïve and nostalgic venture, a ruralistic oasis for a Mary McCarthy to satirize; they recount how ridiculous they were as amateur trail clearers or well-intentioned emissaries to unenlightened Vermont villagers. Indeed the fear to be thought naïve today, or a do-gooder, has been in many ways as corrupting as fears in an earlier day to be thought evil-minded or agnostic—correspondingly, I know it is far harder to interest college students in a work program than it is to interest high school students, and it is harder to interest high school students than eighth graders. But my point here is not to denounce the skepticism of the young today, which has many positive aspects, but rather to indicate how hard it makes their task of finding challenge in the work of conservation and, in general, in fighting for and against nature.

One enormous advantage of a period of some sort of compulsory service, foreseen by Bellamy, beyond the advantage to the young people of having their energies made use of rather than dissipated, lies in the possibility of justifying through this service future periods of voluntary paid unemployment. Most of us, once out of college, never have another chance for a moratorium during which we can reflect on our course and perhaps reshape it, getting such additional training as may be requisite. (And incidentally, as colleges get better and harder to get into, they become less of a moratorium, too, and courses interfere with one's education.) I'm thinking not only of the millions of young people who are trapped in their careers, and of the older people, too, who cannot afford the risks of change, including many housewives with children, who are captives of their spouses. I am thinking also of the many people who would welcome a change from their particular specialty (a change which I have myself enjoyed). The only way in which, for instance, many academic people, many doctors, many engineers can change jobs at present is to become administrators. They are seldom able to switch to an entirely different specialty which requires extensive preparation. But if such people had in their youth contributed to a kind of social insurance fund, they would then be both morally and financially free to live for an equivalent period on the labor of others and have this period in which to retrain themselves for some other activity. Possibly if they would loaf for a time they might purge themselves of the dream of effortlessness; at any rate, they could try another form of life without undue hazard for themselves or their families.

Perhaps you will see what I am getting at here—namely, that each particular stage of life requires its own particular forms of tradition and change, challenge and surcease. In the dialectic between specialization and wholeness, people should be encouraged not so much to change jobs, which Americans do all the time, as to change the very forms of work. In the last great war, that is, in World War II, an extraordinary number of Americans discovered gifts that they had for all sorts of activities they would never have dreamed of or only have dreamed of. And many returned dissatisfied with old occupations and prepared to risk entering new ones. Here the G.I. Bill is a model that I am looking for—it justified retraining at public expense for millions of men who had been introduced during the war to new experiences and opportunities which they would never have thought they were capable of. What I am seeking, in other words, is the basis for a G.I. Bill for everyone—women as well as men—not as a handout but as a right earned through arduous service as youngsters.

Let me refer in this connection to those management training programs in which men are taken out of middle management positions and sent for a period to a university, not to study techniques or a specialty, but to obtain a liberal education. I visited some years ago the most exemplary of such programs, that of the Bell Telephone Company at the University of Pennsylvania, where there were a number of men, some twenty in all, there for a year in one of the most uncompromisingly humanistic programs one could find in any liberal arts college. Many of the men there had not been to college, or worse, had been to engineering school, that is, a narrow-minded engineering school. They were suddenly faced with a program equivalent to two or three years of the most avant-garde intellectual fare—plunged into reading Joyce, hearing Bartok and Hindemith, studying cultural anthropology and reading Lewis Mumford. It amazed them, as well as their teachers, that they could in the majority of cases rise to the challenge, rise to the point of discovering capacities in themselves they had no idea of. Like college students, or like some college students, they would stay up most of the night reading and discussing an assigned book and plaguing themselves with its obscurities. No group I have ever talked to was more alive and responsive than these men.

If we examine these instances, we see some of the problems of creating challenge when the natural environment no longer forces us to struggle. In the first place, there is a group, there is support for the work and for the temporary miseries and agonies found in the work. It asks too much of people today, I think, to expect them to find these challenges alone. In the second place, there is an assignment—a norm is set by the group. The norm is set outside oneself, so that one is not running alone around an unmeasured track to an unknown destination. In the third place, there are models provided in the books themselves and in the mentors who are lecturing or coming to the group from the outside. All these things are concessions to human frailty. Most of us have to make a game of work, to set deadlines for ourselves, to put ourselves into situations, as a skier does, from which it will take exertion and skill to get through and extricate ourselves. Indeed, many of the important choices in life are those we make to create conditions in which we develop under something like forced draft, and for many of you I imagine that the choice of college was such a choice. In fact, college provides at its best the closest thing we have to an initiation, one in which the cultural heritage is not so much stamped onto the bodies of the young (although I understand that that has not too recently left Kenyon!) as transmitted to their minds and senses. Of course, it happens in high school, too, but there is no definite date for the initiation when we begin to accept responsibility for making the culture a part of ourselves. Some of us, of course, accept more of the culture than others. This, unlike my notion of Camp William James, is a more selective service which is at once obligatory and an opportunity.

In this connection I would like to mention a notion which I once discussed with a group at Antioch—that students during some part of their college life be locked up in the library alone with books, adequate food and drink, for a week at a time. Though I think some of you might go stir crazy in the absence of audio-visual aids and chatter and study dates, still I would like to see the experiment tried. For I regard the arts as capable of providing many of us with tasks more than sufficient to challenge us, even were our industry and farming and commerce to become more nearly automatic. In the library, and in the whole experience of becoming part of the process of cultural transmission, one discovers one's own mountain, one's magic mountain, which creates as one climbs it. In this perspective we can view a curriculum, whether of the traditional studies or of the less usual ones, as a series of mountains set down in Chicago, Kansas City, Columbus or anywhere else by the work and imagination of earlier generations as well as the present one.

If books were the only such vehicle, many young people would, of course, be entirely excluded—either because of lack of native talent for literacy or, more usually, because the reading of books somehow got involved with struggles against parents or other adult figures. The same is true of the language of numbers—not because there is anything inherently difficult about it, because learning arithmetic or algebra has somehow got involved with wishes to be taken care of by others or to make life hard for others or for oneself in all sorts of complex ways, or for girls to define their femininity, as by letting men read the timetable for them. The learning of music also may have its blockages, but it is usually outside the formal curriculum and often thus provides a second challenge for some young people, one increasingly made use of in our own day with the immense growth of group singing and playing. As with the authors of books, so with the composers of musical scores, though they may have been dead 200 or 300 years, their spirit is kept alive, their imagination, their sense for form, by being bred into the fingers and bones and voices of the young amateur. Of course, as I have already implied, there are children who are forced, let us say, to practice piano and they respond by learning-blocks. But there is a difference between those subjects one has to learn and the arts one generally learns out of inclination. Thus while any subject, any discipline, can become an arena for struggle between adults and children, the arts are relatively free, as compared with the academic program, of the kind of misplaced parental vanity which wants the child to do well.

I realize fully that the better and more exciting graduate and professional training becomes, the greater the demands put on later life to live up to expectations. A first-rate college often seeks to make us dissatisfied with what we do later. What I am driving at here is that provided each stage of life offers challenge and as we therefore grow to meet the challenge, we demand challenge in the next stage. I've heard good prep schools criticized because colleges aren't as good as the best prep schools, and now I am saying that colleges are sometimes criticized as breeding discontented intellectuals who are too good for this world, whether "this world" is the graduate school to which they go on or a career in business or the professions. But I would be much happier if more colleges put more of this kind of pressure on later life to live up to college; that is, if more people got out of college who insisted that the world live up to the expectations created by college. I think one reason such insistence is muted is that people, once in a job and in a marriage, have no financial leeway to make a radical break and therefore the criticisms they might otherwise make simply don't occur to them; and this again goes back to my thought that if one had a period of compulsory service doing such work as building mountains, one could then later in life have a claim on society on the basis of that service. Now, actually, our society is rich enough so that we don't need that basis, we don't need it, that is, economically although we do need it psychologically or politically. Today, if people find their job undemanding, their temptation is not to seek for a demanding job or to struggle politically for a world in which jobs are more demanding and more interesting and in which industry and the professions do less in the way of stockpiling talent than they now do. Rather I think people flee into what I have called the Utopianism of private life, of domesticity. The trouble with this is that it puts too much of a burden on domesticity, because if one wants to live at the height of the times in work, one has to in leisure and vice versa.

To return to the beginning, it comes as a surprise to Americans that when we are faced with plenty we still find problems no less grave. It still takes nine months to produce a baby; it still takes time to develop anything worthwhile, whether this be a painting or a friendship or a talent or an interest. Walt Whitman wrote: "It is provided in the essence of things that from any fruition of success, no matter what, shall come forth something to make a greater struggle necessary."

REFERENCES

Conant, James Bryant. *Slums and Suburbs*. New York: McGraw-Hill Book Company, Inc., 1961.

Cook, Lloyd. *School Problems in Human Relations*. New York: McGraw-Hill Book Company, Inc., 1957.

Cuber, John F., and William F. Kenke. *Social Stratification in the United States*. New York: Appleton-Century-Crofts, 1954.

Davis, Allison. *Social Class Influences Upon Learning*. Cambridge, Mass.: Harvard University Press, 1948.

Drake, St. Clair, and Horace R. Clayton. *Black Metropolis*. New York: Harcourt, Brace & World, Inc., 1945.

Gallagher, Buell G. "The Pathological Impact of Caste." *Social Foundations of Education*. William O. Stanley, B. Othane and Smith, eds., New York, Holt, Rinehart, and Winston, Inc., 1956, pp. 173–180.

Grambs, Jean D. *Education in a Transition Community*. New York: National Conference of Christians and Jews, 1955.

Lund, S. E. Torsten. *The School-Centered Community*. New York: Anti-Defamation League, 1949.

New York City Board of Education. *The Puerto Rican Study 1953–1957*. New York: Board of Education, 1958.

Passow, Harry. *Education in Depressed Urban Areas*. New York: Columbia University Press, 1962.

Quinn, J. A. *Urban Sociology*. New York: American Book Company, 1955.

Schreiber, Daniel. *The Higher Horizons Program: First Annual Progress Report*. 1959–1960. New York: Board of Education, 1961.

PERIODICALS

Berston, H. M. "School Dropout Problem." *Clearing House,* 35 (December 1960), 207–210.

Druding, Aleda. "Stirrings in the Big Cities; Philadelphia." *NEA Journal,* 51 (February 1962), 48–51.

Education and the Disadvantaged American. Educational Policies Commission. Washington, D.C.: National Education Association, 1962.

Havighurst, Robert J. "Metropolitan Development and the Educational System." *School Review,* 69 (Autumn 1961), 251–267.

{Chapter Five}

THE TEACHER AND
THE URBAN SCHOOL

Urban society and its schools do not clearly define the role of
the teacher. In a pluralistic society undergoing rapid transition, the aims and purposes of education are sometimes confused and often in conflict. The continuity of a culture from
teacher to student breaks down in the transient urbanized
setting, and an effective curriculum cannot be based on a commonly shared past. In this setting, it is difficult to teach with
assurance and conviction. Today's teacher can never be sure
what is expected of her; she cannot even be sure she is
realizing her own expectations, because urban life rarely allows
her to interact with her students in any context other than the
classroom.

Current criticism leveled at the teacher is not only unjust,
it is misplaced. The present crisis in education cannot be
resolved in the classroom. Teachers need a clearly structured
field in which to operate, and they must be provided with
more realistic training and preparation for teaching effectively
in urban schools. The wide social and economic differences
that exist among urban communities have rendered general
teacher education inadequate. Training must become more

specialized, with preparation for a specific kind of community setting.

Some teacher institutes have recognized this need and are providing in-service training in inner-city schools. As the field of education becomes more specialized and complex, continuous in-service training will undoubtedly become an essential part of the teaching profession.

What values and aspects of our culture does a teacher transmit to her students? Our society no longer holds a common expectation of the American teacher, particularly the teacher who finds herself in a large loosely organized metropolitan district. In a cross-cultural analysis, Margaret Mead gives the often confused teacher a rare insight into herself, her culture, and her own particular value system.

THE SCHOOL IN AMERICAN CULTURE /
Margaret Mead

If we turn from images to look formally at the history of American education, of its theory and its practice, the conflict between the school oriented toward the past and the school oriented toward the future, with the seldom obtainable dream of a school which would hold the world steady, will be found to be a prevailing theme. This theme is expressed in many forms: in the struggle between the classics and modern languages, in the struggle between "at least one foreign language" and none at all; in the struggle between academic studies and vocational preparation; in the arguments about required courses versus electives, in which shared conformity to a common past is opposed to selectivity which is a preparation for an unshared future.

Before I go on to discuss the part which this threefold picture of the school has played and is playing in American educational theory and practice, I should like to turn for a moment to the contrasts and comparisons provided by primitive societies on the relationships between the generations. Primitive societies are our models for slowly changing homogenous societies in which the children's lives faithfully repeat,

Reprinted with the permission of the publishers from Margaret Mead, The School in American Culture. Cambridge, Mass.: Harvard University Press. Copyright 1951 by the President and Fellows of Harvard College.

gesture for gesture, and experience by experience, the lives of their parents and grandparents. Through the investigation of such slowly changing societies, we can form a picture of type relationships between the old generation and the new, against which such relationships, when they occur in an age of rapid change like our own, take on additional meaning. In these slowly changing primitive societies we find great variation as to which age group inducts the young child into his society; the baby may spend most of its time with its mother or father, or in the arms of an older sister or brother, or by the side of a grandmother or grandfather. Each is a possible way to learn the intricate, beautiful patterned way of perceiving the world and acting within that set of perceptions which a culture offers each child born within it.

But if we examine in detail some of the implications of the parent-child, sibling-child, and grandparent-child rearing situations, we find certain systematic differences. Those societies in which young children are reared by grandparents—of which certain North American Plains Indian tribes are typical—have an enormous degree of conservatism. The culture survives, even as the buffalo disappear; the land is taken away by the advancing white peoples, and the tepee is displaced by the shack. Still the language, the way of thought, of the past endures. This conservatism, this cherishing clinging to the old, can be related to the role which the grandparent played in the lives of Indian children, to the way in which the child, even as it struggled and wriggled in an ecstasy of beginning movement, apprehended in the tonus of the grandparental arms the sort of pact which its lively little body would someday make with death. As old hands and old voices, speaking with the gentleness and resignation of a people who saw human lives as like grass which grew up in the morning and at night was mown down, informed the child of the way that men and animals, the sun and the moon and the stars, seeking and power, vision and practicality, life and death were to be viewed, so the child was able to incorporate in early childhood all that his culture had to offer him. In such a rounded understanding, nothing was left unexplained, uncontemplated, which later would challenge or threaten. And the Indian has remained as one of our chief examples of the tenacity of a people who, robbed of every condition of their lives, still clung to the form, to the pattern, meeting night after night to gamble for buffalo nickels where once the stake was a war horse.

At the opposite extreme, we find the cultures in which it is the child nurse—the elder sister or less frequently the elder brother—who carries the younger child about on a hip almost too slight to bear the burden. Instead of the tremor of old age, there is the tenseness of the hands which can hardly lift, the hands which are almost unable to readjust the carrying sling, or shift the baby from one hip to another. These child nurses, far from having learned the nature of the whole life cycle from their old grandmothers, are just out of babyhood themselves, and were reared by other children. The child on the hip is not something infinitely young and remote, waiting at the end of memory, but the child whom one was yesterday, with all the fears and urgencies which have just been partially mastered in the self. These are the cultures in which the growing child is kept close to infancy, sometimes only by way of keeping a great awareness of the rhythms of its own body, so that later dancing and love-making will be equally easy and graceful, as in Samoa. Sometimes also the child is kept close to the images of infancy, so that the ritual resolutions of its early terrors are expressed in the theater by conflicts between witch and dragon, who re-enact on a stage the conflicts which the child experiences in its relationship to father and mother, as in Bali. Or the child nurse may help the child retain its passivity, in a world where every adult is egging it on to continuous unremitting displays of energy and anger, as among the Iatmul.

The child nurse may be seen not as the guardian and ally of any particular aspect of early childhood, but rather as a way in which the child's response within its culture is kept intact in spite of the pressures which will later fall upon the adolescent and the adult. From the child nurse there passes to the native child a kind of license to be itself, from one who has not yet departed far enough from that closeness to the experience of early childhood to be able to withdraw the license. And so we have a second model, the society in which the resources of early childhood, whether in directness of bodily expression or richness of phantastic elaboration or denial of the adult structuring of the world, are preserved for children, and therefore for adults also, because the child learns not from someone who has traversed the whole round of life, but from someone still very close to its beginning.

The third model, the model which echoes the little red schoolhouse image, is that in which children are reared not by grandparents who represent the whole traditional definition of life, or by children whose own eager little mouths have hardly left the breast, or by nurses whose own peasant standards of eating and drinking perpetuate the pleasures of the breast with a frank enjoyment which is banished from ballroom and audience chamber, but by parents, by people of early maturity, the present possessors and inheritors of the adult world. This is the typical middle-class position: a family economically well enough off so that the mother is not burdened down with field or farm duties— or overwhelmed with more children than she can feed and care for, in which the father is making his way, actively, in a world of change and commerce, a world of entrepreneurship and profit. In such a rapidly changing world, grandparents are likely to be out of date, behind the times, and also to a degree rejected, as it was they who reared the present parents, and reared them purposefully and deter- minedly to become responsible, time-bound, goal-oriented adults. In such a world also elder siblings are busy themselves learning to outstrip their parents. They have too much to do to be efficient baby tenders; they must learn the skills and arts which will be necessary for success. Furthermore, the middle-class parent will distrust the child nurse, as also the servant girl is distrusted. The child who is to be inducted into a world where life is real and life is earnest must be exposed from the beginning to the model parent, who must herself, and himself, punish and reward the growing child. This middle-class picture is not only true of our own American middle-class life, but also can be found in primitive societies like that of the Manus of the Admiralities, a tribe of stone-age fishermen. The Manus are efficient, profit-seeking, earnest, moral people, concerned to rear their children to follow the same pattern—not so much of life, as of goal seeking. And among the Manus the older children practice in play the arts of adult life, and the parents care for the children, who learn to think of adults as persons who are completely masters of their environment.

The child who is reared according to this third model—reared by parents who are at the height of their careers, far from childhood, and facing an old age about which they know little and expect little— grows up, far from its infant awareness of its body, far from the memory of the childhood fantasies which fed eagerly and hungrily on the very meagre set of symbols which such a culture possesses, but alert and ready to face a relatively new and uncharted world, in a thoroughly learned and thoroughly charted way. Close contact with the grandparent leaves little room for welcoming change or sailing strange seas. Close contact with child nurse or peasant nurse keeps the child so *en rapport* with its body and the arts and rituals whose meanings it is able to retain that it also will be, on the whole, uninterested in change and conquest. But parent-rearing produces a child who faces toward a partial future, who can conceive life as an unwritten chapter of a book that is unfinished.

But these three models which I have been discussing are models drawn from slowly changing homogeneous societies; I have been able to speak of a life in which those who rear were similarly reared, in which all the lullabies one sings to children are the lullabies one heard as a child. If such models are to be of any use in considering the problem of the teacher in the American school today, we must add to them from the actual situation in our own society, the condition of rapid change. We must add to them both the reflection in all adults, whether of the parent or of the grandparent generation, the changes through which they have passed, the fact that they were reared by parents whose hands were already fumbling before unfamiliar doors, or with hands which lay flaccid with despair in a world they had not dreamed of and could not cope with. We must picture the adult who has been reared in a dozen tones of voice, reprimanded, rewarded, cajoled, and teased and appeased according to half a hundred systems, who has learned to move about somehow, in a series of rooms in which the very arrangement of the furniture either diagrams the lack of harmony in the tastes which gradually assembled it or in its per- fection of harmony will give him a pattern which he is not likely to repeat. And to this picture of an adult who in personality is the expres- sion of the great heterogeneity and rapid changes in our current society, we must add the picture of children who differ from the children who came ten years before them, and differ also from the children who will follow them, as children reared on schedules are followed by children rocked to sleep, to be in turn succeeded by children reared according to some new one of the prescriptions through which a newly self-conscious society is attempting to meet newly realized needs. The condition in our society today is dramatized by the late-born child, whose mother finds that nothing that she learned ten years ago about how to treat children or of what to expect from them, can be applied to this newcomer, who seems even to have learned to cry with a new note in its voice, who will have to have different clothes, will display different tastes, and will weep for quite different reasons. Where, in slowly changing societies, the adults are confronted by children whom they know—for were they not such children themselves, just such children with the same fears, the same joys, the same bits of mischief and rebellion—the adults in the modern world face children who are not only unlike their own past childhood, but who are actually unlike any children who have ever been in the world before.

How then does the teacher—the teacher who may stand at the door of the academy, or its successor the academic high school, ready to induct these unknown children into the tradition of the past, and the teacher who stands at the door of the crowded slum school, ready to prepare her pupils to enter the future by leaving their past—how does this teacher fit into the changing world in which she is called upon to play so sensitive and significant a role?

We may consider for a moment the way in which the teacher can approximate to each of the three generation positions: the grandparent who has seen the whole of life, the parent who is living it day by day, and the child or nurse who is the custodian not of the child's future so much as of the child's immediate past.

The type teacher who comes closest to the grandparental role is the teacher of the classics, or the teacher who treats mathematics and science as if they were classics, fixed and immutable, as unchanged and unchanging as the figures on Keats' Grecian urn. The gifted teacher of the classics conveys to the child a sense of the roundedness and relatedness of life, of the way in which each period repeats in its own way an old story that has already been written in a more gracious and finished way in the past. Any budding desire to explore the new, to make new conquests, can be gently, benignly reduced to the expected, by a reference to Diogenes or to Alexander. As man has been, man will be; one can learn to write different but not better sonnets in a world which has dignity and form. The teacher in the academy was typically such a teacher laying the groundwork for an orderly acceptance of a world which, however different today's version seemed, was mercifully never new.

The teacher in the overcrowded city school—where there were too few seats and too few books in a room filled with strange smells from foreign eating habits and foreign sleeping habits—is closest to the parent model, as she struggles to get her pupils to face away from the past and toward the future. She teaches her pupils to acquire habits of hygiene and of industry, to apply themselves diligently to prepare to succeed, and to make the sacrifices necessary to success, to turn a deaf ear to the immediate impulse, to shatter any tradition which seems to block the path to the goal, but to shatter it in a way and with the sanctions of the entrepreneur. This teacher is closest to the model in which the parents rear the child to a kind of behavior rather than to fit within a tradition. When she imitates the teacher of the academy and teaches her pupils to learn memory gems, she will find she faces confusion, because she is teaching them the past of older Americans in order to give them a future, and this contains contradictions. How will these children born in hospitals, treated at clinics, who celebrate a holiday in the biggest movie theater, use such memory gems as "I remember, I remember the house where I was born," or "over the river and through the wood to grandfather's house we go; the horse knows the way to carry the sleigh through the white and drifting snow"? She will be happiest when she teaches modern history, with the next pages still to be written, in a "current events" class; or when she teaches science as a way of looking at life which is constantly changing, constantly discarding what has been the best hypothesis for a better one. She—like the middle-class parent—faces forward into a future that is only partially charted, and so she must furnish her children with a kind of behavior, a method of exploration, rather than with the parchment map, with its lines drawn in lovely fading colors, that is available to the teacher in the academy classroom.

The third model, the child nurse or the peasant nurse, the teacher whose task is to stay close to the young child's bodily impulses and exuberant imaginative attempts to take in the world around him, is a new type of teacher. She has come into being as one gifted thinker after another—Froebel, Montessori, Anna Freud—rebelled against the price which modern, urbanized, industrialized Europeans and Americans were paying for their new kind of civilization. From Germany, from Italy, from Vienna, from England, and from the United States there came a demand for some form of education which would fit the little child—a chair and table to fit his body, materials with which he could work out his groping attempts to relate inner and outer world, and teachers who would kneel beside him, give him a shoulder to cry on or a body which could be turned into a steed, who would be allies of his infancy, rather than surrogates either of the finished world of tradition or of the fluid world-in-the-making of the entrepreneur. First in the kindergarten, and later and much more articulately in the nursery school, we have developed an educational pattern which contains some of the values of the child nurse, or the peasant nurse, in which sensitive teachers, who must almost always be young because of the strenuous physical demands of working with little children who are permitted to move about freely, are taught how to ally themselves with the immediacies of the world of the little child.

But in all three parallels which I have drawn, parallels which, like all figures of speech, impose an extra degree of order and so distort the reality—for in the teaming schoolrooms of America we find all three types of teacher and every possible blend, in every sort of situation—I have still ignored the changing children and have spoken as if the children who face these different kinds of teaching were themselves all of the same stuff as the teachers from whom they learn. If the children to be taught were of the same stuff as the teachers, we would still have a problem in initially training teachers for any one or any combination of the roles which I have outlined. The teacher who is adequately to represent the order of the past, the dignity and beauty of tradition, must, in the course of her training come to terms with her own past. The Latin lines she wrote so unwillingly, the theorems in geometry which were resented, the parents and teachers who were responsible for making her learn her lessons, must all be re-examined, the rebellion exorcised or transformed, so that she can become the whole-hearted and resigned exponent of traditional learning.

The teacher who is to help a generation go away from and beyond their parents, who is to be forever exhorting her pupils to be up and doing, has a different task; she must relive her childhood and exchange the specificity of the demands which her parents and teacher made upon her for a new set of demands, which she will make, in the same tone of voice, upon her pupils. Where the teacher who represents the past and tradition must accept directly and finally both what she herself has been taught and those who stood for the past, the teacher who must urge her pupils to desert or surpass their parents has to abandon the matter but, in a way, keep the manner. She comes to terms during her training, if that training is to succeed, not with her own parents as they themselves were with all their weaknesses and strengths, but with the demands which parents and teachers in the abstract have a right and a duty to make on children. She must give up any overfaithful clinging to the particulars of her own past, if she is to face a roomful of children for whom it is her duty to wish a future very different from that which their own parents' lives offer them.

Congruently, the type teacher of our city and town schools today is a girl who is—in the words of the contemporary class analysis—mobile upward, moving from lower class to lower middle class, or from lower middle class to a better middle-class position. She is someone who must transcend her own past and so in a sense is the better prepared to help her pupils repudiate theirs and become mobile also. The type teacher of the academy or the academic subjects in a modern high school is, on the other hand, mobile downwards, clinging to a past she is in danger of losing, as a family that has fallen on hard days clings to the family portrait and the grandfather's clock.

The type nursery-school teacher is the girl from an upper middle-class background, who finds herself desperately out of sympathy with the verbal facility and concern with things rather than with people that seem to her a predominant characteristic of her world. Very often inarticulate and academically "slow," better able to communicate with a touch of the hand or the slant of a painted line than with words, she can become a nursery-school teacher only if she can come to sufficient terms with her own rebelliousness against adult standards—against, indeed, the whole adult world—so that while she acts as the little child's ally, she does not hold the child back. Very often the nursery-school teacher, and also the child therapist, is not a special kind of adult who has kept a closeness to his or her own childhood, which however is completely reorganized and made anew, but rather a young adult who is continuing to live out an unrealized childhood, and who, after a few years, wearies of the repetitive game and becomes a supervisor, or teaches teachers, or decides it is more rewarding to deal with adults than with children. The teacher who within the school fulfills one of these roles which have a formal relationship to the child-rearing practice of the grandparent, parent, or child-nurse patterns seems to be the more successful the less she is acting out some unresolved and overdetermined past, and the more she has reassimilated and revised her past to fit into the teaching role which she has chosen.

But what then, when the teacher, of whatever type, in whatever type of school, has come to terms with her own past, has clearly seen her own role and is well equipped and ready to carry it out, year after year, as one class succeeds another in her school room—what then, when she meets, year after year, different children? In a more slowly changing society, the good teacher, the *guru* of India, for instance, is typically old, wise, patient, grown mellow with teaching the young about whom he has learned more and more each year. When the pupils remain the same, the teacher has only to keep alive her capacity for lively observation and response, and each year will add to her wisdom, her understanding, and her gentleness. But the world that the modern teacher confronts is a world in which each year serves, not to reinforce and amplify what she is slowly learning about the nature of ten-year-old boys or ten-year-old girls, or about the differences between ten-year-old boys, and ten-year-old girls—constancies which will give her something firm on which to base her methods—but serves rather to disorient her. What seemed to be true as she observed the fifth grade five years ago is no longer true; the children's behavior becomes not more predictable—as it should as she grows more experienced—but less predictable. Ten years ago older teachers expressed their bewilderment and resentment at the circumstances that years of teaching were crowned not with wisdom and the gentleness that comes with wisdom, but with increasing ignorance and an accompanying shrillness of voice and manner; they complained that children hadn't any manners any more, were badly brought up and undisciplined, had no respect. A dozen other familiar complaints come readily to mind. Today, in 1950, the phrasing is altered and teachers now complain of the number of "disturbed children" who complicate their teaching problems. But the terms "lack of manners," "lack of respect," "unwillingness to work," which reflect the more moralistic tone of the past, or the words "disturbed children," which reflect the psychiatrically oriented thinking of the present, refer substantially to the same condition. If the words used today sound more frightening, perhaps it is because the teachers of today are even more appalled at the unpredictableness of their mysterious charges. For all these phrases are ways in which the teacher says that each year she understands her children, not more, as she might reasonably expect, but less. A kind of nightmare reversal has been introduced into life, like an escalator which insists on running backwards; age and experience become not orienting factors but disorienting ones, so that the teacher of twenty years' experience may face her class less confidently than the teacher with only two.

This is, of course, no more than the normal accompaniment of the fantastic rate of change of the world in which we live, where children of five have already incorporated into their everyday thinking ideas that most of the elders will never fully assimilate. Within the lifetime of ten-year-olds the world has entered a new age, and already, before they enter sixth grade, the atomic age has been followed by the age of the hydrogen bomb, differentiated from the atomic age in that many of those who failed to understand the dangers of the atom bomb are painfully beginning to take in the significance of the hydrogen bomb. Teachers who never heard a radio until they were grown up have to cope with children who have never known a world without television. Teachers who struggled in their childhood with a button-hook find it difficult to describe a buttonhook to a child bred up among zippers, to whom fastnesses are to be breached by zipping them open, rather than fumblingly feeling for mysterious buttons. From the most all-embracing world image to the smallest detail of daily life the world has changed at a rate which makes the five-year-old generations further apart than world generations or even scores of generations were in our recent past, than people separated by several centuries were in the remote past. The children whom we bear and rear and teach are not only unknown to us and unlike any children there have been in the world before, but also their degree of unlikeness itself alters from year to year.

Faced with this unwieldy circumstance that the modern teacher becomes not more but, in a sense, less fitted to teach the longer she teaches, we then, as a society, and particularly as those of our society professionally interested in education, have a problem to solve. How can we set up some pattern which will enable the teacher to grow through the years, instead of becoming stunted and distorted, affrighted by the increasing gap between herself and her pupils, which is not a gap of chronological age but a gap of difference in period? Once recognized and named, it should be possible to devise, not refresher courses, which provide the teacher in service with new ways of looking at subject matter, but orientation excursions that would enable the teacher continually to readjust her picture of the sequences which the children she teaches have gone through and will go through. This would mean that the fifth-grade teacher would have regular opportunities to visit the prenatal and postnatal clinic, the playgrounds and parks where mothers take care of infants, so as to revise her picture of what parents are expecting of children and how they are treating them. She would also spend time in day-care centers, nursery schools, and kindergartens, learning how the kind of child with which she had once been familiar has been replaced by a child with new skills, new expectations, and new problems, all of which will take new forms when those same children reach her in the fifth grade. And as she is given a chance to change her picture of her pupils' past, so also she needs an opportunity to change her picture of their future, to visit the seventh grade, to visit high school. The fifth-grade children who face her today are forming their picture of what high school will be like from the experience of their older brothers and sisters who are in high school *now*, not on the picture of high school which their teacher carries in her head, from her own high school days or her practice teaching. And the teacher will also be given a chance, a patterned practical way, to visit other parts of her pupils' lives— Sunday school and scout meetings, and children's chaperoned movie showings; she will be encouraged to watch the television and listen to the radio programs which interest her children this year.

All of this orientation will take time; it will have to be organized and rewarded. Some of it will have to take the place of much of the present in-service credit for any sort of miscellaneous learning. It cannot simply be visiting, but must instead be supervised and interpreted by those who know what is there to be seen, who can save time by proper preparation and emphasis. But just as surely as we have needed a teacher education which permitted the prospective teacher to spend several years learning to teach, learning about her own relationship to her past and to her future, to her parents and her teachers and her peers, and to children and adolescents, so now we need a form of in-service training which will permit the teacher to keep abreast of a changing world, to be what she has every right to expect to be— a better, not a worse, teacher with the years.

This may seem radical and difficult enough, this demand for what amounts to a whole new institution of in-service training, an institution which consciously and delicately corrects for the extraordinary rate of change of the world in which we live—and yet, even this picture which I have drawn so far is, in a sense, a picture which is already almost out of date. For I have made it apply to a teacher who would in her single person reach some sort of synthesis of the three models which I have sketched, who would combine respect and love for the traditional with a willingness to open new doors and send children forth on uncharted seas, while preserving in them part of that closeness to themselves and to their imaginations characteristic of early childhood. Such a teacher, if she had the additional opportunity to keep herself eternally abreast of a changing world, with the latest song on her lips and the latest and most amazing scientific discovery to wonder about, could in a way re-create the nostalgic image of the teacher in the little red schoolhouse.

But to have such an art we need to keep alive a type of awareness which it was once enough to cherish in childhood, so that the gifted artist and philosopher might use this access later, as he built new symbols for his generation. We must devise ways not of cherishing awareness of the self a little longer, which is all that the current nursery school really tries to do and which is all that the child nurse and the peasant nurse did, but instead ways of making that early awareness a continuing part of the personality into adulthood and old age. We need, in fact, to do for many men what accidents of gift and history made possible in the occasional great geniuses of the past.

And finally, and perhaps most difficult of all, we need from the teacher who has relied on teaching how a tried method can be used on new material, a totally new kind of teaching—a teaching of a readiness to use *unknown* ways to solve unknown problems. We are facing a world which this adult generation is unable to grasp, to manage, to plan for. The most we may reasonably hope for is that somehow the old unsuitable methods will get us through until another generation is able to tackle the job. But throughout history, each generation has stood on the shoulders of the past, each new learning has come from an old learning, if only by way of contradiction and explicit rejection. How are we who do not know what to do, who do not know how to live in one world, who have no faintest trace of habituated capacity to operate in a world which may actually destroy itself, who do not know how to carry in our hearts the weight of those who died yesterday in Burma or who may die tomorrow in Prague, or how to cope with the spectacle of machines which can do problems which the men who design the machines could not do— how shall we, who are so unfit, prepare a generation which will begin to be fit to face the new problems which confront mankind? At first sight, it seems a hopeless dilemma, for men can teach only what they know. And yet it need not be, because what we need to teach is a technique which can perhaps be well communicated if we ourselves fully realize our own position. We need to teach our students how to think, when you don't know what method to use, about a problem which is not yet formulated. And is not that in a nutshell our actual position? So if we, who live now, can fully realize and incorporate into our every teaching word and gesture our parlous state, we will, as we transmit it to our pupils and students give them just the freedom, just the sense of an unguessed-at process which nevertheless *must be found*, which if they incorporate it, should equip them as no generation has ever been equipped to make the new inventions which are necessary for a new world.

The changing urban culture has altered the class structure of the faculty. In recent studies it has been shown that urban teachers are no longer predominantly middle class. One might conclude from this that the "middle-class bias" is disappearing. Robert Doherty's article deals with attitudes of teachers toward organized labor; but especially salient to education are the underlying reasons given for such attitudes. Self-conscious in newly gained status, the upwardly mobile teachers of urban schools may not feel free to move into the marginal streams of their changing society where many resolutions of educational crises are to be found.

ATTITUDES TOWARD LABOR / *Robert E. Doherty*

Organized labor for a long time has smarted under the treatment it has received in the public schools. History textbooks, labor spokesmen complain, emphasize the violent role played by American workers and eschew the more positive part that labor has played in the nation's progress toward social and economic democracy. School boards, composed mainly of representatives of the professions and the business community, select administrators who safeguard professional and business interests in implementing educational policy. Teachers, drawn primarily from the middle class, reflect, if not impose, their class biases when dealing with the labor movement or current problems of industrial relations.

There are signs, however, that in the future labor will find considerably less reason to complain. Textbook publishers, as sensitive to market demands as any producers of consumer goods, have eliminated much of the anti-labor bias. In recent years unions have succeeded in placing members on school boards, and they no doubt modify the influence of professional and business members in shaping educational policy.

But more important is a change in the social and economic backgrounds of beginning teachers. Traditionally the domain of middle-class offspring, teaching is being plenished by sons and daughters of blue-collar workers. The demand for teachers and the relative financial ease of securing a teacher education suggests that even more working-class children will avail themselves of teacher education.

However, there is some evidence that an increase in the number of worker's offspring in the teaching profession may hinder rather than help labor's cause.

In 1960, a labor-management attitude scale was administered to 150 students majoring in the teaching of social studies at a New York

Robert E. Doherty, *"Attitudes toward Labor,"* The Education Digest *(October 1963), as reprinted from* The School Review *(Spring 1963), pp. 4–7. Copyright © 1963 by The University of Chicago Press.*

State college of education. The results revealed that students whose fathers were union members as well as blue-collar workers shared a strong anti-labor bias with students from farm and white-collar backgrounds. Further, the responses that union members' children made to most statements on the scale showed that they felt an even greater degree of hostility toward trade unionism than did their farm and white-collar counterparts.

An identical scale administered to students who were not majoring in the social studies showed that anti-labor hostility was, for the most part, more pronounced among these groups than among the social-studies majors. Only students majoring in the teaching of English showed a less unfriendly attitude toward labor than the social-studies group.

What is crucial to labor, however, is not the attitude of those who have little opportunity to deal with industrial relations, but the attitude of social-studies teachers. It is in their courses that organized labor receives the most attention. How thoroughly the subject is treated and how objectively it is handled depend in no small part on the biases of the teacher. The views these teachers bring into the classroom, whether they impart them deliberately or unconsciously, have some effect on the perspectives of their students. It would be ironic if labor unions were to find that the teachers most antagonistic to them were the very teachers that their members had nurtured as children. Yet results suggest that this might be true.

Why do the sons and daughters of union members appear to be more antagonistic to labor unions than students whose parents have no trade-union connections? The overwhelmingly negative response to two propositions in the survey provides us with some clues.

CLUES TO ANTAGONISM

The proposition that "Organized labor has retained its idealism and continues to instill a feeling of elan among its members," for example, found only 4 percent of the "labor" students in even slight agreement; 38 percent disagreed slightly, and 58 percent disagreed completely. Students with farm and white-collar backgrounds also rejected the notion, but at the same time indicated far less cynicism; 7 percent agreed completely, 25 percent agreed slightly, 26 percent disagreed slightly, and 42 percent disagreed completely.

The highly negative attitude on the part of blue-collar students suggests that the students who had the most intimate knowledge of labor organizations were convinced that whatever idealism may have once characterized the trade-union movement had now declined in significance. If the blue-collar fathers were motivated by a high sense of elan, they had not conveyed it to their children. The response also suggests that the image of trade unionism that rank-and-file members carry to their families is that of a highly institutionalized bureaucracy.

Moreover, there can be a vast difference between the attitudes of a union member and a "union man," just as there can be a great difference between a "company man" and an individual who finds himself working for a particular company. A union worker may resent the president of his local as much as he resents his foreman or his supervisor. Unless there are periodic crises, such as strikes or lock outs, the tendency is for workers to become estranged from their unions. When children of union members do hear about their father's union, it is quite often in disparaging terms.

Even more suggestive of the reasons behind the anti-unionism of "union" students, however, is the response to the statement "Affiliating with a teachers' union would be one of the most effective ways for a teacher to improve his professional and economic status."

White-collar and farm students showed little inclination to join the American Federation of Teachers (3 percent agreed slightly, 71 percent disagreed slightly, and 26 percent disagreed completely). In contrast, 22 percent of the students with union backgrounds disagreed slightly, and 78 percent disagreed completely. No "union" student gave any indication that he would like to join his father in the ranks of organized labor.

PROBABLE EXPLANATION

This response probably brings us as close as we can come to an explanation of the antipathy that students with union backgrounds have registered toward trade unions. It has become a commonplace to many Americans that as a nation we have been gripped by a status panic. Certainly the strong status aspirations of these working-class children played a large part in motivating them to study to become teachers. For many students, then, teaching is not a way of life. Rather it serves as an entree to a way of life. It provides the means by which they can surround themselves with all the paraphernalia of middle-class respectability.

A blue-collar student's dreams about the future are not confined to the professional role he hopes to play. He also dreams of an attractive home in a nice neighborhood, membership in the country club, smartly cut suits, the camaraderie of professional and business men, and perhaps, an invitation to join Rotary. He dreams of the things that the mass media and the college milieu have taught him to admire, the very things denied him as long as he remains in the working class. For a blue-collar student, a teacher's fringe benefits must appear to be limitless. In college he is learning to make a psychological adjustment to a new style of life. And in this sleek new world, he believes, people do not take kindly to labor unions.

The old style of life, of course, is the antithesis of the new. It is a world of greasy overalls, of ungrammatical English, and of calendar art. And among all these ingredients of the working-class syndrome is the union. The union is not bad in and of itself, but it is a part of the social accouterment, and it, too, must be sloughed off if there is going to be an easy accommodation to the middle-class style.

It is curious that this sloughing-off begins at this particular time in this particular place. While blue-collar students preparing to become teachers are making firm commitments to the middle class, their younger brothers, still in high school, are strongly pro-labor; and low-income students attending leading universities are considerably more pro-labor than fellow students from the better income groups.

Admittedly, a survey on the attitudes of a handful of students does not anticipate major social trends, either in the selection or the education of teachers, or in industrial and labor relations. But there may be enough evidence to indicate to those responsible for the education of teachers that they should do some serious thinking about the value system under which many of their students operate. Union leaders might ponder the reasons why at least some of those whom they had most depended on to brighten the image of labor are turning out to be the least dependable.

Unless one has had experience in the inner-city school, it is difficult to appreciate the demands made upon a teacher in this setting. Many teachers find most of their energies expended in maintaining order and are inclined to become cynical. Much human resource is left untapped in such a school—not only the resources that remain locked away for-

ever in the child but also those in the teacher who never
realizes himself as an educator. Bertrand Sandweiss accurately
describes the various ways in which teachers capitulate to
conditions in the "custodial" school.

THE TEACHER ADAPTS TO THE CUSTODIAL
SCHOOL / *Bertrand Sandweiss*

A perceptive observer of public education can sense, within the central core of our great cities, the cynical resignation to defeat that grips a substantial part of our teaching force.

The teacher finds that his students are not what he expected. The "bell shaped" distribution curve of student ability, interest and achievement, so neatly diagrammed in his textbooks, is somehow not valid. He sees almost universal low achievement, poverty, instability, violence, and immorality. The impulses conducive to school success— the desire to pursue knowledge as a means toward a better life, the identification with American idealism, morality, civic responsibility and patriotism, are somehow absent from the motivational complex of his students. Well, he had heard about problem schools and low achievers and maybe he had just had the misfortune of being placed in such a situation. But from conversation with the old-timers he learns that his school is somewhat representative of the greater part of the city, and that only in the peripheral areas of the city can one really "teach."

There are several adjustments that our new teacher can make. If by inclination he has always thought of his role as teacher in terms of the subject matter in which he has a vital interest, and by temperament is somewhat inflexible, he (1) begins his quest for the "Holy Grail" by a series of transfers from school to school, (2) projects the difficulty upon school administration's standards and promotion policy (How can you pass them if they don't know anything?) or (3) cynically compromises with the situation, "If I can't teach them, I'll join them. All I have to do is keep school. I'll maintain order in the classroom, go through the motions of teaching, keep myself in good standing with my superiors. Even though I know that I am not

Bertrand Sandweiss, "The Teacher Adapts to the Custodial School," in
Educational Issues in a Changing Society. *A. Kerber and W. Smith, eds.
Detroit: Wayne State University Press, 1962, pp. 159–162. Reprinted with
the permission of the author.*

performing any great service, I'll join the mock heroics *they* call education."

Our second novice has a different perspective. His training and experiences are broad enough for him to sense that education is more than subject matter and keeping school. He has absorbed enough psychology and sociology to help him adjust to this difficult situation. He is familiar with educational platitudes of "individual difference," "start from where they are," "a mental health approach." He quickly learns that teaching is part social work, guidance, parenthood, instruction, policing, moral training, public health, etc.

He accepts it and *really* wants to do a good job. He looks for help and examines the resources at his disposal. He finds an overcrowded classroom, a traditional, rigid curriculum, unsuitable instructional material, an apathetic group of colleagues, and a lack of special education facilities. He looks to his past training for guidance and finds, almost universally, that the literature dealing with the low-achiever is based upon the assumption that this student is placed in a class in which he is confronted by a host of average and above-average students, classes in which he is a potent, but, nevertheless, a minority force. He searches for studies dealing with classes in which the slow learner represents the bulk, and even the entirety of the class, and the only things that he finds are written in the context of special education, i.e., the mentally retarded, ungraded classes, etc. (Interestingly, in doing the research for this paper, this writer found that the designation used in the *Educational Periodical Index* for the kind of student being studied in this paper is "Children-Backwards.")

Soon he asks himself: "Wherein lies the motivational uniqueness of the class composed almost exclusively of slow learners?" If peer acceptance is as important as he thinks it is, he is confronted with a group of students quite satisfied that, in this particular situation, they fit in very nicely. Class achievement is low, but its lowness is not appreciated by the students, they are unaware of any pressure from the group to do better.

The only one who is not satisfied is the teacher. Using the traditional tools and techniques, he fights a losing battle. He struggles to put across a concept, an attitude, and finds the next day that he has accomplished nothing. Repeated enough times, the experience affects the teacher. He, too, accepts the situation, and decides that the pupils are uneducable. The day by day traumatic intrusions of lower-class life upon his own sense of order take their emotional toll. In the absence of even periodic satisfactions to take him over the rough moments, our teacher builds his own emotional defenses: rejection of the children, rejection of his own teaching role, and rejection of the hostile "system." He tends to become cynical. His professional conversations with his colleagues are unending dialogues of grim, sometimes humorous desperation which mutually reinforce each other's acceptance of the fact that they have actually "quit" teaching.

There are, of course, creative teachers who can face these monumental odds with insight and perseverance, whose idealism and sense of social service carry them through. However, they are frequently and deservedly picked off for administrative posts which take them away from front-line effectiveness.

When one sees the education of these children as only a single thread at the core of a great social complex: delinquency, shrinking vocational opportunities, the breakdown of family life, the glittering materialism, prejudice, transiency, poverty, etc., one can truly understand how palliative our "solutions" have been.

What have our solutions been? (1) Gerrymander the problem right out of the school. This is not our responsibility. Look to government, to the home, to the church, to the people themselves for solutions. (2) "Keep school" with these children. As long as we supply supervision for them between 8:30 A.M. and 3:30 P.M., we're doing all we can. (3) Teacher education projects through conferences, workshops, and experimental programs, all looking for the new insight and the new gimmick, that will work within the "old" traditional realities and the "old" budget. (Interestingly, here at Wayne State University, geographically and spiritually itself at the core of this problem, we cannot find one course which deals centrally with this, the biggest individual educational problem in Detroit. We have the background fields of education, sociology, psychology, abnormal psychology, special education, etc. But we cannot find in the catalogue a single course which synthesizes these areas and focuses itself specifically upon the problem of the culturally deprived, a problem which faces over half of the teachers and trainees who work in Detroit. Our student teachers will have contacts with this kind of student. They will get the impression that this is a "tough" situation. They will pick up the general cynicism of the school faculty, and they will hope that the lottery of school placement will keep them out of similar situations. Should they seek new insights from further study, there is little that they can find. Perhaps this is what is meant when we hear that teacher-training is not practical.)

The teacher is often frustrated as he attempts to structure solid educational experience upon the shifting social ground of his culture. But the discontent of today's teacher is not entirely due to current social conditions. Robert Snow points out that certain factors inherent to the very nature of teaching deny teachers recognition and a sense of achievement.

ANXIETIES AND DISCONTENTS IN TEACHING / *Robert H. Snow*

Today the teacher is being recognized as the key to school improvement, and commendable steps are being taken to help teachers operate more effectively. Instructional materials and equipment are being improved. Students are grouped to permit greater efficiency in teaching. Teachers are being relieved of some clerical duties. Salaries have been increased appreciably. Abundant opportunities for advanced professional training have been established.

Still, no broad-scale transformation of classroom practice has occurred. By and large, teachers across the nation still teach much as they have for the last quarter century. While notable changes have been occurring in medical practice, in merchandising, industrial production, and virtually every other field of human endeavor, the practice of teaching remains essentially unchanged.

Persons concerned with improving our schools and colleges are wondering why this is so. Financial limitations undoubtedly play a part, but do not tell the whole story. The many problems involved in educating all youth rather than only a selected few place tremendous burdens upon teachers. However, these problems are not insoluble, nor do they constitute the sole reason why progress is painfully slow. Explaining the failure to achieve excellence in teaching by citing the laziness, indifference, or stupidity of teachers is transparently foolish. Some causes lie deeper, and to find them we must examine the teacher's problems in greater detail.

A teacher is, by the very nature of his work, denied clear-cut, indisputable proof of his effectiveness. He has no dependable means of tracing the consequences of his teaching, of discerning the precise

Robert H. Snow, *"Anxieties and Discontents in Teaching,"* Phi Delta Kappan *(April 1963), pp. 318–321. Reprinted with the permission of Phi Delta Kappa, Inc.*

extent to which his efforts have helped students learn. Even when gains made by students during the period of exposure to a teacher's services can be measured, the teacher cannot be confident that such progress is directly attributable to his efforts. Other factors may have been responsible. He must face the possibility that his own contribution may have been negligible, or even negative.

Many of the teacher's perplexities and frustrations stem from this fundamental predicament. Because he has no satisfactory means of evaluating his performance by results produced, he must resort to supposition and inference. In teaching, he must choose among alternative courses of action somewhat blindly, trying to decide which course he can reasonably assume will be most effective. And having done so, he can gain no clear indication, through observation of results, of whether he is proceeding correctly. In effect, he is steering a ship in semi-darkness, with a compass he can scarcely see.

In this circumstance it is not surprising that teachers generally follow traditional practices and resist innovations. When it is impossible to demonstrate that one method of operation is superior to another, custom tends to prevail. Stereotyped methodology becomes perpetuated. How can one seek out a better mode of operation when "better" and "worse" appear to be indistinguishable?

This uncertainty may have profound effect on the attitudes and conduct of the teacher. In subtle ways, he may be tempted to neglect teaching in favor of other activities, both within and outside the school, which will afford more positive assurance of his competency. He may be reluctant to examine indirect evidence which might shed light on the effectiveness of his teaching and serve as a guide to improvement. Finally, his equivocal position may lead him into routinized habits which are actually detrimental to good teaching.

Despite pious pronouncements about the nobility of his calling, the career teacher in America finds it difficult to attain a favorable self-concept through his efforts in the classroom. He lives in a dynamic, work-oriented society, where reputation is gained and a sense of personal worth is established largely through achievement, and in particular through achievement in one's vocation. Competency in work performed is a major criterion by which we judge ourselves and others, and the normal craving for a favorable self-image will rarely be fully satisfied unless vocational achievement confirms and justifies the image. The difficulty in finding evidence of vocational proficiency becomes a source of frustration for many teachers.

SELF-EVALUATION BASED ON OTHERS' JUDGMENTS

Because the teacher is committed to an enterprise in which he cannot hope to establish objective proof of his competency, he must base his self-evaluation largely upon the implied judgments of other persons. In this respect, his position is not totally different from that of the physician, the lawyer, or any other professional worker. A craftsman who fabricates a product may know his success by examining the product. A salesman may judge his success by the amount of his commissions, the merchant or manufacturer by the profit on his books. In the main, professional work does not offer such possibilities for direct evaluation of performance by results. Accomplishments are vague and indeterminate. But in most occupations, indirect measures of achievement and various forms of recognition and reward serve as tokens of fulfillment and guides to future action.

Although the physician cannot be absolutely certain that he deserves credit for the recovery of his patient, he has gratifying confirmation of his expertness in the fact that patients continue to seek his services and are willing to pay for them. Although the lawyer may not be sure that agreements are consummated or conflicts resolved entirely through his intervention, he is sustained by the realization that his services are in demand, and he enjoys the deference accorded him as a member of an honored profession.

The teacher, similarly unsure that he has produced whatever learning has taken place, does not even enjoy the knowledge that his students came to him freely. For the teacher a repeat customer is a sign of failure, not success.

The prevailing cultural judgment of the teacher's worth, reflected in his financial rewards and in the patronizing manner so often displayed toward teachers, suggests that public endorsement of his work is less than enthusiastic. The immediate beneficiaries of his services do not seek him out. Ordinarily he operates within a bureaucracy, public or private, and his "clients" suffer exposure to his services, in many instances with obvious reluctance, as they pursue broader objectives. Students pay little tribute to his work, often displaying the utmost indifference as he attempts to assist them. The fact that he has been singled out for employment within a school or college and is continued in his job offers slight gratification. He knows that many incompetents are also employed because scarcity of candidates makes it difficult to keep positions filled. Increases in salary imply no recognition of personal merit, because they are granted to all teachers in the system according to years of service. Promotion, if it comes, ordinarily takes him out of the teaching ranks and into administrative echelons. The very fact that he remains a teacher seems to imply that he is unworthy of promotion.

With little assurance that his classroom services are valued by others, and unable to refute adverse judgments with clear evidence of accomplishment through teaching, the teacher may find other pursuits more attractive. He may throw his energies into coaching an athletic team, staging dramatic performances, or engaging in other school-related activities where his services are more conspicuous and recognition is more easily achieved. The proliferation of team sports, public performances, and gala special events within our schools has been deplored in some circles as a distraction from serious study. We forget the contributions these activities make to the sponsoring teacher's ego.

Some teachers develop sidelines outside the profession, engaging in business ventures, officiating at sporting events, or holding public office, and not merely to supplement their incomes. Success in these undertakings may compensate for disappointments in the classroom. If substantial income can be derived from them, competency is further attested.

PUBLICATIONS THE BADGE OF PROFESSORIAL SUCCESS

One suspects that the marked inclination of college professors to devote attention to matters outside the classroom is, in great part, similarly motivated. Publication is often cited as the route to academic advancement. It may also be noted that a book or article in print stands as tangible evidence of accomplishment, more conspicuous testimony to the author's ability than he can hope to gain through classroom service. Even without financial inducements, engagement as a consultant gives comforting reassurance that one's services are in demand.

However, as the teacher's energies are diverted from the classroom, the essential teaching function of the school is weakened. Less attention is given to the improvement of instruction. Routine procedures become established. Practices of questionable value in teaching but demanding little ingenuity or resourcefulness on the part of the teacher are adopted, and the students are deprived of the assistance to which they are entitled.

Improved performance by any teacher requires some method of gauging relative success or failure so that corrective action may be taken. If a rifleman on the firing range should be blindfolded and denied information as to whether his shots were striking the target, his marksmanship would not improve.

NO IMPROVEMENT WITHOUT INFORMATION

If teaching is to improve, there must be a continuous channeling back to the teacher of reliable information about the effectiveness of his efforts so that future teaching may be adjusted for better results.

The teacher meets many discouragements. The achievement of most students under his tutelage falls far short of his aspirations for them. His status within the cultural *milieu* is a modest one. His daily encounters often suggest that he is regarded as ineffectual. Under such circumstances, the teacher may well become defensive, insecure, and sensitive to criticism.

It is easy for him to conclude that all appraisals of his work are apt to be unfavorable. Hence, he may resist strenuously any systematic attempt to evaluate his performance as a teacher. The mere presence of an outside observer in his classroom becomes a threatening invasion of privacy. The rating of his performance by supervisors or by students may be regarded as humiliating.

When such attitudes take over, the teacher may deprive himself of valuable information which could heighten his effectiveness and even sustain him in a more gratifying self-image. Yet there are few signs of eagerness on the part of teachers for information about their teaching and many indications of active resistance. For example, pre-testing of the students' knowledge at the beginning of a course will permit comparison with scores at the conclusion and provide some basis for measuring progress made during the period of study. In many subject areas, standardized tests are available for this purpose. Such tests will also supply the teacher with useful information for individualizing instruction, selecting topics for special emphasis, and avoiding needless repetition. However, pre-testing is extremely uncommon. Apparently most teachers prefer to assume that students begin in a state of total ignorance and that all learning which can be demonstrated at the conclusion has been acquired during the course.

Opinions of students regarding the way educational programs are conducted and the kinds of experience they find helpful can be another source of valuable information for the teacher. Yet even on advanced college levels student opinion is rarely solicited in a systematic manner. More commonly, elaborate safeguards are erected against the overt expression of student judgments. On the pretext that students are unqualified to form sound opinions, the teacher's "dignity" is preserved, and as a result useful insights are sacrificed. Once past the period of apprenticeship, a teacher seldom receives counsel from another adult who has observed that teacher in action for an extended period. It is difficult for a teacher to make an accurate appraisal of his own performance. The perceptions of a sympathetic and knowledgeable colleague can be immensely helpful. Unfortunately, few teachers avail themselves of such assistance. The emotional overtones are too great.

Improvement in teaching often demands a break with tradition, a willingness to discard conventional practice in favor of innovations. The teacher's anxieties can seriously impede necessary experimentation. When confidence is shaky, the *absence* of reprimand offers some semblance of approval, some confirmation that one is not hopelessly astray. There is always the possibility that, if one attempts something different, results may be less favorable than at present. Therefore it appears unwise to alter existing procedures and jeopardize what little security has been achieved.

Emotional considerations often cause barriers to be erected between teacher and student. Many students are enrolled against their will. Because of legal compulsions, parental pressures, fear of economic and social consequences attendant upon withdrawal from school, students find themselves trapped in a relationship with teachers. Some experience a continuing succession of failures within the academic setting. Rebelling against a situation not of their choosing, they may display undiscriminating resentment toward many aspects of the school environment, including their teachers. They may be disorderly, uncooperative, reluctant to pursue assigned tasks, and apparently indifferent to learning. Such feelings may be shared by half the students enrolled in the later elementary grades and early high school years and by a considerable number who complete high school and enter college. To work effectively with these students, the teacher must demonstrate exceptional emotional stability.

RIGID DISCIPLINE REASSURES THE TEACHER

In the face of many uncertainties, the teacher may feel a desperate need for exercising rigid control within the classroom to insure that at least the outward appearance of constructive effort is maintained. When students seem orderly and attentive, it is easier for the teacher to feel assured that he is teaching successfully. Deviations from accepted behavior patterns may be sternly suppressed, because they destroy this sense of confidence. Furthermore, evidences of sloth or recalcitrance are interpreted as personal provocations, because they suggest that the teacher's services are not appreciated.

Some teachers appear to live in dread of insurrection, obsessively concerned with preserving order in the classroom at all costs. Coercive measures predominate; reproaches fill the air. Inordinate amounts of time are spent enforcing minor regulations. The examination becomes a punitive device, chiefly intended to place students on the defensive rather than to measure achievement. The student regards the teacher not as one who guides and assists but as one who threatens and invokes penalties. A gulf widens between students and teacher. The classroom becomes an arena of opposing forces rather than a laboratory for learning.

It is equally unfortunate when teachers, bedeviled by pressures and anxieties, become contemptuous of students. If students are viewed as unworthy of attention or incapable of learning, the cause is lost. A teacher can perform at his best only with sincere interest in the welfare of his students and hopefulness regarding their potentialities. When the teacher must shift responsibility for failure to students in order to preserve some remnants of self-esteem, the foundations of good teaching are undermined.

Certainly many dedicated teachers do focus their talents and energies upon their work with students, seeking no reward beyond the intrinsic satisfactions of a life of service. Yet it is sheer sentimentality to believe that teachers are a race apart, noble and selfless, transcending normal human appetites. The nation cannot build an adequate educational system upon a false assumption of this magnitude.

If professional service is expected of teachers, financial rewards must match those of other professions. If the teacher's role is central in education, this role should be recognized and other functions made subordinate to it. In our present organization, the teacher is lowest on the educational totem pole. Sometimes he is paid less than the janitor and usually less than the football coach. In an educational institution, business managers, counselors, administrative officers and other service personnel have one basic responsibility: to sustain and facilitate the work of the teacher. Our operating procedures often suggest that the teacher's function is less significant than many of these supportive efforts. Even on the college campus, where academic prerogatives are more clearly established, the primacy of teaching is given little more than lip-service.

TEACHERS MUST EARN STATUS BY EXPERTNESS

However, teachers cannot achieve the respect and recognition which they ought to have, and which they *must* have if they are to function as true professionals, if they are content with low standards of performance. They must *earn* status by demonstrating what they can do, by indisputable proof of expertness. We insist that the physician shall be able to accomplish more than the barber and the midwife. Unless the teacher's efforts can produce results distinctively superior to those attainable by the intelligent layman, he has no rightful claim to professional status.

The improvement and further professionalization of teaching will require significant changes in the attitudes of teachers themselves. They must assume much greater responsibility for improving the quality of instruction than they have thus far been willing to accept. Instead of resisting attempts to evaluate the effectiveness of teaching, teachers should be in the vanguard of such efforts, resolving the complex problems of evaluation and establishing more precise means of identifying superior performance.

A major cause of low teacher compensation, and of the patronizing attitudes toward the profession, is the fact that the teacher's contribution is vague and indeterminate. No clear distinction is made between skilled performance and incompetency. Without means of judging the teacher's effectiveness, it is convenient to assume that none are especially effective and to treat them all accordingly. Inadequate teaching on any level, anywhere, weakens the structure of the profession and casts a shadow on the work of all teachers. The good teacher's sole defense is a sound evaluation system whereby excellence can be recognized and shoddiness exposed. Our present scheme of bureaucratic leveling, in both private and public institutions, shields the incompetent and victimizes the superior performer.

No substantial progress will be made toward the elevation of teaching standards without vigorous and sustained efforts within the teaching profession. Legal requirements serve only to set the barest minimums. Administrative officers of educational institutions, even though they are deeply concerned, can have only limited influence upon the quality of instruction. Major responsibility must rest with teachers themselves.

The major task for urban education remains that of effectively educating the culturally disadvantaged child. The schools desperately need teachers who have the skill and the facilities at hand to do so. Miriam Goldberg discusses the kinds of teachers and teacher training needed to meet this overwhelming problem.

TEACHERS FOR DISADVANTAGED CHILDREN / *Miriam L. Goldberg*

Three assumptions underly this paper: The first maintains that a pupil's learning is, in large measure, a function of the kind of teaching to which he is exposed. Thus, the extent to which a pupil masters a given set of academic tasks reflects not only his aptitudes and attitudes, but also the appropriateness of the particular approach by which he is taught.

The second assumption, implied by the title, rejects the notion of the universally "good" teacher, equally able to adapt his style to varying pupil populations, and substitutes a conception of a variety of "good" teachers, differentially suited (by temperament and training) to teaching differing groups of students.

The third assumption proposes that children from culturally disadvantaged backgrounds though highly variable, nevertheless represent a describable pupil population in need of teachers who are uniquely "good" for them.

TEACHERS FOR DISADVANTAGED CHILDREN

In discussing the problem of "teachable groups" Thelen (10) points out that despite great individual differences in teachers' perception of who is teachable, there are some pupils—from 10 to 25 percent of

Miriam L. Goldberg, *"Adapting Teacher Style to Pupil Differences," Abstract (May 1963), Mobilization For Youth, Curriculum Center, 271 East 4th Street, New York 9, New York. Reprinted with the permission of the author and the Merrill-Palmer Institute.*

the average school whom *no* teacher includes among the teachable. His description of this group is reminiscent of what we know about the school behavior of children from disadvantaged areas, from city slums and rural backwoods. Similarly, Heil's "opposers" and to some extent his "waverers" remind one of typical behaviors of disadvantaged children. In the great cities these children represent an increasing proportion of the total pupil population, far more than the 10 to 25 percent suggested by Thelen. And it is expected that by 1970 one out of every 2 pupils in large city schools will be "culturally disadvantaged."

For this increasing number of school children who are too often perceived as unteachable, teachers must, nevertheless, be found; not just warm bodies to mind the classes—although even this is no small problem—but people who have the will and the skill, the appropriate "style" to change the "unteachable" pupil into an active learner.

The approach to the problem of staffing schools in depressed areas requires several sequential efforts: The first step is to gain broad public acceptance of the assumption that disadvantaged pupils, though widely variable in their abilities and personal characteristics, nonetheless represent a describable group: a group which, although it overlaps other groups in many ways, has unique characteristics, stemming from common backgrounds, values and experiences. The second step is to characterize the teacher who is successful with culturally disadvantaged pupils—successful because the pupils in his classes achieve better than similar pupils in other teachers' classes and have more accepting attitudes toward school, toward the teacher and toward learning.

There are no systematic data on what such teachers do, and in what way their teaching styles differ from those of less successful teachers in similar schools or from the styles of successful teachers in more favored communities. Such descriptive information would provide the necessary guide posts both for seeking and for training teachers.

However, it may be worth while to create a hypothetical model of the "successful teacher of disadvantaged children" constructed of implications from available research on teacher behavior, insights from impressionistic observations and inferences from investigations of the characteristics of disadvantaged pupils and their social world. It may well be that several models of successful teachers will be needed to account for the great variety of pupils within the disadvantaged population. What is suggested here is a general outline which may have to be refined and sub-divided to achieve optimum "fit" between pupils and teacher.

HYPOTHETICAL MODEL OF THE SUCCESSFUL TEACHER OF DISADVANTAGED PUPILS

The teacher who is successful with any group of pupils is the one who respects the children in his classes and they, in turn, respect him. As teachers in slum schools look at their pupils they see many children who are discouraged and defeated, even in the early grades; children who express their alienation from the school and the society it represents by aggressive acting-out behavior or by a kind of tuned-out lethargy and listlessness. There are frequent transgressions against the ethical, moral and legal codes of society. Pupils seem to be making little effort to learn, show no desire to better themselves, to break out of the limits imposed upon them by their ignorance. The teacher may feel sorry for them, realizing the limiting circumstances of their lives. Or, he may be angered by their laziness, their lack of effort, believing that they could if they would, but they won't. Or, he may write them off as hopeless, too dumb to learn, taking up time and resources that could be better utilized by pupils with more ability and greater motivation.

But the successful teacher of disadvantaged children does respect his pupils, and not because he sees them through the rose colored lenses of the romantic, finding "beauty" and "strength" where others see poverty and cultural emptiness. On the contrary, he sees them quite realistically as different from his children and his neighbors' children, but like all children coping in their own way with the trials and frustrations of growing up and, unlike middle class children, struggling to survive in the ruthless world of their peers, confused by the conflicting demands of the two cultures in which they live— the one of the home and the street and the neighborhood, the other of the school and the society that maintains it.

Like the anthropologist, the successful teacher views the alien culture of his pupils not as a judge, but as a student. He understands the backgrounds from which the children come, the values placed on various achievements, the kind of work and life to which they aspire. He recognizes and understands the reasons for their unwillingness to strive toward future goals where such efforts provide little reward in the present.

He knows that many of the children bear the scars of intellectual understimulation in their early years. Familiar with the home life of the children, he knows how rarely they are helped to name the things they see and feel and hear, to recognize similarities and differences, to categorize and classify perceptions, learn the word for the object, the phrase through which to express an idea or a feeling.

The successful teacher is aware of the various family structures from which the children come: the matriarchal family in which no father is present or where several men may follow each other for short periods, the home where there are two parents, but both working; where one or both parents are able bodied but out of work, recipients of relief, where the father is disabled and stays home while the mother works, where an extended family—grandparents, aunts, uncles, and other relatives live together. This teacher has seen the physical conditions in which the children live: their lack of privacy, the poor facilities, the absence of basic amenities. He knows the kinds of jobs the parents have, their aspirations for themselves and for their children, and what role they attribute to the school in shaping their child's future.

The teacher is aware of the ethnic group membership of his pupils and how such membership shapes the child's image of himself and of his world. He knows something about the history, traditions and social structures of the various ethnic groups, their unique culture patterns, their status in American society, the blocks and frustrations which they confront and their perceptions of what life has in store for them.

He knows that the language of his pupils is closely tied to the life they lead. While it may represent a complete lack or a distortion of acceptable English, he recognizes its functional qualities for the pupils. Though this language is not "the coin of the realm" it often represents the only known and acceptable medium of exchange in the child's home or neighborhood.

In addition to his knowledge about the child in his environment, the successful teacher has a sophisticated understanding of how a child's abilities are assessed and therefore a realistic perception of what these measurements describe and predict. He knows that native potential intelligence is, at least thus far, unmeasurable; that what tests measure is learned behavior, and that the learning results not only from the child's native ability but also from his total experience. Further, he is aware that intelligence and aptitude tests set out to tap mainly those learnings which are related to verbal reasoning ability; the power to see relationships, to generalize, to apply logical thinking, to deal with abstractions. Thus, he knows that some kinds of intelligent behavior which may be highly adaptive in the life of disadvantaged children is untapped by the tests. In fact, he realizes that many intellectual abilities, like some of those which enter into creative functioning are not measured by existing intelligence tests.

But he is also aware that the tests provide a fairly accurate description of the child's present ability to handle material and, unless there is a significant expansion and reorganization of his experience, the tests will predict with reliability how the child will function academically in the future. Because he is sophisticated in these matters, the successful teacher accepts the test scores as a fair and valid measure of the child's present academic ability, rejects them as a measure of native intelligence.

These and many other anthropological and psychological data affect the style of the successful teacher of disadvantaged pupils. But while the anthropologist's task is to describe and compare behavior of various cultures and the psychologist's to understand individual behavior, the teacher's job is to modify it. Therefore, he must use his knowledge about his pupils and the world in which they live to guide him as he attempts to open more and more doors for them and help them acquire the skills and knowledges with which to enter the new and open spaces which lie beyond. The successful teacher sees his task as preparing his pupils to make competent choices among potentially available alternatives. And he knows that the alternatives increase in number and in variety as the individual increases his academic competence and learns the behaviors expected in various social contests. The teacher is aware that with every passing year the rapidly automating economy affords less and less opportunities to the minimally educated and more and more to the academically and technically trained, and he communicates this understanding to his pupils. Rather than join the camp of those who seek the elusive "culture fair" test, the model teacher bends his efforts toward expanding the pupils' learning experiences in order that they may develop the abilities needed to deal with increasingly difficult abstract, symbolic material.

The successful teacher meets the disadvantaged child on equal terms, as person to person, individual to individual. But while he accepts, he doesn't condone. He sets clearly defined limits for his pupils and will brook few transgressions. He is aware that, unlike middle class children, they rarely respond to exhortations intended to control behavior through invoking feelings of guilt and shame. He, therefore, sets the rules, fixes the boundaries, establishes the routines with a minimum of discussion. Here he is impersonal, undeviating, strict, but never punitive. Within these boundaries the successful teacher is business-like and orderly, knowing that he is there to do a job. But he is also warm and outgoing, adapting his behavior to the individual pupils in his class. He shows his respect and liking for his pupils and makes known his belief in their latent abilities.

He realizes the danger of the "self-fulfilling prophecy" of expecting, and consequently finding a low level of achievement. He, therefore, lets each pupil know that he expects more than the pupil thinks he can produce, but his standards are not so high that success cannot be achieved and the attempt fraught with frustration. He rewards each tiny upward step, alert to every opportunity for honest praise, and, as much as possible, withholds harsh criticism and censure when progress is slow or entirely lacking. Above all, he is honest. He doesn't sentimentalize, doesn't pretend that a pupil's work is good when it isn't, doesn't condone unacceptable behavior.

The successful teacher is also something of a showman, coming to his task with an extensive repertory of carefully constructed scripts and props into which he breathes a sense of drama and high interest to capture the imagination of his pupils and hold their attention.

Unlike the teacher in the suburban school who has, from his experience and from objective studies, some bases for deciding which procedures will produce learning on the part of most of his pupils, the teacher of disadvantaged children has to try a great variety of yet unproven strategies, materials and methods, often quite different from those which work with middle class children. For example, recognizing that lower class children tend more often to be motoric than verbal in their approach, he will draw out of his repertoire learning experiences which will develop verbal skills through motor activities. Since the available books which are on the children's reading level are too unsophisticated in content, he will unearth, or if necessary produce more suitable reading materials. He will make use of some of the developing technological aids—loop films which provide individual drill, tape recorders which help to hear one's own speech and correct it, TV programs or movies which present vivid descriptions or illuminate concepts, teaching machines or programs which allow for individual progress when children become ready to work on their own. He will use approaches which will enable children who are highly concrete and "thing" oriented to move toward a grasp of the abstract and the symbolic. Especially at the elementary and junior high school level he makes extensive use of non-verbal media such as drawing and painting, singing and dancing through which his pupils can achieve immediate success and gratification. But, wherever possible he uses these success producing experiences to lead his pupils into verbal, ideational, abstract learning.

His repertory is not only extensive, providing a great variety of materials and teaching procedures tailored to learning patterns of his pupils, it is also carefully catalogued allowing him to find what he needs quickly and efficiently.

As do other successful teachers, our model teacher has extensive knowledge of the content of the subjects he teaches. In fact, he knows it so well, that he has no need to rely on study guides. Like the knowledgeable native, he guides his pupils through his country without a Baedeker, relying rather on his own familiarity with its terrain to take them to the important sights by paths and highways not often known to the less sophisticated.

Like all composite portraits, this hypothetical model presents an idealized version of reality. The hypothetical teacher is described as a mature, well-integrated person who respects his difficult, unmotivated and apparently unteachable pupils. He communicates his respect by setting high, but reachable expectations, by his impartial and consistent firmness and honesty and his warm personal regard for each individual. He combines the detached but completely accepting stance of the anthropologist observing cultural determined reformer, the educator, in the sense of one who *leads* his pupils *out* into the wider world. Though not a specialist in any one of the behavioral or social sciences, he gleans from each of them knowledge which helps him understand the behavior of his pupils, the meaning of their scores on tests of intelligence and aptitude, the realities of their present and future world, the demands which various social and vocational alternatives will make upon them. In addition, the model requires the teacher to have a wide repertoire of materials and procedures, the ability to devise new ways, to deviate from accepted procedures and courses of study, but always to be aware of the knowledges and skills the pupils must eventually acquire. And in working with his pupils he combines the flair of the showman with the sobriety of the pedagogue, the firmness of the proverbial headmaster with the warmth and concern of the friend. If the hypothetical "successful teacher" were to be characterized in a single phrase, it would be *ordered flexibility*.

APPROACHING THE MODEL THROUGH EDUCATION

To what extent are the attributes of the model teachable? At least three of the aspects are of a cognitive nature and, for the reasonably bright and motivated student, can probably be approached through instruction: 1) mastery of subject matter, 2) the acquisition of an understanding of the major concepts from the behavioral and social sciences and their relevance to teaching disadvantage children and 3) the development of a repertoire of teaching strategies which hold promise for working with disadvantaged pupils. But to accomplish these three purposes alone would require a considerable reorganization and revision of undergraduate and graduate programs of teacher education, both pre-service and in-service.

Such revisions however, cannot even be approached until educators and the public openly recognize 1) that schools in disadvantaged areas do, indeed, present unique problems which differ from the problems faced in more affluent sections of larger cities, in rural areas or in the suburbs; 2) that although disadvantaged children show wide variability in aptitude, achievement and general school functioning, often overlapping groups of children from more advantaged circumstances, as a group they present learning and behavioral problems which distinguish them from their more socially and economically favored agemates; 3) that therefore, those who teach the disadvantaged child need, in addition to the knowledge required of all teachers, specific knowledges and skills which are particularly suited to the learning needs of disadvantaged pupils. Once such acceptance is gained, then courses of study can be constructed to prepare the new teacher for his special job and provide the practicing teacher with new insights into the pupils he teaches and more effective methods of working with them.

REFERENCES

National Society for the Study of Education, N. B. Henry, ed., *Juvenile Delinquency and the Schools*. Forty-seventh Yearbook, Part I. Chicago: University of Chicago Press, 1948.

Sexton, Patricia. *Education and Income: Inequality in our Public Schools*. New York: The Viking Press, 1961.

Smith, Wilfred R., and August Kerber. "The Forgotten Ones." Unpublished monograph, Wayne State University (Detroit), 1961.

PERIODICALS

Adlow, Elijah. "Teen-Age Criminals." *The Atlantic Monthly,* CXCVI, 1 (July 1955), 46–50.

Haber, Robert A. "From Protest to Radicalism." *Venture,* II, 1 (September 1960), 15–18.

Remmers, H. H., and D. H. Radler. "Teen-Age Attitudes: With Biographical Sketches." *Scientific American,* CXCVIII (June 1958), 25–29.

Samuels, Gertrude. "The Schools, the Children, the Dilemma." *The New York Times Magazine* (February 16, 1958), XIV, 75–77.

Silverman, H. L. "The Psychological and Psychiatric Factors in Delinquency as Related to School Administration." *Education,* LXXVI (November 1955), 175–180.

Toby, Jackson. "A Way Out of the Blackboard Jungle." *The Nation,* CLXXXVI (March 8, 1958), 205–207.

Van Til, William. "Combatting Delinquency through Schools." Educational Leadership, XVIII (March 1956), 362–367.

{Chapter Six}

IMPROVING URBAN SCHOOLS: PROGRAMS AND PROJECTS

Through no fault of its own, the urban school is no longer an effective acculturative force in the lives of in-migrant children. Recognizing that the urban child has a greater need of formal education than his counterpart of a generation ago and yet is faced with greater barriers to learning, several urban systems have attempted to provide more realistic opportunities to disadvantaged children who are unable to learn in a traditional school setting.

The big city project aimed at equalizing educational opportunity has been criticized as a "crash program." That is, the typical program incorporates countless theories which attempt to give reasons for the learning difficulties of disadvantaged children, although many of these theories and concepts have not been verified by careful and extensive research. Evaluation, too, is difficult. Is success due to field trips, community involvement, both factors, or neither?

In the defense of such projects, it must be kept in mind that public education, by the very nature of its normative function, encounters difficulty in applying scientific findings to existing educational practice. The social sciences have only recently directed their attention to problems in areas of urban education, but education is faced with the urgency of a crisis which does not stand still for research. The school has no choice but to extend itself into every conceivable direction and hope to reach the disadvantaged child at some point along the way. Despite criticism, the adaptations of metropolitan schools are constructive and promising. They are realizing some success and they have reversed the directions in urban schools toward capitulation to the situation.

The picture of education in American urban centers is not entirely discouraging. Education is moving closer to the ideal of education for all as it now attempts to provide educational opportunity for all. Metropolitan school districts throughout the country are meeting the challenge head on with extensive and intensive projects. The following four articles are accounts of projects in New York, Philadelphia, Flint, and Detroit. Each differs in detail, but one common idea runs through all of them: expectation. The enormous effort being expended on the culturally disadvantaged child indicates a full commitment to the belief that he can and will be educated.

EDUCATING THE DISADVANTAGED CHILD / Morris Krugman

In large metropolitan areas, particularly those with mobile populations living in substandard sections of the city, many children enter school seriously handicapped educationally.

An educational program designed for children from middle class socioeconomic homes does not yield satisfactory results with deprived children. Not only do such children enter school with handicaps, but these handicaps are increased with time, and the educational gap between them and other children is constantly widened.

For example, in city-wide group testing in New York City schools, the third graders in a large, low socioeconomic district had a median

Morris Krugman, "The Culturally Deprived Child in School" (original title), NEA Journal (April 1961), pp. 23–24. Copyright © April 1961 by the National Education Association. Reprinted with the permission of the author and The Association.

IQ ten points lower than that of all third graders throughout the city. The median IQ of sixth graders from the same area was seventeen points lower and that of eighth graders, twenty points lower than the median IQ for the entire city.

City-wide reading tests showed similar results. The low socioeconomic children were retarded one year in reading in the third grade, almost two years in the sixth grade, and more than two and a half years in the eighth grade.

Lowered group intelligence test results and retardation in reading do not tell the entire story for these children. They present more problems in behavior than do other children; many more of them find their way into the children's courts; they leave school at an earlier age and in greater numbers; fewer of them complete high school; and very few of them enter college.

When they leave school, more of them enter unskilled occupations; their incomes, when these young people are employed, are lower; they are unemployed much longer than others; their job dissatisfactions are greater. Their self-concepts and their aspirations are lower.

Although all community agencies have responsibility for improving this situation, the schools feel a special urgency. What then can they do? A New York City experiment, begun in 1956 and known originally as the Demonstration Guidance Project, seems to throw light on this question.

Originally involving one junior high school and one senior high school, the project was "designed to identify and stimulate able students from a culturally deprived area, and from generally low income families without an educational tradition, to reach higher educational and vocational goals."

After four years, the results are most heartening. Achievement improved, behavior improved, self-concepts changed for the better, many more students were graduated from high school, and many more entered college than before. Because of this success, the New York City school system extended the program—in a less intensive form— to sixty-five schools and named it the Higher Horizons Program.

These programs and their methods cannot be discussed thoroughly here, but experiences in six areas seem particularly pertinent to the education of children from low socioeconomic homes.

1. Appraisal of ability and teacher outlook. We began by heeding the long-standing warning by psychologists that group intelligence tests are inadequate for measuring the educational potential of children who are culturally, socially, and economically deprived. Instead we relied on individual psychological examinations, nonverbal intelligence tests, and simple subjective rating procedures.

Teachers, constantly reminded that group intelligence tests could not be taken at face value with these children, began to search for clues of ability and to lose their morbid outlooks about the children, who, in turn, tended to live up to the higher expectations.

2. Early identification. Realizing that junior high school is a crucial point in the education of deprived children and hoping to find out whether, at this age, educational goals could be raised to include high school and college, our original experiment began with a junior high school.

In spite of considerable success, the following factors led us to start succeeding programs in the early elementary school years: Elementary group intelligence tests contain less verbal material and so provide better estimates of ability; negative attitudes toward education have not yet been set; education efforts are less costly and more productive with younger children than with older.

In short, we are convinced that identification of talent and efforts at overcoming cultural handicaps must begin early.

3. Self-concepts, aspiration levels, and educational sights. From the first, we realized that the children we were trying to help have characteristically low self-concepts which in turn adversely influence school achievement and the level of school reached. We set out, therefore, to use educational and guidance approaches that would raise their opinions of themselves and their levels of aspiration. Appreciable changes resulted. As students succeeded where they had formerly failed and as they sensed greater acceptance by the school personnel, they displayed greater pride in themselves and improved their behavior markedly.

A frequent explanation given by the students for their change for the better was "Nobody cared before." They were motivated to better achievement and adjustment, not by direct motivation techniques, but by the feeling and the proof that the school cared about them and provided an educational atmosphere and program that made it possible for them to succeed.

4. Raising educational achievement. Motivation alone, we discovered, did not raise educational achievement among the pupils with whom we were dealing. Neither did normal teaching approaches in classes of usual size—particularly at the high school level.

In our original project, remedial services, both individual and in small groups, were provided whenever necessary. In the senior high school, the youngsters were taught in small instructional groups—not more than fifteen in a class.

They had two English classes each day because their greatest difficulty was in written and spoken English. Part of one of these periods was combined with group guidance. Expense was not spared, since it was necessary to learn which techniques would work with these groups. In the second experiment, it has been possible to reduce expenses materially because of what we had learned.

5. Adequate guidance. The original counseling program was built on the recognition that children from low socioeconomic levels need sympathetic persons to whom they can easily relate and who will help them overcome obstacles and correct antisocial, self-harming behavior. Not more than 250 students were assigned to a full-time counselor in the junior high school and 150 in the senior high school. When problems became acute, social, psychological, and psychiatric services were available.

For youngsters such as these, intensive guidance service is essential, but it can never function effectively without intensive instruction. The students were brought to recognize the need for exerting sufficient effort to succeed, and the standards of academic achievement were never lowered. What is most heartening is that so many of the formerly failing students accepted this challenge and later expressed gratitude for the opportunity.

6. Raising the cultural level. Culturally deprived children are frequently wise in the ways of the slum street but have little awareness of the world beyond their immediate neighborhood. Their experiences are limited. Their horizons are circumscribed. Their tastes and appreciations leave much to be desired. Their contacts with books, music, art, people, and places are extremely limited. It became clear early in our project that this was due, not to low tastes, but to lack of opportunity. When private funds made possible a variety of cultural activities, the youngsters (and their parents) at first demurred, but when they began to partake of them, their horizons expanded immeasurably.

After a slow start, trips to museums, Broadway theaters, the Metropolitan Opera, Carnegie Hall, scientific laboratories, libraries, college campuses were enthusiastically participated in and enjoyed.

Classroom work was correlated with these activities. It was no longer "square" or "sissy" to attend a symphony concert. Boys were not "queer" if they carried paperbacks, which they bought at nominal fees and retained as their own.

In the senior high school, the pressure of serious school work was accepted for the regular school day and for preparation after school; trips and other cultural activities were engaged in on week ends and holidays. Giving up their free time became a gauge of their interest in and enthusiasm for the cultural activities. Their own cultural backgrounds were carefully woven into these activities, so that their pride in themselves and in their groups grew at the same time that appreciation of other cultures developed.

Can schools compensate for the meager backgrounds that children from deprived social and economic homes bring into the classroom? The answer must be a clear "yes," but this compensation is costly when compared with the average educational program. It is not as costly, however, as failure, loss of educated man power, delinquency and crime, maladjustment, and mental illness.

It is probable that such projects as ours in New York City would not be necessary if our education programs were not leveled chiefly at the large middle-class community and if education took seriously into account the assets as well as the liabilities which each child brings to school. However, until practice catches up with already known theory, special programs for deprived children will be required.

STIRRINGS IN THE BIG CITIES: Philadelphia /
Aleda Druding

Paul Laurence Dunbar School is a Philadelphia elementary school. Built in 1931, Dunbar stands near the corner of 12th Street and Columbia Avenue, in the north central part of the city.

A Dunbar School committee describes its community and its neighbors as "Negroes who live in substandard, three-story, absentee-owned multiple-family dwellings. In many blocks there are vacant, dilapidated buildings and unsanitary empty lots. . . . The stores are operated by white merchants who do not live in the community. In short, the school

Aleda Druding, "Stirrings in the Big Cities: Philadelphia," NEA Journal (February 1962), pp. 48–51. Copyright © February 1962 by the National Education Association. Reprinted with the permission of the author and The Association.

serves an encapsulated Negro community where the contacts of its residents with other groups are temporary and seldom occur in a peer relationship. The area can be described as depressed and culturally impoverished."

Other schools in North Central Philadelphia describe their communities in similar ways. For example, a report from the James R. Ludlow Elementary School, which has a pupil population of Negroes, Puerto Ricans, and whites, says: "Most of our children come to school from very depressed housing conditions. Their homes are generally marginal, three-story tenements. . . . Parents are preoccupied with earning a scanty living, and many of them have had to get aid from the Department of Public Assistance."

What do these descriptions mean?

Translated into daily school life, they mean:

That children may come to kindergarten without knowing their own names. "Big Boy" or "Brother" is the only name they have heard at home.

That medical and dental checks will show hundreds of children who have never brushed their teeth or bathed regularly. Mother has never shown them how or encouraged them to brush or wash.

That many children—perhaps most—have vocabularies so limited that they are unable to speak in sentences. "Huh?" "Out!" "Go on." "Shush!" plus a number of curse words may be their entire repertoire.

That many children will fall asleep in class because they find it difficult to sleep at night in the noisy room they share with three or four other children and adults.

That emotional problems are not unusual. One little girl, for example, will not go near the lavatory because she saw a dead woman's body in the bathroom her family shares with the rest of their building.

That the experiences children have had are so limited that stories in their primers will not make sense to them. The majority of these children—and many of the parents—have not been farther from their tenement homes than twenty-five blocks. They have not seen motion pictures, eaten in a restaurant, or ridden in a bus; they have never lived in a situation where a mother and a father work together to rear a family. Of course, they do not identify with the middle-class Dicks and Janes in the typical reading books.

What can be done in situations like these? Until 1960, Philadelphia teachers in schools like Dunbar did their best, with the funds available, to teach these children with limited backgrounds. Here and there, skilled, interested teachers and hard-working principals toiled long hours to bring their pupils up to levels which would enable them to get something more from life than their parents have gotten.

But it was, in the main, an uncoordinated task and a nearly impossible one. Many children were classified as "poor risks"—difficult to reach. Teachers who recognize children's physical and mental health problems had limited time to follow up to ensure that the child and his parents took steps for correction.

Some teachers left the Central City area to teach elsewhere in the city, in the suburbs, or across the river in New Jersey. In some cases morale was affected adversely. It became clear that the situation demanded a larger measure of assistance from specialist teachers, and that a heavier concentration of in-service education on school time had to be provided.

Today, in the words of Marcus Foster, the quiet, energetic principal of Dunbar, "there are no poor risks, only good risks. We eliminated the term *poor risk*," he says, "and we began to work with all the children. We have found that they all have capacity to learn."

This change in viewpoint began in the summer of 1960, when Philadelphia received grants from the Great Cities School Improvement Program, sponsored by the Ford Foundation. Starting in September of that year, the Dunbar, Ludlow, and Harrison elementary schools and the John Wanamaker Junior High School were made the test cases for the Great Cities Program in Philadelphia. Recently, four more schools have been added to the list, and Ford money has been offered for a three-year extension of the program in that city.

What have schools like Dunbar been doing that has produced good risks from poor risks?

Six goals were set from the beginning of the project, according to the project director, Louis R. Ballen. These goals were: (a) to motivate parents to assume increasing responsibility for the solution of family, community, and school problems; (b) to develop interest and understanding of the democratic way of life among parents by a program that coordinates the efforts of the school and all other social agencies; (c) to identify and meet the unique and pressing cultural and social needs of the families in these communities; (d) to raise pupil achievement; (e) to provide opportunities for children to achieve recognition, security, and a sense of belonging; and (f) to decrease juvenile delinquency.

To carry out these goals, the staff of each school was reorganized around a school-community coordinating team. Headed by the school principal, the team includes the counselor, the school nurse, the teachers, the school-community coordinator, the language-laboratory teacher (a reading specialist), and others.

During the school day, the program functions through a combination of team teaching, demonstration teaching, in-service classes, and traditional classroom teaching. Each teacher takes part in one in-service language-arts session each week. Specialist teachers come into the regular classrooms and teach literature and language arts while the classroom teacher observes and learns better techniques.

Reading-adjustment classes are scheduled for poor readers; enrichment classes for better pupils. From the beginning of their school experiences, pupils are encouraged to speak in full sentences, instead of answering merely yes or no. Puppets, films, toy telephones, and other equipment are used to strengthen speaking skills.

Much testing is done. In all of the schools in the project, a difference was discovered between the reading level of children and their listening-understanding level: The children could understand concepts that they heard which they were unable to understand when they read them. The teams worked hard to raise children's reading ability.

At Dunbar, after a readjustment which allowed movement between classes for reading instruction, improvement was obvious. From February to June 1961, the number of pupils reading at the preprimer or primer level dropped from twenty percent to eight percent. The language-laboratory teacher reported that the greatest improvement was among those pupils previously thought of as poor risks.

A club program has been set up during school hours, built around the special talents of the teachers. Forty bell instruments have been purchased for a music club. A chorus has been set up. Literature clubs are studying books and reporting on them. Sewing instruction, centered on practical work such as apron and curtain making, is offered.

To help the children in experiencing beauty—something rarely a part of their home and community environment—emphasis is placed on art. Reproductions of art masterpieces hang on the school walls, and other reproductions circulate among the classes accompanied by biographies of the artists.

The program at Dunbar, and at the other schools, has spilled over beyond the school day. Two buses are available for class trips during the week and on Saturdays, often with parents accompanying the children. Trips are made to museums, industrial plants, the UN headquarters in New York, libraries, health and welfare agencies, airports, farms, and dozens of other places commonly seen by middle-class children, but of new and vital interest to these children—and to their parents.

Reading centers provide extra help after school for poor readers. A library center, created to stimulate children's interest in reading for pleasure, regularly attracts over eighty children at Dunbar. Forty-one Dunbar pupils meet four afternoons a week for extra help in arithmetic.

Meanwhile, beyond the school, the school-community coordinators are at work, trying to involve the pupils' parents in the project. The school-community coordinators in Philadelphia are lay members of the community. They are not college trained, but were selected because of their ability to communicate with the people who live in the school area.

Eloise Holmes is the school-community coordinator for Dunbar. A thin, quiet woman, Mrs. Holmes serves as the link between the project team and the parents of the pupils. Like the other coordinators, she has organized the Dunbar neighborhood block by block. In each block, a block commander assists her, keeping tabs on the school-community activities in that area.

Most of Mrs. Holmes' time is spent visiting parents in their homes—often as many as fifteen or twenty a day. She explains the Dunbar program, asks for cooperation, and encourages parents to attend meetings and adult-education classes sponsored by the project. She informs parents of their duty to send their children to clinics for correction of defects. (By the end of her first year, the number of children reporting for correction of defects increased by 280 percent.)

Mrs. Holmes appeals to parents' pride in their children and tries to overcome the habitual apathy of those living on marginal incomes. Sometimes she shames them into cooperation. One early morning, when she called at a home, she asked the child if he had had breakfast. The child informed her that "mama didn't feel like making any." Mrs. Holmes went directly to the kitchen, prepared breakfast for the child, then left. Next day, mother made breakfast without being asked.

At the end of the first year of the Great Cities Project in Philadelphia, Director Ballen noted that "perhaps the most marked sign of growth is in the attitude of the teachers of the four schools. Enthusiasm and a greatly improved outlook toward teaching have captured them individually and collectively. They reflect the conviction that children of limited backgrounds can learn and be taught so that they want to learn."

Individual teachers are enthusiastic. Language laboratory teachers, in particular, are impressed with the quality of learning possible under the project. And they appreciate the eager cooperation of the classroom teachers. "Most teachers agree that they find the meetings with me helpful," says the Dunbar language-laboratory teacher. "One said to me, 'Every time you talk I learn something new.'"

As the project continues—expanded—through its second year, improvements are being made, within the limits of the personnel and funds available. But more remains to be done. Principal Marcus Foster points to four improvements he sees as still needed: "We must increase the number of books available for the children. It is essential that every school have a library of its own. We have to cut the size of the reading classes down to a maximum of thirty pupils. And we need more in-service training."

Other goals of the project also remain to be completely fulfilled: Parental involvement is as yet built on too narrow a base; additional effort is needed to get and hold good teachers in the central city area; more facilities for study centers and meetings need to be found. But the project has made an important start in an area too long neglected by America's big cities. Its very existence is a morale builder for education.

While the teams at schools such as Dunbar are working to bring their pupils beyond the preprimers and primers, schools in other parts of Philadelphia are facing very different problems.

At J. Hampton Moore Elementary School in Northeast Philadelphia, for example, a first-grade teacher says, "This is the first year that none of my children were reading when they came to school. That makes it so much easier for the children to learn good reading habits together." Usually, she reports, some of the children have learned to read at home and she must set up separate groups from the start.

In the third and fourth grades at Hampton Moore, children have been studying Russian. Sixth graders in one class learn some of their arithmetic by playing chess—nearly every home in the area has a chess set, so there is no shortage of equipment. Last year, one of the sixth-grade arithmetic groups gave a demonstration of how an atomic-energy plant operates—complete with a model of the plant. Another group demonstrated the use of binary mathematics.

At Hampton Moore, according to Principal Isadore Snyderman, the problem is grouping the children in order to offer the strongest program for each of them. During the 1960-61 school year, Hampton Moore teachers met by grade groups to organize a program which has set up two top sections in each grade, with opportunities throughout the year for changes as pupil abilities develop. Community involvement is not a problem at Hampton Moore: Every parent seems to want his child in a top group, Mr. Snyderman points out.

Hampton Moore is typical of many elementary schools in Philadelphia. Since 1957, a city-wide Committee for the Academically Talented, headed by Russell M. Leonard, superintendent of District Eight, has been examining and re-examining Philadelphia's programs for gifted students. The emphasis, Mr. Leonard says, is on the top students in every school, not merely on those who rate in the top ten or twenty percent on national tests.

Philadelphia programs for the gifted extend from first grade through high school. At Samuel S. Fels Junior High School, for instance, students are offered various tracks in mathematics, English, and other subjects. The advanced track in mathematics, according to Fels Principal William Kaplan, allows top students to complete four years of algebra in their three junior-high years. Top students in English have similar opportunities, and advanced science students can take tenth-grade biology in the ninth grade.

Fels programs for the talented extend into the arts, also, with music opportunities, for example, in a symphony orchestra, a concert band, and a glee club. Language programs are extensive, too. Students in the Spanish classes, for instance, publish a Spanish-language edition of the school paper, which they call *El Pedacito de Fels*.

Students from a number of junior high schools with programs similar to the one at Fels feed into the Abraham Lincoln Junior-Senior High School. At Lincoln they find they have a chance—depending on their grades and on examinations—to enter a block group for enrichment studies. Most of the students in the enrichment block, according to Frances Fink, testing director at Lincoln, are in the 95th or higher percentile in tests such as the Scholastic College Aptitude test.

These top students—about forty in the seventh grade, twice that number in the higher grades fed by neighboring junior highs—are offered as challenging an academic program as Philadelphia can devise. In eighth grade, they study Latin, algebra, and get additional depth in other subjects. In ninth grade, they move to another language (plus Latin if they wish) and must choose five major courses.

As they proceed through twelfth grade, they take advanced science, advanced biology, computer mathematics, and a special English composition course (in addition to the regular English classes). They also receive skill training in typing and in speed reading.

Not surprisingly, ninety percent of the block students go on to college. Principal Charles Williams believes these students have as strong a secondary background as any in the country—in private or public schools.

Philadelphia has not been ignoring the students who are in between the nonreaders at Dunbar and the speed readers at Lincoln High. Vocational schools are active, and solid academic programs are under way for the bulk of the students. In fact, during the past few years, the city has recognized its responsibility to offer more to its children at all levels, but with special emphasis on the Great Cities Program and the programs for the academically talented.

NEW PATTERN: COMMUNITY SCHOOLS / Leo E. Buehring

People who have learned to live together in a neighborhood can live together harmoniously as a nation and as a world. On this premise is based the community school program of Flint, Mich. After more than two decades of experimentation, the people of Flint are convinced of the soundness of this philosophy.

The Flint plan has attracted national, even international attention. The thinking behind it is as follows:

The school's job begins with the families and homes of its attendance area. Within a 10 block school area can be found most of the problems and resources of society. The problems of society are the problems of the public school. Public schools are the most effective instruments for bringing together a community's tremendous human and material resources, for the public school is the only agency left in this country today that can reach a true representation of all the people of its community. By showing its people how to live together at the local level and by putting them in touch with the community resources that can help solve their problems, the community school can clear the way for city, state, national and international harmony. . . .

PROGRAM IN ACTION

As evidence of community-centered thinking, a visitor to Flint may observe such sights as these: neighborhood elementary schools that are busier on almost any evening than during the day; 500 youngsters attending junior high school on Saturday mornings of their own accord to acquire skills they haven't found time for during the regular school week; an elderly woman going back to high school (one of 3000 persons enrolled each year in adult high school education); a family reupholstering dad's easy chair in the school's arts and crafts room (part of 35,000 enrolled annually in 776 adult education courses); community players rehearsing their next production in the auditorium of an elementary school; a school person making neighborhood calls.

The Flint community school also provides the facilities for regular sessions of the neighborhood Teen Club (one of 43 such groups with a card carrying membership of 13,000); for 7000 children on tot lots during the summer; for meetings in the community room of men's clubs, P.T.A.'s and various other organizations; for square dances for parents, teen-agers and the younger ones, and other recreational activities held in the large gymnasium; for a Christmas party attended by 700 adults in a school with an enrollment of only 500.

LAY PARTICIPATION

Flint's community schools constantly are reaching out to their people, encouraging them to determine what they want for themselves and for their children. Every opportunity is utilized to enlist the active participation of parents and other adults.

Parents can take part in the community surveys, serve as representatives on the community council, or work on a wide range of committees designed to promote school and community improvements.

Other parents are depended upon to help in most of the following activities: transporting children, making costumes, publishing the school paper, chaperoning parties, providing furnishings for the community room, working with children in art or music groups, acting as consultants in curriculum building and other areas, working on the health program (including the well baby clinic), maintaining a toy library, setting up displays, serving as volunteers with the teen clubs. Usually there is some place in the building where adults may drop in, even while classes are in session, to visit with one another and with the school staff over a cup of coffee.

Businessmen often find themselves providing materials and supplies for various activities. TV dealers may furnish sets and antennas. A trucker may haul in fill dirt and sand for the community playground or the baseball diamond. Men's clubs have taken on such projects as building ice skating rinks, buying athletic supplies, and coaching sports. In several areas the entire community has participated in park building bees to clear wooded school property for picnic areas.

The nerve center of all the various activities is the meeting of the community council. The latter, made up of the school principal, the community activities coordinator, and representatives of all the clubs that use the building, also is a sounding board. . . .

HOW IT ALL BEGAN

The Flint community school concept developed during the Depression years as a program of recreation. As late as 1935 this typical factory town was having a one-third population turnover every four years, and 30 different nationality groups had to be considered. Hard hit by unemployment, the schools' services had been abbreviated to a minimum, and delinquency ran high. Mr. Manley, then head of the physical education system, sought desperately to raise the funds needed to unlock the doors of the schools' unused gymnasiums and the one swimming pool for use during the evening and on week ends.

A turn in the tide came with a $6000 gift from Charles S. Mott, Flint industrialist. The contribution made it possible to use the schools' play facilities and to employ instructors and supervisors of recreation during after-school hours. Success with this activity led to the opening of several school shops to offer diversion to men out of work.

Convinced by this experiment that it is sound business to help the community help itself, Mr. Mott in 1926 created the Charles Stewart Mott Foundation. In 1935 the foundation began working through the school system, supplying the board of education with risk money with which to undertake pilot projects.

Foundation monies generally have not been invested in school buildings, but rather in expanding and improving recreational and educational services. Funds are made available only when the school board can demonstrate that new activities are needed and that funds not provided by the school budget can be administered in an effective and businesslike manner. Once the merit of a particular undertaking has been established, the pump priming by the foundation ceases and the activity becomes a regular part of the program of the school system.

Stimulated by the foundation's example, support has come to the school system also from other individuals and industry, an example being the $764,942 Ballenger Field House.

In planning its community schools, Flint gives top consideration to community facilities. Each of the nine new elementary schools constructed since 1950 has a community room, a kitchen, an auditorium, and a gymnasium planned with the needs and size of the neighborhood in mind. Of one-story, fire-resistant construction, a community school building's design is an outgrowth of the expressed wants of the individual neighborhood, as well as of its formal educational needs.

Eleven existing buildings have been adapted to community use by the addition of "community wings," others through internal remodeling. The community program comes first. Improved facilities and housing follow as an offshoot of the program.

For the five years 1957-62, the "necessary maximum cost" of school construction is expected to amount to $26¼ million, financed with part of the income from a 2½ mill levy voted during June 1957. Included will be community wing additions at 10 more existing schools and of five new schools.

PATTERN FOR NATION

From virtually all over the globe visitors find their way to Flint to study the city's community school system. Educators there are confident that the program will work equally well in other communities. In fact, they believe that the community school idea will have to be transplanted to other parts of the country if this nation is to demonstrate to the world that our kind of democracy really works.

At about this point some reader may say: "This program is fine for Flint, but our city does not have a Mott Foundation." Flint answers: The program began on a small scale—with $6000 and six boys clubs, to be exact—and it has grown to the present size over many years, always in response to public demand.

The average taxpayer in Flint pays roughly 30 cents a day for his public school program. The cost of the Mott Foundation's enrichment of the program represents only 6.89 percent of the board of education's operating budget. Thus, Flint schoolmen stress, were the taxpayer to assume his proportionate share of the Mott program, his taxes on the average would be increased by only 6.89 percent, or 2.06 cents extra a day.

Regardless of whether pump priming support can be obtained from local donors and industry, Flint educators believe that any school district can make at least a beginning, that no community can afford *not* to look into the community school approach to today's school, community, national and world problems.

CONSIDERATIONS FOR EDUCATIONAL PLANNING / *Carl A. Marburger*

THE DETROIT PROJECT—WORKING TOWARD MORE EFFECTIVE EDUCATION

The objective of the Detroit Great Cities School Improvement Project is to increase the competence of children with limited backgrounds. By competence, we mean not academic competence alone, but competence of the "whole child" in the Harold Taylor meaning of the phrase—social competence, urban living competence, and job, or work skill competence—including the ability to learn new job skills if needed. In addition to the five points of the great cities hypothesis, the Detroit Program has these special emphases:

1. A program of teacher-school-community improvement is more effective if all levels of a school system serving an area (kindergarten through grade 12) are involved. Therefore, the seven schools in the Detroit Project include three elementary schools (kindergarten through grade 6); one elementary school (kindergarten through grade 8); two junior high schools (grades 7 through 9); and one senior high school (grades 10 through 12).

Carl A. Marburger, "Considerations for Educational Planning," Education in Depressed Areas, *A. Henry Passow, ed. New York: Bureau of Publications, Teachers College, Columbia University, 1963, pp. 303–314, 320–321. Reprinted with the permission of Teachers College.*

2. The program should be one which can be financed within the resources of the school budget over a long period, if it can be shown (as we anticipate) that the results of the project warrant the program's continuation and extension into other areas of the city whose school populations have similar problems and needs. Therefore, the yearly budget for the five years of the demonstration project represents an increase of less than 10 percent above normal costs per pupil for the city. Thus, the budget, including the Ford Foundation grant (30 percent of the total budget), is realistic in terms of the fiscal support expected for schools in the Detroit area.

3. Any program designed to solve the problem of educating the child with limited background must operate intensively for several years. Solution of the educational problem involves making long-term changes in family and community attitudes and behavior, as well as changes in a more-or-less immediate nature in the pupil-teacher relationships and services available to the pupil. Time is needed to assure that systems of change shall be functional and lasting in effect. Therefore, Detroit's is a six-year project in the three pilot project schools, and a five-year project in the remaining four. Further, there is a commitment to evaluate the working effect of the project far beyond the actual completion date of its program.

With regard to the Great Cities hypothesis, the Detroit projects make use of several major approaches to the solution of the problems of educating children with limited backgrounds.

One major approach is our work with teachers. Improvement of schooling depends to a great extent upon more effective teaching. Therefore, we strive to modify the perceptions of the teachers of children with limited backgrounds as this perception relates to these children, their community, and their curriculum. Many teachers initially perceive these three negatively; that is, in the light of their own experiential backgrounds. Teachers may bring to their work a rigid value system different than that of the populace of depressed urban areas—a value system, for instance, which presupposes certain limits on the intelligence and ability of the child with limited background. Some teachers have been reared in a different socio-economic situation, and have difficulty in objectively assessing the child with limited background. Other teachers have, through their profession, moved up the socio-economic ladder, and may possibly (and paradoxically) reject the all-too-familiar values of the children they teach. In any case, it is not unusual to find in the classroom a critical need for belief in the universal learning ability of humankind, regardless of socio-economic condition.

Our first attempt to bring about appropriate changes was through a series of workshop experiences. Competent consultants were secured in many disciplines: education, sociology, social work, and psychology. Our experience leads us to believe that very few significant changes in the behavior of teachers take place as a result of listening to experts. Those teachers who were tuned in to hear the experts believed and behaved in terms of what they had heard. Those teachers who were not tuned in to hear the experts did not change their behavior to any noticeable degree as a result of hearing them. The key to modification of behavior seems to be involvement.

Our workshops and in-service experiences have, therefore, been structured around local school curriculum problems and have usually involved only a single school staff. We have found that curricula vary from school to school, from community to community, and from school staff to school staff. To achieve the kind of involvement that brings positive change, *each* school staff must look seriously at its unique community, the unique problems of its youth, and its own unique strengths and weaknesses as a staff. Then the school staff may search for appropriate curricular and organizational modifications to strengthen its own school situation.

Our attempts to assist staffs to do this have taken several forms. We have provided workshop experiences through the local university. If teachers and administrators wish to have a course for credit toward an advanced degree or a number of hours beyond the Bachelor's or Master's, they may pay tuition to the university for the workshop experience. If they wish to take part in the workshop but do not wish the credit, the Detroit Great Cities Project pays their tuition so that they may audit the course.

Other local school-curriculum workshops have taken place on Saturdays, and also during the summer months. As a part of the Detroit school policy, teachers involved have been paid for their time on Saturdays and during the summer. Furthermore, some released time has been devoted to in-service education. Indications are that more released time is now an essential need.

As a result of these in-service experiences, some organizational and curriculum changes have been made. We have instituted the non-graded primary in two elementary schools. Block-time and core classes are being held in the junior high schools. Team teaching is being tried in two of the schools.

Curriculum modifications come more slowly. One significant curriculum change has taken place in our early elementary reading materials—but not without difficulty. It has long been felt that children might read with greater facility if the material with which they were dealing was more nearly related to their own real backgrounds. Negro youth, for example, rarely have an opportunity to see a Negro child illustrated in the little picture books with which they learn to read. Through a series of writing workshops we set out to build a series of pre-primers which would focus on the life of a working-class family, living in a typical, racially mixed, urban neighborhood. In spite of the sophistication of the writing committee members, we now know first hand the perils of revolutionary primer writing. The artist doing illustrations for the series depicted some typical housekeeping situations (brooms leaning in the corner, a kitchen sink with exposed pipes beneath it) and this—at least relative to other pre-primers, which do not treat the realities of housekeeping quite as fully—was taken simply as poor housekeeping, and thereby as a derogation of the Negro since this was the home of a Negro family.

The first pre-primer was only one-third the length of a normal pre-primer, because we wanted each child to have the satisfaction of completing a book in a short time. Thus, we inadvertently left the father out of the first pre-primer; indeed, we did not even refer to him. This was also interpreted as a derogation, not only of the Negro family depicted, but of Negro families in general. Finally, we called the little-boy hero of the series "Sammy." It was an unfortunate choice, since it was seen by middle-class Negro families as "stereotype by insinuation."

Having gleaned some important lessons from this experience, we expanded our primer writing committee with a number of consultants, both lay and professional, and revised the series. The first three pre-primers of this series were available in four-color reproduction in September of 1962, for experimental testing.

Other minor curriculum changes have taken place at different levels. We have produced some units for block-time classes at the secondary level, which have been found to be very useful throughout the entire school system for block-time classes.

Perhaps the only significant change in curriculum is what happens when the individual teacher closes the door of her classroom. Assuming the requisite skills in teaching the basic materials, the teacher's attitude is the most crucial factor.

At this point in our project, we conceive the formula that teacher-expectations have surprising impact on pupil-achievement. Indeed we might even say that teacher expectations have a similar impact on pupil intelligence scores. The teacher who expects achievement, who has hope for the educability of his pupils, indeed conveys this through every nuance and subtlety of his behavior. The teacher who conveys hopelessness for the educability of his children usually does so without ever really verbalizing such an attitude—at least, in front of his pupils.

With regard to expectations of pupil ability to learn, a significant experiment was done recently by Robert Rosenthal and Kermit L. Fode of the University of North Dakota. In a carefully controlled experiment, twelve senior division students in experimental psychology were assigned a group of five albino rats for running through a maze ten times a day for five days. Although the rats were randomly selected, each student was informed that the rats were either "maze-bright" or "maze-dull."

> Results indicated that on three of the five days and for the experiment as a whole, E's [experimenters] believing their S's [subjects] to be bright obtained performance from them significantly superior to that obtained by E's believing their S's to be dull. The S's believed to be bright appeared to be learning the problem while those believed to be dull did not. These results occurred in spite of the fact that on the level of verbal report *both* groups of E's wanted their S's to perform well. In addition, a research assistant following the identical experimental procedure, was able to obtain, without "cheating," performance from her S's superior even to that obtained by E's believing their S's were bright. Comparing the degree of correlation between what each E specifically expected to obtain from his S's and what he actually did obtain from them for the "Bright" and "Dull" groups suggested that these groups were about equally biased although, of course, in opposite directions (4).

Thus, even when dealing with non-human subjects, the experimenter's expectations, seem most significant in determining the performance of the subject. Certainly the expectations of the teacher for her pupils can determine, particularly in depressed-urban-area schools, the school survival or non-survival of the youth. If nothing else, teacher expectations affect the time spent in preparing to teach, the amount of real concern for individual students, and the degree of "soul" the teacher gives to his work.

The involvement of an almost total staff, including administration, would seem then to be essential for innovation in curriculum, and for modification of behavior to insure truly effective teaching. We obviously cannot expect anything approximately 100 percent involvement of staff, but the nearer we come to this ideal, and to the contagion of enthusiasm which results from it, the greater the possibility of creating the milieu in which youth, particularly disadvantaged youth, can learn.

In order that teachers of children with limited backgrounds may maintain enthusiasm for teaching, and hope for the educability of their children, they must be continually reinforced. The teacher needs adequate resources to combat the corrosive influences of emotional and physical poverty with which many of his students live day in and day out. The teacher needs help to teach effectively in spite of the inadequate facilities which often seem typical of inner city schools. High transiency rates and the generally low achievement of pupils beset by out-of-school difficulties which carry over demonstrably into the classroom can overwhelm the most conscientious teacher.

The Detroit Project does provide some reinforcement to teachers. Additional personnel, whose duties are discussed at length later in this paper, provide some aid in working with children whose reading, speech and arithmetic disabilities are pronounced, in developing stronger ties and understanding between families and the school, and so forth. Referrals of children with physical or emotional difficulties can be made more readily by the classroom teacher in Great Cities Project schools. After school and evening programs, with clubs, remedial and enrichment classes, and recreational activities tend to provide a more beneficent climate for the child than street play might provide, and to orient the child more specifically to the school and the teacher than would otherwise be so. A full summer-school program involving a large percentage of the school population not only provides interesting learning and recreational experiences for the child, but helps him to carry over what he has learned, in behavior as well as in actual knowledge, from one school year into the next.

One more concrete means of reinforcement is the addition to the general fund of each school a sum ranging from $350 to $450 to be used by the staff for the purchase of small supplies and materials which are not available through normal requisition channels. Another is the provision of funds and transportation for an additional four to five hundred bus trips to farms, parks, museums, and the like for the seven schools in the project.

Significant though these additions may be, they are basically without purpose if the teacher does not have the opportunity in his classroom to be experimental, to be innovative, to be free to do those things which are important for the children. Such freedom to do what is needed is there, or is lamentably lacking, in accordance with the administrative style of the principal of the school. Is the school's administrative staff restrictive or non-restrictive, authoritarian or democratic, legalistic or expeditious? These are knotty questions to ask, difficult questions to answer, but they are important since they are germane to the nature of the teaching and learning processes which exist in each school. It has often been stated that the most important single individual in any community is the elementary school principal. I would extend this to all levels of school administration, elementary and secondary. To illustrate, the most obvious deterrent to enthusiastic and imaginative teaching is the authoritarian who sees his school as an armed camp which admits a school population in the morning, regiments them until early afternoon, and then sends them home, five days a week. More insidious and difficult is the legalist, who represses his staff, who processes each decision with perfect logic and imperfect premises, who operates exclusively through a tight chain of command, who so dampens enthusiasm and subverts innovation that any external assistance provides only short-term palliative results.

Documentation of the statements made above regarding teacher attitude and administrative behavior is very difficult. We have considerable evidence to support these statements. However, because of the experimental nature of the project there is need to preserve a modicum of security since release of research data could indeed contaminate the results of the experiment, particularly with our control schools. Some of the methodology used in our research will be discussed later in this paper.

WORK WITH PARENTS AND COMMUNITY

The second primary focus of our attention is upon the parents and the community. Once again, this is a question of involvement. Parents who are not involved, who do not know what is taking place in the school, can certainly not reinforce what the school is doing with their children. We also see a need to involve parents and the community so that we may raise the aspirations of the parents and their children with regard to academic and social achievement. Parents in depressed urban areas typically stay away from schools. They stay away from school because their own experiences have been either unpleasant or short-lived or both. They are fearful of the institution of the school and they lack information about what is taking place in the school. They do not typically join organizations and therefore do not normally attend parent-group meetings, do not participate in adult-education classes—they generally avoid all school contacts.

We have tried to make our Great Cities Project schools true community schools. This means that the schools must necessarily be open from eight o'clock in the morning until late at night. One of our first approaches to parents was to ask them to tell us the kinds of experiences they would like to have in the afternoons and evenings for themselves and for their children. The parents so contacted were normally those who were more articulate and more solvent economically and who had higher aspirations for themselves and their youth. The so-called hard-to-reach parents were not particularly interested regardless of what the school might offer. Using those parents who could and would respond to our inquiries, we first provided free clubs and classes which were of the upgrading nature. These classes were designed to help parents gain more skills. Often parents had unrealistic expectations about these classes, believing that jobs would become available to them as a result of their classwork. A few have gained some skills through these classes and have been able to obtain, if not better employment, at least techniques which enhanced their leadership potential and communications skills. These first classes included shorthand, speech, typing, sewing, millinery, cake decorating, and the like. The parents then told us that such classes were fine, but asked if it might be possible to provide some classes in reading and arithmetic so that parents could refresh these skills and help their children in their studies. This we did.

Even more crucial than these skill classes were the informal groups, clubs, and classes which were organized around parents' newly expressed needs. Simply the opportunity to meet together, to plan for their youngsters, to take short-term enrichment classes, to learn how to budget, how to prepare food, how to repair furniture, to be more efficient and effective in household tasks and family relations—all of these provided the adults with opportunities to bolster self-esteem and to raise aspirations for themselves and their children.

These clubs and their classes have been taught by teachers on both a voluntary and paid basis and by lay persons from the local community and from the total metropolitan area. In addition, many youth from the community have been hired as baby-sitters, teacher's aides and assistants for afternoon and evening classes and clubs. Altogether there are more than two hundred after-school clubs and classes for youth and adults in the seven schools.

Each school has had to organize after-school and evening activities in terms of its own community and the needs of that community. Some of the schools have put a greater emphasis on the enrichment programs for youth in the afternoon, others on adult programs in the evening. The greatest difficulty in involvement of youth and adults has naturally come at the secondary level, where the ambivalence of youth toward their parents and the size of the school attendance area mitigate against parental participation in school functions.

We have reached not only the "parents who go to PTA meetings"; we have been able, through the skills of some of our additional personnel, to involve a great many of the so-called hard-to-reach parents. The number of people involved in these after-school and evening activities varies, because of the short-term duration of some of the classes and clubs, but it averages between fifteen hundred and two thousand youth and adults each week.

One of the dangers inherent in such involvement of parents is the over-involvement of certain parents. We found that many of our adults would attend as many as four and five evenings a week, with the result that our program tended to fragment rather than bind families closer together. We have gone a long way in solving this problem by scheduling family nights, when the entire family participates in the available activities. We further restrict the number of evenings any family may be involved. We have also experienced some difficulty as a result of the hiring of local people. The moment that one hires people from the local community, one gives them a status which then raises them above their peers and sometimes causes a degree of rejection and considerable resentment of their new leadership capacity.

A further difficulty is the tendency to develop "programs for program's sake" rather than in the terms of the needs of the community. Competition often sets in between schools and results in the scheduling of classes without any inquiry into the needs, expressed and otherwise, of the local school community.

One additional hazard that is very real in this community-school sort of operation in urban depressed areas is the danger of making the parents too dependent on the school. Parents must become dependent on the school initially, if they are to be involved at all. They must see the school as a resource for helping them with their personal and community problems. This project will not succeed if it does not develop an indigenous leadership, which assumes responsibility on its own for the problems of individuals and the local community. We have no intention of relieving parents of their responsibilities as parents, but we want them to ask for help so that they can find ways of working out the solutions to their problems themselves. We attempt in this manner to revive the positive parent-child relationship which is so often lacking in the disadvantaged family.

In order to accomplish both the teacher and parent reinforcement, we must have additional help for the regular staff of each school. This we have provided by adding three additional personnel to each of the school staffs: a school-community agent, a full-time visiting teacher, and a full-time coaching teacher or language arts consultant.

THE SCHOOL-COMMUNITY AGENT

Theoretically, the school-community agent should be a trained social worker with experience in both community organization and group-work. We were not able to achieve this ideally, but have some persons with this background and others with professional training (usually in education) and considerable experience in community organization and group-work activities. The school-community agent is, simply enough, a liaison between the community and the school. This person interprets to the community the functions of the school and interprets to the staff of the school the realities of the community. One of the agent's most important functions is to work with organized block clubs, community councils, and parent groups, if these exist, and to help organize such groups if they do not exist. In addition, we have asked these agents to assume responsibility for the after-school and evening programs for youth and adults. Often these two roles are in serious conflict. The administrative and supervisory functions which are part of the after-school and evening programs do not allow the school-community agent the freedom he requires to become the detached worker; a role which we have found is essential to successful organization of a fragmented and uncohesive depressed-area neighborhood. Further, the administrative style of each school can limit the agent to a program director's capacity or free him to become a detached expert doing constructive work in the neighborhood.

The visiting teacher is the school social worker. This person has had specific training in the case-work methodology and operates primarily with children and the parents of children who have crucial school-adjustment problems. The visiting teacher is normally assigned in the Detroit schools; but she is usually assigned to six or more schools and spends perhaps a half a day a week in each school attempting to handle an unrealistic case load in this fragmented fashion. In the Great Cities Project, the visiting teacher is assigned full time and is thus able to establish roots in the neighborhood and to work closely with the specific problems of the school and the community, its youth and parents. She is able to deal more successfully with fewer cases, to know and understand the school staff and politics, and to become identified with her school and hence with parents. As we examine the role of the visiting teacher in the new five-day-a-week involvement in a single school, we are asking additional questions about the training and certification of these persons. A Michigan law requires that visiting teachers be certified as teachers and, in addition, have Master's degrees in social work with emphasis in case work. We are questioning the necessity for the teaching certificate and are examining the possibility of a combination case and group-work training because the needs of the clients often dictate group-work rather than case-work therapy.

The coaching teacher is actually a language-arts teacher who is performing special remedial functions with children who are retarded in reading. She often conducts small classes ranging from five to fifteen children working on the particular skill deficiencies of children. Once again, the coaching teacher's role is changing. She often finds its more effective to work less specifically with small groups of children and more with total staff in helping all teachers gain the necessary skills to work with the reading deficiencies of children regardless of the subject matter area.

We have seen some startling results show up in achievement in the relatively short period of a semester or a year as a result of this individualized attention given to students by the coaching teachers. We cannot make any claims about this progress in achievement until we have a look at it over a long period to see if there is a retention of the gain.

SCHOOL-AGENCY COOPERATION

In addition to the use of these specialized personnel we have also had intensive public and private agency involvement. The success of any community-school venture depends in large measure on the concentrated use of available public and private agency personnel and resources. The Detroit Great Cities School Improvement Project has therefore developed these programs:

1. In cooperation with the Neighborhood Service Organization and the Detroit Behavior Project, day camps were conducted at one of our schools during the summer of 1961 for fifty-five emotionally disturbed children from the project schools.

2. We have used the YMCA and YWCA programs and facilities. In addition to the use of their busses and physical facilities, we have many YMCA and YWCA groups meeting in our after-school program with agency, school, and lay personnel involved in leadership capacities.

3. We have shared facilities and personnel with the Detroit Parks and Recreation Department. We use one of their large recreation centers, and they use the swimming pools in the school buildings. The Detroit Parks and Recreation Department, a municipal agency separate from the schools, has also provided new programs in project schools where no recreation program had existed before.

4. We have increased the school's use of public library facilities, by shuttle-bussing children in "library caravans" to inner-city libraries. Parents served as assistant librarians on these ventures.

5. We are conducting intensive research into the relationship between physical and nutritional needs of children and the learning process, in cooperation with the Detroit Department of Health, which is a separate city agency. The health examination clinic, which was established in one of our schools by the Pilot Club of Detroit, contains all of the equipment and facilities necessary to do a complete physical examination of the school population. The Detroit Department of Health is providing funds to reimburse the examining pediatricians.

6. We have had continuing contacts with local churches as an integral part of the school-community agents' function.

Often in urban depressed areas there is a tendency for churches and both public and private agencies to move their services from that area to other areas where progress is more easily identified. The agencies which remain in the depressed area often provide overlapping services to the hard-to-reach parents of the community. This leads to the duplication of financial aid and conflicting advice being given to families.

As a result, the Detroit Great Cities Program has developed a theoretical rationale clarifying the role of the school as it relates to the agencies and social work methodologies. This rationale is dynamic, in that it changes as new insights and role definitions develop.

We feel that the public schools, particularly the elementary schools, provide the structures in which social-work functions may best be performed. The encapsulated, or limited and defined, elementary-school *population* and the inclusion within elementary school *boundaries* of a relatively fixed population, offer one of the best field situations presently available. The school has other assets. It is established, it has access to the home, and its records for each child will automatically provide information on a large percentage of the population in the school's boundaries. Such boundaries do include the families of parochial and private students and citizens whose children have gone through school. In these cases, even though the social work contact is not as readily made, at least the boundaries are fixed and provide a localized area for social work operation. The elementary school, therefore, could provide the basis of operations for case-work, group-work and community-work functions. These functions could be operated by school personnel or by public, private, and agency personnel. Yet at the present time, exclusive of this project, Detroit's schools are involved only in limited casework through the Visiting Teacher Program.

CONCLUSION

What are the "short-term" forecasts for the Great Cities Project in Detroit? It is believed that a considerably larger number of children attending project schools will leave them with positive self-images, higher goals, greater scholastic achievement, and improved citizenship; they are expected to be more adequately prepared for continuing school or going to work—independent rather than dependent citizens.

It should be stressed that the Detroit Great Cities Project is not unique in its premises or in its purposes. Individual teachers and schools in Detroit and across the nation are striving to meet the needs of the child with limited background. With little organized help, and no extra funds, their work has been done with dedication and enthusiasm. Such efforts are inspirational, but they are often a stopgap, and we cannot hope that they will resolve a dilemma which has grown to such proportions that it can be met only with concerted, total-community effort. Now, as the community becomes fully aware of wasted manpower, the hard core of unemployed, the high-school drop-out and his inability in most cases to compete for a place in today's overcrowded, skill-demanding job market, it will turn more and more to educators, first for explanations, and then for positive and workable solutions. And educators must be able to provide these solutions, by bridging the gap between what the schools now offer and what life with increasing technology and urbanization demands of an individual.

And that gap does exist. In spite of the fact that more youth are finishing high school and going on to college, increasing numbers of young men and women, including a good percentage of the most able and most intelligent youth, do not find what they need in school, do not learn, lose purpose and direction, and drop out. They are abetted by indecisive parents, tolerated by an apathetic community, often tacitly disestablished by the school.

Certainly we have a commitment as a society to these youth. We should live up to that commitment, preferably before the sad decision to drop out is made. We should consider ways to prevent this crisis. It is far more wasteful of human and fiscal resources to wait until rehabilitation is necessary; particularly when we know the ways we must go to reduce drastically the number of drop-outs, and to make schooling more effective as preparation for life.

Perhaps the most significant thing about the Detroit Great Cities Project, and similar projects in many great cities, is that it stands as a statement of need, as a formal attempt on the part of a superintendent and a board of education to establish a structure which has the funds, the personnel and the support to do a thorough job of proving that all children, no matter how difficult their situation may be, can be well-educated and positively motivated.

I will close with a short list of observations about youth in today's society, made by Professor Earl Kelley (1). He states that all adults, and educators in particular, need to keep always before them these points:

1. Our culture is in jeopardy unless we can adequately care for our young.
2. Our young people are all right when we get them. If all is not well with them, it is due to what has happened to them in an adult-managed world.
3. If youth have not been too badly damaged by the life that has been thrust upon them, they enjoy and desire a good society as much as we do.
4. In urban society, our young live under more difficult circumstances than they used to.
5. The amount of juvenile delinquency in any community is a measure of that community's lack of concern for its young.
6. There is really no valid, responsible place in our urban communities for youth. They are a displaced segment of our society.
7. A place must be made for them and it seems to me that the only feasible place is the school.

It is our hope that the Detroit Great Cities School Improvement Project, in consultation and coordination with other Great Cities projects, can make schools in depressed urban areas the really "feasible place" for youth to grow to independent competent citizenship.

———

A school's success in educating culturally disadvantaged children depends on its administration. Jack Cohn has imaginatively applied the Higher Horizons program to his own grade school and has realized, with a well-motivated faculty, remarkable results.

INTEGRATION OF SPANISH-SPEAKING NEWCOMERS IN A "FRINGE AREA" SCHOOL / Jack Cohn

Ours is a large elementary school in a fringe area. That is a euphemistic way of saying we are on the edge of segregation. Nearby is Harlem. The geographical contour of our community has made it not easily accessible from the Harlem area.

A DIVERSIFIED POPULATION

Many groups now make up the community of which our school is a vital part. The largest group in our school is Puerto Rican—a little more than 55 percent of our present total of 1200.

The Puerto Ricans are not the only ones of Spanish-speaking background in our school. We have another bloc of Spanish-speaking pupils, 9 percent of the total enrollment, about half of whom come from Cuba, the rest from other Hispano-American countries—Dominican Republic, Colombia, Ecuador, Nicaragua, and other Central American, South American, and Caribbean countries. To the Spanish-speaking group we must add a small number of children of Philippine background.

The remainder of the school population, 36 percent, is about evenly divided between Negro pupils and pupils of very heterogeneous ori-

———

Jack Cohn, "Integration of Spanish-Speaking Newcomers in a 'Fringe Area' School," National Elementary Principal (May 1960), pp. 29–33. Reprinted with the permission of the Department of Elementary School Principals, National Education Association.

gins. Some of the Negro group were born in the neighborhood; others came from the West Indies; some have moved in from other Northern cities and an increasing number are coming from the South. Something more than 3 percent are Oriental—Chinese, Japanese, a few Koreans. About 15 percent form a very mixed group—Greeks, Armenians, Jews, Irish, others—a conglomerate and endlessly fascinating variety. Some 30 different national backgrounds are represented in our school population. The alert faces in any of our kindergartens show clearly that our roots are many.

CLASSIFYING FLUENCY IN ENGLISH

There are other basic factors that must be taken into account before any school organization can be drawn up. There are more than 425 non-English-speaking children out of our 1200 total according to a recent census using the classification developed by The Puerto Rican Study. The classification scale of The Puerto Rican Study has been accepted as the criterion on which additional State Aid Funds are allotted. It is a scale which we refer to frequently for organizational and instructional purposes in the school. The scale follows:

PUERTO RICAN STUDY SCALE

A Speaks English, for his age level, like a native with no foreign accent.

B Speaks English with a foreign accent, but otherwise approximates the fluency of a native speaker of like age level.

C Can speak English well enough for most situations met by typical native pupils of like age, but still must make a conscious effort to avoid the language forms of his native tongue. Depends, in part, upon translation and therefore speaks hesitantly upon occasion.

D Speaks English in more than a few stereotyped situations, but speaks it haltingly at all times.

E Speaks English only in those stereotyped situations for which he has learned a few useful words and expressions.

F Speaks no English.

G Child has been in class less than a week, and cannot be accurately rated at this time.

ORGANIZATION OF NON-ENGLISH-SPEAKING CLASSES

To organize the school to optimum advantage, a variety of factors must be taken into account. The non-English-speaking youngsters have to be placed, in the main, in classes of registers of 25 or less which include 50 percent non-English-speaking pupils. These classes have been set up in accordance with a special New York State Aid formula.

Additional state funds are alotted conditional upon the maintenance of the low registers indicated. The 1959 census, taken in part for the purpose of determining the additional State Aid that the City of New York is entitled to, showed that 37 percent of the children in our school fell into the categories C-G on The Puerto Rican Study Scale. These figures were arrived at by careful briefing of all teachers with close follow-up by our teacher-coordinator of education for non-English-speaking children. She is a fine, experienced teacher, assigned full time to our school for the purpose of working directly with teachers of these children. She worked closely with The Puerto Rican Study throughout the four years of that experiment. We have had this position since 1952 when the school opened.

Because of the large number of children listed as non-English-speaking, about two-thirds of our classes have had to be established as so-called "NE" classes, i.e., classes in which at least half of the children are in various stages of learning English. The rest, of course, are of English-speaking background.

The "NE" children assigned to these classes are generally not the more recent arrivals. For those who have come to the mainland within the past three or four months, we have found other patterns of organization more suitable.

Two classes—in past years it has occasionally risen to three—consist of recent arrivals 9 to 13 years of age who come almost entirely from countries where Spanish is the official language. These classes, which have proven to be very successful, are the responsibility of two teachers who have had considerable experience with such children. The teachers understand and speak Spanish competently. Initially, for communication purposes, they use some Spanish in the course of instruction. Occasionally, Spanish is used by older arrivals to prevent loss of knowledge already acquired in countries of origin. Parents of the children in these classes are encouraged to meet with the teachers. Because they learn that the teacher will be able to understand them, most of the parents take advantage of the chance to find out more about our way of life.

These two classes for new arrivals have been of particular benefit to the bright non-English-speaking pupils. Many have found their place among bright English-speaking children within the relatively short period of one year.

For the non-English-speaking children in the lower grades, other organizational patterns are in use. We find that most new arrivals do rather well in regular class organization. For those who need special help, there is a short period of orientation under our Puerto Rican teacher.

Like the "NE Coordinator," the Puerto Rican teacher (officially designated as Substitute Auxiliary Teacher) is assigned full time. About 40 percent of her time is utilized in the orientation program. Daily for one hour at a time, she gathers together and works with two groups, each consisting of 10 lower-grade children who appear to need such help. This orientation program lasts from two to six weeks. Through it, these children gain some knowledge of their school and community and a feeling of confidence in their regular teachers and in their ability to cope with their new surroundings. Teachers have frequently commented favorably upon the change in the children in the orientation program. During this period, there is constant consultation between the Puerto Rican teacher (Substitute Auxiliary Teacher) and the regular teacher.

For the "NE" children, then, our organization requires their placement in "NE" classes, maximum register 25, with at least half of the pupils falling into the "NE" category on a specially devised scale. The other half of each "NE" class consists of English-speaking children who are neither the advanced learners nor the slowest in the grade. This organization has been found most effective as a result of an intensive experiment made by The Puerto Rican Study. With a skilled teacher, neither the English-speaking nor the non-English-speaking group is held back.

CURRICULUM FOR "NE CLASSES"

What of the curriculum for the non-English-speaking? Here The Puerto Rican Study has made a notable contribution. For each grade level, a bulletin containing a series of resource units has been developed, based on the regular curriculum for that grade. Suggested material and activities for the orientation of the "NE" child are also included.

Accompanying these bulletins is a parallel series of language guides worked out for double grade levels, such as 1-2, 3-4, 5-6. These guides contain suggested vocabulary and language patterns to be used with the resource units.

Perhaps the most important task of the "NE" coordinator is to assist individual teachers in the implementation of the program outlined in these bulletins. This specialist is directly responsible to the head of the school but receives further information and training through a central organization.

We have found that there is a need for broadening of experience through many trips, programming of certain periods with other classes (e.g., gym, and assembly), and special activities such as ceramics which lead to considerable use of language under the guidance of a skilled teacher. The supervisor assumes responsibility for organization of all of these, arranges demonstrations, and, if necessary, does not hesitate to handle some demonstrations personally.

Broadening of experience, intensive study of carefully selected vocabulary, and constant use of common language patterns are provided for in the bulletins prepared for teachers who have non-English-speaking children in their classes. The supervisor of a school in which there is a substantial percentage of non-English-speaking pupils is perforce obliged to give much time to the supervision, organization, and administration of a worthwhile program for these children.

Flexibility in placement is of special importance. Children who are ready for continuous work in English are moved to classes to meet their needs. The time for this is determined by the teacher in consultation with one of the supervisors. Readiness is indicated if a pupil has reached at least the "C" level on the Puerto Rican Study Scale, if, in his teacher's considered opinion, he seems to have adjusted to the environment of the metropolis, and if he has begun to show progress in basic academic areas as revealed by informal and standardized tests.

The pattern that evolved was to organize Spanish-speaking parents as a direct and important committee of the parents association within the school, gradually helping the Spanish-speaking to discover their own leadership. Several times a year, the committee of Spanish-speaking parents met separately. Three classes in "English for Adults" were established and still meet regularly. Many parents have learned to speak English and most business of the parents association is now conducted in English. Parents of Spanish-speaking background have taken their place in the leadership of the parents association.

The Substitute Auxiliary Teacher (Puerto Rican Teacher) has performed yeoman service in establishing good rapport with parents and community. Most of her time is devoted to social service work under the supervisor's direction. Home visits are made when they are found to be necessary. Many parents now come into our school to see the Substitute Auxiliary Teacher and daily office hours have been established. Problems related to the health of children, to establishment of understanding between child and school and between parent and school are taken up the by "S.A.T." (Substitute Auxiliary Teacher). Our S.A.T. has become a one-woman social agency. She confers constantly with supervisors regarding the cases with which she is currently involved.

The parents have also found that the teachers are very receptive to their needs. They soon become aware that the teachers bring understanding to their children's problems. They have found that about one-third of our faculty are now able to communicate with them in Spanish. This accounts in part for the lengthy visits by 850 fathers and mothers during the last Open School Week. The "S.A.T." and the "NE" coordinator have acted as interpreters whenever called upon to do so.

We have not forgotten the parents of the English-speaking. We have found that the parents of these children had to be convinced that their children were not lost in our zeal to take care of the overriding problems presented by the "NE" pupils. We realized early that only as the needs of the English-speaking were met could we hope to deal successfully with the problems presented by the non-English-speaking.

PROVISIONS FOR THE ENGLISH-SPEAKING

How can the supervisory staff take care of the needs of the English-speaking in a school with a large percentage of non-English-speaking? Advanced learners are kept together. We find about 10 percent of our pupils fall into this category on each grade level. Gifted teachers are selected to work with them. They are identified early, even from the kindergarten on. We have carried on an experiment in the acceleration of one group to determine whether the first three years can be completed successfully in two. Children talented in art and music have been identified and special programs arranged for them. The junior high school to which our sixth-graders go continues the programs for advanced learners and for talented children.

Organization of classes for normal and slow learners of English-speaking background does not differ from that found in many schools. Slow learners are generally placed in classes of small register with a sympathetic teacher. Normal children are classified according to reading ability. We try to limit the reading range to two groups in any one class. Experimentally, over the last three years, we have established five classes on grade levels three to six on an individualized reading program. These classes have proven to be very successful for normal and slow learners.

With a faculty of very talented teachers, willing to put their talents to the service of children, we have been able to develop a program of enrichment which would not otherwise be possible. We have encouraged the development of science learnings in our children. Their eager curiosity and the developing ability to think have been fostered. The district mathematics coordinator, a fine resource person, has set up a special program for bright youngsters in grades two to six. Our teachers have nurtured interests in the arts. An elaborate ceramics program has been developed in which the children learn processes from wedging clay to glazing to turning pieces on the potter's wheel. We now have three small kilns. Our children have been represented in a number of exhibits of painting and ceramics. A talented musician-teacher has brought forth the best in these youngsters musically.

We have not forgotten basic tools in the learning process. Our brightest readers in the sixth grade read well above grade level on standardized tests. The same holds true in mathematics. For the last four years, 10 percent or more of the pupils in the sixth grade have been placed in special progress classes or schools for the gifted. Another 10 percent have been placed in classes for children showing talent in art or music.

Much of the organization and planning for English-speaking children does not differ from that found in many public elementary schools in New York. It is in the combination of programs for the English-speaking and the non-English-speaking that a whole new series of problems arises in supervision, administration, and teaching. We seek some reasonably satisfactory solutions to the tremendous variety of pupil needs in order to integrate our Spanish-speaking newcomers into the mainstream of American life.

REFERENCES

Anderson, N. *The Urban Community: A World Perspective*. New York: Holt, Rinehart and Winston, Inc., 1959.

Beers, H., and C. Heflin. *Urban Adjustments of Rural Migrants*. Lexington, Ky.: Agricultural Experiment Station, Bulletin 487, June 1946.

Grambs, Jean D. *Education in a Transition Community*. New York: National Conference of Christians and Jews, 1955.

Mumford, Lewis. *The Culture of Cities*. New York: Harcourt, Brace & World, Inc., 1938.

Quinn, J. A. *Urban Sociology*. New York: American Book Company, 1955.

Weaver, Robert. *The Negro Ghetto*. New York: Harcourt, Brace & World, Inc., 1948.

PERIODICALS

Blessing, Charles A. "Two Cities: Designs for Life in Milan and Detroit." *Graduate Comment,* Wayne State University, IV (October 1960), 6.

Dodson, Dan W. "The Changing Neighborhood." *Educational Leadership,* 18 (May 1961), 497–501.

Dotson, Floyd, "Pattern of Voluntary Association among Urban Working Class Families." *American Sociological Review,* 16 (October 1951), 687–697.

Havighurst, Robert J. "Metropolitan Development and the Educational System." *School Review,* 69 (Autumn 1961), 251–267.

{Chapter Seven}

CONTROVERSIAL ISSUES AFFECTING EDUCATION

All adaptations of education are being made in the context of a changing society which seeks to give greater meaning to the democratic ideals and to better fit some of those ideals to an emerging social system. As courts and legislative bodies attempt to resolve the conflicts involved in this process, social ends become clarified. The expectation of education is that it will become an instrumental means to these ends.

A clarification of societal goals, however, does not necessarily solve the problems of adaptation which face education. Although the mandates of society come from a state and national level, education operates in the limited frame of local districts. Ideals of the greater society are often translated into problems within the local ethos.

The obvious example of such a situation is that of the racially segregated South. But what of the suburban community, mostly Catholic or Lutheran, where the public school must because of local tax structure and national edicts virtually compete with the parochial system for financial support? How

277

is a district to serve community interests if that community regards religious observances as a necessary part of formal education? How can a system resolve the inequalities of de facto segregation in the urban community which has a long-standing tradition of neighborhood schools? The following chapter discusses problems of this nature which have been raised in urban education as a result of recent public attention given to controversial issues of our society.

As a culture undergoes change, ideological conflicts arise. Education becomes a major arena of controversy and debate. George Spindler analyzes the value shifts occurring in our culture today and tells how they affect education.

EDUCATION IN A TRANSFORMING AMERICAN CULTURE / *George D. Spindler*

The American public school system, and the professional educators who operate it, have been subjected to increasingly strident attacks from the public and from within its own ranks. My premise is that these attacks can best be understood as symptoms of an American culture that is undergoing transformation—a transformation that produces serious conflict. I shall discuss this transformation as a problem in culture change that directly affects all of education and everyone identified with it.

The notion of social and cultural change is used persuasively, if carelessly, by too many writers to explain too much. Generalized allusions to technological change, cultural lag, the atomic age, the mass society, are more suggestive than clarifying. We must strike to the core of the change. My argument is that this core can best be conceived as a radical shift in values.

The anthropologist, and I speak as one but not for all, sees culture as a goal-oriented system. These goals are expressed, patterned, lived out by people in their behaviors and aspirations in the form of values —objects or possessions, conditions of existence features of personal-

George D. Spindler, "Education in a Transforming Culture," Harvard Educational Review, *XXV, 1955, pp. 145–156. Reprinted with the permission of the author and the* Harvard Educational Review.

ity or character, and states of mind, that are conceived as desirable, and act as motivating determinants of behaviors. It is the shifts in what I believe to be the core values in American culture, and the effect of these shifts on education today, that I wish to discuss. These shifts in values will be seen as the conditions of life to which education and educators, whether progressives, experimentalists, conservatives, or in-betweens, must adapt—and to which they are adapting, albeit confusedly. My emphasis within the value frame-work will be upon shifts in the conception of the desirable character type, since education can never be freed from the obligation to support, if not produce, the features of personality and social character deemed desirable in society.

There is a body of literature on American culture. M. Mead (1942), C. and F. Kluckhohn (1947), C. Kluckhohn (1949), L. Warner (1953, 1959), G. Gorer (1948), D. Riesman (1950), M. Lantis (1955), S. Lipset and L. Lowenthal (1961). These writings range from the highly intuitive to the observation-based. Though there is consensus, and a surprising degree of it, on the part of these students of American culture, little they say can be or is intended by them to be taken as empirically demonstrated. These writings are useful as a starting point but most emphasize static patterning in values more than change in values. To extend the factual baseline I have been collecting relevant data from college students for the past eight years. The sample consists of several hundred students, ranging in age from 19 to 57 years, mainly participants in professional education courses, and representing socio-economic strata describable as lower-middle to upper-middle class. The sample is as representative of this professional group and these economic strata as any regionally biased sample can be. I have used two simple value-projective techniques. The aim has been to find out what features of social character (the term I will use to designate those personality elements that are most relevant to social action) the students in the sample hold as being valuable and that presumably influence their behavior in classrooms. The first of these techniques is a series of 24 open-ended statements; such as "The individual is ———," "Intellectuals should ———," "All men are born ———." The second of these techniques is to require each student to write one brief paragraph describing his (or her) conception of the "Ideal American Boy."

The statements to be made now about American values, their shift, and the effect on education, are based upon the varying responses of different age groups in the sample, upon person-to-person variation in responses, and upon variations in response and particularly contradictions of response within single individual protocols (the total set of responses for a single individual). On the basis of these kinds of data, in the context of wider observations on institutions and culture patterns in the United States, it appears that a major shift in American values is taking place.[1] I find it convenient to label this shift as being from *traditional* to *emergent*, though no basic cultural change of this kind is actually linear. The values thus dichotomized are listed under their respective headings below, with explanatory statements in parentheses.

TRADITIONAL VALUES	EMERGENT VALUES
Puritan morality (Respectability, thrift, self-denial, sexual constraint; a puritan is someone who can have anything he wants, as long as he doesn't enjoy it!)	*Sociability* (As described above. One should like people and get along well with them. Suspicion of solitary activities is characteristic.)
Work-Success ethic (Successful people worked hard to become so. Anyone can get to the top if he tries hard enough. So people who are not successful are lazy, or stupid, or both. People must work desperately and continuously to convince themselves of their worth.)	*Relativistic moral attitude* (Absolutes in right and wrong are questionable. Morality is what the group thinks is right. Shame, rather than guilt is appropriate.)
Individualism (The individual is sacred, and always more important than the group. In one extreme form, the value sanctions egocentricity, expediency, and disregard for other people's rights. In its healthier form the value sanctions independence and originality.)	*Consideration for others* (Everything one does should be done with regard for others and their feelings. The individual has a built-in radar that alerts him to others' feelings. Tolerance for the other person's point of view and behaviors is regarded as desirable, so long as the harmony of the group is not disrupted.)
Achievement orientation (Success is a constant goal. There is no resting on past glories. If one makes $9,000	*Hedonistic, present-time orientation* (No one can tell what the future will hold, therefore one should enjoy

[1] In my formulation of value trends and the interpretation of my data I have been particularly influenced by the writings of David Riesman.

TRADITIONAL VALUES	EMERGENT VALUES
this year he must make $10,000 next year. Coupled with the work-success ethic, this value keeps people moving, and tense.)	the present—but within the limits of the well-rounded, balanced personality and group.)
Future-time orientation (The future, not the past, or even the present, is most important. Time is valuable, and cannot be wasted. Present needs must be denied for satisfactions to be gained in the future.)	*Conformity to the group* (Implied in the other emergent values. Everything is relative to the group. Group harmony is the ultimate goal. Leadership consists of group-machinery lubrication.)

American culture seems to be undergoing a confused transformation, producing many disjunctions and conflicts, from the traditional to the emergent value systems outlined above. It is probable that both value systems have been present and operating in American culture for some time. But recently, and under the impetus of World Wars, the pressures exerted by the "radical right" and the "radical left," the external communist threat, atomic insecurities, and a past history of "boom and bust," the tendencies in the emergent direction have gathered strength and appear to be on the way towards becoming the dominant value system of American culture. At the same time, there is a minority resurgence of extreme versions of the traditional values as some people reaffirm allegiance to them as a reaction to the threat of rapid culture change.

Like all major shifts and schisms in culture, this one has consequences for people. Culturally transitional populations, as anthropologists know from their studies of acculturating Indian tribes, Hindu villages, and Samoan communities (among others), are characterized by conflict, and in most severe form—demoralization and disorganization. Institutions and people are in a state of flux. Contradictory views of life are held by different groups and persons within the society. Hostilities are displaced, attacks are made on one group by another. And this applies as well to the condition of American culture —the context of American education.

The traditionalist may view the emergentist as "socialistic," "communistic," "spineless and soft-headed," or "downright immoral." The emergentist may regard the traditionalist as "hidebound," "reactionary," "selfish," or "authoritarian."[2] Most of what representatives of either viewpoint do may be regarded as insidious and destructive from the point of view of the other. The conflict goes beyond groups or institutions, because individuals in our transitional society are likely to hold elements of both value systems concomitantly. This is characteristic, as a matter of fact, of most students included in the sample described previously. There are few "pure" types. The social character of most is split, calling for different responses in different situations, and with respect to different symbols. So an ingredient of personal confusion is added that intensifies social and institutional conflict.

I hypothesize that the attacks upon education, which were our starting point, and the confusion and failure of nerve characterizing many educators today, can be seen in clear and helpful perspective in the light of the conflict of traditional and emergent values, and particularly in the extremes of both forms that have been described. It is the heart of the matter. The task then becomes one of placing groups, institutions, and persons on a continuum of transformation from the one value system to the other. A simple diagram will aid comprehension of what is meant.

The diagram conveys the information that different groups operating in the context of relations between school and community, educator and public, occupy different positions on the value continuum, with varying degrees and mixtures of traditional and emergent orientations. It should be understood that the placements indicate hypothecated tendencies, that no one group representing any particular institution ever consists of "pure" value types, but that there is probably a modal tendency for the groups indicated to place on the transformation, or continuum line, in the way expressed in the diagram.

School boards are placed nearest the *traditional* end of the continuum because such boards are usually composed of persons representing the power, *status-quo,* elements of the community, and of persons in the higher age ranges. They are therefore people who have a stake in keeping things as they are, who gained their successes within the framework of the traditional value system and consequently believe it to be good, and who, by virtue of their age, grew up and acquired their value sets during a period of time when American culture was presumably more tradition-oriented than it is today. They

---

[2] Irrespective of this kind of name-calling, the dichotomy of values employed in this analysis is not the same as "conversative" and "liberal" or politically "left" and "right." It is certainly very probable, for example, that some political liberals are traditionalists in respect to core cultural values.

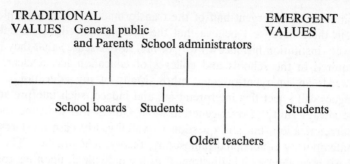

TRADITIONAL VALUES — General public and Parents — School administrators — EMERGENT VALUES — School boards — Students — Students — Older teachers — Younger teachers

may be driven to extreme forms of traditionalism as a response to the pressures mentioned previously.

The general public and parent group, of course, contains many elements of varying value predilection. It is therefore unrealistic to place this public at any particular point in the value continuum. But I hypothesize that the public *tends* to be more conservative in its social philosophy than professional educators are. The placement to the left of center of the continuum takes on further validity if it is seen as a placement of that part of the public that is most vocal in its criticism of educators and education—since many of the criticisms made appear to spring out of value conflicts between traditionalist and emergentist positions. Parents complain that their children are not being taught the "three R's" (even when they are), that educators want to "socialize" the competitive system by eliminating report cards, that children are not taught the meaning of hard work. These all sound, irrespective of the question of their justification or lack of it, like traditionalist responses to change in an "emergent" direction.

Students are placed at two points on the transformation line because it is clear that those coming from traditionalist family environments will tend to hold traditionalistic values, but hold them less securely than will their parents (if our hypothesis for over-all change is valid), while other students who come from emergent-oriented families will tend to place even further, as a function of their age and peer groups, towards the emergent end of the line than their parents would. This is only partially true, indeed, for such a rationale does not account for the fact that offspring in revolt (and many American children from 6 to 16 are in a state of revolt against parental dictums) may go to extremes in either direction.

School administrators, older, and younger teachers, place at varying points on the emergent half of the transformation line. I have placed them there because I believe that the professional education culture (every institution has its own way of life, in this sense) that they have acquired in the schools and colleges of education has a clear bias towards an emergent-oriented ethos. Many of my educationist colleagues will reject this interpretation, and indeed, such interpretations are always guilty of over-generalization. Others will welcome such a characterization, but still question its validity. My case must rest on contemporary educational philosophy, theory, and practice. The emphasis is on the "social adjustment" of the individual, upon his role as a member of the group and community. Most of the values listed under the *emergent* heading are explicitly stated in educational literature as goals. Some of them, such as conformity to the group, are implicit. This value, in particular, grows out of the others, is more or less unintended, and constitutes a *covert* or *latent* value, by definition. This is, admittedly, a little like accusing a man of hating his mother, but not knowing it, and such accusations are usually rejected, or rationalized out of existence. But I believe that it is literally impossible to hold the other values in this system and avoid placing a strong emphasis on group harmony, and group control of the individual. My data, at least, gathered largely from students in professional education courses, indicate that this is the case.

But educators and schools do not all come off the same shelf in the supermarket. Older teachers will tend, I hypothesize, to hold relatively traditionalist views by virtue of their age, and time of their childhood training (when they acquired their basic values)—a period in American culture when the traditionalist values were relatively more certain and supported than they are at present. Younger teachers were not only children and acquired their personal culture during a relatively more emergent-oriented period of American history, but they have been (I hypothesize) exposed to a professional education culture that has become emergent-oriented in its value position. They are therefore placed near the extreme of the transformation line in the emergent direction.

School administrators came from a different shelf in the same section of the supermarket. They, to be sure, range in age from young to old, come from different family backgrounds, and have been exposed in varying degrees to the professional education culture. But sociological and anthropological studies of the influence of status and role on behavior and perception indicate that these factors tend to over-ride others, and produce certain uniformities of outlook. The school administrator's role is a precarious one—as any school principal or superin-tendent knows. He faces towards several different audiences, each with different sets of demands—school boards, parents, power groups, teachers, and students—as well as other administrators. He has to play his role appropriately in the light of all these demands. The fact that many cannot, accounts for the increasingly short tenure of person-ages like school superintendents. But to the extent that he plays *across the board* he will place somewhere towards the center of the line of transformation. Furthermore, his dependence upon the school board, and the power groups in the community, in many cases will tend to make his outlook relatively more conservative, and probably more traditionalistic, than that of his teachers—at least the younger ones. There are many exceptions, of course. I am only claiming *tendencies*.

My thesis, I hope, is clear by now. I am attempting to explain, or help explain, the increasingly bitter and strident attacks on schools and educators, and the conflict and confusion within the ranks. I have claimed that this situation can better be understood in the context of conflicts in core values. And I have tried to show the direction of the values shift in American culture and place the various actors in the drama upon a transformation line within this shift.

In this perspective, many conflicts between parents and teachers, school boards and educators, parents and children, and between the various personages and groups within the school system (teachers against teachers, administrators against teachers, and so on) can be understood as conflicts that grow out of sharp differences in values that mirror social and cultural transformation of tremendous scope—and for which none of the actors in the situation can be held personally accountable. This is the real, and perhaps only contribution of this analysis. If these conflicts can be seen as emerging out of great socio-cultural shifts—out of a veritable transformation of a way of life—they will lose some of their sting. To understand, the psychiatrist says, is to forgive.

I have tried to make it clear that not only are there variations in values held by groups and different parts of the social body and school institutions, but that there are also various values, some of them con-tradictory, held by single individuals as diverse streams of influence in their own systems. This is always true in rapid culture-change situ-ations, as the anthropologist and philosopher know.

This means that the situation is not only confused by groups bat-tling each other, but that individuals are fighting themselves. This has certain predictable results, if the anthropological studies of personal adaptation to culture change have any validity. And I believe that those results can be detected in the behaviors of most, if not all, of the actors in the scene. Let me try to clarify this.

I will deal only with teachers, as one of the most important sets of actors on this particular stage. I hypothesize that the child training of most of the people who become teachers has been more tradition than emergent value-oriented. They are drawn largely from middle to lower-middle social class groups in American society, and this segment of the class structure is the stronghold of the work-success ethic and moral respectability values in our culture (even in a culture that is shifting away from these values). Furthermore, it seems probable that a selective process is operating to draw a relatively puritanistic element into the public school teaching as an occupation. Self-denial, altruism, a moralistic self-concept, seem to be functional prerequisites for the historically derived role of school teacher in American society (I might have said "school-marm").

If this can be granted, then only one other ingredient needs to be added to explain several persistent types of personal adaptation to value conflicts observable among school teachers. That ingredient is one already spelled out—the relatively heavy emphasis, within the professional education culture, on the emergent-oriented value system. Teachers-to-be acquire their personal culture in a more tradition-oriented family environment, but they encounter a new kind of culture when in training to become school teachers—in the teacher-training institutions. This is a particular kind of culture-conflict situation that anthropologists have recently begun to study, but mostly in non-western societies undergoing acculturation under the impact of the western way of life.[3]

On the basis of observations of teachers in coastal communities and in the middle west, I hypothesize that three types of adaptation to this personal culture-conflict situation and experience are characteristic.

> *Ambivalent:* This type is characterized by contradictory and vacillating behavior, particularly with respect to the exercise of discipline and authority. The type tends to be *laissez-faire* in some classroom situations, and authoritarian in others, depending upon which behavior is called into being as a defense against the threat of loss of control of self or of the classroom.
>
> *Compensatory:* This type is characterized by one of two modes of behavior. The teacher overcompensates consistently

---

[3] *Acculturation* is used here to refer to the changes brought about in the culture of groups or individuals as adaptation to a culture different from their own takes place.

either in the direction of the emergent or the tradition-centered values. In the first mode he (or she) tends to become a member of a *group-thinkism* cult—a perversion of progressive educational philosophy in action. The total stress is placed on social adjustment. Individualism is not sanctioned to any significant degree. Conformity to the group becomes the key to success. The type, in its extreme form, is a caricature of the emergent-centered value set. The second type compensates for internal culture conflict in the opposite direction and becomes an extreme traditionalist. Tight dominance is maintained over children. Relationships with them are formalized and rigid. No deviation is allowed, so curiously enough in this reactionary caricature of the tradition-centered values set there is convergence in the demand to conform in one instance to the group, in the other to the teacher.

Adapted: This type can be either traditional or emergent value-oriented. But the compensator and ambivalent mechanisms operating in the first two types are much less intense, or absent. The teacher of this type has come to terms with the value conflict situation and experience and has chosen (consciously or unconsciously) to act within the framework of one or the other value set, or has achieved a workable synthesis of both. There is consequently a consistency of behavior, and the mode of classroom management and teacher-student relationship is not a caricature of either value system.

No one is in a position to say which of these types is represented in greatest numbers among American public school teachers today, and there are few "pure" types. Certainly there are many traditional and emergent-oriented teachers who have adapted successfully to the personal culture-conflict situation and discontinuity of enculturative experience described. But equally certainly there are many school teachers who fall more clearly into one or the other typologies. It would be asking too much to suppose that a cultural values-conflict situation as intense as the one transforming American culture could be handled without strain by a key agent of the culture-transmission process—the school teacher. But again, to understand is to forgive.

In any event it seems clear that if conditions are even partially of the nature described, the group culture-conflict situation resulting in attacks by representatives of those groups upon each other is intensified and at the same time confused by the personal culture-conflict problem. Both processes must be seen, and understood as the results of a larger culture-transformation process.

In conclusion to this incomplete analysis, let me make it clear that I am not attacking either the emergentists, or the traditionalists. Value systems must always be functional in terms of the demands of the social and economic structure of a people. The traditional mode has been functional in our society, and there is a staunchness, and a vitality in it that many of us view with considerable nostalgia. But rugged individualism (in its expedient, ego-centered form), and rigid moralism (with its capacity for displaced, hate) become dysfunctional in a society where people are rubbing shoulders in polyglot masses, and playing with a technology that may destroy everything with a pushing of buttons. The emergentist position seems to be growing in strength. Social adaptability, relativistic outlooks, sensitivity to the needs and opinions of others, and of the group, seem functional in this new age. We need, as citizens, educators, anthropologists, and parents, to examine our premises more closely. The emergentist can become a group conformist—an average man proud of his well-rounded averageness—without really meaning to at all.

And lastly. I would like to reiterate the basic theme of this article. Conflicts between groups centering on issues of educational relevance, and confusions within the rank and file of educators, can be understood best, I believe, in the perspective of the transformation of American culture that proceeds without regard for personal fortune or institutional survival. This transformation, it is true, can be guided and shaped to a considerable degree by the human actors on the scene. But they cannot guide and shape their destiny within this transformation if their energies are expended in knifing attacks on each other in such a central arena as education, or if their energies are dissipated in personal confusions. I am arguing, therefore, for the functional utility of understanding, and of insight into the all-encompassing transformation of American culture and its educational-social resultants.

The decision of the Supreme Court regarding prayer in school involves a confusion of moral and social values. The concept of separation of church and state becomes obscured by those who see it as a part of encroaching secularization which accompanies urbanization and/or further usurpation of local determination. Dale Doak gives adequate legal justification for the decision, but education continues to straddle the divergent streams of changing value and power structures.

DO COURT DECISIONS GIVE MINORITY RULE? / *Dale Doak*

On June 17, 1963, the United States Supreme Court issued an opinion which renders unconstitutional the prescription, by law, of reading from the Bible and/or reciting the Lord's Prayer in public school classrooms. These actions were held to violate the First Amendment as made applicable to the states by the Fourteenth.

The citizens who originally initiated the suit were Edward L. Schempp *et al.* and William J. Murray III *et al.* Schempp as a Unitarian and Murray as an atheist represent religious or non-religious groups which constitute only a small percentage of the U.S. population; yet they have forced action which, to judge by letters in the popular press, is disagreeable to a large majority. Superficially, this appears to be a clear-cut case of minority rule, but let us examine this concept more closely.

Mrs. Murray filed suit to compel cancellation of a rule of the Baltimore school board which required daily reading from the Holy Bible and/or use of the Lord's Prayer in opening exercises. She holds these views toward the Bible and God:

> We find the Bible to be nauseating, historically inaccurate, replete with the ravings of madmen. We find God to be sadistic, brutal, and a representation of hatred, vengeance. We find the Lord's Prayer to be that muttered by worms groveling for meager existence in a traumatic, paranoid world.

Edward Schempp, the Unitarian from Pennsylvania, objected to Bible reading in public school classrooms on the ground that specific religious doctrines are perverted by a literal reading of the Bible.

FACTS OF THE CASE

The Schempp family objected to this 1913 Pennsylvania law:

> At least ten verses of the Holy Bible shall be read, without comment, at the opening of each public school on each school day. Any child shall be excused from such Bible reading, or

Dale Doak, "Do Court Decisions Give Minority Rule?" Phi Delta Kappan (October 1963), pp. 20–24. Reprinted with the permission of Phi Delta Kappa, Inc.

attending such Bible reading, upon the written request of his parent or guardian.

At Abington Senior High, attended by the Schempp children, opening exercises each morning included the reading of ten verses from the Bible and recitation of the Lord's Prayer in unison. Although students remained in their home rooms, the intercom system made the all-school ceremony possible. The King James, Douay, Revised Standard, and Jewish Holy Scriptures versions of the Bible were used. No prefatory statements, questions, comments, explanations, or interpretations were given during the exercises. Recitation of the Lord's Prayer was followed by the flag salute and general announcements to the students. Attendance at these exercises was voluntary.

Schempp chose not to have his children excused from such exercises on grounds that such a request would: 1) cause the children to be labeled "odd-balls" before their teachers and classmates each school day, 2) connote atheism and communism instead of a difference in religious belief, 3) cause the children to miss the daily school announcements, and 4) force the children to stand in the hall while the exercises were conducted, an action which "carried with it the imputation of punishment for bad conduct."

Mrs. Murray and her son William objected to a 1905 rule of the Board of School Commissioners of Baltimore. The rule required ". . . reading, without comment, of a chapter in the Holy Bible and/or the use of the Lord's Prayer." At their insistence the rule was amended to allow children who objected to such practices to be excused upon written request of the parents. William Murray was subsequently excused from the opening exercises.

This, then, set the stage for the court action. In both cases, the Supreme Court declared that the law and rule in question violated the First Amendment as applied to the states by the due process clause of the Fourteenth Amendment.

OPINION OF THE COURT

Mr. Justice Clark delivered the court's majority opinion, which reviewed many of the previous cases concerning religion in public education. The First Amendment is, in the delivered opinion of the court, divided into the establishment clause and the free exercise clause. The establishment clause acts as a barrier to all legislative power respecting religious belief or the expression thereof. The free exercise clause withdraws from federal or state legislative power the exertion of any restraint on the free exercise of religion.

The court concluded as follows:

> ... in both cases the laws require religious exercises and such exercises are being conducted in direct violation of the rights of the appellees and petitioners. . . . The breach of neutrality that is today a trickling stream may all too soon become a raging torrent and, in the words of Madison, "it is proper to take alarm at the first experiment on our liberties. . . ." Finally, we cannot accept that the concept of neutrality, which does not permit a state to require a religious exercise even with the consent of those affected, collides with the majority's right to free exercise of religion. While the free exercise clause clearly prohibits the use of state action to deny the rights of free exercise to *anyone*, it has never meant that a majority could use the machinery of the state to practice its beliefs.

Mr. Justice Stewart dissented on the basis that the records in the two cases before the court were fundamentally deficient and that the cases should be remanded for the taking of additional evidence. He also said:

> ... permission of such exercises [religious] for those who want them is necessary if the schools are truly to be neutral in the matter of religion. As a refusal to permit religious exercises thus is seen, not as the realization of state neutrality, but rather as the establishment of a religion of secularism, or at the least, as government support of the beliefs of those who think that religious exercises should be conducted only in private.

SHOULD THE MAJORITY RULE?

Throughout the nation one hears cries of "minority rule," "atheists and deists are forcing their views upon us." But is majority rule what these persons really want? Suppose you lived in a community where, if the majority ruled, instead of the Lord's Prayer the required prayer began "Hail Mary, full of grace, the Lord is with Thee," or suppose it began "Sheme Israel. . . ." Or it might be a Mormon prayer, a Buddhist prayer, or any other prayer of the religious sect which happens to be in the majority. Then what would you think of majority rule? Should the majority rule in such a religious issue, the ultimate result would be establishment of a state church, the very concept that James Madison was fighting against in his "Memorial and Remonstrance" and that Thomas Jefferson was seeking to prevent in his

"Bill for the Establishment of Religious Freedom" back in the 1870's.
In 1943 Mr. Justice Jackson said:

> The very purpose of a Bill of Rights was to withdraw certain subjects from the vicissitudes of political controversy, to place them beyond the reach of majorities and officials and to establish them as legal principle to be applied by the courts. One's right to . . . freedom of worship . . . and other fundamental rights may not be submitted to vote: they depend on the outcome of no elections.

Jefferson held that a "Bill of Rights is what the people are entitled to against every government on earth, general or particular, and what no just government should refuse, or rest on inference."

This is what the court has reaffirmed—that majority rule is not in effect in matters of religion—that government may not prescribe religious exercises—that the individual is entitled to worship or to refrain from worship—to believe or disbelieve in a supreme being—in any way he chooses. This is what the First Amendment says, that "Congress shall make *no law* respecting an *establishment* of religion or *prohibiting* the *free exercise* thereof. . . ."

Powell Davies states it in still another way. He holds that "the right to disbelieve is inherent in the right to believe."

VIEWS OF CHURCH LEADERS

As we all know, this court decision brought varied comment from church groups and leaders throughout the nation. It would appear that most but not all are favorable toward the decision.

The president of the Central Conference of American Rabbis, Rabbi Albert G. Minda of Minneapolis, said:

> We are gratified to learn of the two decisions. . . . We believe that these decisions will strengthen the voluntary religious life in America and trust that they will be accepted by all groups in the spirit of good will.

The view of the National Council of Churches is that the decision

> . . . serves as a reminder to all our citizens that teaching religious commitment is the responsibility of the home and the community of faith [church or synagogue] rather than the public schools. Neither the church nor the state should use the public school to compel acceptance of any creed or conformity to any specific religious practice.

However, the World Methodist Council president, Bishop Fred

Pierce Corson of Philadelphia, said: ". . . the decision penalizes religious people who are definitely in the majority in the United States."

OPINIONS OF EDUCATORS

Finis E. Engleman, former executive secretary of the American Association of School Administrators, stated recently:

> The Supreme Court decision on Bible reading and prayer in the public schools has strengthened religious freedom in the United States. Rather than prohibiting the Bible from the public schools it authorizes its reading as a part of the curriculum.

Mr. Engleman is obviously referring to Mr. Justice Brennan's concurring opinion which gave clearance for non-devotional use of the Bible in the public schools.

The decision effects only the proscription of Bible reading and recitation of the Lord's Prayer. It does not prohibit voluntary prayers, religious observance of various holidays, baccalaureate exercises, or non-devotional use of the Bible in the curriculum.

Max Rafferty, California State Superintendent of Public Instruction, views the recent decision with alarm. He said:

> The June decision should not, in my opinion, be looked at as an isolated case, but rather as merely the latest in a long series of high court dicta. . . . Little by little, a trend has been established which unless interrupted by factors at present unforeseeable, will lead inevitably to complete secularization of America's schools. Already in my state suit has been filed to eliminate the phrase "under God" from the Pledge of Allegiance, and school superintendents are banning the singing of Christmas carols on the school grounds. . . .
>
> To sum up in one sentence: It is not the last Supreme Court decision which disturbs me: it is the next one, and the one after that.

A professor of law at the University of Chicago, Philip B. Kurland, has interpreted the Supreme Court's opinions in the school prayer case (*Engel* v. *Vitale*) as follows:

> The states may not prescribe the conduct of religious ceremonies in their public schools. To read more into the opinions, as the court's detractors attempt to do, to see the opinions as destructive of religious life in the United States, is so patently absurd as to deserve to be ignored.

PRESENT LEGAL STATUS OF BIBLE READING

Prior to this decision the U.S. Supreme Court had never ruled upon the issues of Bible reading or recitation of the Lord's Prayer in public school classrooms. On at least two previous occasions cases concerning these issues were presented to the court but were not ruled upon because of legal technicalities. The writer proposes that the chaotic pattern of laws and practices concerning these matters is at least partially the result of the court's failure to face this issue squarely.

At present eleven states require by statute the reading of the Bible in public school classrooms. Most of these laws provide for reading without comment, and also for voluntary attendance at such exercises. A representative statute states:

> The teacher in charge shall read or cause to be read a portion of the Bible daily in every classroom or session room of the common schools of the state in the presence of the pupils therein assembled, but no child shall be required to read the Bible against the wish of his parents or guardians.

Mississippi is the only state whose constitution mentions Bible reading in the public schools. It forbids its exclusion.

Statutes in five states authorize, but do not require, reading from the Bible in the public classroom.

Various legal bodies in twenty-three states have upheld practices of and laws requiring or authorizing Bible reading in the public schools.

In eleven states legal bodies have declared Bible reading a sectarian practice forbidden by state and/or federal constitution.

The total legal picture then finds twenty-six states which require or authorize Bible reading in the public school classrooms and eleven states which forbid such practices.

The legal status of recitation of the Lord's Prayer or of other prayers is somewhat less complete than is that of Bible reading. Three states authorize the repeating of the Lord's Prayer in the public schools, while legal bodies in twelve states have approved such recitations and have disapproved it in five others.

In summary, thirteen states authorize recitation of the Lord's Prayer in the public school classroom while some five states forbid such a practice.

THE OPENING DAY OF SCHOOL, 1963

The Associated Press reported that despite the Supreme Court's ban against required religious devotions, thousands of children in public school classes began the first days of school with Bible reading and/or prayer. The AP concluded that most schools merely continued practices followed before the decision.

The one case of open defiance of the decision appeared in Alabama. Governor George C. Wallace said, "We don't care what the Supreme Court says."

Other states have handled the issue in various ways. Arkansas and Delaware are still requiring Bible reading or prayer. In Texas, South Carolina, and Florida local school officials are permitted to use their own discretion but generally with the understanding that neither Bible reading nor prayer be required; Vermont, Massachusetts and Pennsylvania have substituted "moments of meditation," while children in Washington, D.C., public school classrooms will have inspirational readings; in California regular courses of study dealing with the Bible and religious literature, as specifically sanctioned in the Supreme Court decision, have been adopted.

A United Press International survey showed that in the West most schools are abiding by the Supreme Court decision. But in New Jersey school devotions were "blatant and arrogant defiance," according to an attorney for the American Civil Liberties Union. And the UPI reported that at least nine Pennsylvania school districts have voted to continue Bible reading, despite warnings by the state attorney general that the high court left no loopholes in its decision. The Pennsylvania Department of Public Instruction said "the trend" is to abide with the court's and attorney general's opinions.

City schools in Newport, Kentucky, sported signs saying, "Bring back the Bible." When the signs were taken down, students showed up with cards on shirts and dresses saying the same thing.

Tennessee has a state law requiring home room teachers to begin each school day with the reading of a Bible verse. Local school superintendents have interpreted silence from state officials as the green light to continue reading.

School officials in Kansas and Missouri said they did not issue special instructions on prayer or Bible reading. They said it was left on a voluntary basis and left it up to the individual teacher.

EFFECT OF THE DECISION

One can only hypothesize about the ultimate effect this court decision will have upon laws and practices in the states. As the preceding paragraphs show, there is a real question whether the court's voice will be heeded. The legislature in at least one state, Alabama, has moved to defy this decision. Whereas Alabama did not require, by law, reading from the Bible in the public school classrooms, its public officials have now moved to do so. I suspect, however, that most states will eventually comply, realizing that the court's decision was the only one possible if religious freedom of the individual is to be protected. Should the slightest weakening of Jefferson's envisioned "wall of separation" be allowed, the torrent of abuse to follow will destroy the wall so firmly established. And with the destruction of the wall of separation between church and state would come, in my opinion, the ruin of the public school system of America.

The shared-time system is a recent development in metropolitan school districts. It is an honest attempt of public and parochial schools to share the costly burden of educating all children in their community. Leonard Gordon examines the plan, in light of democratic principles which separate church and state, and finds it wanting. Small systems, struggling to realistically solve the unrealistic financial problem, find that they are damned if they do share and damned if they do not.

SHARED TIME—AN ANALYSIS AND EVALUATION
/ Leonard Gordon

In his major Senate address of May 20th, 1963, on the subject of the need to resolve the religious controversy in education, Senator Abraham Ribicoff made reference to the concept of "shared time." Specifically, the Senator suggested that a shared time plan could be one of the techniques to break the deadlock between public and parochial school supporters over federal aid to educational institutions. Of underlying importance is that Sen. Ribicoff's presentation is symptomatic of a major division in perspective that has arisen in our society over what direct or indirect public aid, if any, should be given to religious institutions, including their educational programing. Shared time has come into sharp focus in the context of debates that revolve about this division.

Leonard Gordon, "Shared Time." Unpublished paper, 1964. Reprinted with the permission of the author.

It is the concern of this article to evaluate some of the more substantive pro and con arguments that have been advanced in regard to shared time. Before considering these arguments it is necessary to consider the nature of the concept. What is basically meant by shared time is some arrangement by which parochial school students would attend public schools for a portion of their schooling. The subjects usually suggested to be "shared" with parochial students in public schools are those with the least theological implications. Subjects most often mentioned are math, the physical sciences, shop, home economics, gymnasium and vocational courses. Shared time programs exist in such cities as Pittsburgh, Philadelphia and Hartford, although they are limited in numbers of students and program content. The most extensive program to date began in the fall of 1963 in the Cherry Hill School District near Detroit. The Cherry Hill plan involves several hundred parochial students. This particular plan as well as the others have resulted in widespread editorial and religious comment. Fears have been raised by public school supporters over possible violation of church-state separation and injury to the independent growth of public schools. On the other side, parochial school supporters, mostly numbering Catholics who support most of the parochial schools in existence, have expressed concern over the possible undermining of a totally integrated religious schooling program.

As a major issue it is important to see shared time in the context of related public concerns. In this manner its merits and demerits will stand out more sharply. It is clear that shared time is part of the constellation of church-state concerns relating to the proper relationship in our democratic society between the institutions of religion, education, and government. Other related issues include public school transportation to parochial schools, using public tax funds for parochial school construction and paying parochial school teachers out of the public tax till. Through these issues runs one theme: religiously controlled schools would receive significant financial relief should any one of these proposals be widely adopted. However, of these issues, only shared time involves no direct aid to privately controlled religious institutions. It is perhaps because of this factor that it has engaged so much attention and resulted in so many conflicting views. This point is elaborated on in the context of the following three crucial considerations:

WOULD A SHARED TIME PLAN ABROGATE THE TRADITIONAL PRINCIPLE OF CHURCH-STATE SEPARATION?

Protection of the principle of church-state separation is generally argued on grounds of any given proposal being constitutional or unconstitutional. There does not seem to be a serious question of this point about the shared time concept. Although there has been no court test of a shared time plan, the concept appears to be constitutional on the basis of the *McCollum* and *Zorach* "released time" decisions since parochial schools would receive no public funds or property. Yet, our Constitution can be, and occasionally is, changed by amendment if thought to be desirable by the citizenry. Therefore, it is necessary to consider the historical and contemporary importance of the principle of church-state separation in our society and whether or not the shared-time concept affects it.

The separation principle as written by James Madison into the First Amendment to the Constitution and interpreted over the years by the Supreme Court, is designed to protect the free and independent religious consciences of all groupings and individuals within our society. The principle is particularly vital from the point of view of religious minorities such as Jews, Moslems, Hindus, Unitarians and, at least historically, Catholics as well as non-believers. More generally the principle of church-state separation contains the essence of classic Jeffersonian democratic theory, i.e., the inviolable right of an individual or an individual group to hold views contrary to prevailing custom and thought. It is generally accepted that to a large extent our society's flexible strength to meet new challenges over the years has rested on the process of free and open exchange of minority-dominant view expressions. Thus, it is unlikely that any shared time proposal would be acceptable if it clearly breached the principle of church-state separation. It can be argued that with certain qualifications the shared time concept can meet this test. In this argument the point is made that it is necessary to remember that the church-state separation principle is a double jointed one constitutionally. While the First Amendment guarantees the "free exercise of religion" it also prevents the government from aiding or hindering any "establishment of religion." The free exercise clause, in this line of thinking, would not be touched so long as there were no religious observances in public schools.

Concerning the "establishment" clause, there exists a conflict between the church-state separation principle and generally accepted traditional practice of allowing students to substitute parochial education for public school education in deference to the "free exercise" provision. Under a shared time program this situation, supporters say, need not be altered in any significant way. Private aid for direct religious practices and teachings would continue along past patterns for it is not suggested that expenses or facilities be shared. Children would have to go back to privately supported parochial establishments to receive religious instruction. Also, supporters contend that by allowing school children to substitute parochial education for public education in the first instance, we have automatically always sanctioned indirect government support of an establishment of religion. Thus, the very existence of parochial schools as substitutes for public school education is aiding a church establishment. Therefore, what seems historically to be the case in this view is really a concern with no direct aid to a church establishment in support of the clause protecting the "free exercise" of religion.

There is a contrary view to the concern with the "establishment" clause. Public school officials are responsible to and derive their authority from all the people. Traditionally, public schools have dealt with individuals rather than with any groupings along lines of class, ethnicity, race or religion. It appears inherent in shared time that public school officials would be in a position of working out schedules and coordinating school operations with parochial school officials who are not responsible to the entire public, but rather to a particular church establishment. This is in fact the manner in which the shared time programs, e.g., in Cherry Hill and Pittsburgh function.

WOULD THE AID AFFORDED PAROCHIAL SCHOOL SYSTEMS BY SHARED-TIME PROPOSALS RESULT IN A STRENGTHENING OF PAROCHIAL SCHOOLS TO THE DETRIMENT OF THE GROWTH AND VIABILITY OF PUBLIC SCHOOL EDUCATION?

It is a well-established historical proposition that the public school systems have proved extremely valuable as an educational and social meeting ground for the various group elements in our pluralistic society. Consequently, any plan that would do injury to the public education concept would have much opposition to it.

Along this line, one opposition argument states that allowing parochial school students to attend public schools for certain classes would add intolerable expense to the public school system and result in impossible administrative complications. Supporters say that this argument has to be considered in the context of our commitment to the public school system being open to all regardless of expense or administrative difficulties. For example, there is no question about the public schools taking in all parochial school students if they so wish to go to the public schools at any time. This was rather chaotically illustrated in the Spring of 1963 when parochial school parents organized mass entries into the public schools of Jefferson City, Missouri, in order to protect Missouri's public school bus policy. Whatever the merits of the case, the public schools were legally and morally obligated, and did, enroll the Catholic students. Supporters go on to say that shared time would work to the advantage of both parochial school and public school students. In such classes as physics, chemistry and home economics, parochial school students would receive the benefit of better facilities and a generally better paid staff. On the other hand public schools would more likely receive tax backing from parochial school parents than is now the case. As a *Michigan Catholic* editorial stated in supporting the Cherry Hill shared time plan: "It would be difficult for someone to vote an additional tax for himself from which he will receive no direct benefit." Shared time would, presumably, present this benefit.

Opponents have voiced the opinion that by the very nature of our society widely adopted shared time programs would do injury to the public schools. There are over 300 religious denominations in the United States. It is argued that shared time would release the financial burden on church schools of teaching the more expensive subjects such as physics, home economics and vocational courses. This would enable many more parochial schools to be created. The long range effect could be a proliferation of parochial schools that would add enormous administrative costs to the support of formal education generally and have an ultimately deleterious effect on its general quality, public or parochial. If this proliferation did occur the public schools could turn into vocational centers with all of the essential humanities courses taken out of the curriculum. Also, shared time could lead in many communities to joint operation of the public school system by public and church school officials. Such a consequence would be fatal to the integrity of an independent secular public educational system that could effectively offer service to all individuals and groupings in our society.

Another opposing point relates to the interracial tensions existent in our culture. Many public school supporters who live in urban centers with large Negro populations, argue that shared time would enable many white people to take their children out of the public schools for part of the day. Thus, shared time could serve as a stepping stone toward abandonment of the public schools by middle class white people in our large cities in order to avoid full integration. With concurrent withdrawal of tax support carried to its fullest, this could leave the large city public school systems in a pauper state.

CAN A SHARED-TIME PROPOSAL HELP BREAK DEADLOCKS OVER NEEDED ADDITIONAL TAX AIDS FOR PUBLIC EDUCATION?

As property tax rates reach their saturation levels in local school districts, it is becoming more and more obvious that additional federal and state aid to education is needed. Attempts at passage of a bill to this end have generally been blocked by the controversies over school desegregation and over the issue of federal aid to parochial schools. Shared time, for the above stated reasons, could be one of the "techniques" (as Senator Ribicoff refers to it) of resolving the second controversy. If this occurred perhaps there would result the necessary support to pass appropriate school aid bills. Secondarily, in so far as it is possible local millage and bond issues may stand a better chance of passage in various communities as earlier noted.

Opponents argue that parochial school authorities have given no substantial indication that demands for inclusion of parochial schools in any federal or state school aid bills would cease as a result of a shared time proviso. If this is so, shared time would not break the stalemate, and any direct aids to parochial schools would meet the sharp opposition of proponents of both the separation principle and a strong, independent and viable public school system.

It is evident at this point in time that the shared time concept is likely to be tried in various school districts. The programs in existence or being planned for in and around such cities as Pittsburgh, Detroit, Philadelphia and Hartford substantiate this contention. As earlier stated the public schools have been historically one of the key institutions in the maintenance and growth of our culturally differentiated and pluralistic democratic society. Consequently, as shared time programs are expanded and new ones are created a number of questions emanating out of the above outlined concerns need to be confronted.

In the midst of today's affluence, the schools operate out of an unrealistic and inadequate financial base. Under the present system education can increase its budget in only one way: request, by public election, a mileage increase. Alfred Meyers examines the forces at work in the city which frequently defeat mileage.

FINANCING THE URBAN SCHOOLS / *Alfred Meyers*

At a time when the public school attendance of Americans is the highest in the history of our nation, the very survival of our public educational system, as the preeminent educational force in the country, is in doubt. This threat to public education can be most readily seen, at the present time, in our large urban centers. Here racial tensions are most evident. The Negro minority here is most vocal in seeking the full benefits of American citizenship. Here school enrollments are growing, though the remaining white population is aging. In the urban center, the public schools are rapidly acquiring a majority of Negro pupils, and large numbers of white parents send their children to parochial schools. Welfare costs have taken an increasingly larger share of the local taxes. Add to the above, antiquated tax structures, a vacuum in community leadership, rurally oriented legislatures, a loss of higher-income families to the suburbs, and increasing social needs of the city, and we understand some dimensions of the inner city atmosphere which is developing social dynamite. A continuing problem of adequately financing local government services, including those of public education in the urban centers is becoming more aggravated all the time. Large urban centers are accumulating an increasingly dependent group, the younger and older segments of the population, while the productive elements of the community are decreasing in number.

There are many complex problems confronting the schools in large urban communities, over which the schools have little if any influence. The problems have an effect upon the vote on school issues. Keeping the above in mind, there are many implications for future action by those responsible for the public schools.

It is apparent that public education is threatened by a combination of attitudes and circumstances found in our country at the present

Alfred Meyers, "Financing the Urban Schools." Unpublished paper. Reprinted with the permission of the author.

time. In most school districts, in comparison to all other major governmental services, the schools must ask the voters to approve an increase in their revenues. A voter unhappy about taxes in general can make his displeasure felt in a school tax election. Many parents who send their children to parochial schools, caught in a financial crisis of their own, advocate the allocation of school tax money to private and parochial schools. Some communities in the south are deserting their public school systems as they are threatened with desegregation. Many white families in the north are sending their children to private or parochial schools as desegregation takes place in their communities. Some Negro extremists urge drastic measures to bring an end to what they call "de facto" segregation. At the same time, many responsible Negro leaders feel that the white community does not really understand or care about the effects of segregation and, therefore, does not really concern themselves with the problem.

The problems listed above could bring about a combination of forces in the national Congress which would provide federal aid to pupils of non-public schools and/or to the non-public schools themselves. The logical consequence would be the eventual adoption of the principle of aid following the child at the state and local level as well. This could prove to be a mortal blow to the future adequate support of public schools, especially in the large urban centers.

In addition to the threats they face, the public schools are called upon to meet the challenges of the times. They are expected to transmit our social, political and cultural heritage. They are expected to solve the problem of the school drop-out, overcome the handicap of the culturally deprived child, and at the same time provide worthwhile experiences for those blessed with special abilities. Each of the above responsibilities cost large sums of money, money which voters in the large urban centers have been increasingly unwilling to grant. Yet the parent who is dissatisfied with the ability of the public schools to handle these problems, and blames the schools and those responsible for running them, often still refuses to vote additional necessary funds for overcoming his dissatisfactions. In this manner a vicious cycle has been started which has had disastrous effects upon the financial support given the public schools.

It becomes obvious that the demands of the local community and the nation for a highly educated youth have doomed the concept of local support for education. It must be recognized that ignorance cannot be quarantined in modern America. The youth of our nation, as well as the adult population, has become so mobile that among other reasons localism has no political or sentimental validity. The education of the youth of our country is a national problem. Local communities, have had increased state aid, and we are apparently unable to finance an adequate educational program to meet the needs of the times. It is becoming more apparent that federal aid is vitally necessary in solving the over-all financial problem. School leaders have the responsibility of taking the initiative in bringing about the recognition of the need for federal assistance to the public schools and in refuting the arguments of those who cling to the antiquated concept of localism.

As less family units in the urban centers have children in the public schools it becomes necessary for school officials to develop means by which the entire community becomes aware of the benefits of a good public school for all citizens. They must open channels of communication between the schools and these families. They must provide a means through which such people may participate in democratic decision making processes affecting the public schools.

School boards are more than ever faced with the need for developing a system of communication with all segments of the community. Such a system must enable the board to strengthen the community's belief and faith in public education. Such a system would inform the citizenry of the local, state, and national aspects of the problems of free public education; it would provide that degree of participation and understanding to make men strive to preserve the preeminence of the public school system in the large urban centers and the nation.

Cyril Tyson discusses the timely issue of open enrollment. Busing children into other districts is an honest attempt on the part of the school systems to remedy educational inadequacies. The idea was never conceived as mere token integration. But any major educational change gets caught in the crossfire of traditional and emergent interests of the entire society.

"OPEN ENROLLMENT: AN ASSESSMENT" /
Cyril Tyson

The "Open Enrollment" program of the Board of Education of New York City provides an opportunity to examine the major issues inherent in the pursuit of school integration. The "Open Enrollment" program is an endeavor to provide an integrated educational setting for children of Negro and Puerto Rican parentage, by permitting them to transfer from "de facto" segregated schools to schools in white communities.

The basic question is whether the Board of Education has the right to exercise its prerogative to provide the best and most realistic education for its students. In today's world "best" and "realistic" are interchangeable with "integrated." The assumption that the Board of Education had the right and responsibility to provide the integrated educational setting and experience met with hostile reaction in some quarters. This position was confused in the minds of many with the Supreme Court's decision in the *Brown* case in May 1954. The Court finding that ". . . to separate (Negro children) from others of similar age and qualifications solely because of their race generates a feeling of inferiority as to their status in community that may affect their hearts and minds in a way unlikely ever to be undone . . ." was taken by many to imply that race could not be a factor in the moving of children even for integration. Since "de facto" rather than "de jure" segregation existed in northern communities, some held that the Board of Education was powerless to effect integration without violating the Supreme Court decision.

Judge Irving Kaufman, alluded to just such a situation in reaction to the New Rochelle Board of Education's concern over providing services specifically to a given minority group. Judge Kaufman stated in part, ". . . the Constitution is not this color blind . . . there are instances where it is not only justified, but necessary, to provide for such allegedly 'unequal treatment' in order to achieve the equality guaranteed by the Constitution." This was clear recognition of the need to provide unequal treatment (in New York City's case recognition of "race") in order to achieve ultimate equality.

Cyril Tyson, "Open Enrollment: An Assessment," Journal of Educational Sociology, 35, 2 (1961), 93–96. Reprinted with the permission of the Journal.

The role of Education is recognized as crucial in the development of an informed public and viable democracy. Through our country's history various educational trends have evolved in attempts to maintain this viability. The drive to eliminate illiteracy, which induced the compulsory educational law; the development of the Vocational Schools, resulting from industrialization; the emphasis on Americanism and assimilation, flowing from the previously dominant "melting pot" approach to the non-Northern European immigrant. The educator's main responsibility involved creation of the administrative procedure, curriculum, and climate to properly prepare the student for the demands made upon him by recurring societal change. Where social innovations fostered new demands, educational approaches were adjusted to meet the challenge. Today, social change in our country and throughout the world has initiated an entire new order of demands upon the educational ingenuity of America. The attempt to forge positive relationships with the emerging non-white countries of the world, the programs designed to uncover scientific talent and our anxiety concerning the development of the "specially gifted" student, manifest our determination to meet this challenge.

The Supreme Court decision on school desegregation constitutes another force for social change. The *Brown* decision contributed to our realization that no group can be set apart from the remainder in educational institutions, without damaging all those involved in the educational process. To the Negro this damage openly manifests itself through inferior facilities, teachers, curriculum, achievement levels and per capita expenditure. Psychologically, both the Negro and white students are affected. Self-evaluations on the part of the white student are unrealistic and result from the superior position held in the social structure because his skin is white. The Negro is a product of a value system which regulates certain phenotypic manifestations, over which he has no control, to the lowest level of the system.

Again, in curriculum, the Negro and the white student are adversely affected. This occurs in the segregated white and Negro educational institutions as well as the "integrated" schools. The white person's view and expectation of the Negro, as indeed the Negro's view of himself, is affected by the treatment of the Negro in curriculum. There is evidence of but a scattered mention of the Negro's real role in the development of our society. The dignity of his African heritage; language, customs, folkways, traditions, is destroyed through an historical approach which roots the Negro's development to slavery; rather than viewing the condition as a transitional phase from one culture to another. Our elementary school readers still do not include illustrations of Negroes. Today, such approaches to learning can no longer be tolerated. Students must be prepared to function in a pluralistic society. In order to achieve this, the best and most realistic education is one which is integrated.

Properly instituted *integrated education is the organic uniting of administration, teachers, curriculum, and students of diverse cultures and colors into an educational whole.* It transcends the mechanical moving of students. It is a commitment to a new educational concept. If the Board of Education in northern communities recognized this concept, the issue of "race" as such would not be *the* factor in the moving of children. The Board of Education would be recognizing their responsibility to provide the best education for its students, and to spell out the ingredients of such an education. The greatest mistake that could be made is the assumption that it is "business as usual" in the desegregated school. The failure to articulate the integrated educational experience is crucial in securing Negro and white community support for such an experience.

Basic to the integrated educational experience is the acceptance of "cultural pluralism," which replaces the old "melting pot" approach to people of diverse cultural heritage. Cultural pluralism is a recognition that the threads of intrinsic unity, long sought in our ethnocentric approach to people of different cultures and colors, exist in the essence of man and is not a function of cultural monoism. Under cultural pluralism the problem is no longer one of "assimilation" on the part of the "out" group, but rather preserving those elements of the "foreign" culture which contribute to the development of a society. Education within the integrated setting assumes a character quite different from its role when the "melting pot" psychology was prevalent. Instead of the suppression of the customs, traditions, folkways . . . yes, and even the language of a people; education moves to identify these elements of culture, creating an atmosphere for understanding appreciation and acceptance of them. Cultural pluralism permits the essentials of culture to manifest their dignity as a contribution to the integrated educational experience.

Society is continually changing in scope and intensity, making it extremely difficult to develop citizens capable of effectively functioning with others of diverse cultures and colors without adequate preparation. Since all the skills needed to exist are acquired after birth, we must alter the view that education is measured by achievement levels and scholarship alone. We should recognize that the ability to accept the equal essence of man, cultural differences, and self images unbiased by prejudice and misconceptions of self worth, are all intrinsic to good education. Man must learn to live with others in dignity before his capabilities can be fully manifested. Education can, and *must* provide the tools, techniques and avenues through which such existence can be assured.

"Open Enrollment" then as a process, is just one aspect of school integration. It provides the educational setting conducive to the integrated educational experience. It is folly to assume that the mere proximity of students to each other is the only requirement necessary to undo generations of inadequate education. Now, as in the past, physical integration without a sound commitment will not provide the education necessary for this generation of children. Only when there is consensus on the educational ingredients inherent in the process will we properly prepare our children for the demands which will be made upon them in their time.

One of the significant trends in recent years has been the increasing militancy and activity of teacher organizations. In the face of the growing financial crisis that confronts the teaching profession, teachers are somewhat belatedly using their collective strength to influence major policy decisions in the educational enterprise. To remain unorganized in a society in which all other professions and groups are highly organized is to ask for increasing exploitation. In modern society where contending factions jockey for positions of vantage, the old adage that "power yields only to power" is all too true. Floyd Adams describes the basic struggle for teacher loyalties in the following article.

TEACHER ORGANIZATIONS AND COMMUNITY POWER STRUCTURE / *Floyd Adams*

"Most teachers' organizations exist in order to send flowers to the survivors of deceased parties." This "joke" was, for many years, not regarded as a joke by large numbers of teachers, but as a statement of fact.

Floyd Adams, "Changing Patterns of Teacher Organization." Unpublished monograph, Wayne State University.

While social activities (picnics and frolics the NEA Local Association Reports call them) are worthwhile activities, they hardly convey the picture of vital organizations interested in teacher welfare or educational problems. For years teachers attended a seemingly unending series of meetings called by subject-matter organizations in order to discuss "mutual problems." That the results of these meetings have often seemed to have had less effect on boards of education than one brief phone call from the chamber of commerce has long been resented by teachers. Boards of education and superintendents are well aware of the power structure in public education. With some exception, educational organizations—and especially teacher organizations—have not been included in this power structure.

Eventually, due to a number of changes in American society, teachers began to demand a more realistic approach to their professional problems. The founding of the American Federation of Teachers in 1916, and the application of the militant tactics of labor to education was one of the first examples of a "change" in teacher organizations. The NEA countered in 1917, with the Classroom Teacher Association; less militant perhaps than the AFT, but oriented to the practical problems of teachers.

In the years following the Second World War, the AFT won collective bargaining agreements with several boards of education. The NEA through various of its branches took an active part in teacher-board relations and matters of teacher welfare. However, it was the winning of a collective bargaining election by an AFT local in New York City in 1961 that, more than any other single event, illustrates the new power and direction of teacher organizations.

The success of this agreement has been instrumental in an unprecedented growth in the size of the teachers' union. AFT locals in several of the nation's largest cities, and in some of its smaller ones, now bargain with boards of education on issues ranging from teacher salaries to curriculum. The NEA has been equally active, and under a slightly different, but increasingly militant, format now demands a voice for teachers in a manner unheard of just a few years ago. The very active Urban Affairs Project of the NEA is designed to assist the city teacher in a wide range of day to day problems.

For years, teachers have observed other segments of society making gains through the application of organizational pressure. It is to be expected that teachers might now use the same kinds of pressure. Both of the major teacher organizations have shown, that if they feel it absolutely necessary, they will engage in a work stoppage. The contest that is developing for teacher loyalty between the NEA and the AFT will serve to drive both organizations into a more militant posture. The modern teacher organization with its continuity of leadership, effective fund raising procedures and increasing awareness of its own power is a far cry from the old "teachers club." Not that it is any less interested in good education, indeed it is probably more interested than ever before.

Teachers are no longer willing to be left outside the educational process and they are making increased demands on their organizations for what they believe to be their rightful place in matters of policy. Educators now expect the organization of their choice, regardless of the nomenclature it might use, to bring about fundamental changes in employer-teacher relationships and they expect their organization to press with vigor in all areas of teacher welfare. Teachers have tasted success, and things will never be the same again.

REFERENCES

American Association of School Personnel Administrators. *Standards for School Personnel Administration*. Preliminary first ed. Kansas City, The Association, 1960.

Beauchamp, George A. *Curriculum Theory*. Wilmette, Ill.: The Kagg Press, 1961.

Becker, Howard S. "Career Patterns of Public School Teachers." In Blaine E. Mercer and Edwin R. Carr, eds., *Education and the Social Order*. New York: Holt, Rinehart and Winston, Inc., 1957.

Brim, Orville G., Jr. *Sociology and the Field of Education*. New York: Russell Sage Foundation, 1959.

Butler, T. Donald. *Four Philosophies and Their Practice in Education and Religion*. New York: Harper & Row, Publishers, Inc., 1957.

Conant, James B. *Slums and Suburbs: A Commentary of Schools in Metropolitan Areas*. New York: McGraw-Hill Book Company, Inc., 1961.

Education Policies Commission. *An Essay on Quality in Education*. Washington, D.C.: National Education Association, 1959.

Erickson, Erik H. *Childhood and Society*. New York: W. W. Norton and Company, 1950.

Fletcher, Warner G. *Sociological Background for Community Improvement*. New York: Institute of Administrative Research, Teachers College, Columbia University, 1955.

Green, Scott. *The Emerging City*. New York: The Free Press of Glencoe, 1962.

Griffiths, Daniel E. *Administrative Theory*. New York: Appleton-Century-Crofts, 1959.

Gross, Neal. *Who Runs Our Schools?* New York: John Wiley and Sons, Inc., 1958.

Gwynn, T. Minor. *Curriculum Principles and Social Trends.* New York: The Macmillan Company, 1960.

Halsey, A. H., ed. *Education, Economy and Society: A Reader in the Sociology of Education.* New York: The Free Press of Glencoe, 1961.

Hare, R. M. *The Language of Morals.* London: Oxford University Press, 1952.

Havighurst, Robert J. "Social Class Influences on American Education." In Nelson B. Henry, ed., *Social Forces Influencing American Education.* Chicago: National Society for the Study of Education, University of Chicago Press, 1961, p. 139.

Kitsuse, John, and Aaron V. Cicourel. *The Identification of Talent in the High Schools.* Indianapolis, Ind.: The Bobbs-Merrill Company, Inc., in preparation.

Mayer, Martin. *The Schools.* New York: Harper & Row, Publishers, Inc., 1961.

Mumford, Lewis. *The City in History: Its Origins, Its Transformations, and Its Prospects.* New York: Harcourt, Brace & World, Inc., 1961.

Parsons, Talcott, and Edward A. Sails, eds. *Foundations of Modern Sociological Theory.* New York: The Free Press of Glencoe, 1961.

Pepper, Stephen C. *The Sources of Value.* Berkeley, Calif.: University of California, 1958.

Polley, John W., Joseph O. Loretan, and Clara Blitzer. *Community Action for Education.* New York: Bureau of Publications, Teachers College, Columbia University, 1953.

Sherif, Muzafer, and Carl I. Hovland. *Social Judgment: Assimilation and Contrast Effects in Communication and Attitude Change.* New Haven, Conn.: Yale University Press, 1961.

Smith, John Blackhall. *Team Teaching: An Approach to Elementary Instruction.* Greenwich, Conn.: mimeographed by author, January, 1960.

Thayer, V. T. *The Role of the School in American Society.* New York: Dodd, Mead and Company, 1960.

Thibaut, John W., and Harold H. Kelley. *The Social Psychology of Groups.* New York: John Wiley and Sons, Inc., 1959.

White, E. B. *Here Is New York.* New York: Harper & Row, Publishers, Inc., 1949.

Wittich, Walter A. *The Wisconsin Physics Film Evaluation Project.* Madison, Wisc.: School of Education, University of Wisconsin, 1959.

{Chapter Eight}

NEW DIRECTIONS IN URBAN EDUCATION

For the most part, directions in education have been shaped by urban development rather than the development of new educational concepts. In adapting to the urban crisis today, educators have had to assess the entire field of education. Adaptation, although stemming primarily from the crisis in the inner city, has become an attempt to improve the field of education; for recent assessment of education has shown that it is no longer a realistic extension of society. As society has undergone transformation, the role and tasks of education have been dramatically altered.

This final chapter is not intended to suggest solutions to the problems set forth earlier in this book. Rather, it attempts to show in part the directions education has begun to take in the present urban setting. Actual programs are not dealt with extensively here, for education stands today at the point of carefully considering how it can effectively be related to its society. Education, in a way, enjoys a rare opportunity today. Crisis lends support to education to institute long-needed changes in an unprecedented fashion. The final challenge to education, once it defines properly its relation to contemporary society, is to seize that opportunity which now permits it to actively participate in shaping the educational directions of American society.

Today the curriculum strives to incorporate an ever-increasing body of factual knowledge. Roger Leatherman notes that this is not the real issue for education. In the face of our growing knowledge of the physical world, the human problem of how to live in that world is greater than it ever was before.

THE EXPLOSION IN LEARNING AND ITS IMPACT ON INSTRUCTIONAL MATERIALS AND RESOURCES / *Roger L. Leatherman*

Everyone is today highly conscious of a major explosion in learning. Before [We] can begin to consider the impact and consequences of this explosion, we must, as in the explosion of an atomic bomb, consider the nature of many parameters. As heat, radiation, shock waves, altitude of blast, even psychology become necessary fields of concern in studying an atom bomb, the explosion of learning must consider not only the gross quantitative increase in facts about our universe but also the negation of previous understandings and the consequent need for correcting these misunderstandings, while at the same time exploring the many newly uncovered fields of potential human productivity which have lain totally uncultivated throughout human time.

Questions about current subject matter, materials, resources and curriculum rarely take more into account than how to handle the quantitative increase in factual knowledge; yet this aspect is the smallest and least dangerous parameter of the learning explosion. As Peter Drucker has pointed out, it is probably a fallacy to equate this quantitative growth of factual knowledge with a growth in understanding, since it accomplishes, practically, the wholesale confusion of scientists, citizens, and teachers. Ignorance of many fields with

Roger L. Leatherman, "The Explosion in Learning and Its Impact on Instructional Materials and Resources." Mimeographed working paper for the American Society for Curriculum Development Seminar on a Theory of Instructional Materials, Washington, D.C.: 1959, pp. 1–3. Reprinted with the permission of the author.

their growing specializations, unique languages, etc., leads one rapidly to the understanding of none, for the mental organization of the mass of data from all these areas requires a superhuman ability. Even if we hold that quantitative increases in knowledge have some minor part in the education and we wish to promote growth of this sort, we run immediately into major problems of technique.

We know from simple arithmetic that if we attempt to add more items to an established course or curriculum that amount of time available per unit item decreases. We further know (or should know) that increases in the classroom in quantity of subject matter (beyond fairly small and well-defined limits) will decrease the student's interest and ability to interrelate into pattern these many items, and will definitely be measurable in lowered retention and consequently in both lowered understanding and use. Even should we develop techniques in curriculum planning or subject matter presentation (which we do not now possess) that would make it possible for the student to retain more knowledge from more fields of growing diversity, we may have provided further insurance of intellectual confusion to that student. So we return again from this practical concern with method to the knowledge that we dare not be terribly concerned with increasing the volumetric capacity of students but rather must concern ourselves with the human changes this revolution has brought about. For the real issue in this entire matter is not that an expansion of knowledge has occurred, but that a diminution of understanding has come about in our entire society.

The central hub of this issue is simply that multiplication of knowledge frequently multiplies the alternatives of possible human behavior, yet weakens the rationale for any one selection. A growing knowledge of our universe is therefore associated with a drop in the specific utility of (or necessary dependence upon) any one (or group of) fact (s), and heavier demands are necessarily placed upon means for arriving at social consensus independent of the facts. Said simply, the more facts we possess, the more relative they become in terms of employment—like the child with a penny to spend who unhesitantly spends it if but a single selection is possible but who may spend an hour in front of twenty varieties of penny candy and then leave dissatisfied because he is sure he made the wrong decision.

The consequences of this chronic dilemma are many; all are indexes of the rate of change in knowledge occurring in modern society. Rapid growth of decision-making groups, committees, etc., with diminishing abilities to provide objective reason for the decisions they arrive at, is one of the hallmarks of our time. Determination of human goals by such groups becomes increasingly characterized by a priority —be these goals research achievement, educational achievement, or whatever. No longer can future direction be extrapolated from past research results, for they are too numerous, and no group could finance further research in all areas. It also becomes difficult to say whether one line of endeavor will be more profitable than another. Increasing concern with the possible permutations and combinations of known data along with differing opinions of best human directions leaves less time for speculative work on unknown areas. Computer facilities and men alike cheat themselves more each year by spending larger amounts of time and money sorting previously collected data of progressively (through time since collection) questionable validity. This is done of course because of the felt need to find common denominator understanding from mountains of data, but the frequency with which this is in fact the product is very low, and more frequently even more data of a more questionable nature is spawned from the process—that which was intended to solve a human problem has actually intensified the crisis. . . .

As curriculum standards are raised and the basic skills needed for an urbanized society become more complex, teachers are going to find that they must either spread themselves too thin or bring additional assistance into the classroom. Lee Cronbach assesses programed instruction as one possible aid to teaching.

WHAT RESEARCH SAYS ABOUT PROGRAMED INSTRUCTION / Lee J. Cronbach

It is extremely difficult at present to arrive at a just evaluation of proposals for programed instruction. Techniques are changing month by month, and the research studies available provide only sketchy answers to our major questions.

Some devices now being promoted are little more than old-fashioned

Lee J. Cronbach, "Programed Instruction," NEA Journal (December 1962), pp. 45–47. Reprinted with the permission of Harcourt, Brace & World, Inc., New York.

workbooks. At the other extreme, a system is undergoing trial in which the pupil is shown a complex scene, map, or object on a television screen, is asked a question, and punches his answer on a keyboard wired to an electronic computer. The computer evaluates his answer and decides what explanation or question should next appear on his screen.

One feature of these devices is *active response* by the pupil, immediately scored—in other words, continual trial and correction. Even more important is the sequencing of material so that every question will elicit a response *readily available to the pupil*. The program of instructional material is more significant than the physical device for presenting it. A program is a prearranged sequence of explanations and questions. A program, whether for a brief unit or for an entire course, is a carefully planned progression of ideas, beginning with elementary notions and working up to relatively complex theories or applications.

Sufficient cues and sufficient initial explanation are given to eliminate groping or guesswork. The initial items are easy. Difficulty is introduced by gradually withdrawing some of the cues or by bringing in more complicated examples.

Ideas and questions appear in a carefully planned sequence. Successive questions are pitched just within the learner's reach; if he has done well at one level, he should be able to stretch his knowledge to succeed on the next. Questions are pretested to eliminate points of difficulty and to determine the criterion for moving ahead to the next set of questions.

Programed instruction takes the principle of readiness more seriously than does any other teaching procedure. Ideally, the pupil moves to a new idea only when he individually has demonstrated his intellectual readiness for it. And—in theory—no question is presented until sufficient readiness has been developed by the preceding question to prepare him for almost certain success.

A well-designed program is a thoroughly orderly arrangement of questions and explanations. Every lesson, and every question within the lesson, is built on interpretations and associations that preceding questions have supposedly taught. In most textbooks, the teacher can take up chapters in whatever order he prefers or can omit lessons he considers unimportant. In an integrated program, this is impossible. It is precisely this systematic, cumulative sequence that distinguishes modern programed instruction from old-fashioned repetitive drill on fragments of information.

The program is a highly redundant communication. Redundancy is achieved by sheer repetition, by repeating the same thought in new language, and by developing logical interconnections so that the answer to one question follows meaningfully from the preceding explanations and responses.

In the most common type of program, there is just one "route" through the material. Every pupil responds to the same questions, save that some pupils must repeat sections in which they have made many errors whereas others go straight ahead.

In contrast to this linear sequence, some programs branch. The answer the learner gives to a question determines what stimulus is next presented. If he is correct, he moves forward. If he is wrong, the nature of his error suggests where he is confused. He is given a fresh explanation and a series of questions to test and to fix in mind his revised interpretation.

Branching procedures assume that there is a reason behind each error and that the program should make intelligent use of that information just as a teacher would. The linear program seeks to produce its effects entirely by eliciting correct responses, ignoring errors rather than discussing them.

The present formal research on programed instruction is fragmentary. One of the chief merits of programing is that it specifies each step in teaching so that it can be thoroughly pretested and then revised and standardized in the form that proves best. But since few of the programs used in experiments to date have been put through patient tryout and editing, programing at its best has not been tested.

Furthermore, there has been no adequate test of the claim that when pupils proceed through programs at their own rates, bright pupils progress further than slow learners in the same period of time. Nearly all the experiments have compared groups studying the same instructional material, presented in different ways. We have no adequate histories of long-continued programed instruction, in which each pupil is working at his own level, and no adequate observations on the integration of programed instruction with class instruction.

The studies now available suggest that automatic, programed instruction teaches facts and verbally mediated responses as effectively as conventional procedures do. There have been, for example, reports of success in teaching factory assembly operations, a highly verbal psychology course, and bridge playing.

One set of programed mathematics textbooks for traditional high school curriculums was developed by mathematicians and tried in dozens of classes. Each pupil proceeded through the book at his own rate, with help from the teacher as needed.

At the end of the year, these classes took a standard test, the results of which were compared with those of similar groups taught from a conventional text. The preliminary report by Allen Calvin states that when teachers are favorable to the new approach, student performance is at least equal to that of conventional classes and sometimes quite a bit superior. When teachers are unfavorable, student performance on programed materials is inferior.

Other studies report that small-step programs produce somewhat greater learning than large steps; but the small-step program takes longer, and it appears that making the steps *extremely* small has a bad effect.

Students rarely reach 100 percent mastery of programed material. Indeed, followup studies after use of some programs show startling deficiencies of learning, with some students passing no more than one-third of the test questions. In one study, half of those who had worked through the programs had scores no better than those in a control group who took the test without instruction. Educators, therefore, will have to look closely at evidence on programed instruction as it accumulates in the next several years. More than that, they should ask publishers for test data to show the effectiveness of the particular programs they are considering for adoption. One of the chief virtues of programed instruction is that the process of tryout necessarily generates such data.

We are not able to greet teaching machines, self-teaching texts, and the other products of this new movement as a great breakthrough comparable to the invention of printing. These devices are designed primarily to present information, and seem to be neither better nor worse for this purpose than conventional methods of presentation. They may, however, prove to be especially convenient for some remedial work and individual instruction.

The evidence now available gives little support for the original view that instruction calling for one active response after another will teach better than a straightforward lecture or text. In several studies some students had to respond actively to the programed text (e.g., fill in a blank and check against the correct answer), while other students studied the same program with the blanks filled in. That is to say, the second group was merely asked to study the text material in the usual manner. (Sometimes the words that constituted "answers" were underlined.)

These experiments showed that reading a programed text produces as much learning as does making active responses to the program. Moreover, the reading accomplishes the same results in less time. Very likely, a well-motivated student will profit more from reading a programed text than from giving equal time to programed response-plus-reinforcement.

But this is true only with a very superior textbook. Programed explanations have great clarity if properly pretested, because any confusing sections have been discovered and remedied during the tryout period. No textbook or lecture is checked out in such detail. Once the program is in good sequential form, with every step of reasonable size, the pupil who is motivated can learn merely by reading it.

Overt response is of little importance when a presentation is so highly meaningful that the right response is readily discriminated from all others. The teaching machine is only a technique of classroom management, whereas the programed sequence of ideas is a technique of *instruction*.

The trial-and-feedback step seems most important (a) with learners who have to be kept at the task by artificial controls or (b) with subject matter that cannot be put in words (a complex map, for example) or (c) with instructional materials that are unclear. Nothing in these findings diminishes the importance of active response in learning sensory discriminations. In acquiring a motor skill, the student cannot possibly learn to respond to cues arising within his own body save by active trial. The findings do imply that active response is less necessary in intellectual learning than psychologists have previously believed.

We have no reason to doubt the claimed advantage of presenting ideas in a tightly knit, carefully sequenced and pretested program. But there still is the large and unanswered question: What interpretations and responses can be adequately taught through programed presentation?

Programing works well for highly structured material where there are fixed stimuli to respond to and a definitely correct response. One can program spelling and vocabulary, and also the more complicated skills of arithmetic, choice among grammatical forms, and balancing chemical equations. We know little, however, about the extent to which programs can develop insight into the nature of a subject or ability to solve problems creatively. A pupil can be drilled to the point of applying the techniques of arithmetic perfectly, yet have little concept of the number line and little ability to organize a new experience in a meaningful manner.

The views of Piaget and other psychologists suggest that numerous trials of both wrong and right responses are an essential part of arriving at deeply understood concepts.

Programs, like all other instruction by presentation, are predicated on the identification of a definite right answer, constructed out of responses the learner already possesses. It is difficult to see how programs can contribute to divergent thinking and creative imagination, although experiments are now being conducted in this area.

Some programs are attempting to build general understanding and to teach pupils to discover principles for themselves. A recent publication showing imaginative uses of programed instruction is *Programed Learning and Computer-Based Instruction*, edited by John Coulson. (Wiley, 1962.) One impressive report is that of Keislar and McNeil, who used a program to teach first graders the theoretical principles behind condensation. The success of the training was judged by the pupils' ability to explain, in a final interview, phenomena they had never studied to which the principles of molecular attraction and coalescence apply. The mean score of these pupils was 66 percent; an uninstructed control group averaged only 22 percent.

Few of the programs now being tried make any provision for the ultimate transfer of generalized, verbal concepts to concrete, nonverbal situations. The research on transfer leads us to doubt, for example, that a medical education confined to words, pictures, and tape recordings would prepare the student to recognize, in the flesh, an early case of chicken pox. Nor could it develop in him an encouraging, confident bedside manner. Somewhere, verbal concepts must be blended with observations on and responses to concrete reality.

The more that imagination and creative thought are involved in the responses to be developed, the less one can teach by presentation alone. We can judge each response right or wrong when teaching the pupil to avoid grammatical errors. But when we want him to compose interesting sentences in a style suited to his audience and topic, there is no scoring key.

Programed teaching can make the pupil a master of the facts about the Fifth French Republic. It can even indoctrinate him with the view of the programer on the desirability of close cooperation between France and West Germany. But interpretation and appreciation of history cannot be reduced to certain "sound" answers.

Programs to date reward the student only for agreeing with what the programers believe. If composition, literature, languages, social studies, and science are reduced to responses that can be evaluated by a clerk, education will have settled for considerably less than half a loaf.

I see no danger that the school will reduce itself to a fact-dispensary, with machines in rows like gasoline pumps. Attitudes, reasoning powers, and creative responses will remain important in the minds of educators and parents. The school does have a great deal of factual material to teach and many definite skills to be developed. It is surely possible to prepare standard programs that will be as effective as the lessons a typical teacher might personally prepare. The best hope is that these programs will free the teacher to help the pupil develop intuition and judgment by adventurous problem-solving.

Let me emphasize once more that not all programs will be equally sound. A program dashed off rapidly is not likely to communicate in a truly clear and accurate manner. It will be slow and expensive— but necessary—to revise every program after tryout, removing sections that lead to misconceptions, smoothing out the difficult spots, and quickening the pace where the author's first approach was too leisurely. We will have brilliant programs and run-of-the-mill programs. The quality of teaching is more important than the form it takes.

The burgeoning problems in metropolitan school systems have resulted in a number of innovations in administrative practice and procedure. Breaking down the monolithic structure of large school systems into more manageable units, together with improving methods for handling school-community conflicts, are typical of the efforts being made to achieve more effective administration. The urban school administrator must deal with problems that are unique in their force and complexity. It has been apparent for some time that the quality of educational services is directly related to

*the level of administrative excellence, and that strenuous
efforts are needed if any improvement is to be made. Gerald
Boicourt suggests in the following article that more is required
of school administration if the current crisis is to be met.*

NEW DEVELOPMENTS IN ADMINISTRATION OF METROPOLITAN SCHOOLS / Gerald W. Boicourt

Current research regarding educational innovations indicates rather clearly that organizations, like single cells, seek equilibrium with their environment and that changes in relationships and methods occur largely as a result of external pressures. Within local school systems it also appears that administrators are the most important figures in introducing and implementing changes and that teachers are relatively unimportant in charting new courses in the educational sea. These two statements may be somewhat unpalatable to the average educator; but they do provide some explanation of the great ferment that has been bubbling in the public schools for the past ten years, and suggest some of the directions in which urban administration seems to be moving.

The fear of Russian burial, the spectre of widespread unemployment in the most affluent society on earth, the general *angst* engendered by automation, and problems posed by the "urban sprawl" all combine to exert tremendous pressures upon all educational systems in general, and the public schools in particular.

Decentralization. The clearest example of the reaction response in urban schools is the trend toward decentralization of administrative control and the diffusion of the representative function of local boards of education. An organization's adaptability to change is quite clearly proportional, inversely, to the size of the organization itself, and, especially, to administrative hierarchy. For this reason large corporations such as General Motors have, for years, spread certain functions among semi-autonomous units operating under the umbrella of the parent body. Similarly, in recent years, large-city school systems with thousands of teachers and hundreds of thousands of students have been reorganizing into "administrative units" headed by an assistant superintendent or his equivalent who has broad decision-making authority. The obvious objectives here are to expedite decision making

Gerald W. Boicourt, "New Developments in Administration of Metropolitan Schools." Unpublished paper. Reprinted with the permission of the author.

and to increase the two way communication that is necessary to encourage understanding and creativity.

Related to this trend, but coming more directly as a result of community pressures, is the development of techniques to spread the representative function of local boards of education. Historically, Parent-Teacher Associations and Mothers' Clubs have occupied this role, but since the end of World War II there has been a proliferation of various kinds of citizen advisory groups. The majority of these have been in cities where people, increasingly, have felt divorced from the cherished tradition of "local control." Such groups have usually been task-oriented—to recommend curriculum changes or building programs, for example. These groups usually have had short tenure. Some cities such as New York, have established continuing "local boards" to advise the central elected body. Currently plans are being made in Detroit, Chicago, Cleveland and San Francisco to create communities within large cities and establish autonomous governing bodies for all aspects of city government. This area, of course, is a battleground of political scientist, and the implications for city school administration are not clear. It does seem, however, that increasing pressures will be exerted to bring certain kinds of decision making and policy formulation closer to the citizens in metropolitan areas.

Any large city has hundreds of organizations and agencies which have an interest in (or whose purposes are related to) the public schools. Youth bureaus, delinquency control centers, and employment agencies are but a few. Attention given to juvenile delinquency and school dropout, state and national attempts to meet the problem of youthful unemployment, and "The War on Poverty" have resulted in a startling increase in the number of such organizations and agencies. In addition to this, national foundations have established still other kinds of groups to deal with metropolitan problems—many of which are related directly to public education.

The need for city-wide and regional planning. These facts present a bewildering array of problems for the urban school administrator as he attempts to develop and organize programs for culturally deprived children and other community action programs. In medium-sized cities such as Flint, Michigan some successful programs have been developed which coordinate the efforts of many community agencies. However, too often, schools operate independently or in ignorance of other community organizations or city departments and find themselves in competition for financial support, working at cross purposes, or undertaking tasks which might better be performed by other agencies. The wide-spread acceptance of public school driver education programs might be taken as a case in point. Undoubtedly, such programs are successful, but the question of whether or not city police departments or state highway departments should, more logically, have done the job was seldom adequately reviewed.

Similarly, the Great Cities School Improvement Program has highlighted serious school and community problems and sponsored school programs to help solve them, but the responsibility of city government to share in such programs on a continuing basis has not received sufficient attention. In fact, there is considerable evidence that real solutions to slum-engendered school problems must involve massive programs that include all branches of city government and be designed to correct neighborhood and home conditions which affect the child at a very early age.

Clearly needed then, is city-wide or region-wide planning and cooperation of the kind that is being done by Greater Cleveland Area Research Council, The New York Metropolitan Goals Committee, and The Form For Detroit Area Metropolitan Goals.

The weakness of current approaches is that these organizations do not constitute a legal entity and must act solely in an advisory capacity. The success which Toronto has experienced in establishing a metropolitan authority responsible for region-wide planning and coordination of many city and suburban agencies, including schools, is most promising in this regard, and should be studied carefully by both city and school administrators.

Program leadership. The ultimate function of school administration is to provide the climate in which sound educational progress can flourish and the machinery by which such progress can be expedited. This returns us to the opening statement of this paper. One educator-revered cliché is that curriculum is determined by the teacher and the student in the classroom. Yet modern students of educational innovation are agreed that very little such determination has occurred in the past. Almost all of the present program changes have been initiated by national committees of academicians and implemented by foundation or government grants. The implementation consists of a "package" including financed teacher-training and materials and equipment.

The significant trend here in administrative program leadership has been the willingness and ability of local administrators to adopt programs developed nationally or regionally and vigorously pursue their implementation at the classroom level. Coupled with this has been the growing willingness of local boards of education to provide sabbatical leaves and significant periods of released time for curriculum improvement. The number of districts which pay teachers for summer work on curriculum study geared to regional or national programs is increasing yearly.

School building planning. During the past ten years urban school systems have faced an acute shortage of classrooms in addition to the obsolescence of many existing facilities. Providing new buildings and adapting existing structure has been a staggering task. It has been complicated by urban renewal projects, with high rise apartments replacing single dwellings; by mobility within the city and mobility between the city and its suburbs; by changing sociological patterns within the city and resultant shifts in population density; and by citizen resistance to the costs of building programs. The classroom shortage will apparently plague metropolitan areas for sometime to come. The U.S. Office of Education reports a 1964 classroom shortage of over 124,000 classrooms. As the 1945-46 "Bumper baby crop" begins to have children of its own, and if families continue to increase in size, the need for additional classrooms may increase geometrically.

However, many imaginative, exciting and economical programs have been developed to deal with this persistent problem. The development of such programs has been aided by the growth of state and national agencies devoted to improved planning, increased research, and the publication of the results of such study and cooperation. The American Association of School Administrators, The National Council on Schoolhouse Construction, The Association of School Business Officials, and the Educational Facilities Laboratory have all made significant contributions to improved planning and building design. Most state departments of education and many universities have competent consultants and conduct continuing research in the field. Finally the quality of planning staffs in local school districts has steadily improved, with the result that school buildings have shown marked improvement in construction.

Building design changes are most marked in three areas:

Provision for flexible grouping of children—ranging from individual study spaces to large group meeting areas.

Provision for community use of buildings.

Provision for re-locating buildings within the district as population and needs change.

Features in schools which contribute to flexibility in grouping include movable partitions between rooms, rooms clustered around resource centers, the provision of study carrels and conference rooms, and the provision of rooms of various size.

More and more school buildings include community facilities such as kitchens, recreation rooms, storage facilities in shops, public access to libraries, and facilities for the public use of gymnasiums.

Movable buildings come in many different packages, and over 36,000 are in use in the nation schools. Some are very satisfactory, other less so, but their use to meet a pressing problem will undoubtedly expand.

Two other developments should be noted: the use of new materials or methods such as the geodesic dome or inflatable structures and the joint occupancy of buildings—usually apartments where the school occupies the ground floor. It might be expected that rapid progress will occur in both cases. Because of these developments, the school taxpayer is getting slightly more space for his dollar, but a great deal more which contributes to excellence in an educational program.

Breaking the educational lock step has been a dream of educators for a long time. The movement toward individualizing the program of instruction has been in effect on the elementary level, but implementation in high schools has been less successful. B. Frank Brown has developed a nongraded program in the Melbourne Public Schools that has been successful and is offered here as an example of what can be done.

AN ANSWER TO DROPOUTS: THE NONGRADED HIGH SCHOOL / B. Frank Brown

In the not too distant past, the only path for a school to follow was the well-worn and repeatedly traveled road of conventional education. The idea of a school going any other route was inconceivable heresy. The change at Melbourne High School actually preceded the technological revolution by several years. Our program of experimentation was launched in 1957, shortly after the Russians slammed the

B. Frank Brown, "An Answer to Dropouts: The Nongraded High School," The Atlantic Monthly, *November 1964, pp. 88–90. Reprinted with the permission of the author.*

first man-made hardware into orbit around the earth. An important side effect of the Russian breakthrough was the creation of a national climate conducive to educational innovation and change in America. To a school operating in the shadow of what was then Cape Canaveral the launching of Sputnik was most provocative indeed.

Melbourne High School is a fifteen-hundred-pupil senior high school located in the Cape Kennedy complex. The proximity to the Cape gives rise to the myth that the students are all sons and daughters of space scientists. While there is a modicum of scientific personnel in the area, the vast majority of students are the children of technicians and laborers. What most of America does not realize is that the creative genius behind the missile industry is concentrated at missile design and space centers in California and Huntsville, Alabama. The chief function of the John F. Kennedy Missile Test Center is to provide a firing range where the efficiency of missiles can be tested.

While the impact of Cape activity on the school has been conspicuous, its contribution is far more apparent in the quantity than in the quality of students. The school has been literally clobbered by the explosion in population created by the teeming influx of Cape workers. Each of the past five years has brought four hundred new students. Twice the school has been split to form new high schools in order to accommodate the deluge of incoming students.

While the enterprise at the Cape has brought an agglomeration of people to the area, it has also succeeded in bringing about a compensating community coalescence. The unifying element is the extensive support for space activities which has been generated in the area. This bond of like-mindedness has led indirectly to a profound community appreciation for the value of a good education.

Within less than a month after the first hole had been punched in space, the faculty at Melbourne High School had begun to debate the question whether we dare attempt to make advances in education comparable with the achievements in space. When a school develops heretical notions, the first obstacle which must be surmounted is the problem of how to bypass the trip wires that keep schools conventional. Our move to overcome this barrier was to develop a strategy for change. The mechanics of this maneuver were based upon a process which we have since dubbed the "spin out," a technique whereby, instead of replacing an old practice with a new one, a new practice is introduced alongside the old. The cataclysm of the new tends to obscure or "spin out" the older course of action. This operation comprises a kind of innovative test boring. Its effect is to give the entire school program an innovative tug.

Since the immediate impetus of Sputnik kindled a national concern for the education of the gifted, our first "spin out" was designed to break the grade lock step which has for so long restrained bright students. We simply removed all grade barriers and let the school's talented students pursue any course that they were capable of passing without reference to the grade to which they had been promoted.

The outcome exceeded all expectations. Increasing numbers of students eloquently met the challenge, and their parents were enormously pleased. Community approbation was so swift and convincing that in an unbelievably short time the whole process of grouping students into grades had "spun out" of existence. Once the stumbling block of the grade had been removed, we were able to concentrate in earnest on the development of a new brand of education.

What we were after was to reorganize learning on a radically different basis from the conventional plan which classifies youngsters into grades largely on the basis of age. The idea of grouping students by age into grades has never been more than a poor piece of technology. For this reason the most urgent problem facing education has for a long time been the issue of how to gear the curriculum to what the students actually know rather than to the grade to which they have been promoted. Only after this is accomplished can youngsters be taught to learn for the right reasons for devotion to learning rather than for marks and promotion.

The new anxiety which Sputnik generated gave us a blank check to realign the curriculum in a manner best suited to the needs of students. Using the task-force approach, we probed a number of possibilities. We concluded that what was needed was a reorganization of the school around the knowledge and past accomplishments of the students. Subsequently, every student was rescheduled according to the degree of his past learning as measured by nationally standardized achievement tests.

We named this revolutionary new organization a "phased" rather than a "graded" curriculum. The word "phase" was carefully chosen since it fit our intent to make all learning situations temporary and to allow students to move up the ladder of learning continuously without being restricted by the limitations of the grade.

In the plan for phased learning, the curriculum of each student is linked to his personal achievement rather than to his chronological age, as is customary in the graded school. The notion of phasing deposes and refutes both the graded organization and the concept of annual promotion. The purpose is to replace stops and starts with continuous learning and constant advance.

The class situations created by the new phased structure for learning are as follows:

Phase 1. Subjects are provided for students who perform from 0 to the 20th percentile on nationally standardized achievement tests, indicating that they need special assistance in small classes.

Phase 2. Subjects are organized for students who range between the 20th and 40th percentile in achievement and who need more emphasis on fundamentals.

Phase 3. Courses are arranged for students who score between the 40th and 60th percentile on standardized achievement tests, indicating that they have an average background of accomplishment.

Phase 4. Subject matter is planned for extremely well-prepared students who achieve between the 60th and 80th percentiles and who desire education in depth.

Phase 5. Courses are available for students who attain above the 80th percentile and who are willing to assume responsibility for their own learning, pursuing college-level courses while still in high school.

Phase Q. Students whose creative talents are well developed should give consideration to the Quest phase of the curriculum. This is an important dimension of the phased organization in that it gives thrust in the direction of individual fulfillment. In the Q phase, a student may register for independent study in any area in which he is deeply and sincerely interested.

The underlying philosophy of the phased curriculum calls for student learning to be deliberately variegated in accordance with the response of the individual. For example, a particular student may be programmed into Phase 1 for social studies (achievement below the 20th percentile), Phase 2 for language arts (achievement between the 20th and 40th percentiles), Phase 3 for science (achievement between the 40th and 60th percentiles), and Phase 4 for mathematics (achievement between the 60th and 80th percentiles).

Professor Jerome Bruner, director of the Center for Cognitive Studies at Harvard, reports his impressions of the program in his forthcoming book, *Education for the Space Age.*

In the multiphased school, courses have been reorganized into a system of phases that reflect not the grade in which they are taught but the student's ability to grasp the subject and his willingness to throw his weight into the task. Phase 1 is the remedial section and it is designed for students who need special assistance in small classes. When a student feels ready to try something more advanced, he is encouraged to set forth to the next "phase." His willingness is a major criterion. Phase 2 is for students who need more emphasis on the basic skills of a subject. Phase 3 is for those who are ready to have a go at the major substance of the curriculum in the field. Phase 4 is the subject in depth and with concentration. Phase 5 is independent study for the exceptional student willing to assume responsibility for his own learning and ready to use all available resources in doing so. He is supervised by a teacher with whom (as in any tutorial system) the student makes an appointment when he has finished a stint of work. The phase system operates in the four basic intellectual disciplines: mathematics, science, English, and history. They are the core of the process.

Virtually every one of the major curriculum efforts of the last decade has been incorporated and fitted to the needs of Melbourne's multiphased school—the Physical Science Study Committee course, the Chemical Bond course, the Biological Sciences Curriculum Study, several experimental mathematics programs, and some homegrown innovations in social studies and humanities. These courses can and are being adapted to different phase levels. There is no reason why the new curricula cannot be adapted to this broader use more generally.

But the realignment of students on the basis of achievement changes course content in the nongraded school in subtle ways. The school perforce resorts to a much wider range of materials than those used in the graded school. Standard textbooks aimed at a grade level are inappropriate and have been abolished. A multiplicity of materials has replaced the rigid text.

Professor Bruner's statement that the school teaches the new subject matter at different phase levels is worthy of further comment. It is to the nation's discredit that every one of the new curriculum projects sponsored by the National Science Foundation has been designed for the above-average student. Since no new curriculum has been devised to appeal to the lower group of America's students, our own teaching staff has taken on the task of adapting subject matter, designed for the gifted, to the various levels of ability with which the school must cope. The approach has been to tease out the major principles from the new material and to focus on the big themes which tie the subject together. When great emphasis is placed on the large ideas, the basic skills and principles become more interesting.

In effect, fundamental knowledge has been re-tooled around important new concepts, and these considerations are presented at multiple phase levels through the discovery method. When a youngster discovers a new concept by himself, it whets his curiosity and makes it easier for him to make a discovery the next time. Subject matter learned in this fashion is more realistic and meaningful to students.

A certain amount of anarchy has been deliberately introduced into the curriculum. This agitation-of-learning situation makes it possible for learning to be approached in violently different ways. Subject matter for some students is no more complex than the mastery of basic skills; for others subject matter becomes so intensively a problem-solving process that it acquires the sophistication of a Rorschach test. The ancient shibboleth that all students are equal and should study the same phenomena and learn the same details has been thoroughly dissipated. The intent of a nongraded brand of education is to provide a curriculum with differing clefs and keys. We are convinced that the only way to organize a school is on the basis of student achievement.

While in the past one of our major problems has been how to persuade talented teachers to work with the less talented students, the effect of a multiphased curriculum on this problem has been striking. As learning became more variegated and individualized we found teachers stepping forward to say, Give me the ungifted, for I am a professional and I can teach students of varying ability.

The forward projection of education can only be in the direction of a nongraded model. There is simply no other place to go. The major function of nongraded education is to give students a litheness of attitude and a suppleness of mind. Prognosticators forecast that the rapidly changing technology will require that students now in school be retrained three times. The intent of our curriculum is to equip students with "built-in" second-chance mechanisms. In the age of automation, each individual must possess a kind of expertise which will enable him to shift quickly when new skills are developed and old skills become outmoded. Such an environment demands a ground swell in the direction of flexible education. Because we operate in the Cape Kennedy area, we are convinced that an important function of the school is to develop individuals who are adaptable. Unless we succeed, our society will be too rigid to deal with the future.

Any discussion of changes in the curriculum must eventually come to the point of what is being done about reading. This is the central intellectual obligation of the educated person and the most important subject in the curriculum, yet educators are unable to agree upon how it should be taught. While we in Melbourne do not claim to have all the answers to the reading debacle, we are deeply committed to the notion that reading is a high school problem. The high schools of the country are literally overrun with students who are unable to read above the third- or fourth-grade level. Training in this subject should not be relegated solely to the elementary school. It is a matter of extreme urgency for high school students with reading handicaps to receive particular attention. When students are phased instead of graded, those who do not read competently are scheduled for two or more hours a day in a reading laboratory. Here an intensive effort is made to increase reading efficiency.

Second in importance among the needs of high school students is a thorough understanding of the principles of mathematics. In the phased curriculum, students with a poor background in mathematics are scheduled for increased time in this subject. This extra time is provided in small classes where students receive as much personal attention as is needed in order to learn the subject effectively.

The phased curriculum, bracketed by a nongraded organization, denotes a big push in a new direction for the educational enterprise. But much more is needed. We found that the role of the teacher must also change to meet the dynamics of a changed establishment. The need for a new breed of teacher is as urgent as the need for a revolutionized curriculum.

Our teachers have been compelled to abandon the mass of trivia which directs the way conventional classes are taught. I am referring to the monotonous practice whereby the teacher conducts a class by asking questions to which he has pat answers. Over the years this technique has become so thoroughly ingrained as a method of pedagogy in the public schools that the publishers of many school materials prepare canned questions for teachers to ask. These trite questions are supplied in teacher manuals accompanying textbooks. It is a prescriptive kind of learning, which we found to be too ineffective to be useful in the classroom of a school with a phased curriculum.

Another major stumbling block to learning which we had to overcome was the extreme and exaggerated overuse of the lecture as a style of teaching. The lecture as a teaching technique was introduced into the secondary schools in the nineteenth century at a time when the public schools were educating only the intellectually elite. Its effectiveness has receded as a result of compulsory education laws, which have brought into the schools the general population with their exceedingly wide range of abilities.

Lectures are unprofitable in dealing with the mass population unless they are delivered in very small quantities. As a matter of fact, this method of teaching would have vanished a decade ago had it not been for the shot in the arm given by the team-teaching fad.

The lecture as a manner of presentation is far more appropriate to the setting of the college, where students usually have no more than two or three classes a day. High school students must face from five to eight classes a day. There is a decided limit to the amount of learning which can be absorbed through the process of being "talked to." Furthermore, many high school teachers are dull and uninteresting, while colleges attract the best and the most creative minds in the teaching field.

Another factor making the lecture more appropriate to college learning is the makeup of the college population, which is highly selective. The epitome of the matter is that the students in colleges differ vastly, both in intellect and sophistication, from the general population which comes within the province of the high school, where only a third of the students are going to college and where another one third of the students often are handicapped by cultural disadvantages. Since high school learning activities must deal with the general population, we found it expedient to organize instruction around shirt-sleeve types of activities in which students are personally involved.

While it is extremely important to allow the individual teacher flexibility of method in attaining the goals of the course, there are several basic principles which buttress viable learning in the classroom of the phased program.

1. Teacher presentation of materials generally may not occupy more than 20 percent of the time in the course. (This includes time spent in viewing films as well as lecturing.)

2. Discussion in analysis groups constitutes approximately 40 percent of the class time.

3. Individual work and reading encompass roughly 40 percent of the class time.

Now what can we say about the differences which these changes have wrought?

The most reassuring result has been the complete disappearance of discipline problems. The act of placing students in learning situations closely linked to their achievement has resulted in a remarkable improvement in their attitudes and behavior. Certainly the reading laboratory, where many students spend several hours of the day receiving personal attention, has made a tremendous difference to the youngsters in the low socioeconomic bracket.

At the other end of the spectrum, the achievement of the more able students has been spectacular. Such subjects as Greek and differential equations have been added to a curriculum which has become rich in variety. In each of the last five years the school has won first-place honors in the Florida State Science Fair. In national competition, students have twice won the Westinghouse Talent Search. Last year we produced a Presidential Scholar. The number of students enrolling in college has jumped from 30 to 70 percent. There is an ever-increasing flow of able students to the high-prestige colleges. Alumni are presently enrolled at Harvard, Yale, Princeton, Amherst, and Smith. Reports from colleges reveal that most of the school's graduates are making creditable college records.

In addition to the intellectual changes which have taken place among the students since the establishment of the nongraded pattern, there are several important plant changes which are worthy of note. With students taking more responsibility for their own learning, we found that the conventional high school library was no longer appropriate. It became necessary for us to construct a new library which, in the words of the faculty, had to be "as large as the gymnasium." This new facility was built deliberately on the lawn of the school. The purpose was to make it available to students in the afternoon and evening after the school is closed. We have also found it necessary to construct new science laboratories in such a way that they could be made accessible after school and in the evening. When we took the limits off learning, many students began to ask for longer school hours. The school under the nongraded program has indeed undergone some revolutionary changes.

In conclusion, I feel compelled to mention one distinct drawback to a serious commitment to the notion of innovation and change. When a school ventures to undertake new programs, it can expect to be ostracized from its neighbors. Most schools are so tethered by the fetters of convention that they "would rather fight than switch." Through its adherence to a concept of heresy, Melbourne High School has indeed suffered the loneliness of the long-distance runner.

For all that has been said of transformation and revolution, classroom technique has remained relatively untouched; consequently, many students remain untouched. Loretta Jones and Richard Wisniewski outline the changes that are needed in the curriculum of slow learners in order to provide effective learning experience. We offer this article as an important consideration for all children. In the words of the authors, "nothing needs to be done for the slow learner that should not also be done for all students."

CURRICULUM NEEDS OF SLOW LEARNERS /
Loretta B. Jones and Richard Wisniewski

In examining the curriculum needs of slow learners, we would ask a basic question: Who *are* the slow learners—the students or the teachers? Neither facetiousness nor disrespect engenders this question. It is simply an expression of our conviction that the attitudes of teachers and school systems toward slow learners is the basic problem. Until these attitudes are at least acknowledged, there is little hope for implementing the wide range of instructional and organizational changes necessary if we are to more effectively challenge the abilities of all students. We propose to answer the question we have raised but only after we have presented our views regarding changes that are obviously needed.

Regarding teacher attitudes toward slow learners, it should not be necessary to elaborate at length on the overwhelming desire of most teachers to teach the brighter students, the college-bound students (readily discernible in the elementary grades), and the middle-class students who conform to the regimen and expectations of the school. The fact that some exceptional teachers, fortunately, actually derive satisfaction from working with slower groups, does not alter the "Beta press" in the profession. Far greater prestige and satisfaction are accrued by those who teach the upper third of a given school's population. Student teachers, for example, are readily conditioned to this prevailing attitudinal ethic. They are often appraised of their classes by competent and well-meaning professionals who apologize that this or that group is "the slowest group in the school" or is "just average, but there are a few bright ones in it!" Even the so-called average class is *not* good enough for many teachers, and students in the lower third

Loretta B. Jones and Richard Wisniewski, "Curriculum Needs of Slow Learners." Unpublished monograph. Reprinted with the permission of the authors.

of the school's grade-ranking system are clearly second class citizens.[1] The perceptive neophyte will quickly learn that many of his colleagues are both consciously and unconsciously disturbed, depressed, and often blatantly intolerant of those students who learn more slowly than others.[2]

Social class and racial biases complicate the question of teacher attitudes toward slow learners since many of these students come from the growing number of culturally different or culturally deprived children. The influx of Puerto Rican, southern white, and Negro families to urban centers presents serious problems in intergroup relations. To ignore biases toward these children held by many teachers is as pointless as attempting to ignore social class, racial, and/or religious biases in our society as a whole. They exist and must be challenged. There is some hope that the increasing concern with culturally disadvantaged children within our profession will help many teachers to develop more positive attitudes toward all slow learners, whether or not they come from a minority group. Attitudinal changes take time, however, and meanwhile tens of thousands of children are either passed-over or passed-on, both alternatives wasteful to the individual and to society. Our first premise, thus, is painfully clear: too many teachers do not want to work with slow learners. These students, purely and simply, do not reflect the academic and/or social graces that attract many of us to teaching. And attitudes are crucial, for it is our expectations that often determine how far any group will develop in particular skills or areas of knowledge. Unfortunately, the expectations of many teachers toward slow learners are so low as to preclude much in the way of real learning.

A second basic premise of this discussion is that nothing needs to be done for slow learners that should not also be done for *all* students. Concentrating on curricular changes that may better "reach" slow learners should not cloud the principle that good curricula and instructional techniques are needed for all students. We are concerned that teachers who work with brighter students sometimes restrict their teaching to very routine techniques simply because these students *appear* to respond so well. These students read the text faster, learn to use reference materials, do extra work, and participate more in

---

[1] Compare G. Orville Johnson, *The Slow Learner—Second Class Citizen?* Syracuse, N.Y.: Syracuse University Press, 1962.

[2] For an insightful analysis of the difference between poor and slow learners, see Frank Riessman, *The Culturally Deprived Child.* New York: Harper & Row, Publishers, Inc., 1962, Ch. VII.

discussions. The teacher of a bright group will often feel that this type of response "makes up" for the period later in the day when he has to "teach" the slow learners—the school rejects. This teacher will too often attempt to use the same materials and techniques with the slower group but will expect poorer reading, poorer participation, poorer discussions, and so on. The question here appears obvious: how many of these teachers critically examine the curriculum in which even the bright students do well? Our answer is twofold. First, we question *any and all* of the approaches traditionally used by teachers. The fact that they *seem* to work better with the brighter groups does *not* necessarily mean they are good. In point of fact, if they don't work well with *all* students, there is probably something wrong with the curricula and the techniques rather than with the students. Unfortunately, it is almost axiomatic that the latter conclusion will be drawn by most teachers, that is, "What's wrong with these kids?" We seldom hear the other question: "What's wrong with what we're doing to these kids?" Both questions may need to be asked, but the ratio is very one-sided at present. Second, the myth of homogeneous grouping is most assuredly omnipotent. Many of us simply do not recognize the range of abilities that appear in any group. Even if this range is recognized, we tend to ignore it in practice. Hence, even in a so-called homogeneous group, slow or bright, not all of the students will be responsive to the rather traditional techniques that characterize most instructional programs. Until we are willing to repeatedly question any and all of our assumptions and traditions in building social studies curricula, we will *not* be doing much to better educate all of our students.

In short, we believe that good teaching means taking a group "where they are," whatever the criteria used to establish this fact, and then proceeding in *any and all* directions necessary to build upon and extend the capabilities of these students. To achieve this level of effectiveness, we must be willing to work with all children—and this is the rub, as we have attempted to point out. But even if we were all willing to do so, we would not really succeed until we were far more receptive to new ideas than is now the case in education. As is true of all institutions, the imprint of the past is far deeper than the willingness to face the problems of the present. As has been said a million times, we must meet individual differences, but the very organization of schools precludes real individualization to a great degree. Can schools be organized so that *more* individualization can take place? We believe the answer can be in the affirmative if and when some fundamental changes in school organization and instructional programs take place.

It has been said we are experiencing a revolution in instruction,[3] but as we view the evidence in classrooms we have serious doubts as to the impact of the revolution.[4] Is it not mainly a paper revolution thus far? In any case, we are convinced that a revolution *is necessary*. Until some fundamental changes take place, the needs of all students must suffer. Meanwhile, slower students will suffer more, for they are least able to conform and perform in the existent programs. In our view, we need to develop curricula and instructional techniques far more flexible than those now in existence. To achieve this flexibility, we need to examine, evaluate, and adopt far more rapidly than we do those suggestions that appear to offer some hope for revitalizing our profession. Team teaching, flexible groupings, nongraded classrooms, programmed instruction, and more intensive use of electronic devices represent some approaches to better teaching. We cannot discuss here the virtues and drawbacks of these newer approaches, but we are convinced that many of the electronic devices, for example, teaching machines, films, video tapes, etc., can present "basic knowledge" or "facts" far more efficiently and in a more individualized manner than that which is usually achieved in the classroom. We need to lose our fear of the new instructional technology. Rather than a threat to our existence, it probably offers some solutions to the frustrations of attempting to mold thirty-five or forty individuals into a given curricular offering in a limited time. Frustration is inevitable when we know all too well that each person needs more of one skill, set of facts, or time to ponder than does another. We simply must find ways to break through the lock step, factory systems of education that characterize most schools in our nation. In short, we must be far more open to promising innovations. Good intentions are not enough, however, for change comes only through action.

Fundamental changes in school organization will take much time to achieve. In the meantime, we have to operate within existent organizational and curricular patterns. While the balance of our discussion focuses on aspects of the social studies curriculum, our major field of interest, the suggestions offered are tacitly applicable to all subject-

---

[3] Lindley J. Stiles, "Revolution in Instruction." In *Education in Urban Society*, B. J. Chandler, L. J. Stiles, and J. I. Kitsuse, eds. New York: Dodd, Mead and Company, 1962, Ch. XI.

[4] Compare Martin Mayer, "Last Chance for our Schools?" *Saturday Evening Post*, CCXXXVI (Sept. 14, 1963), 24–26.

matter areas. Literature in social studies education offers many leads as to what can be done by persons who *care* about the problem. Many of these ideas are models worthy of emulation. We, certainly, are not prepared to offer a model curriculum for all slow learners. No such model exists or will ever exist, for curricula must be continually evaluated and changed for all children. Each school needs to examine its curriculum in terms of the unique configuration of students, problems, community, and personnel factors operative in that school. So long as we look to "others" to solve our problems, we can be sure we will be derelict in our responsibilities to the schools in which we teach. Further, so long as "curriculum changes" amount to little more than changes in textbooks or changing American history from the 9th to the 10th grade, we will be missing the more basic issues we are attempting to raise in this discussion. Because the problems in building a curriculum are complex, we propose to offer only four general guidelines that we believe are useful in meeting the needs of all students, and slow learning students in particular.

First and foremost, *all* learners need to understand the point of what they are asked to study. The social studies are overwhelmingly historically oriented. The chronological development of ideas, whether it be in history, American government, economics, or other disciplines is the most common pattern in the field. If we have not yet learned that it is the here and now that is crucial to all of us, students and teachers alike, we see no hope for any meaningful curricular changes. The fact that current events and controversial issues are encouraged or at least given lip service in the social studies does not obviate the tremendous and overriding traditions that force us to concentrate on the past. We do not intend to engage in the inevitable debate that would cite some sound reasons for examining ideas chronologically nor are we "anti-history" in any shape or form. The issue simply revolves about decisions that determine where we begin and what we will emphasize in any given course. We believe that social studies curricular offerings for *all* students need to be overwhelmingly "present minded," dealing with the sociological, economic, religious, and political issues of today. We need to look upon historical antecedents as a means to understanding and reinforcing the present rather than as ends in themselves. We are not convinced by those who would say that this *is* what we do now in the social studies. We are far more convinced by what we have observed in classrooms during our combined professional experience, and that which we see is almost always content that is "dead" rather than "alive." Until social studies teachers deal with the present 99% of the time, students will continue to look upon our area as a stultified one. Readers may disagree with our "percentage," but the point we are attempting to make is far more important. The goal of the social studies, after all, is to develop informed citizens who will be able to function in *this* society and not in societies of times past, no matter how many interesting and perhaps instructive historical antecedents may be cited. In a word, we need to teach history backwards, beginning with major issues of the day and including those historical aspects that apply to these issues.[5] We need to realize that even dealing with the present is a somewhat "dated" procedure, for our students are destined to live in a world different from that of this generation. But, we can at least begin at this point.

Second, we need to concentrate on skill development to a vastly greater degree. Skill development *is*, of course, a part of all social studies curricula now, but we are suggesting a far greater emphasis on this aspect of our goals. Slow learners are at least partially so labeled because they lack the "know-how" that would permit them to move more rapidly through the materials which we present. We need, therefore, to make skill building an integral part of *all* social studies classes. If a group of students does not have the skills we believe necessary, then we must develop them regardless of the grade or content with which we are dealing. This procedure is clearly in keeping with our injunction to "take students where they are." Blaming previous teachers or the students themselves for not having taught or learned the skills is of no value (except in terms of demonstrating the need for more cooperative curriculum planning). Slow learning students will never be free of this label with all of its negative connotations until we help them to acquire the skills they need.

The slow learner is faced with problems in the communication skills, that is, reading, writing, and speaking. He needs to learn how to find materials, to analyze them critically, to participate in group undertakings, and to use maps, globes, and other "tools of the trade." He cannot achieve any competence in these skills unless we design a wealth of materials and lessons to help him to apply them. The fact that skills are learned must be remembered and teachers must discard the timeworn idea that teaching skills take time and emphasis away from the subject matter. How can one expect to teach one or the other without including both? It cannot be done, and until we emphasize

---

[5] For a concrete illustration of how this procedure can be effected, see James Wallace, "Making History Relevant." *Social Education*, XXVI (1962), 17–18.

this elemental fact much more, we will be doing very little to help the slow learner. The alternatives are clear: we either develop the skills these students need, or we condemn them to second class citizenship both in and out of the school.

Third, we need to integrate the content of the social studies even more than has already been done. We need to do this despite vocal opposition which demands more *real* history, more *real* geography and more *real* civics as discrete course offerings. We have no quarrel with demands for "depth" in all social studies courses so long as the interrelationships between the concepts are clear to all students. In point of fact, there is *no* depth unless the interrelationships are taught. While very bright students appear to be able to interrelate the concepts they learn, our experience with slow learners indicates that they cannot do so without help. We are not even sure that the so-called bright students can fill the gaps we so assiduously seek to develop in the typical high school social studies program. If we wish our students to have a comprehensive knowledge of mankind, we need to interrelate the concepts and findings of the social sciences at every conceivable opportunity, whether it be in our individual classrooms or in planning the entire curriculum. These interrelationships just do not "happen." In order for them to be understood, they must be taught and applied. To expect the slow learner, in particular, to put together all he has learned in the separate course offerings is indeed a serious error on our part.

Some courses, for example, sociology, cultural geography, and world affairs or "problems" type courses make attempts at achieving this integration. Often, varied approaches and materials are used in these courses and teachers are perhaps more willing to experiment and put their creative talents to work. We believe there is a need for the expansion of courses of this type, especially bringing to bear the sociological and anthropological insights that cut across disciplinary lines. The integrated or block of content type of course also holds promise for all learners and especially for slow learners. It is really so important that our students learn about every fact, date, event, or personality described in the text, or is it more important that they understand the interrelationships and meanings thereof? We believe that the integration of the separate disciplines can produce a more practical, logical, and meaningful study of man for the slow learner. There are many reasons, of course, why any given group of slow learners may be difficult to handle or stimulate, but we will at least untie our hands in terms of the content we are offering if the integrated approach is accepted. Further, the integrated approach is conducive to the use of problem solving techniques as a means of "covering" the content. In posing the problems and seeking the solutions, students can draw upon all the areas and acquire some skill in discovering the relationships which gain meaning through application.

Fourth and last, we need to orient the curriculum to the community from which our students are drawn. We suggest this not as a general goal but as an operational aspect of the curriculum. It might be suggested that most slow learners will not go to college, hence "give them a course in 'the community,' for example, employment opportunities, civic problems and responsibilities, etc." These types of information are highly desirable for *all* students, but our proposal goes deeper than any single course offering. We believe that the community is the laboratory in which the concepts developed in the social studies *must* be tested, not on a haphazard basis, but as an integral part of the curriculum. If we do attempt such a use of the community in the curriculum, we can expect certain outcomes. For example, we will be attempting to close the gap between schools in general and their communities. Students may finally begin to see some connection between what their teachers say and what the students experience. They will begin to learn about the ecology of their community and how they fit into it. They will learn about the services available to them as well as their responsibilities as members of the community. They may, in short, begin to see the links between their lives and the ideas discussed in school. Again, some would say that this is already our goal in the social studies. We must reply that the goal is far from being achieved. When *all* students engage in community studies as a normal and expected part of *all* their social studies classes, rather than as special assignments by outstanding teachers, we will acknowledge that the goal has been implemented.

In the same vein, America is a pluralistic society made up of many subcultures. Yet, social studies curricula are notoriously bereft of any real emphasis on the accomplishments of minority groups. When social studies teachers indeed begin to recognize this fact, students from all segments of our society will more likely feel "at home" in school far more than is now the case. It goes without saying that if the social studies take the lead in this regard, opposition will be forthcoming from those segments of the community that are not interested in having students learn "too much." In our view, social studies teachers who would fear such opposition are not achieving the goals of their calling.

None of these guidelines are new nor are they the whole answer.

What is essentially needed is a systematic and continuous evaluation of the curricular needs of *all* students. When each school and each teacher undertakes such an evaluation as a routine part of the year's operation, the slow learner will stand to benefit as much if not more than anyone else. The purpose of such evaluations is to fit the curriculum to the needs of the children who are to learn from it. If any sizable segment of the students are not learning, the fault is with a curriculum which is not flexible enough to meet changing needs. School curricula, however, are tradition bound, influenced by pressure groups, restricted by textbook choices and by college demands, and they are *always* behind the times. Because of these factors, implementing changes is an uphill and difficult task. Happily, it is becoming more and more obvious to a greater number of teachers that the schools are not meeting the needs of slow learners. Once enough teachers are convinced of this fact, they will be amenable to and active in efforts to bring about some of the changes suggested herein, despite the difficulties they will need to overcome.

We see one danger in the concern with the curricular needs of slow learners, however. There is always the possibility that once we identify and label the lower third of our students, we will devise special programs for them, which in effect, *will keep them slow learners*. We realize that all good teachers want to raise the abilities of their students and hence such an injunction may not seem necessary. Nonetheless, we also realize that schools are very slow-changing social systems; and once a program is implemented, it *will* be continued long beyond its use and, further, it *will* stigmatize those students within it. We believe that the way to avoid such an outcome is to be concerned with the curricular needs of *all* students. When this is the case, a flexible curriculum within a flexible school organization is more likely to emerge and within such a school, all students will be learning, slow or fast. The solution to the curriculum problems of the slow learner, hence, lies in an examination of how effective we are with *all* of our students. Once we begin to recognize the gulf between what we profess in the curriculum guides and what we accomplish, the slow learner will not appear to be such a problem. Meeting the needs of *any and all* learners will be challenge enough.

In light of this discussion, we are now prepared to answer the question posed in the first paragraph: who are the slow learners—the students or the teachers? The answer is obvious in our view. Students, after all, are the constant in education, that is, there is a ready supply of them to be educated and they represent the full gamut of abilities.

In point of fact, they vary as much in ability and interest in school as do we—their teachers. We, however, are trained and hired to work with *all* children, yet we prefer the bright ones. Further, many of us operate as if *all* children can basically learn *all* the same material at exactly the same rate. This is simply not the case. It was not true of us when we sat in the rows of seats we now teach, nor will it ever be true. Many of us in the profession must indeed be slow learners ourselves if we have not learned this elemental pedagogical fact.

There are some extenuating factors, of course. We recognize the multitudinous forces that make the factory system of teaching a hard reality in our society. We recognize the enervating and frustrating task of trying to meet the needs of slow learners when the pressures about us force us to move quickly, to handle groups often too large, to deal with seriously maladjusted children, to be limited in terms of materials and organizational inflexibility, and so on. We recognize, too, that slow learners are often harder to work with since many of them are intimately involved in the social upheavals of which we are all a part. Whatever the problems in working with slow learners, however, we must get beyond the symptoms and attack the causes.

There is some reason to hope that a real breakthrough in school organization and practice is taking place, but the pace is evolutionary rather than revolutionary. We see, therefore, only one real hope for the slow learners in school today. Namely, that more and more teachers "learn faster," that these children can learn if we are willing to change many of our preconceived notions about them, about curricula, and about instructional techniques. Until our attitudes and practices change, the cost in human waste and frustration for students and teachers alike is beyond computation. Articles such as this will not be needed when teachers are positive in their attitudes toward slow learners. Until then, all of us must honestly examine our feelings toward these students. Even if the millennium never arrives, let us at least be honest with ourselves.

Metropolitan school districts are investing heavily in the culturally disadvantaged child. In New York, for example, an additional $200 per child is being spent in inner-city schools to equalize education. Money is being poured into a structure and concept of education which has failed dismally with these children in the past. Spending more money to operate an essen-

tially unchanged curriculum is not the wisest nor the most effective investment that can be made in the education of the culturally disadvantaged child.

PRESCHOOL EDUCATION FOR THE DEVELOPING CORTEX / *August Kerber and Barbara Bommarito*

Today one third of the children in metropolitan centers are not being adequately educated. By default, education is perpetuating a widening gap between social classes. In countless schools these children do not learn the skills and attitudes necessary to fully participate in their society. Instead they learn that they are inferior and uneducable, that society has no need of them, that the "good life" is not for them. They are called culturally deprived, culturally disadvantaged, alienated, slum children—by any name they are the ones for whom educational experiences are not only ineffective but downright debilitative.

It is predicted that the percentage of culturally disadvantaged children enrolled in urban schools will rise to 50% by 1970. This is the crisis which education is meeting head-on at all levels. It has, by the expenditure of enormous amounts of money, time, and energy, shown a striking change in its goals for culturally disadvantaged children. The programs now operating in urban education affirm a belief that culturally disadvantaged children can benefit as fully from education as their middle-class counterparts. It is to the credit of American education that this ideal of an open-class society is finally being actively sought as a reality. But the fact is that the number of children who are being reached is negligible. Thousands of children, in the face of intensive and extensive effort, do not learn to read properly. The majority of them continue to get a poor start in school and drop further and further behind as they progress through the grades.

The problem will never be solved within the present k–12 structure of education. Increasing evidence indicates that by the time the culturally disadvantaged child enters school it is *too late* to alter the course set toward academic failure. The cognitive set of the culturally disadvantaged child, that pattern of perception which handicaps him in learning tasks demanded by the school, is irrevocably cast in preschool years. Before the child—any child—enters school, the cortex has

August Kerber and Barbara Bommarito, "Preschool Education for the Developing Cortex." Unpublished monograph, 1965, Wayne State University.

already developed its system of sorting, relating, interpreting, and perceiving experience. That system remains relatively unchanged throughout life.

This does not mean that education must resign itself to a kind of "cortical determinism." The eager and inquiring mind, capable of sophisticated thought, can now be seen as not necessarily the manifestation of inherent or "native" intelligence. Intellectual activity of this sort takes place in a portion of the cortex which is a blank slate at birth, uncommitted to the raw phenomena which impinges upon it. Here is where language and perception will be written. The greatest percentage of development takes place in the cortex directly after birth. Benjamin Bloom has found that one-half of all growth in intelligence takes place between birth and the age of four.[1] The linguistic and perceptual experiences in these crucial years largely determine the level of mental processes for life. As the neurosurgeon Wilder Penfield has put it, "One might say there is a built-in biological clock that tells the passing time of educational opportunity."[2] These are the years when a basic set toward learning is developed. Later all that takes place is an addition of experience into the "preordained categories." The language set gained in early years largely shapes these categories which incorporate—or fail to incorporate—later experience.

The culturally disadvantaged child, at the peak of his learning development, is rarely exposed to the full range of experiences which his cortex is so ready to learn. Conversation in his home is not used to communicate abstract concepts, relate ideas, or solve intricate problems. The child is not encouraged to express his feelings and emotions verbally. He has little opportunity to make perceptual discriminations, either auditory or visual, because of the lack of order, variety, and harmony in his physical surroundings. Life comes at him in the most elementary form with things to grab, strike out at, or avoid. The immediacy of poverty, and the world perspective which accompanies it, never allows him to experience the highly removed abstractions of life so essential to education—that world of thought as embraced in reading and writing.

The idea that a child is ready to learn these skills at five or six is presupposed in the laws of every state in the nation. What is not pre-

---

[1] Benjamin S. Bloom, *Stability and Change in Human Characteristics*. New York: John Wiley and Sons, Inc., 1954.

[2] Wilder Penfield, "The Uncommitted Cortex." *Atlantic Monthly* (July 1964), p. 78.

supposed in these laws is that a child is ready to learn to read at five or six only if he has had the proper experience for full cortical development prior to that time. The age at which a child is ready to learn anything is now open to debate. Dr. Omar Moore, a Yale sociologist who believes that the most creative and intellectually active years of life occur in the first five years, has successfully taught three- and four-year olds to fluently read and write on automated typewriters. No reading readiness program, no teachers lavishing TLC, no classroom rapport. In fact, nearly every cherished pedagogical concept has been violated in this remarkable program. What Dr. Moore has done is seize the moment of educational opportunity and feed stimulating, carefully programed linguistic and perceptual experience to a voracious cortex.

More than the linguistic and perceptual set of a child is determined in his preschool years. Professor Bloom's book *Stability and Change in Human Characteristics* corroborates what most behavioral scientists have insisted right along: the personality is shaped in the earliest years. The values and attitudes toward self and the greater culture which are learned in the slum home are dysfunctional in the academic setting. Recognizing this, education has tailored its curricula for culturally disadvantaged children from this point of reference. But what education has not fully recognized is that it cannot alter deeply enculturated values.

The entire educational process enjoys success, when and where it does, not because of any bromide of method; but simply because it reinforces the cultural values already within the child. The *kheder* schools of the *shtetl* Jews in eastern Europe turned out countless scholars, yet these schools were the antithesis of a "good" or "proper" learning environment. At three or five years of age, boys began classes in small, crowded rooms for ten hours a day. They sat on hard benches memorizing meaningless passages in Hebrew, a language yet unfamiliar to them. Learning was monotonous and tedious. The rooms were often cold, and most of the children were poorly dressed and hungry most of the time. The boys were cruelly punished on the slightest provocation. Yet they learned, achieving a remarkably high level of literacy. What is more, they retained that which made it possible to learn under such conditions in the first place—the deep and abiding love of learning and knowledge. The Judaic culture regards literacy and education as an ethical necessity. Only through formal education can one come to relate properly to God and the community.

The other side of the coin is the culturally disadvantaged child who, in a sunlit school full of smiling teachers and beautifully illustrated textbooks, does not see education as the key tool needed to relate himself properly to his world. He does not see himself as capable of mastering academic tasks. He can never be convinced otherwise unless education gets to him sooner than it now does. He is the too-late child. He is exposed to reward, attention, remedy, warmth, encouragement, and special technique too late. Education is a lifelong process from birth to death. Where formal education begins is arbitrarily decided. For the culturally disadvantaged child it must begin sooner. If he is to be educated he must be brought into the school during the crucial years of enculturative and cortical development.

The New York system has already set up a pilot preschool academy for Harlem children between the ages of three and five. Under the direction of Martin Deutsch, these schools give the child richer linguistic and perceptual experiences than those found in the home. The children learn to speak in complete sentences and verbally express all experience. They are surrounded with order, relatedness, harmony, clarity, even beauty which they are encouraged to carefully discriminate and verbally identify. The child's sense of self is given special attention also. He is learning, at the time when such attitudes takes root, to trust himself and the school. The program extends into the home by encouraging the parents to carry on involved conversation with their child, take interest in his school experiences, and praise his successes.

Results are encouraging. There has been a significant increase in the I.Q.'s of the children in preschool academies, and teachers report that these children come to kindergarten remarkably well prepared. Now other cities are considering nursery schools for culturally deprived children.

The preprimer nursery must be moved from the pilot level to where it is an essential foundation of public education. Under the present system, projects continue to treat the symptoms while the illness remains endemic to urban education. The culturally disadvantaged child is seen as a major problem in education, but he is far more than that. He and his peers are nearly half of the future adult population in the greater cities of America. Even more he is an individual who, by right of the highest ideals of our society, is entitled to more than a dead-end existence amidst tremendous opportunity. If we do not invest in the culturally disadvantaged child before he begins school, we shall have to subsidize him after he leaves, and boondoggle his time in between.

This is to say, in effect, that there is no alternative for us. Education, to be effective for the culturally disadvantaged child, must be extended downward to the three- and four-year old.

The school no longer operates within a society containing an objective and unified value system. Yet education, to be sound, must operate within a well-structured value system. In view of this fact, conflicts in the choice of values are inevitable —but not, says Harold Dunkel, wholly undesirable.

VALUE DECISIONS AND THE PUBLIC SCHOOLS / *Harold B. Dunkel*

Education as a practical operation is inextricably involved in the problem of values. If, as is often done, we define education as "the process of producing desirable changes in people," criteria of desirability are clearly indispensable, and ultimately these involve fundamental value positions. To some degree at least, the schools attempt to make children "good" in the ethical sense by teaching them their duties as citizens, as parents, and as individuals. But even beyond this the schools attempt to make the child a better person for himself and others to live with: to make him a better parent, a better friend, a better neighbor, a better worker, a better citizen, and better many other things.

Thus, if, for the sake of brevity, in the traditional triad of "the good, the true, and the beautiful," we leave out of account the other two and focus only on "the good," we see that schools can scarcely operate without committing themselves to some view of "the good."

This fact is nothing new. What is new is the increasing popularity in recent years of a view in value theory which says that these decisions do not rest on the nature of things or grow out of some specific intuition or revelation but are simply the non-rational, non-cognitive results of a process of social conditioning. In the area of values, then, we believe what we do merely because our society has so conditioned us. Our codes or our views of man's duties are merely products of the

Harold B. Dunkel, "Value Decisions and the Public Schools," The School Review (Summer 1962), pp. 163–170. Copyright © 1962 by The University of Chicago Press.

customs of our group. While statistics on such matters are impossible to come by and estimates are at best precarious, a sizable proportion of contemporary anthropologists, sociologists, and philosophers (perhaps even a majority) hold to this view.

This answer has been widely accepted by linguistic philosophers who are interested primarily in how words like *good* are used in a given society and by behavioral scientists who wish only to describe what values are in fact held by a culture. But education encounters some difficulties not felt by these other disciplines because the job of education is not descriptive but operative. Education does not describe values; it functions on the basis of a fairly explicit set of values and even attempts to inculcate values directly. For this reason it is itself one of the chief agencies of social conditioning. As a result, the educator is faced with some difficulties which do not beset other workers dealing with the problem of value.

The purpose of the present paper is not to examine or criticize the bases and merits of this particular view of the nature of values. This belief will simply be taken as a datum, as a view widely held by competent thinkers. Rather the effort here will be to examine the consequences which this view produces as problems in the conduct of the educational enterprise.

When a society is sufficiently monolithic that its views on value are essentially unanimous, perpetuating these values through social conditioning in education and elsewhere is not difficult. But the situation in a complicated, pluralistic society like our own is quite different. There no single set of mores or values prevails, but there are competing and conflicting sets held by diverse groups within that culture. Which set of values are the schools to adopt? To be sure, overlappings will occur over considerable areas of the various sets; otherwise the pluralistic society could not hold together at all. But the differences between the sets are important partly because they are conspicuous exceptions to the general area of consensus and partly because these differences tend to constitute the distinguishing characteristics or caste marks of particular subcultures. As a result, for example, a subgroup which believes in cleanliness, neatness, respect for property, and control of physical aggression is not likely to be happy with an educational system which minimizes these values out of deference to some other subgroup which sees these attitudes as mere symptoms of middle-class compulsivity.

Most theoreticians who hold this view of the nature of values will respond to the question, "Which code or which set of norms will be enforced?" by replying, "That of the group which can make its wishes prevail." In other words, the decisive factor is power in some form since rational or scientific methods of reaching a decision are viewed by this position as impossible. Power is not, of course, limited to brute force. It assumes protean forms: the power of money, position, persuasion à la Madison Avenue, personality, and myriad others.

Education must then inquire where this power struggle, at least the parts of it bearing on the educational enterprise, is decided. How does a community decide which value patterns are to be taught in its schools and are to be used as the basis for curricular and instructional decisions?

One possible answer is that a pluralistic society wishes for an obvious and open decision never to occur. A struggle of this sort would be devisive, indicating quite clearly to a number of subgroups that their views were not being adopted by the society as a whole. Thus a pluralistic society may prefer to ignore this question as long as possible in the hope that it will not become too troublesome. Some aspects of our present educational situation suggest that in part we have more or less consciously adapted this answer.

A second possibility for a pluralistic society is apparently to handle the problem pluralistically, that is, for each subgroup to set up its own schools operating on the basis of its own standards of value. The parochial schools set up by various religious denominations and the private or proprietary schools offering some specific kind of training are examples of this procedure in our culture. This device would be more viable if all value positions were represented by schools and if all schools were of this sort. The wider the range of highly diversified schools, the more adequate this multiple answer to the problem of pluralistic values becomes.

Under present modes of operation, however, we do not have complete diversity. Local school authorities maintain out of public funds one set of schools for most of the children of the community. Under these circumstances, how and where are value decisions made? The answers to these questions appear to be quite varied.

In some school systems, the simple situation mentioned earlier does seem to exist. The population of the suburb is often homogeneous to a considerable degree, and the schools of that community can incorporate the system of values espoused by most of the inhabitants. The result is schools which the community considers "very good" and which are much admired by holders of these same values elsewhere. Strong local support (both financial and moral) and nation-wide admiration and publicity are common consequences. These schools so clearly enshrine values which are "right" in the eyes of what is currently a large and influential portion of our population that they are *ipso facto* good.

In the more heterogeneous community (particularly in the urban setting) this simplicity is not possible. (This fact is possibly one of the contributing causes for the commonly held belief that suburban schools are usually "better" than are city schools.) Here again a multiple answer to the problem of pluralistic values is commonly attempted through a variety of curriculums or tracks with their accompanying levels of aspiration, modes of instruction, type of student, and general tone. Thus the academic or accelerated program in the urban high school seeks to be a partial replication of the suburb in the city. To the extent to which different value patterns are embodied in each curriculum, diversification of these tracks is a partial answer to the problem. But at best the solution is partial and somewhat superficial. Values affect the elementary school in an equally fundamental fashion; yet diversified elementary schools (except insofar as they are the by-products of the existence of Negro ghettos) are not common and are probably unthinkable to most citizens. The strong belief of many Americans in the common public elementary school which educates all the citizens reflects the attitude that social cohesiveness should be obtained through the universal inculcation of one set of basic values for the nation as a whole.

If the schools are to incorporate some one set of values, who decides which one of the various sets is chosen?

A seemingly easy answer sometimes used is "the local board of education." Legally charged with the conduct of the local schools, this body would seem to have some claim to be the decisive court of appeal. But whether these bodies can in fact make this decision on behalf of the community and whether they can make this decision in a form in which it is useful are questions worth asking at least.

To a limited extent, American communities do seem to intend to follow this practice. For example, where the school board is appointed by a mayor or some other elected official, there is usually the strong tradition of including in its membership representatives of various major ethnic, racial, religious, and other groups. Obviously this selection is aimed primarily at securing the political support of well-defined groups of voters. Yet this support is probably assumed to be forthcoming on the ground that the views of these groups (and in considerable part their respective value positions) will be advocated by their representatives. Whether school boards as now selected (or even as they could be selected) are competent to perform this task on behalf of the community if they are explicitly charged with making these value decisions is a nice question for the administration of American schools.

Directly in the case of elected boards, and indirectly in the case of appointed ones, solutions through decisions by the school board are affected by some facts of American political life. One of these is the political axiom: avoid divisiveness and nourish majorities by blurring issues which might lead to dissension—a result almost certain in a decision regarding fundamental values. As the national platforms of the political parties demonstrate, the electorate is usually asked to choose between programs worked out with meticulous vagueness. Yet the educational operation demands a fairly definite stand (if only by implication) on certain value problems. Even after a referendum, the teacher or administrator who attempted to justify any educational practice on the basis of some mandate received through a political decision would probably feel that for all practical purposes he was making the decision for himself. The choice would probably never be made in terms sufficiently clean-cut to offer clear guidance.

This situation suggests what is probably the major mechanism by which these value decisions are now in fact reached. The local administrator and the classroom teacher make these judgments on the basis of their own preferences where they feel they can get away with them. When these limits are inadvertently passed, we find the person who gives up the profession or who seeks another school or another community where the extent of coincidence between his value system and that of the dominant group is greater.

Thus we see another multiple mode of answer to the problem of pluralistic values, with the unit this time being the individual teacher. Within those areas where the culture generally shares certain views, the teacher obviously operates with impunity. Beyond those limits, however, the situation becomes more precarious. Clearly the educator cannot make decisions according to his own views in areas where groups more powerful than he have an interest in making their wishes prevail. It would be an unsophisticated teacher or administrator who would attempt to run counter to the views of the local PTA, the local American Legion, the most influential religious denomination, or similar groups if they can enforce their wills against his. According to this value position, their views are more correct simply because their power is greater. In areas where the teacher's opinion deviates from that of the total culture but where no such power groups are mobilized, however, he has greater freedom of action. Groups wishing and able to enforce their positions simply do not exist. In some instances there is also the possibility that conflicting power groups can be counterpoised against each other and thus the teacher will still have room to maneuver because the groups are busy attacking each other rather than him. But by and large the teacher imposes his own value structure, which is, of course, the product of the social conditioning he received. In any areas where he comes from the "wrong" subgroup or where for some biographical reason he deviates from the line espoused by major pressure groups, he operates simply by assessing the power which can be brought against him. He fills or trims his sails accordingly. A glance at American schools suggests that the preceding description is not purely hypothetical.

The foregoing analysis suggests several things. First, we see that American education is to a considerable extent operating on the basis of procedures which are not incompatible with this general view of value sketched. School boards, administrators, and teachers seem not to have adopted this view explicitly. For various reasons we need not go into here, they would probably hesitate to do so. Nevertheless, they act in many respects as if this view were in fact theirs. Possibly analyses like this one, which endeavor to render the issues more explicit, can assist in making the solutions more effective since they can be worked on consciously.

A second result is that we see what is, according to this view, the basis for the attacks so frequently made on the public schools. One man's meat is simply another man's poison. The public schools of a pluralistic society probably cannot please all subgroups in the population at any one time despite the various dodges that have been indicated. And if these decisions in regard to value are arbitrary acts of will, the remedy for those dissatisfied is not to urge the schools to adopt their solution, which is alleged to be rationally or scientifically right. There are no such solutions according to this view. The critics must do what (in large part) they have done in the past. They must generate power in some form to bring pressure on the schools in the areas where they desire change. But clearly the charges often brought against the American public school that it is confused and contradictory in its procedures and that its purposes are unclear are no longer the devastating attack it might be under other views of value. According to this view the public school could be clear in its aims and efficient in its procedures only under some form of government which produced approximate unanimity among all citizens. Since our form of government is not of that sort and since most of us would not be prepared to tolerate one, we must accept the kind of diversity which results in the public schools—a diversity which has close kinship to conflict and muddle.

This view of the nature of value decisions and value judgments is not, obviously, the only one. It is, however, a major one in America today, and it has left its impact on our schools. If it persists and particularly if it wins greater acceptance, the kind of problem and the kind of solution outlined will become more prevalent and those of us working in education would do well to be aware of them.

REFERENCES

Lippmann, Walter. *The Public Philosophy*. Boston: Little, Brown and Company, 1955.

Scott, Stanley, ed. *Metro-Area Problems*. Berkeley, Calif.: Bureau of Public Administration and University Extension, University of California, 1960.

Scudder, Kenyan, and Kenneth S. Beam. *The Twenty Billion Dollar Challenge: A National Program for Delinquency Prevention*. New York: G. P. Putnam's Sons, Inc., 1961.

Tipton, James H. *Community in Crisis: The Elimination of Segregation from a Public School System*. New York: Bureau of Publications, Teachers College, Columbia University, 1953.

Wey, Herbert, and John Cory. *Action Patterns in School Desegregation: A Guidebook*. Bloomington, Ind.: Phi Delta Kappa, Inc., 1959.

PERIODICALS

Champlin, Nathaniel L. "The Attacks Upon Public Education: Their Significance for Philosophy of Education." *Educational Theory* (July 1958), pp. 157–161.

NEA Research Division. "Ten Criticisms of Public Education." *NEA Research Bulletin* (December 1957), pp. 133–174.

Norton, John K. "The Need for Federal Aid for Education." *School and Society* (March 1956), pp. 87–90.

INDEX

357